INDONESIAN
COMMUNISM

A HISTORY

Arnold C. Brackman

FREDERICK A. PRAEGER, *Publisher*

New York

FREDERICK A. PRAEGER, Publisher
64 University Place, New York 3, N.Y., U.S.A.
77-79 Charlotte Street, London W.1, England

Published in the United States of America in 1963 by
Frederick A. Praeger, Inc., Publisher

Second printing, 1963

Library of Congress Catalog Card Number: 63-9391

This book is Number 123 in the series of
Praeger Publications in Russian History and World Communism

Printed in the United States of America

To Aggie

stringer extraordinary

Contents

Introduction: The Setting

The Communist movement of Indonesia, waxing and waning in relative obscurity for more than forty years, is the oldest in Asia. Presently, the Partai Kommunis Indonesia (PKI)—the Communist Party of Indonesia—is the largest in the world outside the Sino-Soviet bloc. Buttressed by a panoply of fronts, it possesses the most elaborate and disciplined political organization in the country. It has honeycombed Indonesia with paramilitary cells, and, directly and indirectly, exerts influence on almost every sector of Indonesian life. By the logic of the Cold War balance of power, the PKI has become an increasingly critical factor not only in Indonesia but also in world affairs.

Communism's gradual erosion of the non-Communist world and the peculiar nature of the nuclear balance of terror have dramatized Indonesia's international political position. There was a time when the Soviet Union was haunted by the fear of capitalist encirclement. Lenin's law of "uneven development" and Stalin's thesis of "socialism in one country" rationalized the concept of the Soviet Union as a Communist island in a hostile, capitalist sea. Khrushchev buried the concept of capitalist encirclement. He holds the emergence of Communism from within the bounds of a single country and its transformation into a world system to be the main feature of the present era. As evidence, Khrushchev has cited the astonishingly rapid expansion of the Communist world order. In less than two generations, the Communists have extended their control to over one-fourth of the earth's land mass and one-third of the earth's population and now account for one-third of the world's total industrial output. "At present," Khrushchev has said, "it is not known who encircles whom."[1]

The crucial question, "Who encircles whom?"—the burning issue of the day—cannot be resolved by war. Nuclear capabilities have canceled out global conflict as an instrument of national policy. The power-politics vacuum has been filled largely by alternating periods of "Cold War" and "peaceful coexistence," an unremitting ideological war of attrition. In the West, the lines between the Communist and non-Communist worlds have hardened; in East Asia, a similar situation prevails. The battle-ground has shifted to the uncommitted, underdeveloped sector of the world, the tropical belt encircling Africa and southern Asia and, to a lesser degree, Latin America. In part, "Who encircles whom?" will probably be determined by the outcome of the struggle among the newly emerging Afro-Asian states.

The Soviet Union clearly recognizes this strategic development. Moscow has proclaimed that the peoples of the East are playing an active part in deciding the destinies of the whole world, that they are becoming a new, mighty factor in international relations. In the North Atlantic community, a similar appraisal has increasingly been gaining acceptance. As Mendès-France expressed it, the newly independent nations may become "the arbiters of the contest." It is in this light, as a potential arbiter in the ideological conflict between the two systems, that Indonesia assumes tactical importance in world affairs. In area, manpower, and natural resources, Indonesia is in the forefront among the under-developed nations in the non-Communist world. Thus, the success or failure of the Communist movement in Indonesia may profoundly influence the world balance of power.

In terms of military strategy, Indonesia is the linchpin of the "Malay Barrier," the formidable chain of peninsulas and islands stretching from southern Thailand to western Australia. Like Suez, the Barrier is one of the great strategic areas on the globe.[2] It shelters primary ports and airfields, road and rail networks. Virtually inaccessible by land, it can be overcome only by sea power—or from within. Although the Soviet Union has challenged United States sea power in the Pacific, showering rockets into a test area near Hawaii on the eve of Khrushchev's first journey to Indonesia in 1960, the oceans, for the time being at least, remain the lakes of the non-Communist world. The Barrier can fall only from within.

D. N. Aidit, the youthful General Secretary of the PKI, clearly recognizes this geopolitical state of affairs. Promulgating an Indonesian variant of the conception of "capitalist encirclement," Aidit states that

> in the vicinity of Indonesia lie fortresses of imperialism, colonial and semicolonial countries. To the north lie Malaya, Singapore, Siam, South Vietnam, Sarawak, North Borneo, and the Philippines. To the south lie Australia as well as the Christmas Islands and the Cocos Islands, which are under British domination. On the east is

East Irian [East New Guinea] under Australian domination, while West Irian is still under the complete domination of the Dutch imperialists. Indonesia has no frontiers with a country which is already completely liberated from imperialist power. All these facts make it all the more necessary for the Indonesian revolutionaries to take their own course in bringing the Indonesian revolution to completion.[3]

Under Communist domination, the Barrier could conceivably tilt the precarious power balance in Asia and the Pacific in favor of the Communist world. A Communist Indonesia would drive a wedge between the Indo-Pakistani subcontinent and Australia by subjecting the lands between China and Indonesia to almost irresistible pressure and seal the fate of a large part of Southeast Asia. It would flank the Philippines in the south and deal South Asia's experiments in representative government and civil liberties an irreparable psychological blow. It would breach the United States defense perimeter in the southwestern Pacific. It would pose a threat to Japan, dependent on Southeast Asia for raw materials and markets. Indeed, the road to Tokyo leads through Djakarta, a reality that has grave implications for the defense of the whole of the Pacific.

By absorbing Indonesia, the Communists would gain a major insular base of operation. Indonesia would provide the Communist forces with the world's largest archipelago. At present, Djakarta claims the area extending from lat. 6° N. to lat. 11° S., and from long. 95° W. to long. 141° E. Distances within the area are awesome. The distance from west to east is 3,107 miles, equal to that between Los Angeles and Bermuda; from north to south, 1,242 miles, equal to that between Berlin and Algiers. Within the archipelago are more than 3,000 islands and 30,000 islets and atolls, ranging from Kalimantan (Borneo), an area almost equal to that of France, to uninhabited, nameless coral reefs. Unwinding along the southern periphery of the Asian mainland, the insular chain is astride the trade routes linking the Indian and Pacific oceans, Western Europe and Eastern Asia, and athwart the air and sea lanes of Southeast Asia and Australia.

Strategic military considerations are not Indonesia's primary significance in the Cold War. Rather, Indonesia has the basic ingredients of power: an abundance of manpower, natural wealth, and potential hydroelectric power. In population, Indonesia ranks among the largest nations on earth, rivaling Pakistan as the largest state in the Islamic world. A bare century ago, the islands contained 12.5 million people;[4] now there are almost 96 million. Moreover, the population is increasing by 2.3 per cent annually. Eighty per cent of the Indonesians are impoverished, credulous peasants, the easy targets of demagogues and masters of deceit; more than 50 million people are crowded onto Java, whose total area is equal to that of New York State, making the island one of the most densely populated places on earth. Thus Java, which constitutes about 7 per cent of Indonesia's land mass, contains three-fifths of its people. By the middle of this decade, the archipelago will embrace more than 100 million people. The Communist world has demonstrated the capability of a rigorously controlled society to organize and exploit large reservoirs of manpower. During World War II, at a cost of 2 million Indonesian lives, Japan showed the feasibility of applying a totalitarian system to Indonesia.

In natural resources, Indonesia ranks as the third-richest nation in the world, after the United States and the Soviet Union. The archipelago is a treasure chest of mineral deposits and reserves (oil, iron, coal, bauxite, copper, nickel, manganese, gold and silver, industrial diamonds). In 1959, the International Atomic Energy Agency found evidence of uranium and beryllium deposits on Sumatra and Kalimantan. Some of the islands are said literally to float on underground, untapped lakes of oil. The archipelago is also a potential storehouse of foodstuffs and commercial crops (rice, rubber, sugar, sisal, coffee, tea, tobacco, ground nuts, palm oil, forest products, and spices). Indonesia's soil, composed largely of volcanic ash, is almost inexhaustibly fertile.[5] Yet many of the larger islands, including Sumatra, are sparsely cultivated and inhabited and covered with rain forests.

The crucial question confronting Indonesia is how her power potential will be developed. Can she achieve economic growth and social reform only by sacrificing her revolutionary political ideal— an independent, democratic republic?

In the Indonesian Communist movement, Moscow and/or Peking have a potentially powerful instrument for bringing about the collapse and integration of Indonesia into the Communist world. The PKI is an orthodox Communist Party and, accordingly, has had a long, though at times troubled, history of fidelity to Moscow. This loyalty has been rooted in the proposition, albeit one that has led to some conflict within the Communist world in recent years, that whatever advances the Kremlin's interests in turn advances the interests of international Communism and, therefore, the PKI's.

Loyalty to the Moscow line has been a paramount feature of the PKI's history. There have, however, been two exceptions to the general rule: one fleeting, the other of unknown duration and consequence. The first exception, if it may be termed such, occurred during the confused initial phase of the power struggle between Stalin and Trotsky. The Indonesian Communists hedged their bets as to the outcome—with calamitous results. The aberration proved short-lived; Stalin emerged triumphant and imposed his will on the international Communist movement. Thereafter, until 1961, the PKI obediently followed the zigs and zags of the line. Then, in late 1961, with the Communist world shaken by the airing of the Moscow-Peking dispute, the PKI's fidelity to Moscow again faltered. As in the 1920's the Indonesian Communists moved onto the fence. They are still straddling it at this writing.

But whatever the impact of the Sino-Soviet dispute on the Indonesian Communists, however prolonged or fleeting the divisive tendencies within the Communist camp may prove to be, the important thing within an Indonesian, Southeast Asian, and Southwest Pacific context is that in the PKI, the Communists in Indonesia control a power-hungry mass organization forged in the crucible of intrigue and revolution. In 1926, the PKI rose in rebellion against Dutch colonialism and was crushed. In 1948, the PKI again acted on the Leninist principle that the central and highest task of revolution is the seizure of power by armed force. On that occasion, during the dark days of Indonesia's struggle for emancipation from Dutch rule, the PKI turned on the embattled republic and was again crushed. Then, in 1951, following a protracted period of rising PKI agitation in what appeared to some as the prelude to still another Communist power play, the republic, for the first time after independence, took the initiative against the Communists, ensuring itself against the probability of another PKI adventure.

Despite these abortive efforts to achieve power in Indonesia, despite the ferment within the Communist world—glaringly exposed in Hungary and Tibet, by Khrushchev's denunciation of Stalin, and by the differences between Moscow and Peking—the militancy and dedication of purpose of the Communist leadership in Indonesia is undiluted. The PKI at present has lost little, if any, of its faith in the *dynamique mystique* of Communism, of its revolutionary ardor and sense of mission, although, inevitably, the schisms within the Communist world must erode these articles of faith and raise doubts about the dogma that Communism is the irresistible wave of the future.

By any political standards, the situation in contemporary Indonesia should be viewed as critical. Its urgency is reflected in the striking similarity between it and China's development in the turbulent years prior to the Communist assumption of power on the mainland. Communism came to power in China largely by default. It came at a time when nationalism was partially spent, either unwilling or unable to resolve the far-reaching social and economic problems arising from nationalist revolution and the founding of the Chinese Republic in 1911. Like China, Indonesia has been in the throes of political, economic, and social disintegration for almost a generation. The situation, within the Indonesian context, has closely paralleled the tragedy of the Chinese Republic. As early as 1953, the nationalist daily, *Indonesian Observer*, commented: "We are gradually resembling the China of Chiang Kaishek."

Indonesia has suffered recurrent cabinet crises, intermittent revolts by extremist factions of the Left and Right, and localized civil conflict. The revolutionary leadership has split on the surface over personal issues, and beneath the surface over the basic question of which political road to travel—the unending pursuit of the general good and individual welfare, or the path of supernationalism, xenophobia, the glorification of the state and its leaders as an end in itself. Amidst this turbulent setting, many of the hopes and dreams of the Indonesian revolution have faded. The results of free elections have been obliterated, civil liberties curtailed. Lately there has been galloping inflation in the seaports and a new wave of unrest in the villages. The central government, an uneasy partnership between President Sukarno and the army, has ruled by fiat and sought to meet financial obligations by the expediency of the printing press, the expropriation of minority capital (Dutch and Chinese), and the indiscriminate solicitation of military and economic assistance from both East and West. Significantly, the Soviet Union, since launching its formal assistance program in 1955, has provided more military aid to Indonesia than to any other non-Communist country in Asia.

A political history of the PKI is obviously indispensable to anybody concerned with the question of "Who encircles whom?" and Indonesia's bearing on the answer. But the library shelf on Indonesian Communism is almost bare. This is not altogether surprising. As Guy Wint has observed, the history of the Chinese Communist movement was neglected until it almost became the master of the country. The first comprehensive book on the history of the Indian Communist Party, by M. R. Masani, appeared only in 1954. Yet the PKI has long proposed a solution for Indonesia's problems, and the Communist package has attracted considerable support within the country. The PKI has proposed the creation of a "people's government, a government of democracy of a new type, a government of people's democracy." The formula guarantees freedom of speech, religion, the press, and assembly, as well as the right to work, to demonstrate, and to strike.

By PKI definition, a people's democracy is a government of the national united front formed on the basis of the alliance of the workers and peasants under the leadership of the working class. Because of the economic underdevelopment of Indonesia, the PKI holds that this government should not be a government of the dictatorship of the people. This was the Communist stratagem in Eastern Europe and China—backed, significantly, by military power.

The PKI prescription is disarmingly simple. The "united national-front government" is to be an alliance embracing workers, peasants, petty bourgeoisie, and national bourgeoisie—Mao's "four-class bloc." In terms of practical power, the PKI would govern the front. Soviet theoreticians have repeatedly stated that a people's democratic regime performs the function of a dictatorship of the proletariat and is a political form of the dictatorship of the proletariat, i.e., a dictatorship of the Communist Party. At the PKI's Sixth National Congress in 1959, Indonesia's Communists reaffirmed confidence in this future, declaring that

> there is no longer any doubt that this objective [a people's democracy] will be achieved because the shining star that illumines the path of the Indonesian people's struggle is the all-powerful teachings of Marx, Engels and Lenin, and because the experience of the two great peoples—the Soviet people and the Chinese people—are examples that give inspiration to the Indonesian people under the leadership of the working class and the Communist Party of Indonesia. There is no other easier or more correct path than this, nor can there possibly be.

Thus, the Party program exhorted Indonesia's

> working class, the peasants, the intelligentsia, the petty bourgeoisie and the national bourgeoisie in the various progressive political parties, organizations, and other progressive forces to unite, to strengthen and expand the national united front in the struggle for independence, democratic freedoms and economic prosperity for Indonesia, in the struggle for a happy New Indonesia.

The PKI appeal is manifold. To toiling, naïve peasants, the "New Indonesia" is a Promised Land; indeed, the peasants are expressly promised land. The peasants are told that Communism is a blessing, as it will free the people from oppression. The appeal evokes response; it was Aristotle, not Marx, who observed that poverty is the "parent of revolution." But the end of poverty is not the only appeal. To many of the bourgeoisie, caught up in the ruinous whirl of inflation and its silent companion, corruption, the New Indonesia holds the promise of perhaps putting a halt to economic and social chaos. The Communists seek to assure the middle classes, constituting barely 10 per cent of Indonesian society, a place in the new order, promising them the prestige and security of the straw boss and bureaucrat. The Communist appeal to the bourgeoisie in the underdeveloped nations also generates response from what Sir Julian Huxley has termed the "revolution of expectation," the ferment growing out of the widening abyss between the haves and have-nots. To the demi-intellectual and, paradoxically, to the crude practitioner of force—the rootless street fighter—the Communists offer an emotional outlet for agitation against the existing order, a formula for resolving the frustrations and problems of contemporary society, an ideological guide to action, association with the "winning side" (i.e., Russia and China), and, above all, the prospect of real power.

The universal appeal to throw off "colonial" (i.e., Western) political, economic, and cultural domination transcends class lines. As the natural foes of Western influence in all its manifestations, the Communists in Indonesia, as elsewhere in Asia, have successfully exploited the colonial past and the nationalist present, portraying themselves as allies of the postwar revolutionary movements in the underdeveloped world. They have judiciously contributed to a psychological atmosphere in which anti-Communism is equated with the heresy of counterrevolution.

A history of the PKI entails obvious pitfalls. The PKI, like Communist parties the world over, is conspiratorial in character. Its decisions are arrived at *in camera*. It operates a legal and an illegal apparatus. Moreover, many of its documents have been lost in the tumult of Dutch colonial rule, Japanese occupation, and Indonesian revolution. To compound the problem, the PKI, like other Communist parties, has a predilection—a dialectical compulsion, if you will—to "doublethink," to rearrange and, if necessary, create "facts" to suit the Party posture at a given time. The Indonesian Party program adopted at the Sixth Congress, referred to "the shining star that illumines the path of the Indonesian people's struggle . . . the all-powerful teachings of Marx, Engels, and Lenin."

That Congress convened in 1959, three years after Khrushchev's denunciation of Stalin. But at the Fifth Congress, in 1953, the PKI found the road "lighted by the rays of Marxism, Engelism [*sic*], Leninism and Stalinism."

In the intervening years, Stalin's star had waned. But who can say that a Stalin will not be reborn tomorrow? What checks and balances in the system of "democratic centralism" can prevent insolence of office in the world of Marxism-Leninism?

The difficulty of writing on the PKI is further compounded by the Party's viewing of all world affairs through the distorting prism of Leninism, which the British political writer George Lichtheim describes as "a system of thought which obscures the facts it purports to describe." An example is the Communists' use of the term "proletarian revolution" to describe the totalitarian rearrangement of society *after* the capture of power.

Communists frequently resort to the term "democracy" in stating their goals and aims. But what do they mean by democracy? The word, controversial as it is in the non-Communist world, is loosely construed as meaning a system in which power with restraint is freely delegated and renewed by consent of the governed. Democracy will probably never be defined to everyone's satisfaction. Representative government is a fair description, and it may take many forms, e.g., parliamentary system, presidential system, etc. But it is not a distortion to say that democracy—as the non-Communist world understands it—is the antithesis of arbitrary rule, government by decree, control and draconic regimentation of every facet of life by an omnipotent, omnipresent state. Yet, in the Marxist-Leninist lexicon, totalitarianism is democracy. In that special terminology, democracy is "centralized guidance," in which decisions arbitrarily drawn by a self-perpetuating autocracy are "promptly transmitted" to the people.

In the following pages an attempt is made to overcome some of these semantic problems by using PKI documents and statements *in extenso*. Given enough words, to paraphrase Lenin, we shall provide enough rope to know the hangman. For obvious reasons, the emphasis will be on the PKI's development and growth in postwar Indonesia, for it was only after World War II and the decline of Western power in the archipelago that hegemony over the East Indies passed into Indonesian hands, enabling the PKI to function freely in a purely Indonesian environment and society. It was only after World War II that Indonesia emerged as a potential arbiter in the struggle between the Communist and non-Communist worlds—as demonstrated by Sukarno's September, 1961, mission to Washington on behalf of the "nonaligned" Belgrade powers—and that, in turn, the role of the Communists in Indonesia assumed critical international importance.

What follows, then, is a general account of the growth and development of the Indonesian Communist Party. The author wishes first of all to acknowledge an obvious and deep debt to the work of journalists and academicians cited in the notes; to a group of "personal encouragers," in particular the late Donald Fagg; to those who provided invaluable suggestions, in particular Lyman Hoover; to those who assisted in the process of producing this book, in particular Malcolm Reiss, Frances Camiano, and Jean Steinberg; and, above all, to the many Indonesian leaders who have taken the author into their confidence for almost a double _windu_, but who, for political reasons, cannot be publicly identified at this time. The author, of course, assumes all responsibility for the book as it stands; any errors of fact or interpretation are solely his.

A word about Indonesian names. The author has employed Indonesian names wherever possible, i.e., Kalimantan for Borneo, Sulawesi for the Celebes, Nusatenggara for the Lesser Sundas, and West Irian for West New Guinea. Similarly, and equally arbitrarily, the author has used the names commonly employed in Indonesia for political figures: Thus, Amir Sjarifuddin is Amir; Sjafruddin Prawiranegara is Sjafruddin; Ali Sastroamidjojo and Alimin Prawirodirdjo are Ali and Alimin, respectively. But Mohammed Natsir is Natsir, Dipa Nusantara Aidit is Aidit, and Sutan Sjahrir is Sjahrir. To complicate matters, many Indonesians have only one name; e.g., Wilopo and Sukarno. The latter, incidentally, still writes his name in the Dutch fashion—Soekarno—whereas Mohammad Roem prefers to be known as Rum. In some cases, Indonesians are known only by full names: The best example is Tan Malaka (also spelled Tan Malakka), who is never called simply Tan or Malaka. However, the author has avoided the extreme of using the most common designation in each instance, e.g., Badio for Subadio Sastrosatomo. The rule has been to make the text readable.

It is the author's hope that this book, in some measure, will contribute to the world's growing knowledge of Communist strategies and tactics, enlighten the general reader, open new avenues of exploration for scholars, and focus attention on the Indonesian phase of mankind's never-ending struggle for civil liberties and representative government—goals the Communists pay lip service to and exploit for their own totalitarian ends.

ARNOLD C. BRACKMAN

Dobbs Ferry, N.Y.
September, 1962

INDONESIAN COMMUNISM
A HISTORY

1

The Road from Semarang

The Bolsheviks' seizure of power in Russia in 1917 was followed by a series of revolutionary actions—some related, some not—in Europe and the Afro-Asian world. Between 1918 and 1927, revolutions flashed in Finland, Austria, Germany, Hungary, Korea, Turkey, Bulgaria, Estonia, Morocco, and Syria; "rice riots" stirred Japan; a general strike engulfed England. In 1928, the Sixth World Congress of the Communist International (Comintern) averred:

> These events, as well as events like the uprising in Indonesia, the deep ferment in India, the great Chinese revolution that shook the whole Asiatic continent, are links in one and the same international revolutionary chain, constituent parts of the profound general crisis of capitalism.

Of these events, perhaps the most obscure occurred in the remote Netherlands East Indies. There, on May 23, 1920, the first Communist Party in Asia was founded under Western guidance, the Perserikaten Kommunis di India—the Communist Association of the Indies—later renamed Partai Kommunis Indonesia. The birth of this organization ushered in six turbulent and formative years for the Indonesian Communist movement, ending with an abortive insurrection that left its leadership divided and the Party itself outlawed and driven underground. Looking back thirty-five years later, D. N. Aidit, the Party's General Secretary, observed: "The PKI was a child of the period in which it was born." [1]

The progenitor of revolutionary Marxism in the Indies was H. J. F. M. Sneevliet, a Dutch radical socialist.* In 1913, Sneevliet arrived at the port of Semarang, on the northern coast of Java, as the employee of a trading association. Whether he chose to go to the Indies for political, economic, or personal reasons is conjectural. But whatever his motivation, Sneevliet found Indonesia fertile soil in which to plant the Marxist idea of a society divided, Aristotelian fashion, into two camps: the oppressed (proletarians), and the oppressor (bourgeoisie).

Sneevliet's Indies on the eve of World War I were a colonial empire over which, with the still-smoldering "pacification" of Bali, the Dutch had just established hegemony, in a process of colonial ingestion dating back to 1596. In 1913, the islands contained about 40 million Indonesians, 900,000 Chinese, and 100,000 Europeans (perhaps 90 per cent of whom were Eurasian). Far from homogeneous, the Indonesian population was composed of 80 distinct ethnological groupings, largely of common Malay stock, who spoke 20 different languages and 200 dialects. About 85 per cent of the Indonesian people lived on Java, an island constituting barely 7 per cent of the archipelago's land mass. The cultural level, then as now, ranged unevenly from the Stone Age of the Papuans in West Irian to the relatively sophisticated society of the Javanese, whose social fabric was woven from animistic, Hinduistic, and Islamic strands. Yet despite these disparate elements, the people of the islands had a sense of oneness. The three most powerful unifying factors were language (Malay was the lingua franca of the islands); religion (almost all Indonesians were nominally Moslem); and the Dutch (whose highly centralized colonial rule extended from Sabang, on the tip of North Sumatra, to Merauke, in West Irian). In the modern political sense, the concept "Indonesia" is largely an unintentional Dutch creation.

At the time of Sneevliet's arrival, most of the Indonesians lived in village clusters and tilled communal rice fields. The country supported neither an industry nor a landed gentry of consequence. About 95 per cent of the population was illiterate, impoverished, unworldly, and politically inarticulate. Nonetheless, unlike most of the Afro-Asian world, Indonesia had minimal problems of food, water, clothing, and shelter; it was neither a desert wasteland like

---

* Sneevliet was a member of the radical "Tribunist" faction of the Dutch Social Democratic Labor Party (SDAP), founded in 1909. In 1918, the SDAP became the Communist Party of Holland; in 1935, the Party changed its name to the Communist Party Netherlands, thereby embracing the Empire, including the East Indies.

the Middle East nor a depressing mass of humanity like India and China.

Considering the Netherlands limited manpower and financial resources,* the island empire was relatively well administered in an atmosphere of *Pax Neerlandica.* In terms of raw power, the Dutch ruled with the blessings of the British, who after briefly controlling the archipelago during the Napoleonic wars, returned the islands to the Dutch. However, any radical shift in the British position in Asia clearly would have an unsettling impact on the continuity of Dutch rule. But this was 1913, and the world order appeared immutable.

Dutch rule exploited the general submissiveness of the people, particularly on Java, and relied heavily on a rigid political, economic, and social stratification of society. The Dutch occupied the apex of the power pyramid, the Chinese the middle, and the Indonesians the broad base. The Dutch had perfected "indirect rule," governing through intermediaries such as the local aristocracy. At the village level, government was administered within the framework of traditional Indonesian forms: *gotong royong* (mutual assistance, a spirit of "all for all"), *mufakat* (decisions by unanimity, a village variant of the veto), and *musjawarah* (deliberations among representatives, invariably elders). In the economic and social spheres, the Dutch discriminated against the nonwhite community, employing the Chinese as a middle-class buffer between themselves and the Indonesians. Two legal systems prevailed, one based, as in the Netherlands, on the Napoleonic Code, and the other on *adat,* or local law, which varied from area to area and encouraged regionalism. Thus, the Dutch political objective was to maintain Indonesia in a state of suspended animation. Dutch scholars, however, recognized that "the people of the Indies form basically one social group, which, in the course of time, will develop into a great and united nation."[2] Nonetheless, in a country of literally tens of millions, the Dutch ruled with a maximum of 10,000 white troops.[3]

Although the Indonesians were politically unaware and unorganized, and their direct contact with the Dutch was minimal, a tremor of nationalism pulsated through the islands in 1905. The Japanese, by their triumph over Russia, had demonstrated that Asians were technically capable of meeting the West on equal power terms. The tremors were transmitted by the Indonesian

* Prewar foreign investment in Indonesia totaled barely $520 million—75 per cent Dutch, 13.5 per cent British, 5 per cent French, 2 per cent German, 1.5 per cent Swedish, 1 per cent American, and 1 per cent Japanese.

"middle class," whose upward surge had brought them into collision with the industrious Chinese and the Indonesian "educated class," which found political, economic, and social advancement barred by the colonial system. Among the Indonesians, frustration and its companion, bitterness, deepened.

The history of international relations is written largely in terms of the attempts of some peoples to dominate others, and the determination of all peoples to resist domination. In 1913, Indonesia was ruled by a minority of an alien race, language, religion, and mores. The logic of history demanded that the Malay majority ultimately assert itself in Indonesia. The only question was *how*.

As World War I approached, the Sarekat Islam (Islamic Association) was in the vanguard of the emerging Indonesian nationalist movement. Its predecessor, the Sarekat Dagang Islam (Islamic Trading Association), had been founded in 1911 in response to the expansion of Chinese economic influence on Java, an indirect outgrowth of the Chinese revolution of that year. The Dageng incited racial riots against Chinese stall owners, and the Dutch outlawed the organization. The following year the Dageng, re-cast in a moderate mold, emerged as the Sarekat Islam. Although these developments went unnoticed in the West, Lenin saw their significance. On May 7, 1913, he wrote in *Pravda:* "A significant development is the spread of the revolutionary democratic movement to the Dutch Indies, to Java and the other Dutch colonies [*sic*], with their population of some 40 million."

Lenin ascribed the phenomenon to the revolt of Islamic reformists in Turkey in 1908, the gradual emergence of an Indonesian intelligentsia during the early stages of "capitalism," and the revolutionary fervor of the emigrants from the Chinese mainland. Although Lenin misread the role of the Chinese, he already foresaw power possibilities in Indonesia. For that matter so did Sneevliet, then living on Java.

At Semarang, Sneevliet made common cause with a band of restless Dutch radical socialists who, morally outraged by the glaring inequities of colonial rule, were eager to apply their Marxist theories to Indonesia. They sensed the explosive revolutionary ferment developing beneath the placid surface of Indonesian life. In 1914, Sneevliet, together with J. A. Brandsteder, H. W. Dekker, and P. Bergsma, founded the first Marxist organization in the history of Southeast Asia, the Social Democratic Association of the Indies (ISDV). Being affluent, the ISDV published its first magazine, *The Free Word*, on October 10 of the following year.[4] Its editors were Sneevliet, Bergsma, and another Dutch radical socialist, A. Baars, a teacher at the Queen Emma School in Surabaya.

The creation of a small revolutionary socialist cadre within the Dutch community was neither surprising, given the growth of Marxist thought in pre-1914 Europe, nor threatening to the Dutch position in the Indies. The ISDV held no appeal for the colonial settlers, and it was doubtful that the ISDV would be able to exert influence on the nationalist movement: The barriers—religious, linguistic, and racial—appeared to be too formidable. Yet, as Sneevliet sensed, the ISDV had to penetrate the Sarekat Islam if the approaching Indonesian revolution was to be guided along the path of revolutionary Marxism. In 1916, Sneevliet developed a novel method of infiltration, the "bloc within" technique of dual party membership, whereby members of the Sarekat Islam would be drawn into the ISDV while retaining their membership in the Sarekat Islam. This tactic was a wide departure from the customary two-party alliance (obviously inapplicable in the Indies context), which the Communists have since described as the "bloc without."

In 1917, Sneevliet established contact with two Indonesians amenable to the tactic—Semaun, the head of the Sarekat Islam's Semarang chapter, and Darsono, an aspiring journalist. Both were Javanese, in their twenties, resentful of the old order, dedicated to promoting a new order, ambitious, and politically capable. By entering the ISDV while retaining membership in the Sarekat Islam, the two men became the first "transmission belt" between the revolutionary Marxism of the West and the Indonesian masses.

Their recruitment into the ISDV coincided with the Russian Revolution, an event that transported Sneevliet to heights of ecstasy. He plunged himself into the politics of revolution, publicly urging the Indonesians to emulate the Russians and secretly trying to build blocs within at different levels of Indonesian society—in the embryo labor movement as well as in the Dutch armed forces. His activities attracted the attention of the Dutch Political Intelligence Service (PID), and in 1918, Sneevliet was expelled from the Indies. Brandsteder followed in 1919, Baars in 1921, and the last of the Dutch radicals in 1923.

While the ISDV maneuvered to infiltrate the nationalist movement in remote Indonesia, revolutionary sentiment burgeoned in postwar Europe. In the hope of exploiting this revolutionary upsurge, Lenin, in 1919, convened the First Congress of the Comintern and sounded the call for recruits to world revolution. Heralding Communist strategy, the manifesto of the Congress set the tone: "Colonial slaves of Africa and Asia! When the hour of the dictatorship of the proletariat in Europe strikes, the hour of your liberation shall have come."

It required no particular insight into Marxist social theories to appreciate Lenin's grand design. The triumph of Communism in the West was equated with the "national liberation" of the Afro-Asian world. On distant Java, the ISDV responded enthusiastically. In a move foreshadowing the conditions for admission to the Comintern adopted by the Second Congress in 1920, the ISDV met on May 23, 1920, and after heated debate voted thirty-three to two, with one abstention, to rename the association Perserikaten Kommunis di India. The historic meeting took place at the Semarang offices of the Sarekat Islam. Semaun was elected Chairman; Darsono, Vice Chairman; Bergsma, Secretary; Dekker, Treasurer; Baars, a board member. A national council was established, and representatives appointed for West, Central and East Java. As Baars explained: "We have long been Communists. The change in party name does not change our goal of Communism—the establishment of a dictatorship of the proletariat, the only possible course for building a socialist society."

Sneevliet's symbiotism was working faultlessly. Semaun was now chairman of the Semarang branches of both the Sarekat Islam and the PKI.

That summer, the PKI was represented at the Second Comintern Congress by Sneevliet (using the alias Maring), who attended as a proxy delegate. Technically, of course, the PKI was not even a member of the Communist International. But on Christmas Eve, it corrected the oversight, voting unanimously to accept the "Twenty-one Conditions" for membership on the ground that to "consolidate our position, an affiliation with Moscow is necessary." The conditions called for the expulsion of "all reformists"; the creation, if necessary, of "a parallel illegal apparatus"; agitation among "workers and peasants"; support of the "movement of liberation in the colonies"; adherence to "democratic centralism," with directives from Moscow to be implemented with "iron discipline"; and, as evidence of international solidarity, changing the PKI's designation from *perserikaten* (association) to *partai* (party).

The PKI looked forward hopefully to 1921, mapping plans to capture the Sarekat Islam and fashion a revolutionary mass movement. The Party had cause for optimism. Sneevliet's demagogy, transmitted by Semaun and Darsono, had struck a responsive chord within the Sarekat Islam, particularly the Leninist dogma that imperialism was the final phase of capitalism and was

responsible for Indonesia's subjugation. Influenced by the nationalist content of Marxism, the Sarekat Islam became increasingly
radical in outlook. In 1917, the association was openly demanding
independence for Indonesia; so attractive was the appeal that
within two years, the ranks of the Sarekat Islam swelled to 2.5
million. But there were subtle and substantive differences between
the platform of the Sarekat Islam and that of its bloc within.
The Sarekat Islam stressed the attainment of independence by
evolutionary, not revolutionary, means. Moreover, in calling for
a struggle against capitalism, the Sarekat Islam specified a struggle
against "sinful" capitalism—that is, foreign as distinguished from
Indonesian capitalism. Thus, Marxism proved attractive in Indonesia not because of its economic and social doctrines but because of its nationalist content. A generation later, with the founding of the Indonesian Republic, virtually all Indonesian leaders,
including the most adamantine anti-Communists, would consider
themselves "Marxist," in the sense of being hostile toward foreign
"capitalism."

As Semaun's influence within the Sarekat Islam deepened, the
moderate Islamic leadership, feeling itself undermined, engaged
in a contest for control with the Communists and drove the
organization further to the left. This, in turn, increasingly attracted the attention of the PID, and the Javanese membership,
traditionally submissive to authority, abandoned the association
in ever-larger numbers. The contest for power at the top was no
longer a competition designed to attract a broader mass following,
but rather a struggle for control of the organization itself. A
showdown between the moderate Sarekat Islam leadership and
the Communist faction appeared inevitable.

The showdown came in October, 1921, at the Sarekat Islam's
Sixth National Congress. The PKI faction, led by Semaun and
Tan Malaka, an aspiring young Sumatran with a flair for prop-
aganda work, made an open bid for control. Their drive was blocked
by a rising modernist, reformist leader in the Islamic world, Agus
Salim, who had contested Semaun for control of the Indonesian
trade-union movement the year before and had lost. At the
Congress, Salim deflated the arguments of Semaun and Tan
Malaka with the historic rejoinder that Mohammed had preached
socialism twelve hundred years before Marx. He then induced the
Congress to pass a resolution barring members of the Sarekat
Islam from holding membership in another party. The Com-
munists resigned *en masse* and in December they set up Red
Sarekat Islam branches in opposition to the parent body. For the

first time, the struggle between the forces of Islam and Communism was openly joined in Indonesia.

Displaying a marked aptitude for demagogy at the rice roots, the Communists overshadowed their rivals in capturing the dwindling number of Sarekat Islam members and demonstrated their militancy by staging a series of strikes that culminated in an abortive general strike in 1925. Thus, in 1923, Tan Malaka could point to "the great crisis developing in our favor in the Sarekat Islam" and inform the Comintern that PKI control already extended to 20 Sarekat Islam sections which once claimed 100,000 members, on 30,000 of whom "we can count." [5] The PKI itself claimed 38 sections and a hard-core membership of 1,140— "Very large," Aidit later observed—compared to the 900 members then in the Chinese Communist Party.[6]

By 1923, the breach between the PKI and Sarekat Islam had become irreparable. The PKI, at its Fourth Congress, in March, 1923, voted to compete against the Sarekat Islam as a separate and distinct political organization and not as a splinter. As a consequence, the Red Sarekat Islam changed its name to the Sarekat Rakjat (People's Association) and campaigned as a new radical nationalist organization. The Party also considered it opportune to extend its radius of activity beyond Java. The PKI opened branches in Padang, Sumatra, and Macassar, Sulawesi.

Despite the over-all advances made by the PKI, two major developments conspired to arrest its growth. One was ideological— and beyond the control of the Party. The Second Comintern Congress had adopted the "Theses on the National and Colonial Questions," which Sneevliet has helped draft. Its gist was the familiar line that one of the main sources from which European capitalism draws its chief strength is to be found in the colonial possessions. Thus the breaking up of the colonial empires, together with the proletarian revolution in the home country, will overthrow the capitalist system in Europe.

However, the theses held that although the revolution in the colonies is not going to be a Communist revolution in its first stages, this did not imply that the Communists should abdicate the leadership of national-liberation movements to "bourgeois democrats." The theses also asserted that the outcome of the revolution in Asia hinged on the attitude of the peasantry and cited the peasantry of backward countries as of "special importance." "Above all," the document stated, "we must strive as far as possible to give the peasant movement a revolutionary character." The Comintern analysis also stressed the concomitant necessity to combat Pan-Islamic and Pan-Asian movements. It called for "war against the attempt of quasi-Communist revolutionists to cloak the liberation movement in the backward countries with a Communist garb." Thus the Comintern attempted to blow and swallow simultaneously. The Moscow directives thrust the PKI into an unenviable position. On the one hand, the PKI was urged to support the revolutionary national-bourgeois liberation movement at home. In a predominantly Moslem country like Indonesia, where Islam served as a rallying point against the Christian colonizer, this obviously implied support of Pan-Islam. On the other hand, the PKI was exhorted to combat Pan-Islam as a "bourgeois-nationalist" manifestation detrimental to the creation of a Communist world order. Among the PKI leaders, Tan Malaka made the most persuasive effort to convince the Comintern of the contradiction in its national and colonial theses, at least as applied to Indonesia. He appealed to the Comintern to endorse Pan-Islam as a fraternity of oppressed, colonized peoples in revolt against the West. At the Fourth Comintern Congress, in 1922, he warned that the "hostility to Pan-Islam expressed by the Second Congress had damaged the position of Communists [in Indonesia]." [7] But the Comintern ignored Tan Malaka's warnings. The PKI was destined to become impaled on the horns of this dilemma.

The other major development restricting Communist growth in Indonesia at this stage was the Party's uncontrollable spin to the left. The PKI had become obsessed by its own left-wing slogans, a condition that Lenin had diagnosed in 1920 as an "infantile disorder." Gradually, the leadership of the PKI had slipped into the hands of a radical clique. The radicals were led by Alimin Prawirodirdjo (the adopted son of a Dutch professor), an activist in the Sarekat Islam and ISDV, and by Musso, a postal clerk who had organized a union of postal workers and had a reputation in Surabaya as a street brawler. One immediate consequence of the increasingly revolutionary Party line was an intensification of colonial harassment. The further left the PKI traveled, the closer the surveillance of the PID. The Dutch, aware of the abyss between the PKI leadership and the masses it sought to control, developed an ingenious policy of decapitation. They expelled Communist leaders from the Indies in systematic fashion in an effort to prevent the PKI, then a disorganized body, from turning into a genuine mass movement. Communist functionaries were arrested and offered the alternative of internment in Indonesia or political exile in a country of their own choosing. Invariably, they chose the latter course, usually opting for Russia, China, or Holland. Thus Tan Malaka, who had been elected

PKI Chairman in 1922, was banished from the Indies that same year; Semaun, his successor, in 1923 (together with the remainder of the Dutch radicals); and Darsono, the Party's Second Chairman, in 1925. There were also flights abroad. In 1925, harassed by the Dutch, Alimin, Musso, and Sardjono (a Madurese Communist leader) fled to Singapore. Once abroad, they shuttled between Europe and Asia as agents of the Comintern, the PKI, or both. Thus, as the PKI tilted to the left, it was being denuded of its Dutch tutors and indigenous leadership. Between the PKI command and the rank and file, a gap was developing.

2

An Infantile Disorder

As the void developed and the party wrestled with the Comintern's confusing directives, Moscow, following the death of Lenin in 1924, was immersed in the titanic Stalin-Trotsky struggle for power. In August, with Stalin in the ascendancy, the Fifth Comintern Congress convened in Moscow. Stalin was instrumental in the preparation of a manifesto stating that "all sections" (parties) of the Comintern were in the throes of ideological crisis, torn by Right and Left deviations. Only Stalin, of course, with Solomonesque wisdom, could resolve these crises. As a starting point, the manifesto called for the creation of parties of a "new type," so-called Bolshevized parties—i.e., parties submissive to the dictates of Stalin. In fact, Stalin was deliberately pitting one faction against another in every Communist Party in an effort to divine those ready to support him.

Semaun, the PKI delegate at Moscow, presumably conveyed the nature of this grim struggle to the Party in Indonesia, for in December, the PKI summoned a congress of its own at Jogjakarta, in Central Java, to review the tense situation. The Party, confronted with problems at home, elected to straddle the Moscow conflict and named a new chairman, Alimin, who had never been outside Java and was therefore "neutral." It also passed two resolutions: One, displaying Rightist-deviationist tendencies, endorsed the eventual dissolution of the Sarekat Rakjat, the PKI's peasant base, and called for the development of a broader proletarian base in the towns and seaports; the other, displaying Left-deviationist tendencies, endorsed an armed revolution and the proclamation of a Soviet Republic of Indonesia. Thus, by driving simultaneously Right and Left, the PKI hoped to navigate the Moscow shoals. It was an absurd performance, since the PKI was simultaneously narrowing its social base while preparing for revolution. Abroad, both Tan Malaka and Moscow were disturbed by the implications of this approach.

Tan Malaka, now the Comintern agent for Southeast Asia and Australia, with headquarters at Manila, was appalled by what he considered a premature adventure that could end only in disaster. It was not that he opposed a violent overthrow of Dutch authority, but that he regarded the moment as inopportune. The PKI, he argued, was small, still preoccupied with the early stages of organization and discipline, insufficiently schooled in Marxist-Leninism, and lacking in both funds and weapons. Moreover, Tan Malaka was convinced that without the support of the peasantry, no revolution in the agrarian Afro-Asian world could succeed—as the Comintern's theses on colonialism had repeatedly emphasized.

The Comintern also perceived the folly of the PKI position. A Moscow directive from the Comintern's Executive Committee (ECCI) in March, 1925, ordered the PKI not to abandon the Sarekat Rakjat, but to transform it into a "genuine national front" under Communist direction, because the "experience of the international Communist movement has shown that there is not a single country in the world where the proletariat can count on success in the struggle unless it obtains the active support of the majority of the peasantry."

Five months later, in his only known public comment on the Indonesian Communist movement, Stalin joined the chorus: "The Communists in Java, who recently erroneously put forward the slogan of a Soviet government for the country, suffer, it seems, from a [Leftist] deviation . . . which threatens to isolate the Communist Party from the masses and to transform it into a sect." [1]

But the PKI appeared oblivious to these criticisms. There are several explanations, albeit conjectural, for the Party's behavior. For one, the Alimin-Musso and Tan Malaka factions had clashed over the control of the Party. It is not inconceivable that the Stalin-Trotsky feud served as a pretext for this struggle. In the ensuing contest, personalities transcended programs. Another factor was Dutch harassment, which was depriving the PKI of some of its ablest leaders; in the process, the strength of the Party was being dissipated. If it was to survive, this erosion had to be checked. But how? Alimin and Musso were convinced that the day could be saved by a seizure of power. The ECCI obviously failed to appreciate the nature of the Indonesian situation. The

Party had no choice in the matter. Moreover, overthrowing the Dutch would strengthen the PKI's position in Moscow. Certainly the moment was opportune. Even the non-Communist nationalists in Indonesia were proclaiming that "we are oriented towards revolution. And it is on this platform that nationalist and Communist find one another. We can perhaps differ in the choice of means by which to win the sovereignty of the people . . . [but] we can stand sympathetically in regard to one another." [2]

Thus, out of desperation more than hope, revolutionary sentiment mounted within the PKI. The 1925 general strike had been a failure; the Party hierarchy was largely in exile abroad; the Party's infrastructure weak. With legal avenues to power blocked by the colonial authority, and with Communist strength ebbing (as Semaun informed the ECCI in February, 1926), the only recourse was a bold move—a revolution.

The revolutionary die was cast in October, 1925, at Prambanan, Central Java, in a travel-folder setting of Hindu temple ruins. There the PKI's Executive Committee, under Alimin, approved plans for an armed insurrection the following June. Strikes on Java, culminating in a general strike, would create the mood. The Communists would rise first on Sumatra, then on Java, with Batavia, the seat of Dutch power, as the ultimate prize. But PKI security was poor. The next month, the PID raided PKI headquarters and branch offices and arrested the leadership, including Darsono, who, with Semaun, had formed Sneevliet's original transmission belt. Alimin, Musso, and Sardjono had already fled to Singapore. The PKI was now in turmoil. Wildcat strikes and minor armed disorders erupted, preparatory to the general strike scheduled for December, but they failed to attract mass support. In Singapore, Alimin and Musso misinterpreted the sporadic strike wave as a manifestation of deep economic and social discontent and became more determined to proceed with their plans for armed revolt. Comintern approval was imperative, for practical as well as ideological reasons. The PKI was in desperate need of moral support, funds, and weapons. Its leadership was confident that when its position was clarified in Moscow, the ECCI would approve its plans. A necessary, though distasteful, first step was to obtain Tan Malaka's endorsement.

Alimin invited Tan Malaka to come to Singapore from Manila for a conference, but the Comintern representative declined. Persisting, Alimin himself went to Manila, his sojourn indicative of the influence Tan Malaka exercised in the PKI as well as in Moscow. At Manila, Alimin explained the reasons for an immediate armed revolt and unfolded the plan for it. Tan Malaka was unimpressed. He held that the Party was incapable of executing such a grandiose scheme at this stage. Later, perhaps it would be feasible, but not until the PKI had generated a revolutionary mood among the Indonesian masses by instigating strikes and mass demonstrations. Alimin was aware of Tan Malaka's views, which the PKI had published at Semarang in 1921 in the pamphlet *Parliament or Soviet?* Tan Malaka had written: "We can defeat the wealth, the intelligence, and the solidarity of capitalists in Indonesia because, although we [Indonesians] lack wealth, there are many thousand times more of us than them."

Tan Malaka was an advocate of mass action; but before the Dutch could be defeated, the Indonesian masses had to be roused to a revolutionary emotional peak. In concluding his criticism, he told Alimin: "We must to the best of our ability avoid a defeat which would paralyze our organization for a long time to come." [3] Tan Malaka presented Alimin with a memorandum on his position, but after returning to Singapore, Alimin, wishing to create the impression that Tan Malaka agreed with his position, suppressed the memorandum. Alimin, accompanied by Musso, then departed for Moscow to solicit the blessings of the hierarchy.

In March, 1926, Tan Malaka arrived in Singapore, and there he learned of Alimin's duplicity from Djamaludin Tamin and Subakat, the PKI goalkeepers in the British colony. Tan Malaka dispatched them to Java to forestall the revolt and forwarded a report to the Kremlin. He also publicized his disapproval of the impending PKI adventure in a pamphlet, *Mass Action*, clandestinely published in Singapore.

In Moscow, meanwhile, Alimin and Musso found themselves drawn inexorably into the Stalin-Trotsky vortex. They had to choose. The atmosphere in Moscow was charged with intrigue, and their activities there can only be conjectured. It would be logical to assume that Trotsky, the proponent of world revolution, supported Alimin's plans, and that Stalin, who stressed the consolidation of the Russian Revolution first, disapproved. It is unlikely that the details will ever be disclosed. But apparently, Alimin and Musso won Stalin's approval of their plans—perhaps in return for their loyalty, or perhaps because Alimin and Musso informed Stalin, then the likely winner, that Tan Malaka harbored Trotskyite sympathies. What we do know incontestably is that Alimin and Musso proceeded with their plans for revolution, that they enjoyed Stalin's confidence during the remainder of his rule, and that when the revolution in Indonesia materialized, they received a warm endorsement from the ECCI (although, of course, the ECCI may have had no alternative but to support a revolution waged in the name of Communism).

In Indonesia, preparations for the revolution were accelerated. The PKI moved its headquarters from Batavia, the Dutch capital, to the mountain city of Bandung, and established a special underground apparatus, the DO (Double or Dictatorial Organization). Also, the Communists increased the volume of their revolutionary, nationalist propaganda, demonstrating the same skill that they were to exhibit during Indonesia's first general elections in 1955. The impending PKI uprising was portrayed as the harbinger of the general good. The ultimate goal was *merdeka* (independence), but everyone defined it differently, and the PKI had a kind word for all:

> The more well to do were promised a Utopia where they would . . . not have to pay any taxes. . . .
> The descendants of the sultans and the other title-bearers were promised the establishment of a new sultanate. . . .
> The followers of the religious leaders . . . were enticed with the prospects of the glories of paradise, the reward which would await them as warriors victorious in Allah's name. . . .
> Everyone was led to expect the blessings of cheap rice or free rice and free transport in cars and trains, etc.

The Communists also employed intimidation:

> Side by side with the illusions of fortune for those who would rebel were of course the threats for those who would not. They would not partake in the advantages of Utopia; on the contrary, they would be oppressed; their property would be confiscated for the founders of the new community.[4]

The PKI claimed that the impending revolt enjoyed Soviet backing and, for the benefit of the Faithful, that Kemal Atatürk would send Turkish airplanes (!) in support of the insurrection.

People were enticed into the revolutionary movement through deceptive maneuvers. First they purchased PKI membership cards, which purportedly would exempt them from the taxes of the Soviet Republic of Indonesia. Later, they were impressed with the knowledge that they had joined "a powerful, awe-inspiring, mysterious, and religious organization, which they would soon know more about." Techniques were devised to create the illusion of mass support, such as the widespread sale of red cloth as wearing apparel. It must be emphasized again that the victims of the Communist propagandists were impoverished, illiterate, and credulous. Moreover, the Dutch practice of labeling any Indonesian who favored an end to colonial rule as a "Communist" inadvertently provided the PKI with nationwide respectability, prestige, and sympathy.

The PKI also mustered bourgeois-nationalist support abroad. In the Netherlands, Semaun, on behalf of the Comintern, entered into negotiations with the Perhumpinan Indonesia (National Vanguard of the Movement for Indonesian Independence), the most powerful of the Indonesian student organizations. These were, of course, revolutionary times in the West. The Indonesian students in the Netherlands were exposed to the reverberations of the Bolshevik seizure of power in Russia and to the postwar wave of militant nationalism sweeping Europe—Wilson's principle of self- determination, the Irish rebellion, and the rebirth of independent East European states. Moreover, to many students in the Perhumpinan, Marxism was nothing more than an expression of Western humanism. Influenced by Marxism, some of the students were drawn into the Comintern; others entered the democratic socialist movement. Among the latter were Mohammed Hatta, then President of the Perhumpinan, and Sutan Sjahrir. Both were destined to guide the Indonesian revolution of 1945–49.

When Semaun approached Hatta and Sjahrir, they were already planning to found a nationalist party on their return to Indonesia. Apparently Hatta and Sjahrir regarded neither the supranational PKI, with its subservience to Moscow, nor the rival Sarekat Islam, with its strong religious overtones, as suitable vehicles for attaining the nationalist ideal of an independent, democratic republic of Indonesia. In December, 1926, with the PKI revolution in motion, Semaun and Hatta concluded a pact of cooperation. Under its terms, the Communists promised not to interfere in the development of the new nationalist party provided it trod an unswerving path toward an independent Indonesia. The PKI regarded the Semaun-Hatta accord as an attempt to build a united front with the nationalist bourgeoisie as the insurrection unfolded.

On Java, meanwhile, Tan Malaka's emissaries were spreading confusion at the Party's lower level, forcing postponement of the revolution from June, 1926, to the following November. On the eve of the adventure, Alimin, en route to Indonesia, arrived in Singapore. There he was apprehended by the British and given the alternative of prison or expulsion. ("Those were reactionary days," he said later.)[5] At his own request, Alimin was put on a ship for China. Despite its thorough disorganization, probably the result of the leadership crisis, the PKI proceeded with the revolution.

On November 13, 1926, at 12:30 A.M. 200 armed men seized the telephone-and-telegraph building in Batavia and severed com-

munications. The capital of the Netherlands East Indies was
isolated from the rest of the world. But at dawn, the Dutch Army
easily retook it. The sabotage coincided with minor disturbances
in Batavia's suburbs. That same night on Bantam, on the western
tip of Java, telephone lines were severed, railroad tracks demol-
ished, and barricades erected on main roads. Several village heads
and petty Indonesian officials in the colonial administration were
murdered. Similar events occurred in West Java (the Priangan)
and Central and East Java (Solo, Banjumas, Pekalongan, Kedu,
and Kediri). There, too, the Dutch encountered little difficulty in
restoring order. By November 19, the "revolution" on Java had
evaporated. In truth, it had never approached the emplaning
stage. The pattern of disorganization was complete when, on New
Year's Day, a PKI branch belatedly rose in rebellion in West
Sumatra (Padang and Padangpandjang). The revolutionary effort
dissipated almost immediately. In Bantam, it sputtered again, but
was quickly extinguished. In both cases, several armed bands
continued to operate for a short period, but their activities were
more in the nature of a "holy war" by Islamic zealots than a
Communist rebellion. In Moscow, however, the ECCI proclaimed:
"From this rostrum, we greet the proletarians and peasants of
Indonesia, the broad working masses of this Dutch colony who
are likewise engaged in a bloody struggle against capital. Our
full support to the Indonesian people!" [6]

The hard fact was that the "broad masses" of Indonesia had
failed to stir. The revolution had buckled, exposing the illusory
nature of the PKI assessment of the political situation. The Communist feint resembled a Javanese shadow play—imagery without
substance. A Dutch razzia followed. Nine persons were hanged for
terrorism;[7] some 13,000 were detained, and of these, about 6,000
were released, 5,000 given light prison sentences, and 1,308 interned;
823, presumably the hard core, were banished to the penal colony
of Tanah Merah (Red Earth) in the malaria-infested swamplands
of Boven Digul in southwest Irian. The Dutch estimated that, at
its crest, fewer than 8,000 persons had participated in the abortive
effort. Obviously, the great majority had had little conception of
what it was about. The Communists had exploited their credulity,
their natural grievances, their deep desire for freedom and a new
life. Sjahrir, who was later exiled to Irian, described his fellow
inmates of Tanah Merah as largely villagers who were politically
and intellectually unsophisticated and would have followed any
"prince or venal quack or lunatic" in rebellion against the Dutch.
"They are," Sjahrir wrote, "simply and fundamentally Indonesians." [8] They must be viewed in this light first, he said, and

only then could their "Communism" be evaluated. He described their Communism as an irrational blend of Hinduistic and Islamic influences, "with definite animistic tendencies." [9]

The Dutch assessed the rebels' Communism similarly.

In West Sumatra, a Dutch sociologist reported that the PKI membership consisted of "socially disillusioned and socially unbalanced persons"; that its leadership was drawn largely from intellectually frustrated schoolteachers and impoverished members of the nobility; that the Party's Agitprop section consisted of barbers, sewing-machine agents, village lawyers, and others "in close touch with village life"; and that the poorest peasant groups provided the rank and file.[10] "This time it was so-called Communists, another time it will be extreme nationalists or others who attempt the same thing," concluded an official Dutch commission of inquiry.[11] "The urge for freedom . . . stirs the best among these people." In effect, the Dutch conceded that the basic appeal of Communism was independence. And to this, the Dutch had no answer.[12]

Although a failure, the revolt had a tremendous psychological impact on both the Dutch and the Indonesians. It shattered Communist illusions about "mass support" and Dutch illusions about "native contentment." It encouraged many Indonesians to reappraise the permanence of colonial rule. The PKI could always claim that, although the revolt of 1926 was a fiasco, "there is one thing which cannot be forgotten, and that is that the revolt showed the Indonesian people that the Dutch could be thrown into confusion, that colonial power could be shaken, that this power was not eternal." [13]

Thus, there is some validity in Aidit's assertion that the affair raised the level of Indonesian political consciousness. Twenty years later, on the revolution's anniversary, a Sumatran newspaper extolled the insurrection, saying: "This day saw the beginning of Indonesia's battle for independence." [14] By 1961, the PKI was claiming that 1926 marked "the first armed national revolt of the Indonesian people" against Dutch rule, a gross distortion of Indonesian history.*

What was the Communist explanation for the debacle? It, of course, vindicated Tan Malaka. Sardjono, who was interned for

---

* The PKI claim was made in a message to the Albanian Workers' Party as broadcast by Tirana, February 15, 1962. For a list of armed national revolts punctuating Dutch rule in Indonesia since the seventeenth century, see *Lukisan Revolusi (Illustrations of the Revolution)*, Ministry of Information, Djakarta, 1950, pp. 14–17.

his complicity in the affair, later held that "we could not exploit the situation because the revolt was spontaneous and uncontrolled." [15] In his rewriting of history, Njoto, the second Deputy General Secretary of the PKI, conceded in 1958 that the basic reason for failure was "inadequate preparation. . . . Another reason was that the PKI at that time did not yet understand the need for uniting with the national bourgeoisie." [16] Aidit concedes further in his Party history:

> During and after this revolt, the weaknesses of the Party became very apparent; for example, the lack of unanimity in the Party leadership concerning this revolt, the lack of preparation to safeguard the Party cadres and leaders, the lack of coordination . . . the lack of any link between the actions of the countryside and those in the towns, etc. Apart from this, there were also such people as Tan Malaka, at that time a leader of the PKI [sic], who did not take resolute action prior to the revolt but blamed the revolt after it had broken out. More that that, he and his clique openly adopted Trotskyite practices.

The PKI misadventure, coinciding with a Communist disaster in China, had repercussions in the Communist world. After the Asian setbacks, Stalin became increasingly wary of "bourgeois" alliances and, through the Comintern, directed Semaun to repudiate his pact with Hatta's Perhumpinan. Semaun implemented these instructions in December, 1927, informing Hatta that he had negotiated the accord without Comintern approval. In reality, the Communists broke the agreement because it limited the PKI's area of activity and allied the PKI with the "unstable national bourgeoisie." The Semaun move was a precursor of the line change to the left promulgated at the Sixth Comintern Congress in 1928. In the four-year interval between the Fifth and Sixth congresses, Stalin had consolidated his power in the Kremlin. At the Sixth Congress, Stalin exuded confidence and, taking the offensive, reaffirmed that the ultimate Communist aim was "a world system of Communism"—under Russian direction and discipline—and in the process denounced the bourgeois nationalists of Africa and Asia. Among the Asians, Stalin assailed China's Sun Yat-sen and India's Gandhi. Stalin was noticeably silent on the PKI fiasco, another indication that Alimin and Musso may have had his approval for the reckless adventure.

The sixth Comintern meeting was of historic importance to the PKI. On hand were the principal figures in the Indonesian Communist drama—Alimin, Musso, Semaun, Darsono, and Tan Malaka. For the independent-minded Tan Malaka, Stalin's resumption of the offensive against Pan-Islam and Pan-Asia—which

Tan Malaka continued to envisage as springboards to power—probably marked the end of the Moscow road. Although the Congress elected him and Darsono to the Central Committee as candidate members, both later defected from the international Communist movement, Tan Malaka to embark on a path leading toward "national Communism." During a heated exchange on Communist policy in Asia, Bukharin (whom Stalin ordered executed ten years later), seared Tan Malaka with the epithet "Trotskyite!" It is probable that after Alimin's duplicity in 1926, Tan Malaka had foreseen the development, for in 1927, he secretly founded a rival underground Marxist-Leninist party, the Partai Republik Indonesia (PARI)—Party of the Republic of Indonesia —at Bangkok. The creation of the PARI was to become an indelible PKI mark against Tan Malaka. As late as 1950, *Bintang Merah* (*Red Star*), the official PKI journal, denounced the PARI as Tan Malaka's "betrayal" of the Indonesian Communist movement, and accused him of deliberately fomenting the 1926 Party rift in an effort to "liquidate" the PKI. Nevertheless, there is evidence that Tan Malaka and Alimin attempted to repair political fences in 1931 and restore a modicum of cooperation. But "personal differences soon arose again and led to a final rupture." [17] Darsono, disaffected and disillusioned, remained abroad until 1950, when he returned to an independent Indonesia and entered the Ministry of Foreign Affairs as a political analyst.

The others who were at Moscow in 1928—the Stalinist trio of Musso, Alimin, and Semaun—remained in Russia. There was no uncertainty about Musso's loyalty; he emerged from the Sixth Congress as titular leader of the PKI and was elected an ECCI member. In 1935 and 1948, Musso was to return to Indonesia on daring missions for Stalin. In 1946, after three years at Yenan with Mao Tse-tung, Alimin returned to Java as the PKI's "elder statesman." In 1956, after the "thaw," Semaun returned to Indonesia, where he plays a prominent role as an adviser in Sukarno's "guided democracy."

Thus, 1928 brought to an end the formative period in the development of the Indonesian Communist movement. The PKI's forward march had been arrested. But Communist prospects in Asia were not uniformly bleak. The Sixth Comintern Congress could, for example, console itself with the deepening of the world-revolutionary situation as manifested by "the rebellion in Indonesia; the maturing revolutionary crisis in India; and, finally, the great revolution in China. . . . The most important of these facts, an event of world historical importance, is the great Chinese revolution."

And the Chinese, who held their sixth "national" congress at Moscow in September of that year, immodestly concurred. A Chinese manifesto described the completion of the Chinese revolution as the prelude to the victory of the world proletarian dictatorship.

"The triumph of Communism in China," the manifesto continued, "could not fail to influence neighboring Asia, particularly India, Indochina, Java, and Korea."

After the abortive events of 1926–27, according to the PKI, the "Indonesian national bourgeoisie, led by revolutionary intellectuals, set up a number of organizations and political parties, continuing the revolutionary struggle which had already been begun by the PKI." [18]

The PKI debacle, followed by the exile or banishment of the Party leadership, presented the Dutch with the alternative of either gradually developing an Indonesian civil service (still virtually nonexistent) and attempting to guide the nationalist movement into moderate, constructive channels in preparation for inevitable independence, as had been done in the Anglo-American colonies, or creating a political vacuum by proscribing nationalist activity and thereby attempting to ensure uninterrupted Netherlands rule. Dutch sentiment overwhelmingly favored the latter course. In Indonesia, the majority of Hollanders in the administration and commerce viewed the disorders of 1926–27 as a by-product of Dutch colonial liberalism, the "ethical" policy adopted in the Indies at the turn of the century. In their opinion, the "natives" were peaceful and content under Dutch rule; discontent was artificially stimulated by "Communist agitators." The Dutch colonial "ultras" banded together in the Vaderlandsche Club and applied pressure on The Hague for more stringent controls over native activities.

But a minority of Dutch intellectuals, largely Indies-born officials in the administration, felt otherwise and formed a rival association to encourage Indonesia's development in partnership with the Netherlands kingdom. Displaying deep political insight, they contended that Holland's colonial task would be fulfilled only when "an Indies Commonwealth shall take up a place of its own among the independent peoples of the world." [19] The society, known as De Stuuw (Forward Movement), after the name of its journal, aimed at "the forging of lasting links between the Netherlands and this Commonwealth." The advocates of this policy included Dr. Hubertus van Mook, destined to be the last (Lt.) Governor General of the Indies, and others who sought an accommodation with the revolutionary republic at the end of World War II. At best, however, De Stuuw reflected the views of a distinct minority. As Van Mook noted later, the tragedy of Dutch colonial policy in this period was "the more regrettable because in the nationalist movement an active middle-class section gained the upper hand after the Communist outburst." [20] He was referring to the two mainstreams that now provided the leadership of the nationalist movement.

One tributary, the Perhumpinan, was in the Netherlands. Among its prominent leaders were Hatta, Sjahrir, Iwa Kusumasumantri, Achmed Subardjo, Ali Sastroamidjojo, and Sukiman Wirjosandro. In the late thirties, the Perhumpinan was to be devoured by a Communist "bloc within." In this early period, many of the students were already active in the League Against Imperialism (LIGA), a Communist front founded in 1926; Hatta and Subardjo served on the executive committee, as did Semaun and a miscellaneous bag of anticolonial intellectuals, including Jawaharlal Nehru and Albert Einstein. However, Stalin's declaration of war against bourgeois nationalism in 1928 "soon put an end to this Indian summer of Leninism," [21] and the following year Hatta and the Perhumpinan broke with the LIGA. The Hatta flirtation with Communism had ended.

The other tributary feeding the nationalist movement was the Indonesian student movement at home. On June 4, 1929, a group of students formed the Perserikaten Nasional Indonesia (PNI)— the Indonesian Nationalist Association. The PNI was the first nationalist-oriented party not affiliated with either Pan-Islam or the Comintern. Its chairman and dominant figure was Sukarno. Born at Surabaya on June 6, 1907,* Sukarno was the son of a Javanese schoolteacher (his mother was Balinese) who had tutored him in Islamic and Western studies. On the eve of World War I, Sukarno's father sent him to a secondary school. For a brief period, Sukarno boarded with O. A. Tjokroaminto, the founder of the Sarekat Islam, whose house was an intellectual haven for students (including Alimin) and political personalities (including Sneevliet and Musso). At this early age, Sukarno was cast into the turbulent stream of the nationalist movement and exposed to Marxist and Islamic influences. Then, in 1915, he joined his first political group, the Young Java Association, one of many regional nationalist organizations. He wrote tracts under the pseudonym Bhima, the redoubtable warrior-hero of the Hindu epic *Mahab-*

---

* A mystic, Sukarno explains his ability to embrace conflicting philosophies— e.g., Islam and Communism—by the fact that he was born under the sign of the Gemini.

harata; attended the Bandung Technical School; and, in 1925, received the degree and title of I.R. (Engineer). At Bandung, his oratorical skill, magnetic personality, and consummate acting ability attracted widespread attention. At one student rally, he whipped the audience to such emotional heights that the police had to interrupt the meeting and remove him bodily from the dais.[22] His professors counseled restraint; he assured them that he would not neglect his studies. His philosophy was eclectic, being compounded of Islam, Marxism, and mysticism. Under his dynamic leadership, the PNI continued the "revolutionary struggle" set in motion by the PKI in 1926. The revolutionary nationalism propagated by the PNI attracted former members of the Sarekat Rakjat and PKI, and also students returning from Holland, among them Sjahrir. Inevitably, the PNI also attracted the attention of the Dutch colonial authorities. In December, 1928, Sukarno was arrested on charges of sedition. In 1930, after a spectacular trial, he was sentenced to four years in prison. In an eloquent defense, later published in Holland as *Indonesie Klaagt Aan (Indonesia Accuses)*, Sukarno drew on his fund of diverse philosophies to formulate a philosophy of his own for a future Indonesian republic. He called this the philosophy of Marhaenism, "a type of socialism . . . which is particularly adapted to the Indonesian community and spirit." [23] Sukarno invented the word *marhaen* as the collective name for Indonesia's "depressed, desperately poor"—the small farmers, farm laborers, factory workers, and other small wage earners who together form more than 90 per cent of the Indonesian population. Sukarno developed the vague concept of a *gotong-royong* state in which people would "share equally in happiness and prosperity."

With Sukarno imprisoned, the PNI withered. Sjahrir recognized that the Dutch were pursuing a policy of thwarting the development of a mass movement by removing its leadership. He believed the nationalist movement could outmaneuver the Dutch by developing a small band of democratic socialist cadres who, like the Roman commander Fabius in the Punic Wars, would strike hard at the right moment. For this purpose, the twenty-three-year-old Sjahrir organized his own PNI, the Pendidikan Nasional Indonesia (Indonesian National Education Club), in 1932. Later that year, when Hatta returned from the Netherlands, Sjahrir stepped aside and Hatta became the chairman of the new PNI.

But a large majority of Sukarno's PNI, nationalist extremist in sentiment, opposed the creation of a small cadre organization and advocated the development of a militant mass movement. Led by men outwardly radical but inwardly conservative, these narrow nationalists endeavored to continue Sukarno's program of organizing the masses. Their stridency notwithstanding, they moved with the prevailing colonial wind, trimmed their sails, and modified the revolutionary content of the old PNI program. Their vehicle was the Partai Indonesia (Partindo), a party dominated by Sartono, Ali Sastroamidjojo, Mohammed Yamin, and Iskaq Tjokroadisurjo. In December of that year, Sukarno was unexpectedly released from prison. An attempt to restore the unity of the PNI failed. Confronted with the decision of whether to cast his strength with Hatta and Sjahrir's PNI or the Partindo, he chose the latter. It is worth noting here that Sjahrir felt that Indonesian nationalism was largely a projection of the inferiority complex that springs from the colonial relationship between subject race and master race and that the noncooperative movement was the purest expression of this colonial nationalism. Thus, he conceded that he never had been really noncooperative, because he felt and understood

> that . . . noncooperation, while it could be a source of strength for our movement, could never really furnish an ideal. It was too bitter, too narrow, and was often connected with baser feelings and instincts. I have always been able to accept noncooperation only as an effective instrument of nationalist propaganda and as a means of spreading the nationalistic idea. I have never been able to base a philosophy upon it.[24]

The debate between the Sjahrir and Sukarno factions proved to be academic. In August, 1933, Sukarno was rearrested and banished, presumably for life, first to Flores and then to South Sumatra. The following February, Sjahrir and Hatta were also interned, presumably for life, first in Irian and later on Banda.

Thus, by the mid-thirties, the secular Indonesian nationalist movement had split four ways—along the paths of international Communism (PKI), national Communism (PARI), authoritarian nationalism (Partindo), and democratic socialism (Sjahrir's PNI). In the nonsecular community of Islam, strains were developing between a modernist, reformist faction and conservative, orthodox factions. Disparate as these groups were, they shared a common objective: Indonesian independence. They also shared a common experience: Dutch harassment. The colonial authorities were determined to create and maintain a political vacuum in Indonesia. Yet it was patently clear that the tighter the Dutch clamped the lid on nationalism, the more devastating would be the explosion when the lid ripped off. Dutch colonialism was living on borrowed time; Japanese expansionism, appeased by Anglo-American sea power, was now approaching disastrous maturity.

3

The "Illegal-PKI"

In the era of Dutch political repression and the nationalist restiveness of the early 1930's, the PKI receded into the shadows, outlawed and disorganized. Although later it made several attempts at recovery, it did not emerge as a serious political factor in Indonesia until after World War II.

In 1927, barely two months after the PKI disorders in West Sumatra had subsided, the Dutch had thwarted Communist plans for a revolt in East Sumatra, the country's richest estate belt; in 1928, they had exposed a PKI effort to regroup at Surabaya behind the fiction of a federation of trade unions; and in 1929, they had disbanded a PKI front at Medan, Sumatra, arresting Iwa Kusumasumantri, who had recently returned from Holland after a sojourn in Moscow,[1] where he had left a wife and child. Despite these setbacks, according to Aidit, a shadow PKI continued to operate. In 1932, the Party adopted an eighteen-point program advocating Indonesian independence, the release of political prisoners, the right to strike, the right to demonstrate, land for the peasants, and other political and economic reforms[2]—demands never granted by Communists when they are in power.

In the half-world, the PKI struggled with Tan Malaka for control of the Indonesian Left. Gradually, the schism in the Communist movement widened and distinct lines appeared. The PKI emerged as a supranational Soviet instrumentality, and PARI as a revisionist movement espousing what was later to be characterized as "national Communism." Despite his nationalist orientation, Tan Malaka was not averse to seeking support from abroad. Whereas the PKI viewed the rise of Japan with misgiving—in part because of the threat it posed to Soviet Asia—Tan Malaka saw in Tokyo a lever for ridding the Indies of Dutch rule. Whereas the orthodox Communists took the global view that they served Indonesia by serving Moscow's goal of reshaping the world in the Soviet image, Tan Malaka took the nationalist view that he served Indonesia by supporting Tokyo's goal of Asia for the Asians. Although aware of the atrocities committed in China by the Japanese, Tan Malaka visited Tokyo and arrived at an accommodation with the Japanese.

The contest between Tan Malaka and the PKI coincided with the Great Depression, which had a severe impact on Indonesia's raw-material economy. An isolated political incident dramatized the temper of discontent. On February 2, 1933, the Dutch and Indonesian crew of the 6,500-ton naval-training ship "Zeven Provincien" ("Seven Provinces") mutinied in Sumatran waters in protest against a series of pay reductions. The mutineers seized the vessel and steamed for the Surabaya naval base. The adventure ended four days later, when the Royal Netherlands Air Force bombed the ship, killing twenty-three ratings and wounding twenty-five.[3] Although it was later found that the incident had been inspired by a non-Communist labor union, it has assumed epic proportions in PKI lore. Its immediate effect was to generate new demands among the Dutch ultras for a tighter colonial rein on "native" activities. Shortly thereafter, Sukarno, Hatta, and Sjahrir were interned.

Aidit has ascribed the ineffectual and uncoordinated nature of the actions against the Dutch in 1928–35 to the PKI's failure to properly reform its central leadership. This is partly correct; the PKI's experienced leadership of the 1920's was either interned or in exile. But perhaps a more serious drawback was the Comintern's line of implacable hostility toward bourgeois nationalism. Without the natural cover of nationalism, Communism is at a serious disadvantage in the colonial world. For the PKI and the other Communist parties in Africa and Asia, 1928–35 were "lost years." In the early thirties, a new menace arose—fascism—and with it the necessity for a new Moscow line. In Indonesia, the new line revived the fortunes of the PKI.

In July, 1935, Stalin summoned the Seventh Comintern Congress, the first to be held in seven years. Now the international Communist movement shifted toward a flexible strategy of cooperation with the bourgeois camp. Stalin called for a "united front from above" against the growing danger of German National Socialism, "the most reactionary, most chauvinistic, and most imperialist" form of capitalism. Fascism superseded the bourgeois democracies of the West and the bourgeois nationalists of the colonies as the main roadblock to the advance of Communism. The new line called for cooperation with the democratic West and the national-liberation movements in the Afro-Asian world. Georgi Dimitrov, Secretary-General of the Comintern from 1935 to 1943, introduced the shift. In facing fascism, Dimitrov said,

> the first thing that must be done . . . is to form a united front, to establish unity of action . . . in every country all over the world. . . . The Communist International attaches no conditions to unity of action except one . . . that the unity of action be directed against fascism. . . . The Communists pledge . . . not to attack anyone, neither persons nor organizations nor parties that stand for the united front of the working class against fascism.

Dimitrov directed Communists to assume the garb of nationalism: "Comrades, proletarian internationalism must, so to speak, 'acclimatize itself' in each country in order to sink deep roots in its native land." He instructed Communists in colonial territories to "take an active part in the mass anti-imperialist movements headed by national reformists."

The new Moscow line afforded the PKI latitude in which to maneuver. For the first time since Semaun's break with the Perhumpinan in 1928, the Indonesian Communists were permitted to enter an alliance with bourgeois nationalism. A prominent student leader of this period was the burly, bespectacled Amir Sjarifuddin, who, like Hatta, Sjahrir, Agus Salim, and Tan Malaka, was a Sumatran. Amir had returned from Holland in 1932 and assumed the leadership of Sukarno's Partindo, for which he later served three years in a Dutch prison. His release coincided with the enunciation of the popular-front line. Among intellectuals in Indonesia, as elsewhere in the world, the Soviet appeal for a united front against the rising German, Italian, and Japanese militarism struck a responsive chord. In Indonesia, democrats such as Sjahrir, then in exile, recognized that both Holland and Indonesia were threatened by Berlin and Tokyo. Here, then, was a common ground for a united Indonesian-Dutch front that, in turn, could advance the Indonesian goal of an independent, democratic republic. The conflict between Indonesia and the Dutch was "overshadowed and depreciated." [4] Moderates and democrats the world over, in a spirit of eternal hope, had accepted Moscow's shift in good faith. Even the impact of the Soviet pact with Hitler in August, 1939, was largely dissipated when, following the German attack on Russia in June, 1941, Stalin reverted to the Dimitrov line. In many respects, the naïveté currently displayed by many of the newly independent Afro-Asian states regarding Communist objectives is not unlike that shown by the West before and during World War II.

The new line in Indonesia implied cooperation with the bourgeois nationalists and the Dutch. Every other consideration, including independence, had to be subordinated to the struggle for Communist survival against the main class enemy—fascism. The application of this doctrine by the PKI is illuminating. In Holland, the Perhumpinan, now controlled by the Communists, dropped the word *merdeka* (independence) from the name of its journal, *Indonesia Merdeka*. And the Netherlands Communist Party (CPN), in the interests of a popular front at home, abandoned its program for immediate Indonesian independence.[5]

In Indonesia, the moment had arrived for a fresh effort to reorganize the PKI, this time within the strategic folds of the new doctrine. The mission was assigned to Musso, who arrived in Surabaya in April, 1935. There, with the assistance of Djokosudjono, Pamudji, and Achmad Sumadi, he established an organization called the "Illegal-PKI." He also set up the PKM, the Party of Communist Youth, to implement the Comintern's order for the training of genuinely Bolshevist leaders in the Communist parties, "so that the parties will be able at the sharpest turn of events independently and quickly to find a correct solution for political and tactical problems of the Communist International."

In Indonesia, meanwhile, the Partindo split over cooperation with the Dutch, a policy now advocated by the Illegal-PKI "bloc within." Like its predecessor, Sukarno's PNI, the Partindo had prided itself on noncooperation. Unable to resolve the disagreement, Amir, its chairman, joined by the erratic Yamin, himself a former Partindo chairman, dissolved Partindo in 1936 and re-formed it as a new party, the Gerakan Rakjat Indonesia (Gerindo) —the Indonesian People's Movement. This group established ancillary fronts such as the Barisan Pemuda Gerindo (Gerindo Youth Corps). The Gerindo advocated the "establishment of an independent social-democratic state to be achieved through a policy of cooperation, if necessary"—a program sufficiently vague to placate impatient Indonesians while adhering to the Communist line. Aidit observed later that the formation of Gerindo gave new strength to the national-independence movement and the antifascist movement—which, stripped of Aesopian language, meant that it infused new life into the parallel nationalist and Communist movements. Gerindo became the voice of the Indonesian Left, operating with reasonable freedom because it advocated cooperation with the Western democracies against the Axis powers.

In 1939, a sixteen-year-old Sumatran, Dipa Nusantara Aidit, the future leader of the PKI, was recruited into the Barisan group. Aidit, the son of a forest worker, was born in East Sumatra on July 30, 1923, of "pure Malayan stock." [6] That year, his family moved to Tandjungpadang, South Sumatra, where Aidit attended primary school. He was then sent to Java to study at the Batavian Commercial High School, where, he has said, he acquired his knowledge of English. But his parents were unable to continue financing his education, so Aidit took a part-time job as a tailor's apprentice, making buttonholes. In 1939, Aidit joined the Persatuan Timur Muda (Pertmu)—the Association of Eastern Youths—one of the small student groups of the period. He displayed a flair for political work and friends urged him to join Gerindo. "Gerindo was not Communist—nor was I—at that time," he has stated. "But many of Gerindo's members were Communists." Apparently he attracted Amir's attention and soon rose to the position of youth leader at Batavia.

When Holland fell in 1940, the nationalist movement perceived an opening. But although the colonial authorities countenanced nationalist activities along "cooperative" lines, they adamantly rejected any suggestion of Indonesian independence. Nationalism, the Dutch said, was not negotiable.

There is scant information available on how the PKI adjusted its course to conform with the switch in the Communist line following the Stalin-Hitler accord. There are clues, however. In Holland, for example, Perhumpinan leaders such as Setiadjit and Maruto Darusman, undercover Communists at the time, joined the CPN in publicly denouncing the "imperialist" Allied war effort. In 1941, when the Germans invaded Russia and the Communists reverted to the popular-front line, they and the CPN entered the Dutch anti-Nazi resistance.

On the basis of this admittedly slender straw plus the PKI's general submissiveness to Moscow (with the exception of 1926—which was a special case since it was entwined with the Stalin-Trotsky feud), it is reasonable to assume that the Illegal-PKI was no more insensitive to the 1939–41 shift than the Indonesian Communists in Europe. Aidit, in his Party history, provides another clue. He laments that following Musso's departure from Java in 1936, because the Dutch had "got wind of his arrival," the Illegal-PKI "worked without any firm guiding lines to build a party of the Lenin and Stalin type." This was his explanation for the PKI failure to organize "mass actions in the form of demonstrations or other action which would bring significant pressure to bear on the Dutch colonial government" after the fall of Holland in 1940 —moves that would have served the Comintern's line. It is possible that the Communists either were too weak to do so by themselves or wielded too little influence within the nationalist movement to promote such action. Whatever the reason for the PKI lapse, the eve of World War II witnessed a revival of Communist fortunes in Indonesia. Musso had re-established the PKI. Gerindo, the advance guard of the Indonesian Left, had been infiltrated, if not captured. Abroad, in Europe, the influential student body— Perhumpinan—had been reduced to a Communist front. After twenty "lost years," Communist prospects in Indonesia were at last encouraging.

4

Asia for the Asians

The year 1940 ushered in the German occupation of Holland, and 1942 saw the beginning of the Japanese interregnum in the Indies. For Indonesian nationalists and Communists alike, World War II was a time of peril, intrigue—and opportunity.

The purposeful Communists employed a wide variety of deceptive tactics, not only to insure the Party's survival during the war, but to exploit the war in such a fashion as to advance Communist power aims in the postwar period. Thus, in occupied Holland, Indonesian Communist students collaborated with the anti-Nazi underground without revealing their Moscow affiliation. In the Pacific, the Indonesian Communists likewise collaborated with the Allies but did so openly. In occupied Indonesia, the Illegal-PKI operated both inside and outside the nationalist movement.

In the Netherlands in 1941, after the Communist change of line, the Indonesian Communist bloc within the Perhumpinan entered the Dutch resistance. Among the bloc's prominent leaders were Setiadjit and Abdulmadjid, both of whom had studied briefly at Moscow, and Suripno and Maruto Darusman. They masqueraded as democratic socialists. It was a masterful deception, and Setiadjit rose to such prominence that he became editor of the Dutch Socialist underground paper, *Vrij Nederland* (*Free Netherlands*). Clearly, the wartime activities of Indonesian Communists in Holland were more in the nature of an infiltration rather than an open collaboration with the West.

It should be recorded in passing that during this period the turbulent career of Sneevliet, the father of the Indonesian Communist movement, came to an end. In 1922, Sneevliet had been instrumental in the founding of the Chinese Communist Party.

In Trotsky's assessment, Sneevliet was the "sponsor of the 'two-class' party for China, later embraced by Stalin with such fatal results for the Chinese revolution of 1925–27." [1] After the debacle in China, Sneevliet returned to Holland and subsequently was elected to the Dutch second chamber. He is credited with persuading the Perhumpinan to adopt the popular-front line. In 1940, he was arrested by the Germans, and two years later he was executed.

Indonesian Communist tactics in the Pacific contrasted sharply with those in Europe. True, the Communists collaborated with the Allies, but unlike the situation in Holland, they operated aboveground, albeit at the invitation of the Allies.

In 1942, with the approach of the Japanese, the Dutch began evacuating political prisoners from West Irian, about 600 in number, many of whom had been interned since 1926. The evacuees were sent to Queensland, where Charles van der Plas, the former Governor of East Java and a political adviser on MacArthur's staff, invited them to join the Allied cause.* The Communist prisoners, under the titular leadership of Sardjono, the Party's former chairman, readily agreed. "I harbored no personal animosity toward the Dutch despite seventeen years of confinement," Sardjono explained later. "My attitude was conditioned by my impersonal ideology. I was glad to have the opportunity to fight fascism." [2] Here was the dedicated, disciplined Communist.

For the remainder of the war, Sardjono and his group worked for the Allies, first at a Brisbane propaganda center and after the reoccupation of West Irian, from Morotai, where they edited the Malay-language newspaper *Penguluh (The Torch)*. Thus in the Pacific, as in Europe, the Communists contrived to occupy important positions in the Allied propaganda apparatus.

The situation for the Communists inside Indonesia, however, was less favorable. Although Sjahrir's faction emerged at the end of the war as the dominant resistance movement, the first Indonesian underground was jointly organized—intentionally or otherwise—by the Dutch and the Illegal-PKI. Amir served as the honest broker and, once again, Van der Plas as the contact.

In January, 1942, Van der Plas proposed to Amir that he develope an underground intelligence network. The Dutch considered Amir a logical, if not wholly reliable, candidate. Amir's Gerindo was, after all, a leading advocate of an Indo-Dutch popular front against fascism. Amir proved receptive and received an advance of 25,000 guilders ($10,000) to finance the operation. In approaching Amir with the proposition, it is probable that the Dutch suspected a liaison between Gerindo and the Illegal-PKI. In 1940, Amir had

* In the prewar period, he had been a member of De Stuuw.

been arrested on the charge of associating with the outlawed Party. Offered the alternative of banishment to Irian or cooperation with the colonial authorities, Amir chose the latter and was appointed to the Department of Economic Affairs in October of that year. There he worked under Van Mook.

During the first year of the Japanese occupation, Amir, too prominent to move underground, assumed the guise of a "collaborating nationalist." But the Japanese mistrusted his earlier conversion to Christianity, his role in Gerindo, and his activities in the prewar administration. In February, 1943, Amir and 300 others, largely Gerindo members, were seized on suspicion of organizing a resistance movement. Among those arrested and later executed were several leaders of the Illegal-PKI. Amir was given the water treatment, but denied a Communist affiliation. In 1944, the Japanese sentenced him to death, but Sukarno and Hatta interceded on his behalf and the sentence was commuted to life in prison.

However, some isolated, small-scale Communist activity continued, largely in the fields of propaganda and recruitment. In Djakarta, the only noteworthy cell still functioning was headed by Wirdarta, a Javanese. "It was Wirdarta who recruited me into the PKI in 1943," Aidit reminisced later.[3] "Until then, Gerindo was the only political organization I had ever joined." As a Gerindo youth leader, Aidit had been instructed not to cooperate with the invader. But he was disturbed by the welcome accorded the Japanese on their arrival. "The Indonesian people harbored the illusion that the Japanese were liberators," he said. "People had heard about their barbarism. Few wanted to believe the stories. But soon the Japanese were detested. I joined the Illegal-PKI because it was resolutely anti-Japanese." Later Aidit also joined the Angkatan Indonesia Baru, the New Indonesian Generation, a radical nationalist student group with headquarters at 31 Menteng Street, Djakarta, an address that was to become famous. He also became a member of the Gerakan Indonesia Merdeka, the Free Indonesia Movement, and the Barisan Pelopor Istimewa, the Special Shock Troop, a terrorist organization formed shortly after the proclamation of independence.

Perhaps the most successful of the remaining cells was the group operating in East Java under the direction of Djokosujono, a hand-picked Musso aide and one of the founders of the Illegal-PKI. The group infiltrated the Sukarela Tentara Pembela Tanah Air (PETA)—the Volunteer Army of the Defenders of the Fatherland—a Japanese-sponsored Indonesian military organization of about 50,000 troops who subsequently formed the nucleus of the republican army. After the revolt of a PETA battalion at Blitar in 1945, the Japanese suspected Communist infiltration and planned a purge. But the purge was frustrated by the sudden end of the war.[4]

For all practical purposes, the Communist apparatus was largely ineffective during the war. Yet throughout the occupation, the Japanese were obsessed with a "Communist" danger and persisted in equating any opposition to their rule as "Communistic." [5] Like the Dutch before them, the Japanese were inadvertently fostering a sympathetic climate of opinion for the Communists while promoting the myth that the Communists were omnipresent and omnipotent.

Late in 1944, with Japan's strategic situation deteriorating rapidly, the Japanese radically revised their occupation policy. A discussion of Japanese wartime policies is beyond the scope of this narrative, but an appreciation of the changes wrought during the interregnum provides an insight into postwar developments in Indonesia and the Communist role therein.

For the Japanese, the Indies were easy prey. On March 9, 1942, eight days after they invaded the islands, the Dutch capitulated on the grounds that resistance was "useless." [6] Java, more densely populated than Japan and containing nearly one-third the population of Southeast Asia, had fallen in almost a week. Dutch prestige in Indonesian eyes sustained an irreparable blow. The unarmed Indonesian population offered no resistance to the Japanese, nor was it inclined to do so—on the eve of the Japanese invasion the Dutch turned down Indonesian requests for arms as "impossible." [7] For most Indonesians, the Dutch surrender was a day of rejoicing. Yet the repressive character of Dutch colonialism paled in comparison with that of Japanese imperialism.

Broadly, the Japanese occupation government was organized along the lines of Mussolini's corporate state. An authoritarian colonial society was transformed into a totalitarian New Order. All labor—professional, white-collar, skilled, and unskilled—was herded into functional "corporations." Normal economic and social life outside the corporations virtually disappeared as labor, goods, and services were funneled through the state mechanisms. Within eighteen months, the Dutch population was in confinement. Life in the internment camps was a nightmare. Civilian prisoners, including women and children, were treated like "paper cuttings spread and lost before the wind." [8] The terror was calculated. The former white rulers were humiliated in front of the "natives," who in turn were intimidated by the excesses of their new overlords. Underground anti-Japanese resistance was enfeebled and fear instilled into the ranks of collaborating nationalists. Yet the harsh treatment of Europeans was relatively mild compared to the terrorization of the civilian population. At the end of the war, the Japanese acknowledged that they had conscripted 270,000 *romushas* (slave laborers), of whom only 70,000 survived. Allied and Indonesian sources place the number of Indonesians who perished during the occupation closer to 2 million.

From the outset, the Japanese made plain that Indonesian independence was not a war objective; within three months, all Indonesian political parties and organizations were dissolved and the population strictly prohibited from participating in meetings "to discuss, engage in activities, encourage, or make propaganda concerning the organization and structure of the government." [9] Only the Illegal-PKI, accustomed to working undercover, was able to absorb the shock of transition from Dutch to Japanese rule and then, as noted, only briefly.

The suppression of the nationalist movement created a political vacuum that the Japanese sought to fill with a nationalist movement of their own. But they failed dismally. As the Indonesians failed to appreciate that their "liberation" was within the framework of Asia for the Asians, and not Indonesia for the Indonesians, the Japanese also failed to appreciate that they had been welcomed as liberators not of Asia but of Indonesia. Yet the Japanese realized the necessity of drawing the Indonesians into the war effort; and the Indonesians recognized that they could probably extract political concessions by collaboration. Both sides explored an accommodation.

Sukarno, the opportunist, counseled cooperation with the Japanese; Hatta, who on the eve of the Japanese attack had urged the people to resist the invader, opposed cooperation. Sjahrir, planning a resistance, appealed to both as the country's popular leaders, to "do everything legally possible to give the nationalist struggle a broader legal scope, and at the same time secretly support the revolutionary resistance." [10] Sjahrir reasoned with Hatta that he was too prominent to remain at large as a noncooperator and that the resistance would require a trustworthy and highly placed contact within the Japanese administration. In the background was Sjahrir's mistrust of Sukarno. As it developed, Sukarno's role in the occupation became a source of controversy. Sjahrir, for example, is vague about Sukarno's wartime activities and has written that "for several months," Sukarno kept him informed about the Japanese but that gradually "there was no longer any immediate reason for [Sukarno] to see me, and I lost touch with him until just before the proclamation of our independence." [11] Undeniably,

Sukarno's objective, his burning passion, was an independent Indonesia. Serving at the head of numerous Japanese-sponsored organizations, Sukarno exploited the elaborate Japanese propaganda machine to establish direct contact with the Indonesian masses, skillfully employing every opportunity to raise the level of Indonesian national consciousness while advancing his own claims to Indonesian leadership. Sukarno collaborated with the Japanese not because he was pro-Japanese; on the contrary. But he felt they represented the wave of the future. He was impressed by Japanese power and until the final weeks of the war cooperated in anticipation of a Japanese victory. Indonesia not only would have to gain its independence under the Japanese, but it also would have to live in a Japanese Asia.

The Communist position on the collaboration issue has fluctuated with changes in the Moscow line. The PKI has alternately denounced and defended Sukarno's wartime role. Although clearly inconsistent with established fact, Aidit, whose current position on Sukarno follows the prevailing coexistence strategy, claims:

> My sympathies were always with Sukarno, not Hatta. Even before the war, Hatta was pro-Japanese; Sukarno was not. But Sukarno was in a difficult position, defenseless in the face of the Japanese, lacking arms and armed forces. Sukarno had no alternative but cooperation. To my mind, Sukarno cooperated with the Japanese for tactical reasons; Hatta, in principle.[12]

In any event, by the middle of 1943, with Tokyo prepared for a protracted war, the Japanese gradually broadened "native" participation in the administration and for the first time brought Indonesians directly into the government machinery as advisers. Ironically, every American victory promoted the cause of Indonesian nationalism.

But it was not until late 1944 that the Japanese began to prepare for the possibility of defeat. The character of the occupation was re-cast and the stage rearranged for Indonesian independence. First, however, the Japanese sought to ensure as best they could that the new nation would pursue a path least inimical to Japan's long-term interests. At this juncture, Tan Malaka re-emerged from the wings as a central figure in the Indonesian Communist drama.

In September, 1944, Tokyo instructed the Japanese Military Administration in the Indies to cease "haughty and arrogant behavior," abandon the "idea of colonial subjugation," encourage "nationalistic activities," promote "racial consciousness" among the people, and impart "political training" to the Indonesians.[13] A central figure in the training program was Vice Admiral

T. Maeda, the head of the Army-Navy Liaison Office at Djakarta and head of Japanese naval intelligence in the Indies. Maeda had established a reputation for unorthodoxy as early as 1938, when he proposed that Japan buy up German claims to its former colonies in East Irian and the Pacific after an Axis victory.[14] Maeda had sought to avoid what seemed like an inevitable postwar collision between Berlin and Tokyo. In 1944, therefore, it is not unlikely that he was preoccupied with the prospects of an Allied victory— and the probability of a postwar Soviet-American clash. Maeda apparently reasoned that in such an eventuality, an independent "national Communist" Indonesia would probably resist both Soviet and American influence. Although it seems implausible, Maeda apparently set about fostering the growth of Tan Malaka's revisionism as a means of advancing his political goal. Maeda simply sought to exploit the Marxist-Nationalist sentiment that had permeated the Indonesian independence movement since the days of Sneevliet. For Japan, it was an act of desperation.

The leading figure in the Maeda drama was, of course, Tan Malaka. According to what purports to be his autobiography, Tan Malaka returned to Indonesia in 1942 and was conscripted into the *romusha* as a coal miner in Bantam, West Java, as unlikely a role as imaginable for a political personality of Tan Malaka's restlessness and caliber.[15] According to Indonesian sources, however, Tan Malaka worked "behind the screen" for Admiral Maeda and Hitoshi Shimizu, the fanatical director of the Sendenbu (the Japanese Department of Propaganda). Tan Malaka broadcast regularly from Bantam as the "Voice of Radio Tokyo." Like Sukarno, Hatta, Sjahrir, and Amir, Tan Malaka exploited the occupation in what he felt was the Indonesian interest. As Amir and Sjahrir before him, he set up a clandestine organization of his own, recruiting such youths as Adam Malik, who directed a "national Communist" cell in the Sendenbu, and attracting the support of erratic radical nationalists such as Sukarni Kartodiwirjo and Chaerul Saleh, both influential figures in the Menteng 31 group. He also drew support from two veterans of the nationalist movement, Subardjo and Iwa, both of whom were to play prominent roles in Tan Malaka's postwar bid for power. Subardjo was then the political adviser to the Japanese Consulting Office on Political Affairs and had access to Sukarno. Like Tan Malaka, Subardjo was identified with both Communism and Japan. He was a former Perhumpinan president who had studied briefly at Moscow and later had broken with Stalin. In the 1930's, he had visited Japan and had become the Tokyo correspondent for the Indonesian daily *Matahari* (*The Sun*). It is doubtful, however, if the story of intrigue on the Indonesian Left can ever be satisfactorily unraveled. To cite an example, Subardjo also worked for the Dutch Economic Affairs Department during the popular-front period. Had he drifted back to the Illegal-PKI? Iwa's background closely paralleled that of Subardjo as well as Tan Malaka's. Iwa had been an editor of *Matahari* and had also studied in Moscow. In 1929, the Dutch arrested him for Communist activity in East Sumatra. In 1942, the Japanese released him from Dutch internment at Macassar, the South Celebes. That year he became a prominent member of the Japanese-sponsored Organization of Public Safety and, in 1943, was sent to Java, where he maintained close liaison with Admiral Maeda. Officially, Iwa was a "solicitor" during the Japanese occupation.

With Tan Malaka at the center, and with the assistance of Subardjo and Iwa in the wings, Maeda spun his web. In October, 1944, one month after the instructions from Tokyo, Maeda opened a "political institution" at Djakarta, where selected students were indoctrinated with Communist ideology, although not with Moscow's version of proletarian internationalism. Instead, Communism of a "national" or "independent" character was taught, a variant later labeled "Titoism." Prominent nationalists, including Sukarno, Hatta, and Sjahrir, as well as Subardjo and Iwa, lectured at the school. Perhaps the most astonishing aspect of the Maeda affair is that for a short time after the August, 1945, proclamation of Indonesian independence, the Tan Malaka forces appeared to be in control of the republic. But their close identification with the Japanese during the occupation was to contribute to their downfall.

In a remarkable piece of counterintrigue, the Illegal-PKI, aware of the Maeda stratagem, infiltrated the school. Wikana, whom the Japanese probably suspected of being a Communist because of his prewar record,* became a director of the school, whose student body included such Communists as Aidit and Mohammed Jussuf, who organized the first above-ground PKI group after the Japanese surrender. Aidit has since said that he has been "Sukarno's pupil," as though preparing to lay future claim to being Sukarno's logical successor:

"During the occupation," Aidit has said, "Sukarno became my teacher." [16] Then amending the remark slightly, he added, "At least, one of my teachers. He taught many members of the Illegal-PKI who, like myself, attended the Japanese school."

* Wikana was arrested by the Dutch in 1940 for organizing Illegal-PKI activities, including distribution of the Party's clandestine paper, *Manara Merah* (*Red Tower*).

It was in this atmosphere of intrigue and counterintrigue that the Indonesian Republic was born.

On July 17, 1945, with the Japanese war effort crumbling, Tokyo set Indonesian independence for September 24 at the latest, to enable the islands to join in "the battle for the common defense of Greater East Asia." Three weeks later, the Japanese installed an Indonesian Independence Preparatory Committee with Sukarno as President and Hatta as Vice President. But on August 15, midway in their plan, Japan surrendered. The A-bomb had ended the war, canceled the scheduled September invasion of Japan at an estimated cost of 1 million Japanese and American lives, liberated thousands of Allied prisoners of war and civilian internees from vile camps, and freed millions of Asians from oppressive Japanese military rule.

By ending the war, the bomb provided Sukarno with the opportunity to proclaim Indonesian independence without Japanese sponsorship.

But Sukarno hesitated. Some say he vacillated out of fear of being brought before an Allied war-crimes tribunal as a collaborationist; others, that he felt "obligated" to the Japanese and naïvely awaited a prearranged Japanese signal for the proclamation of independence. Whatever the case, Sjahrir emerged from the underground and pressed Sukarno and Hatta to issue a revolutionary proclamation. Hatta agreed but still Sukarno vacillated. This, however, is the version of events as recounted by Aidit:

> On August 15, I learned of Japan's surrender from a Eurasian woman who had not been interned. I proceeded immediately for Menteng 31. We discussed our course of action. The bourgeois students argued that this was not the moment for independence. The Communists said it was. We unanimously agreed to send a delegation to Sukarno.
>
> Four persons went—two youth leaders, myself, and Wikana—and two student leaders—Subadio Sastrosatomo and Suroto Kunto. We told Sukarno that the students and people were prepared to fight for freedom. Sukarno wavered. He said he could not act without first conferring with Hatta, Iwa, Subardjo, and the others. We waited.
>
> Hatta appeared first and said he appreciated our feelings, but that while his heart was warm his head was cool. "We cannot accept your proposal," he said. We asked whether this implied Sukarno's rejection. "There may be a difference of opinion," Hatta said. "But I speak for all." I then told Hatta: "You have destroyed the hopes of our generation."
>
> We returned to Menteng 31 in a revolutionary mood. Our leaders, we agreed, were waiting for independence from the Japanese.

We agreed that we must proclaim independence ourselves. The most outspoken students were Chaerul Saleh, Adam Malik, Lukman, and Sidik Kertapati. The students proceeded to Sukarno's residence and persuaded Sukarno and Hatta to accompany us.

I do not call our action kidnaping. It was a matter of consultation. We drove them to a Chinese house at Rengasdengklok [south of Djakarta]. We told them we would act with the people's support, but that without leaders chaos would result. They were convinced. We returned them safely to Djakarta. The rest is history.[17]

Under the circumstances, the only alternative the Communists had was to avert "chaos." The PKI was in disarray, without leadership, funds, arms, or a mass following. In an uncontrolled revolutionary situation, Tan Malaka would probably emerge the dominant figure; his area of influence extended deeply into the ranks of both the collaborating nationalists and the radical wing of the student resistance. Although his version is widely discounted, Shimizu later claimed that the Japanese staged the abduction to impress the Allies with the spontaneity of Indonesia's independence. If this was even remotely the case—and even that is doubtful—they were again promoting Tan Malaka's bid for power.

For the Illegal-PKI, its brightest prospects lay in an "orderly" proclamation of independence. Although relatively weak, the Communists were secure in the knowledge of the moral and material backing of a triumphant world power, Soviet Russia. No other political group in Indonesia enjoyed similar external support. In the long run, in the event of a colonial war between Indonesia and the Dutch, the PKI would be in a position to benefit from its association with Moscow. The probability was that the PKI would assume the eventual direction of the national-liberation movement. Were Aidit and Wikana instructed by the Party to "consult" with Sukarno and Hatta? "There was no time for instruction," Aidit has said. "Later I went to Wirdarta and asked whether I had acted correctly. He commended my action, and so did the Party."

According to other participants in the "kidnaping," the Japanese dispatched Subardjo to Rengasdengklok with the delicate mission of negotiating for the safe return of Sukarno and Hatta to Djakarta. In any event, the two leaders arrived at Admiral Maeda's house on the night of August 16, and the following day, at 4 A.M., completed the draft of the independence proclamation. In addition to the members of the independence committee, Subardjo, Sukarno, Chaerul Saleh, and Wikana attended the meeting. The Sjahrir resistance boycotted the session because the planned manifesto accompanying the proclamation was not resolutely anti-Japanese. Sjahrir sought such a declaration to avoid having the republic charged with being a product of the Japanese. As it developed, no manifesto was issued; later Sjahrir was to write one himself. At 10 A.M. on August 17, 1945, Sukarno read the declaration of independence, which both he and Hatta had signed. It began: "We, the people of Indonesia, hereby proclaim the independence of Indonesia."

The Japanese did not authorize publication of the news of Japan's capitulation in Indonesia until August 21. The Japanese played a double game. They sought to deceive the Indonesian people into believing that independence was a "gift" from Japan; they sought to reassure the Allies that the Indonesians had revolted and that Japan had not violated the Allied surrender terms. It is not inconceivable that the Japanese envisaged the development of a revolutionary Communist society in Indonesia hostile toward both Russia and America and dedicated to Pan-Asianism. These were the three denominators shared by the Japanese, Tan Malaka, and the majority of collaborating nationalists. Although Japan's contribution to Indonesia's independence will remain a source of controversy, Japan undeniably played a part in routing the Dutch from Indonesia. In this sense, the Japanese could claim a positive role in Indonesian independence.

The impact of Japan on the Indies is speculative at best. Although Japanese rule lasted barely forty months, it made a lasting impression on many collaborating nationalists. Japanese authoritarianism was a hint of things to come as Sukarno subconsciously fashioned a similar system in the name of "guided democracy." As the record will show, the Communists not only warmly endorsed Sukarno's concept, but also encouraged the development of "guided democracy." In the end, the distinction in Indonesia between farmer Jones and Napoleon became blurred.

As for the Illegal-PKI, the Communists emerged from the war numerically weaker than before, but in an advantageous position. By their hostility toward the Japanese, the Communists had earned new respect. They had infiltrated the nationalist movement, recruited new cadres, and successfully carried out the Party line, ingratiating themselves with the bourgeois democracies abroad and the bourgeois nationalists at home. As revolutionary sentiment swept Indonesia, Communist hopes appeared reasonably bright. But the Party apparatus had been weakened by the wartime arrests of the leadership. PKI orthodoxy, with its emphasis on proletarian internationalism, was being diluted by Tan Malaka's stress on nationalism. Above all, the first rank of the PKI leadership was either dead or scattered, and, as Aidit noted later, "the Party also had no experience in armed struggle, something very necessary . . . in a period of revolution." [18]

5

The August Revolution

Indonesia proclaimed its independence under ideal revolutionary conditions. For forty years, the Indonesians had groped toward freedom from Western subjugation. Now an abundance of arms were at their disposal and the ruling powers had lost the will and capacity to rule. It was a rich moment for both nationalists and Communists, and richer still for the national Communists; for whereas the orthodox Communists employed a subtle strategy in seeking to usurp the revolution, the Tan Malaka faction boldly moved into the foreground in an open bid for power.

The Allies, as unprepared for peace as they had been for war, did not reach Java in significant numbers until the first British contingents landed on September 29, 1945. The Allies' late arrival, a republican statement conceded at the time, provided an excellent opportunity to the Indonesian Government to consolidate the authority of the republic. In the forty-five-day hiatus between the Japanese capitulation and the arrival of the British, the Indonesians had established a government. The Preparatory Committee had elected Sukarno and Hatta as President and Vice President of the republic, respectively, and had hastily promulgated a provisional constitution providing for civil liberties and representative government with a strong central executive. The Committee also transformed itself into a quasi-parliament with advisory powers, the Central Indonesian National Committee (KNIP). Lastly, on August 31, Sukarno named a cabinet, under the constitution responsible to himself.

The first republican cabinet was heavily influenced by collaborating nationalists and Tan Malaka aides. Its composition angered the resistance movement that Sjahrir had built up during the occupation. Resistance leaders denounced the cabinet as "fascist." They also held that the government was incapable of curbing growing revolutionary excesses as extremist gangs ran amok in the first flush of independence and breakdown of authority to loot and hunt down Dutch nationals who had left the internment camps. The resistance felt that a government of such dubious character could not win the support of the world as the Indonesian revolution must if it were to succeed. Sjahrir demanded the dismissal of the cabinet and the introduction of sweeping democratic reforms. "Having successfully weathered the storm and stress attendant on the initial stages of its assumption of power," Sjahrir declared, "the time is now ripe for the institution of necessary measures aimed at democratizing the administrative structure of the country." [1] In the Sjahrir program, the Communists, conspicuously absent at this stage in the revolution, visualized a means of ousting the revisionist Tan Malaka forces from the government. The Communists wholly supported Sjahrir's "democratic revolution."

Sukarno also cast his lot with Sjahrir. An astute tactician, Sukarno rolled with the ground swell. He realized that he was the only leader of popular national stature and that Sjahrir urgently required his support; for that matter, Sukarno also realized that the republic must confront the Allies with a "resistance" government and that he was in equally desperate need of Sjahrir. Accordingly, in October and November, a democratization program was implemented with a view to weakening the position of the collaborating nationalists and the national Communists. The 150-member KNIP, for example, was enlarged by the addition of 33 members from the resistance, 15 of whom were appointed to a working committee and entrusted with guiding revolutionary strategy. Sjahrir was elected as chairman of the powerful working committee; Amir, as vice-chairman.* The KNIP was also converted into a legislative body. A multi-party system was introduced, and political parties mushroomed. The Masjumi,† established as an Islamic "corporation" in 1943, was reborn as a political party on November 7. The Partai Nasional Indonesia (PNI)—the Indonesian Nationalist Party—was revived on January 29. Both these parties, in the Indonesian context, were bourgeois in content and Marxist-socialist in outlook; the Masjumi was oriented toward Islam, the PNI toward secularism. Finally, on November

---

* Amir had been freed from a Malang jail by an armed band of *pemudas* (youth).
† Madjelis Sjuro Muslimin Indonesia (Council of Indonesian Moslem Associations).

12, Sukarno dismissed his cabinet and the first of three Sjahrir cabinets was formed. Sjahrir held the portfolios of Premier, Home Affairs, and Foreign Affairs ad interim; Amir, Defense and Information (later Information was turned over to Mohammed Natsir, a rising Islamic reformist figure who had first attracted national attention in 1940 with his anti-Japanese tracts).

The image of the republic had undergone a transformation. The government was now dominated by the resistance. In *Our Struggle*, a pamphlet circulated on October 21, Sjahrir moved to shift the ideological moorings of the revolution. "Democracy," he wrote, "not nationalism, should be the primary objective of our revolution." He called for a purge of "all political collaborators of the Japanese fascists," characterizing them as "dogs" who had betrayed the Indonesian ideal of an independent, democratic republic. The term "dog," anathema to even a nominal Moslem, deeply wounded the nationalists who had collaborated; Sukarno suspected the shaft was directed at him. Actually, Sjahrir had referred to the collaborationists as "tools" of the Japanese, but Tabrani, a Left-wing resistance journalist, had altered the phrase just before going to press. On November 1, Sjahrir sought to make amends in a political manifesto issued in the name of the republic. The manifesto drew a distinction between opportunists and true nationalists who had collaborated with the Japanese, emphasizing that the latter "never forsook the nationalist ideal." But the collaborating nationalists never forgave Sjahrir. As Sukarno receded into the background of the revolution, his distrust for Sjahrir and "Sjahrir-minded" groups deepened. Johan Fabricius, a Dutch journalist prophetically recorded in 1946:

> I thought of the gallant little Premier [Sjahrir] with his tired smile. In my mind, and in the minds of many others who believed in his tenacity, there was no doubt of his ultimate victory over his undeclared enemy, Sukarno. But how long was it to be before he succeeded in rooting out from the Indonesian republic ranks the fascism that he dared to challenge? And when the independence of Indonesia was recognized by the world, would perhaps then the greatest disillusionment of his life be awaiting him? [2]

In this atmosphere, as the abyss between the authoritarian Sukarno and the democratic Sjahrir widened, the British landed at Batavia with the declared objectives of releasing prisoners of war and civilian internees and disarming the Japanese. "I have made clear that we are not going into Java to put the Dutch back into power," Lt. General Sir Philip Christison, the British commander, announced from Singapore. Had the Indonesian revolt ended on this note, it is probable that the Dutch would have retained their financial and cultural interests in the Indies. With Western good will and assistance, Sjahrir's program of democratization would have been assured. And, finally, the Communists would probably never have had the opportunity for developing a mass movement; for, as postwar colonial history demonstrates, wherever the West has withdrawn gracefully, the Communists have fared poorly.

But the Dutch were determined to regain their "rightful" place in the Indies. In Holland itself, only recently liberated from foreign oppression, sentiment overwhelmingly favored the repossession of the Indies, by force if necessary. In the wake of the British landings, the Dutch systematically reoccupied the deepwater ports on Java and Sumatra. By November 29, 1946, when the British withdrew, the Dutch had more than 89,000 troops poised on the perimeters of six vital seaports—the Djakarta-Bandung complex, Semarang, and Surabaya on Java; Medan, Padang, and Palembang on Sumatra.

Under these circumstances, it was not surprising that clashes between the Indonesians and Allies multiplied. Armed bands infiltrated the Allied lines, terrorized the countryside, attacked prisoner-of-war camps in the interior, and clashed with each other. It was during this period that the British twice arrested Aidit for terrorist activity. "I was jailed in September but escaped to lead another guerrilla unit," Aidit said.[3] "I was caught again by the British, turned over to the Dutch, and held for seven months on Onrust."

As the disorders mounted, the republic abandoned Djakarta as its capital and on January 4, 1946, transferred the seat of government to Jogjakarta in Central Java, where the youthful, reformist Sultan Hamengkubuwono IX had declared himself on the side of the revolution. At Jogjakarta, the government found sanctuary and would be able to trade limited space for limited time in the event of a Dutch attack. The government was also in a position to counteract the activity of the revisionist Communists, who had reacted sharply to the Sjahrir program of democratization and mapped plans for seizing control of the revolution.

Up to this point in the developing revolution, the orthodox Communists were almost conspicuous by their absence. Not so the national Communists. From the outset, Tan Malaka maneuvered to widen the split between Sukarno and Sjahrir. He first approached Sjahrir and proposed that the resistance forces join with his own group in deposing the "fascist" Sukarno. Tan Malaka was apparently unenthusiastic about making an attempt to seize direction of the revolution without first eliminating Sukarno. As Tan Malaka doubtlessly expected, Sjahrir rebuffed him. Accordingly, Tan Malaka embarked on a daring and amateurish scheme to attain power by duplicity. He sought to capitalize on the growing unrest in Batavia by inducing Sukarno to draft a political will designating him as sole heir in the event that harm befell Sukarno and Hatta, which was probable once such a testament was signed. Sukarno, recognizing the need for some kind of a political will, consented, but he cleverly divided his legacy among four heirs—Tan Malaka, Iwa, Sjahrir, and Wongsonegoro—the last-named a respected old-line nationalist with no following. Sukarno felt that this group was representative of the main currents of the revolution—Sjahrir, the Marxist; Wongsonegoro, the nationalist; and Iwa, a devout Moslem, his Communist background notwithstanding. Sukarno preached that only by a blending of these three forces —Marxism, nationalism, and Islam—could the revolution succeed and the republic survive. In his mind, perhaps, Tan Malaka embodied a coalition of these three forces. Although Tan Malaka was disappointed by the will, the very fact that Sukarno had drafted a testament suited his designs admirably. As expected, the news of the testament spread rapidly, although its contents were kept secret (and have yet to be officially disclosed).

Now Tan Malaka drafted a new testament, in which he alone was named political heir. He then proceeded to the interior and spread rumors that Sukarno and Hatta were captives of the Dutch and that Sjahrir was in the pay of the British. By transferring the government to Jogjakarta, Sukarno exposed the absurdity of Tan Malaka's charges.

Apparently, Sukarno now felt that he could use Tan Malaka to depose Sjahrir, for Sukarno believed that Sjahrir's democratization program and conciliatory attitude toward the Allies had been pursued too far. Sukarno therefore encouraged Tan Malaka to capitalize on the widespread opposition to Sjahrir's policy of negotiations with the Dutch and British by constructing a broad united front behind the government. To achieve this, Tan Malaka organized the Persatuan Perdjuangan (Fighting Front) at Purwokerto. Within a short interval, the Persatuan succeeded in enrolling 141 parties and organizations "without the slightest difficulty." [4] Both the Masjumi and PNI entered the Persatuan, as did the Socialists and other parties of the Left that had blossomed after the introduction of the multi-party system.* No party could afford to dissociate itself from a front that enjoyed Presidential

* Although they had retained the names used during the prewar period and Japanese occupation, respectively, they had no direct connection with the

encouragement and was ostensibly organized to marshal the country behind the government.

By January 28, Tan Malaka apparently felt sufficiently secure to draft a seven-point Persatuan program, which, he felt, the moderate Sjahrir would reject. The "minimum demands" called for

Negotiations on the basis of the [100 per cent] recognition of Indonesian independence.

Composition of the government in harmony with the tendencies among the people.

Composition of the [Army] in harmony with the tendencies among the people.

Disarming of Japanese forces.

Confiscation and exploitation of enemy [Dutch] estates.

Confiscation and exploitation of enemy [Dutch] factories.

Sjahrir confounded Tan Malaka by endorsing the program. Tan Malaka countered by demanding its immediate implementation, a move that made it clear that Tan Malaka's primary objective was to topple Sjahrir. The parties of the Left, Sjahrir's main source of strength, resigned from the Persatuan; the Masjumi, by then in the cabinet, wavered. On February 28, Sjahrir, who considered Sukarno a coarchitect of the Tan Malaka strategy, abruptly resigned as Premier. Sukarno, forced to choose between Sjahrir and Tan Malaka, recognized the ambitious Tan Malaka as the greater personal threat and turned again to Sjahrir. On March 2, Sjahrir returned to office. Tan Malaka, enraged by Sukarno's deception, set about to attain power by a *coup d'état*. His plans were thwarted, however, when the government arrested him and a number of aides, including Yamin and Chaerul Saleh, on March 17. His arrest, meanwhile, generated disorders at Soerakarta, Central Java, largely between the Barisan Banteng (Buffalo Legion) and the Pesindo (Socialist Youth), which supported the government.*

Now the government organized a front behind the republic, the Nasional Konsentrasi (National Concentration). The Konsentrasi

former organizations. The PNI, for example, was a fusion of six minor nationalist groupings.

Amir had founded the Socialist Party of Indonesia on November 6, and Sjahrir the People's Socialist Party on November 20. On December 1, these two groups merged, forming the Socialist Party.

* The Barisan Banteng, a *bersiap* fighting organization, was the radical wing of the Barisan Pelopor, established by the Japanese in 1944 with Sukarno at its head. Chaerul Saleh and Dr. Buntaran Martoatmodjo were prominent members of both organizations, as was Dr. Muwardi. It was not known at the time that the Illegal-PKI had been instrumental in organizing the ostensibly socialist Pesindo.

embraced the Left and middle-of-the-road parties, including the Socialists and the Masjumi. Sardjono, the chairman of the PKI, a recent arrival in Indonesia, was elected chairman, not as a Communist but in tribute to his revolutionary past. Although the front never went beyond the paper stage, its creation symbolized Tan Malaka's isolation. His support was reduced largely to the intransigent PNI, not inconsiderable in view of its size, and to several fighting organizations, notably Dr. Muwardi's Buffalo Legion at Soerakarta. The alliance between Tan Malaka and the PNI, many of whose leaders had been collaborating nationalists, was born of a common hostility toward Sjahrir's "intellectualism" and his moderate policy of negotiation with the Dutch.

When the government announced on June 25 that within a week the police would be transferred from the Ministry of Home Affairs to the Premier's office, Tan Malaka's adherents were so distrustful that they interpreted the move as authorizing Sjahrir to form a private army with which to liquidate Tan Malaka's forces. Many army officers felt that the transfer foreshadowed not only the disarming of the Tan Malaka fighting organizations, but also the dismissal of Japanese-trained officers from the armed forces, perhaps even General Sudirman, the Chief of Staff. Like the former collaborating nationalists, the former PETA officers felt that they had no future in a "Sjahrir-minded" republic. Had not Sjahrir warned the nation in *Our Struggle* not to sacrifice its principles and its revolution for the sake of militarism and fascism? Despite these suspicious responses, the transfer of the police to the Premier's office manifested nothing more than Sjahrir's determination personally to coordinate the campaign against the extremist armed gangs then terrorizing West Java.*

Nonetheless, the June 25 announcement served as a signal for General Sudarsono, the Indonesian Republican Army commander at Soerakarta, to join forces with Tan Malaka and bring the simmering resentment against Sjahrir to a boil. Two days later, Tan Malaka was surreptitiously released from jail by Sudarsono's men. That evening, Sjahrir and three ministers were abducted as they passed through Soerakarta. Sukarno deplored the kidnapings as undermining the republic with the enemy at the gate, and he assumed all powers of government until such time as the cabinet and administrative service would again function normally. On July 2, the coup reached a decisive stage. An attempt to abduct Amir, the Defense Minister, miscarried. At the same time, Tan

---

* This wave of terror culminated in the Tanggerang (West Java) massacre of June 11, 1946, in which 653 Chinese, including 136 women and 36 children, were slaughtered.

Malaka sent General Sudarsono and Yamin to Sukarno to demand the resignation not only of Sjahrir, but to Sukarno's surprise, his own resignation as well. Sukarno ordered the arrest of the two emissaries. The army, including General Sudirman, now realized that Tan Malaka planned not only to depose Sjahrir, but also to overthrow Sukarno and the republic. The high command declared anew its loyalty to the President. A loyalist patrol located Sjahrir and freed him, unharmed. Tan Malaka's bid for power crumbled. The republic had weathered its first Communist power play, albeit "revisionist" Communist. Tan Malaka, Sudarsono, Yamin, Subardjo, Iwa, Sukarni, and Adam Malik were among those jailed. The "national" Communist bloc was to remain confined until August–September, 1948, when the government released them on the eve of a new *coup d'état*—this one staged by the orthodox Communists.

With the opposition apparently neutralized, Sjahrir was free to conclude his negotiations with the Allies. On October 16, 1946, under the aegis of the British, a truce was arranged between the Dutch and republican forces, setting the stage for the withdrawal of British troops. One month later to the day, a political accommodation was arrived at. It provided for Dutch recognition of the *de facto* authority of the republic over Java, Madura, and Sumatra; the formation, by January 1, 1949, of a federal United States of Indonesia (U.S.I.), comprising "the entire territory of the Netherlands Indies"; the creation of a Netherlands-Indonesian Union with the Dutch queen at its head; and the return of Dutch property to its rightful owners. In essence, the Dutch were exchanging political for economic concessions. But a compromise rarely satisfies extremists on either side, and in both the Netherlands and Indonesia the accord generated disapproval.

In Indonesia, support for the agreement came almost exclusively from the Left. The Communists approved the accord at Soerakarta on December 3, 1946. The Masjumi and PNI opposed the federalist settlement as weakening the concept of the unitarian republic proclaimed for the whole of the Indies. In particular, the vision of a union headed by the Dutch crown stuck in the throat of the PNI. The PNI joined the Masjumi to form a powerful front, the Benteng Republik (Republican Fortress), to block ratification of the agreement by the KNIP. The withdrawal of the Masjumi from the Konsentrasi limited the government-sponsored front to parties of the Left. As a consequence, the Left reformed itself into a new bloc, the Sajap Kiri (Left Wing), composed of the Socialist, Labor, Socialist Youth, and Communist parties. Its immediate objective was to mobilize support behind the political accord with the Dutch.

With the Masjumi and PNI in the opposition, it was clear that the Left could not muster sufficient votes in the KNIP to ensure the agreement's ratification. Thereupon Sjahrir, with Sukarno's approval, employed the tactic of enlarging the KNIP by Presidential decree. On February 25, 1947, in a tense session at Malang,* Sukarno, winning tacit approval for the move, defended himself in these terms: "I am neither a president *à la français*, nor *à l'americain*. I am a president of the Indonesian revolution!" The KNIP was expanded to 514 members. The majority of the new representatives were drawn from the Left. The Labor Party, which had had six seats, now had thirty-five; the Communists soared from two to thirty-five seats; functional worker and peasant fronts, previously unrepresented, were awarded eighty seats. The Sajap Kiri gained control of the quasi parliament, and ratification was assured.•

On March 25, 1947, at the hill station of Linggadjati, near Cheribon, the Indonesian-Dutch agreement was formally signed by the representatives of the republic and the Dutch crown. In truth, Linggadjati was a product of negotiation between the liberal *De Stuuw* faction of the Dutch and the democratic socialists of the republic. Under the circumstances, it was a reasonable accommodation—too reasonable for the ultraconservatives in the Netherlands and the radical nationalists in Indonesia.

But what of the Illegal-PKI in this initial period of revolution? True, it had improved its position in the KNIP. But by and large it seemed inactive, despite a long revolutionary tradition in Indonesia and a searing desire for power. PKI tactics appeared inexplicable, on the surface at least. Yet they merely reflected Stalin's immediate postwar strategy.

An understanding of the PKI's initial tactics in the August revolution requires an examination of Stalin's immediate postwar strategy. At the end of the war, Europe was prostrate, its prospects for political stability and economic recovery bleak. Stalin's main hope of Communist ascendancy in Europe was by default. "Communism is like a hotel," Alimin, who turns a phrase as neatly as Khrushchev, once said. "When people at home complain about their house, they move into a hotel."

---

* Ali Sastroamidjojo (PNI) spoke against the concessions. A Pesindo gang visited his hotel later, flashed knives, and warned him against further opposition to the accord. The story circulated in Malang. Amir, who had close ties to the Pesindo, investigated. Ali has said that he told Amir: "Your fascists tried to get me."

After the war, Stalin continued the Dimitrov line in the expectation that Newton's law would induce the ripe European fruit to fall. On the Continent, the Communists practiced moderation. In the colonies, the Communists exercised restraint on extremist nationalism. Communist moderation in the Afro-Asian world benefited the Communists in the European mother countries. In Indonesia, the Communists approved of Sjahrir's democratization of the republic (1945), encouraged negotiation with the Dutch (1946), ratified Linggadjati (1947), and countenanced a resumption of negotiations under the aegis of the United Nations after the Dutch attacked the republic that same year. For the PKI, it was of little concern if the policy of compromise postponed Indonesian independence. The Communists were sacrificing Indonesia for a bigger prize; Indonesia's turn would come later, as the irresistible Communist wave of the future engulfed the globe. If, however, the negotiations prospered and Indonesia acquired independence at the conference table, so much the better.

Thus, at the end of the war, the Illegal-PKI pursued the tactics of concealment and infiltration laid down by Musso at the outset of the popular-front period. A decade later, the PKI blamed these tactics for the Communist failure to capture the Indonesian revolution. In Aidit's words:

> During the revolution, the Party abandoned political, ideological, and organizational freedom and did not attach sufficient importance to its activities in labor and peasant circles. These were the reasons why the revolution failed.[5]

And he added:

> The Party failed to recognize in the August revolution that there was no need for illegality. The Party failed to realize that the Dutch colonial era ended and that a new era opened. This was the first mistake: the failure to declare the Party legal and lead the revolution. The second mistake was to join Sjahrir in creating a Socialist Party. It was a disastrous policy to unite with Right-wing Socialists and not with nationalist and Islamic groups. It was a sectarian, anti–popular-front policy. The Party should have fostered a broad national front. Instead, the Party fragmented its power. In this way the Party weakened its position early in the revolution.[6]

The PKI policy of concealment and infiltration was strongly motivated. But the Party was not compelled to practice deception; on the contrary, Sjahrir invited the Communists to assume an active, legal role in the multiparty system. "The Dutch and the Japanese," he said, "were equally hard on the Communists and the political parties which stood for complete untrammeled independence. The Republic of Indonesia will ban no political organization as long as its tenets or actions do not run counter to recognized democratic principles." [7]

The Communists, of course, were contemptuous of "recognized democratic principles" and chose to remain concealed.

The PKI's immediate postwar policy was conditioned by several factors. Forced to follow the official line, the PKI was committed to restraining Indonesian nationalism and encouraging a policy of compromise with the Dutch. The Sjahrir Socialists at this time were the leading advocates of this approach. Thus, Aidit's subsequent assessment notwithstanding, the PKI could not seek a united front with the Masjumi and PNI, since both parties— the Masjumi to a lesser degree—opposed negotiations unless the Dutch first acknowledged that Indonesia was "100 per cent" independent. The Masjumi and PNI were convinced that the Dutch were negotiating with Sjahrir in bad faith, employing the talks as a cover pending a military build-up in the port areas. The closest the PKI came to alliance with the Masjumi was their common membership in the Konsentrasi—and that front was intended to support Sjahrir against the machinations of Tan Malaka.

A number of reasons dictated the policy of concealment. By playing an open, prominent role early in the postwar Indonesian revolution, the Communists would have handicapped the republic when the time came to solicit Western recognition and assistance. This also would have played into the hands of the Dutch, who, after first seeking to depict the republic as a Japanese fiction, then labeled it a Communist creation. Thus, the Communists would only have antagonized Indonesian nationalism— especially in view of the PKI's supranational character.[8] Then, too, by delaying its emergence above ground, the PKI provided its scattered leadership abroad with time in which to return to Indonesia. Underground, the PKI enjoyed a breathing space while awaiting a clarification of the postwar Communist line and the revolutionary situation at home. It is also conceivable that the PKI chose to remain underground to await the reception accorded the Allies on their landing. If the republic collapsed, the PKI's emergence would have proved premature. Abroad, the Communists were treating the republic disdainfully. Radio Moscow ignored the proclamation of independence,[9] and in Holland, the Communists—Indonesian and Dutch alike—denounced the republic as the handiwork of Japan. Certainly, between August and November, the Indonesian situation must have confounded

Moscow. From afar, the republic appeared to be controlled by collaborating nationalists of Trotskyite coloration.

The tactics of concealment and infiltration did not win complete Party approval. One section of the Illegal-PKI, led by Mohammed Jussuf, rebelled against moderation. On October 21, 1945, Jussuf re-formed the PKI above ground. He shifted from the compromising Right line to an uncompromising Left line of encouraging antigovernment activities and "social revolution" in West and Central Java. In February, 1946, Jussuf organized a *Putsch* at Cheribon, which was suppressed by the republic. Jussuf's actions forced the Illegal-PKI to modify its strategy and to operate in part in the open to restrain Leftist deviationists and divorce the Party from "Left-wing adventurers" who besmirched the PKI's name and sabotaged the Moscow line. On March 3, 1946, the PKI denounced Jussuf's deviations and expelled him from the Party. Later, Aidit, who restored Jussuf to good standing in 1951, contended that "Jussuf was a good Communist who was dubious about PKI policy during the August revolution. He could not comprehend why the PKI must not appear to lead the revolution. He organized his party in defiance of the Party leadership. The Party had no alternative but to condemn him." [10]

The Jussuf affair coincided with the return of the veteran Communist leadership from abroad. In March, Sardjono arrived in Indonesia—over Dutch objections[11]—having been discharged from the Allied propaganda service at Morotai. Sardjono tarried three weeks at Batavia and then crossed into the republic, rejoining the Party at Soerakarta. "I found it was the same Party," he said. On April 29, 1946, under his chairmanship, the Party emerged from the dark—for the first time since 1926. Sardjono established his headquarters at Jogjakarta, in a former hotel; on a small rise across the road, over the doorway of a Catholic church, the republic's flag fluttered. The PKI headquarters, staffed by twenty-five persons, was austerely furnished with battered chairs and tables and threadbare curtains (as were all republican offices). Sardjono explained that the Party wished to strengthen the national character of the revolution, and not its social or economic aspects; that the Party's goals were identical with those of the government; that it was prepared to cooperate with Moslems and Christians. He said that "our policy is no more and no less than the policy of our heart," that the Party did not seek to establish socialism, since prevailing conditions did not warrant such a development. On August 12, 1946, shortly after Sardjono's arrival, Alimin reappeared in Indonesia, after having been absent for twenty years. He was the first emissary from behind the Iron Curtain since the end of the war. Would the "Sardjono line" change? Apparently not. Alimin affirmed:

> Our program is simply to support the government. . . . With the dissolution of the Comintern, the PKI follows an independent course. We wish to cooperate with the Dutch in developing a democratic United States of Indonesia. Three hundred and fifty years of Dutch rule cannot be snapped overnight. We Communists advocate democracy and economic development for Indonesia, with emphasis on the modernization of agriculture.[12]

Sardjono continued functioning as Party chairman, but Alimin directed the Party's affairs. Alimin, endeavoring to de-emphasize his presence, shunned Jogjakarta and settled at Soerakarta. He avoided discussing the 1926 debacle other than to say that after his deportation from Singapore he sailed for Canton, attended the Pan-Pacific Trade Union Congress at Hankow in 1927 (where he met Earl Browder and other Communist luminaries), and spent three months in a Nationalist jail. After Hankow was lost to the Nationalists and Mao Tse-tung began the Long March in search of an "active sanctuary," Alimin left for Moscow by way of Korea. "I remained in Moscow until 1943," he said, "and engaged in practical work, which took me to Germany and England." In 1943, Alimin departed for Yenan and remained there until 1946, returning to Indonesia by way of Tokyo, where, he has said, he visited his comrades and spent several days watching the trial of Hideki Tojo.

In the 1945–46 period, the Indonesian Communist students in Holland also returned home. Ironically the Dutch, impressed by their "moderate" views, gave them free transportation. Rustam Effendi, a Communist member of the Dutch Parliament, for example, was then advocating Indonesian independence within a Netherlands Commonwealth under a common head of state.[13] Setiadjit and Abdulmadjid flew to Batavia; Maruto Darusman went by ship. There were others.

On their arrival at Batavia, the "students," most of them in their late twenties or early thirties, discerned the nationalist character of the revolution and crossed into the republic. Their return to Indonesia represented a sound Dutch investment. Once in the republic, they propagated a spirit of compromise with the Dutch. Some, like Setiadjit, played critical roles in the political negotiations. As in Holland, however, the students continued to conceal their Communist affiliation. At Jogjakarta, they dispersed and infiltrated other parties in what later appeared to be a master plan. Only in late 1948, on the eve of a Communist rebellion, did they disclose their genuine colors. Again, as in Holland, the Communists proved themselves masters at deception. Setiadjit, for example, joined the *Partai Buruh* (Labor Party); Abdulmadjid, Sjahrir's Socialist Party.

Only one of the returning students—Maruto Darusman—openly entered the PKI. It is likely that he did so to allay suspicions that the other students might have been under Communist influence. His joining the PKI made it reasonable to assume that any other Communists in the student group would do likewise. As a Eurasian, moreover, his entry into the PKI demonstrated Communist universality and promoted the idea that the Communist movement was above racism. Although Darusman contended that he was not a Communist when he returned home, his meteoric rise in the PKI belied his disclaimer. In 1947, Darusman was "elected" Vice-Chairman of the Party and entered the Amir cabinet as one of the ministers of state, ostensibly the first Communist to sit in a republican cabinet. Darusman echoed the Sardjono-Alimin line:

> Our Party program is a nationalist, not a socialist program. Our principal plank is to strengthen the nationalist movement and broaden the nationalist front. Socialism patterned on the Soviet model would not succeed in Indonesia. Socialism must adjust itself to local conditions. We cannot copy the Soviet model.[14]

The returning students were not the only Communists infiltrating the Socialist and Labor parties. Members of the Illegal-PKI also dispersed, infiltrating different political groups. Tan Ling Djie, a Marxist theoretician of Chinese extraction, joined the Socialist Party. Wikana, the PKI youth leader, entered Pesindo, which later became the PKI's paramilitary front. In November, 1946, when the mainstream of Indonesian labor was reorganized into the SOBSI—the All-Indonesian Central Organization of Labor—its leadership was dominated by crypto-Communists, among them Harjono, Njono, and Oey Gee Hwat, who, like Tan Ling Djie, was of Chinese extraction. Similarly, when the peasantry was organized into the BTI, the Indonesian Peasant Front, the Communists secretly acquired control; Sadjarwo was a principal leader. Perhaps the most startling revelation was Amir's announcement in 1948 that he had been a member of the Illegal-PKI since the days of Gerindo and the popular front.

Despite the known dimensions of the Communist infiltration of the revolution, it is unlikely that the complete extent will ever be fully plumbed. In analyzing this period, two logical conclusions emerge. First, without the clandestine support of the Communist movement, Sjahrir's policy of negotiation with the Dutch would probably have collapsed. Sjahrir enjoyed the support of the Socialist, Labor, Socialist Youth, and Communist parties, the SOBSI and BTI. Indeed, when Sjahrir's Ministry fell in June, 1947, it was because the Communists felt Sjahrir had outlived his usefulness and the Communist bloc within withdrew its support. Second, the Communists—particularly the Pesindo fighting organization—were instrumental in thwarting Tan Malaka's bid for power in 1945–46. An impartial observer may therefore conclude that the Communists played an important role in the early history of the republic. Neither Sukarno, Hatta, nor Sjahrir, much less any non-Communist foreign observer, suspected the depth of Communist concealment and infiltration. Little wonder, then, that by 1947, Soviet commentators apparently found the situation in Indonesia sufficiently favorable to make such statements as this: "The democratic [Communist] elements in the country have become a major force." [15]

Yet despite the penetration, Communist influence in the republic was more apparent than real. The Communists were seeking to control the revolution from the top; the PKI lacked a rice-roots organization. Throughout the revolution, the republic was clearly dominated by the dynamic of nationalism, with democratic socialism and Islam riding its coattails. Not only did the Communists lack a mass following, as Aidit has conceded, but in the showdown that later developed between the republic and the Communists, the Party found itself devoid of middle-class and intellectual support as well.

6

The First Colonial War

As the Communists pursued their deceptive tactics in jockeying for power, the differences between the Dutch and the republic over the implementation of Linggadjati rapidly approached a deadlock. For the Dutch, Linggadjati served as a pretext for military action. For the Communists, it provided an opportunity to jettison Sjahrir and the "Right-wing" Socialists.

The impasse arose from a dispute over the meaning of Linggadjati. The Republicans interpreted the agreement as recognizing Jogjakarta's sovereignty, the Dutch as affirming Netherlands sovereignty pending the transfer of power to an independent U.S.I. On May 27, 1947, as the split deepened, the Dutch served the republic with an ultimatum incorporating a number of provisions. Sjahrir, in effect, sued for peace and on June 19 acceded in part to Dutch insistence on holding veto power in the interim government prior to the formation of the U.S.I. The Dutch interpreted Sjahrir's concession as weakness and pressed even harder; in the republic, radical and conservative opinion alike interpreted the concession as appeasement and called for firmness.

Unbeknown to Sjahrir, his political redoubt, the Sajap Kiri, had been captured by the Communists. In May, the Left-wing bloc was reorganized and the Communist, Labor, and Socialist parties accorded equal voices in determining Sajap Kiri policy.[1] Given the depth of Communist infiltration of the Labor and Socialist parties, the Sajap Kiri had become a Communist instrument. The time was now at hand for the Communists to depose Sjahrir, which they accomplished on June 26. Sardjono set the pace by announcing that the Communists rejected Sjahrir's concessions;

the Socialist and Labor parties followed suit. That evening, Sjahrir resigned. On the following day, however, Setiadjit returned to the republic from a mission to Eastern Europe. He called a session of the Sajap Kiri at Jogjakarta, recounted his experiences at Prague as a SOBSI delegate to a conference of the World Federation of Trade Unions (WFTU), and endorsed Sjahrir's policy of compromise. The Sajap Kiri thereupon reversed itself and endorsed Sjahrir's actions. The front asked Sjahrir to resume the premiership. But the Communists had shown their hand; Sjahrir realized that he had become a pawn in the Communist game and rejected their invitation.

Sukarno, aware of growing Dutch belligerency, proposed that the republic's major parties, the Masjumi, Nationalists, Socialists, and Labor, join forces to form a government of national unity. On July 3, Amir succeeded—but without the Masjumi, which, under the moderate leadership of Natsir and Sjafruddin Prawiranegara, had thrown its support behind Sjahrir in his hour of need. However, a group of opportunists in the Masjumi broke with their party and entered the cabinet as the PSII, the United Indonesian Islamic Party. This clique endeavored to capitalize on the prestige of the defunct Sarekat Islam, which, in 1929, had changed its name to PSII. Their defection was the first serious weakening of the Masjumi, which nevertheless remained the largest party in the republic. For the radical Left, the Moslem cleavage—a harbinger of instability and indiscipline in the Islamic ranks—was an undisguised blessing. PSII participation in the cabinet provided the government with a needed aura of Islamic respectability.

On paper, the cabinet was ostensibly a Sajap-Kiri–PNI coalition, marking the first active participation of the PNI in a republican cabinet. The cabinet, however—this was known only to the Communists—was a creature of the PKI. It was dominated by assorted Nenni-type fellow travelers. Amir (Socialist) was Premier and Defense Minister; Setiadjit (Labor), Deputy Premier; Miss S. K. Trimurty (Labor), Minister of Labor; Abdulmadjid (Socialist), Vice Minister of Internal Affairs; Mohammed Tamzil (Socialist), Vice Minister of Foreign Affairs; Dr. Ong Eng Die, a Chinese (Socialist), Vice Minister of Finance; Siauw Giok Tjhan, also a Chinese (Chinese Community), Minister of State; Wikana (Youth Congress), Minister of State; Darusman (PKI), Minister of State; Suprodjo (Labor), Minister for Social Affairs.

The cabinet promptly reaffirmed Sjahrir's June 19 concessions and instructed Setiadjit to make further concessions to the Dutch on July 8. Thus, in a single maneuver, the Communists had reaffirmed the Stalinist line of moderation; disposed of Sjahrir;

secured control of the cabinet; and insured that in the likely event of Dutch aggression, they would exercise considerable, if not decisive, influence in the underground republican resistance government then being planned.

Short of open treachery, however, no republican government could possibly yield to the Dutch on one demand—Netherlands insistence on the creation of a joint Indo-Dutch constabulary to police the republic in the interim period. The Amir cabinet, like its predecessor, stalled. At this critical point, the United States directly intervened in the Indonesian dispute for the first time.

Since its inception, the republic had vainly solicited United States recognition and support. American popular opinion was instinctively and overwhelmingly sympathetic to the Indonesian cause, but in the Cold War, the United States frequently fails to act on its beliefs. Thus the United States Government, pre-occupied with the containment of Communism in Europe and fearful of offending the Dutch, treated the republic icily. As early as October 20, 1945, the republic had asked President Truman by cable to mediate the growing dispute between the Dutch and the Indonesians. On November 10, the republic cabled again, this time to protest the misuse of American surplus war matériel by the Dutch. The United States responded by requesting the Dutch to remove American insignia from their armor. This happened at a time when Sjahrir was implementing his program of democratization and was hopeful of a peaceful solution of the conflict with the Dutch.

In Indonesia itself, the official American representation evinced a strong pro-Dutch flavor in 1945–47; the United States Consul General, Walter A. Foote, who served in the Indies before the war, was so ostentatiously pro-Dutch that his behavior embarrassed and offended the sensibilities, if not the political awareness, of consular officials. Thus, there was considerable excitement in Indonesia when Washington addressed itself to the Indonesian dispute in 1947. The impression was that the United States acted to forestall a Dutch military adventure, but, as it developed, American pressure was being brought not against the Dutch but against the republic. In a June 27 *aide mémoire* to the republic, the United States appealed to the Indonesians to co-operate in the formation of an interim government in which the Netherlands would exercise sovereignty; behind the scenes, the British impressed on the republic that a similar formula was being applied in India.[2] What the Anglo-American powers failed to appreciate, however, was that although the United States had withdrawn from the Philippines in 1946, and although the British were preparing to withdraw from the Indian subcontinent that summer, the continental Europeans—Dutch, French, Portuguese— had no intention of leaving Asia. The United States *aide mémoire* also reflected Washington's insensitivity to the dynamic of postwar Asian revolution: the quest for human dignity. The United States promised financial assistance to Indonesia if the republic acceded to the Dutch demands. The logical course, if dollar diplomacy was to be brought into play at all—and its advisability is open to serious question—would have been to sweeten a Dutch withdrawal with financial aid in the form of Marshall Plan funds. But, apparently, Washington felt this to be too crude a method of dealing with the Dutch, but not with the Indonesians.

The tragedy for the West was that in the end, Marshall Plan funds financed the Dutch colonial wars in Indonesia in 1947 and 1948–49 in the face of hostile Western public opinion.

In the republic, the American *aide mémoire* was widely interpreted as supporting Holland. Foote contributed to this feeling a week after it was issued. On July 4, Foote did not hold the traditional Independence Day reception (although he held open house every Sunday) and, instead, attended a "private party" for the small American community, at which Van Mook, then the Lt. Governor General of the Indies, and other Dutch officials appeared. Although Batavia was still under a joint Indonesian-Dutch administration, no Indonesians were present. Shades of the "Ugly American."

On July 20, 1947, at 10:37 P.M., with the republic either unwilling or unable to agree to a joint gendarmerie, the Dutch attacked the republic. At a midnight press conference, Van Mook euphemistically described the aggression as a "police action." Armored Dutch columns, with air support, rolled into republic territory, encountering scanty, if any, resistance. The disheveled republic forces dispersed in orderly (often disorderly) fashion into the mountains flanking the main roads along which the mechanized Dutch columns advanced. The prospect was for a Dutch blitzkrieg and an interminable guerrilla campaign thereafter. The Dutch assault outraged public opinion in the West as well as Asia. On July 30, acting on an Australian complaint, the Security Council took up the Indonesian question and promptly ordered a ceasefire. The Netherlands and the republic complied on August 4. There followed a fortnight of debate in the Council, resulting in a political impasse. The Soviet bloc batted around. In the exchanges, the Stalinists at the U.N. often stood alone on a moral pedestal denouncing the colonial war in Indonesia and calling for a return to the *status quo ante*. While the West's policy of containment was barring the front gate, the bear was lumbering in through the back door. Soviet propaganda not only enhanced the prestige of the Communists in the Afro-Asian world, but, even worse, weakened the moral posture of the West in the West itself.

On August 25, an American "troika" formula broke the stale-mate on the Council. A resolution was passed (with Russia and Poland abstaining) authorizing the creation of a three-power Committee of Good Offices (GOC) to seek a political settlement in Indonesia. Each belligerent was permitted to select one power, and these two powers in turn chose the third member. The Dutch chose Belgium as its representative; the Indonesians chose Australia; and the Belgians and Australians, the United States. Eventually, the Dutch and Indonesians agreed to meet on the "neutral" terrain of the third power, aboard a 15,000-ton American naval transport, the U. S. S. "Renville," anchored off Batavia. The GOC held its first plenary session aboard the "Renville" on December 8. Between the August 4 cease-fire and the opening of political talks, the Dutch had mopped up the extensive Indonesian pockets between their armored columns and, in violation of the truce, had extended their areas beyond the forward lines. The Dutch defended their actions on the basis of the so-called Van Mook Line, an arbitrarily drawn perimeter, which reduced republic territory to about two-thirds of Sumatra (jungle interior), half of Madura,* and one-third of Java. In the interval, the Dutch also proceeded with their grand strategy to Balkanize Indonesia and reduce the archipelago to a conglomeration of puppet entities, each of which would serve as a constituent state in the proposed U.S.I. By doing so, the Dutch irreparably harmed the future political development of Indonesia. Henceforth, the Indonesians, particularly Sukarno and the PNI (with Communist encouragement), would suspect federalism as a "neocolonialist" device. Yet a federal republic, as later publicly espoused by the Masjumi and the Sjahrir Socialists, was and is the obvious solution to the problem of administering and developing the far-flung archipelago through democratic processes in accordance with the Indonesian ideal of an independent, democratic republic.

* In 1945–46, the Dutch had reoccupied sparsely settled Kalimantan, Sulawesi, Nusatenggara, and the Malaku without encountering serious resistance.

7

The Road to Madiun

The Renville negotiations coincided with the first substantive post-war shift in the international Communist line. In 1947, the popular-front line was abandoned. The switch seriously affected the course of events in Indonesia. Given the explosive situation in Southeast Asia at that time, the new line led to an armed Communist bid for power in the region.

In 1947, Moscow's hopes for assuming power in Europe by default lay shattered. The Truman Doctrine bolstered southeastern Europe; the Marshall Plan gave promise of economic recovery and political stability on the continent. Stalin reacted vigorously. He revised his strategy and took the offensive. In effect, he declared war on the non-Communist world. The shift was heralded by growing Soviet intransigence on East-West issues. The founding of the Cominform (Communist Information Bureau) at Warsaw on September 22, 1947, initiated the shift. The new organization postulated an ideological division of the world into two conflicting camps, the "imperialist, antidemocratic camp" headed by the United States, and the "anti-imperialist, democratic camp" headed by the Soviet Union. A Cominform communiqué served notice that the ideological division of the world imposed "a special task" on the Communist parties, i.e., that "they must take into their hands the banner of the defense of the national independence and sovereignty of their countries."

Clearly, the popular-front period of compromise and negotiation was at an end. In a speech to the Cominform, Andrei Zhdanov removed any remaining doubts. Rephrasing Zinoviev's aphorism that the road to Paris was through Peking, and the Marxist-Leninist dictum that "when the 'lower' classes do not want the old way, and when the 'upper' classes cannot carry on in the old way—only then can revolution triumph," Zhdanov declared that World War II had aggravated the crisis of the colonial system, and that this was expressed in the rise of a powerful movement for national liberation in the colonies and dependencies. This has placed the rear of the capitalist system in jeopardy, for the peoples of the colonies no longer wished to continue living as they had in the past. He went on to say that the ruling classes of the metropolitan countries could no longer govern the colonies by methods that in the past had led to protracted colonial wars.

In his division of the world, Zhdanov placed Indonesia in the Soviet camp. Doubtlessly, he was influenced by intelligence supplied by Indonesian Communist exiles in Moscow—Musso and Semaun, for example—that the republic, like the Vietminh, was deeply infiltrated, if not controlled, by Communists.

A comparison of Zhdanov's Warsaw speech with an article for the September, 1947, issue of *Political Affairs* (an American theoretical Communist journal), apparently written the month before by Charles Bidien, dramatically demonstrates the sudden reversal of line. Bidien had enthusiastically, and inaccurately, written in the then-prevailing popular-front vein that

> the Socialist Party of Indonesia, basing its political position on Mao Tse-tung's writings, has worked in harmony with the Indonesian Communist Party. [The line in those days, of course, was that Mao was an "agrarian reformer" and not a Communist, certainly not a Communist in the Stalinist tradition.] This is an Asian example of the new Socialist-Communist coalition in Eastern Europe.

Zhdanov urged the Communist parties to close their ranks and unite their efforts on the basis of a common anti-imperialist and democratic platform. Specifically, he ordered them to break with Right-wing socialists. In Indonesia, this obviously meant Sjahrir. To Communists, Zhdanov's bellicosity sounded the opening of a new phase in the unceasing struggle for world domination. By intensifying the colonial crisis in Asia, Stalin may have foreseen that the metropolitan European countries would divert Marshall Plan funds to finance their colonial wars in Indonesia and Indochina. Moreover, colonial war in Asia would obstruct the flow of raw materials for European reconstruction, e.g., Indonesian and Malayan rubber and tin. And by encouraging tension between Asia and the West, Stalin also may have hoped to promote friction along racial lines and thereby drain the reservoir of Anglo-American good will generated in Asia by the defeat of Japan, the American withdrawal in the Philippines, and Britain's abdication of power on the Indian subcontinent. Lastly, by encouraging disorders in the newly independent states, Stalin may have hoped to weaken the fledgling nations, already beset with the legacies of colonial rule and confronted with demands for radical economic and social reform.

In Europe, the Communist rank and file executed an electrifying *volte face*. There, Stalin was compelled to employ tactics short of war. The West possessed a total nuclear-weapons monopoly. In France and Italy, the Communists fomented general strikes and disorders; in Greece, the "limited" civil war was intensified. By February, after the fall of Czechoslovakia, all of Eastern Europe was under Soviet control; in June, 1948, the Berlin blockade was imposed, testing the endurance of the West for almost a year. In non-nuclear Asia, however, Stalin enjoyed a relatively free hand. There he unleashed war. In 1948, the Communists rose in rebellion in the independent and capitalist Philippines, in colonial Malaya, Marxist-Socialist Burma and revolutionary Indonesia. All these revolts were politically motivated. Nor was Southeast Asia the only area to be involved. In 1949, the Communists overran the Chinese mainland. In 1950, they invaded Tibet and Korea. (It was not until 1953 that there was a return to a "Right" line, reflected in the Korean truce and the Indochina settlement in 1954, culminating in Khrushchev's development of the line of "peaceful coexistence" at the Twentieth Congress.)

The Zhdanov line had seeped into the circulatory system of the Asian Communist movement with relative rapidity. By December, 1947 it was being applied in theoretical terms directly to Asia. The December 15, 1947 issue of *Bolshevik*, the organ of the Central Committee of the CPSU, carried an article by Zhukov, in which he wrote:

> In a number of colonial . . . countries, a people's anti-imperialist front has been formed, consisting of a coalition of parties having the struggle for liberation as their platform, under the leading participation of the Communist Party. It is well known that democratic forms have already been successfully put into practice in large areas of the liberated parts of China, in the unoccupied territory of the Indonesian Republic, and in the inner regions of the Republic of Vietnam.

In India, the Communists shifted to the new line, adopting an aggressive anti-Nehru posture. In China, Mao Tse-tung echoed Moscow and appealed to all the anti-imperialist forces of the various Eastern [Asian] countries to unite to oppose the oppression of imperialism and the reactionaries *within* each country. In effect, the "tough" line called for war on two fronts: externally against the "imperialist, antidemocratic camp," and internally against those who opposed the "anti-imperialist, democratic camp." In January, 1948, Soviet journals were applying the line directly to Indonesia; Moscow characterized Indonesia as "the advance guard of the liberation struggle of the colonial peoples" and as a "people's democratic republic." It described the PKI as "the real leader and organizer" of the Indonesian revolution—doubtlessly swept away by its enthusiasm and misled by the apparent success of the PKI's tactics of infiltration and concealment.

The new line was publicly disseminated in Asia for the first time at the Conference of Youth and Students of Southeast Asia Fighting for Freedom and Independence. The Conference, meeting at Calcutta on February 17, 1948, was sponsored by the World Federation of Democratic Youth and the International Union of Students, both Communist fronts. As a result of the wide publicity given the new doctrine at the WFDY-IUS Conference, it earned the sobriquet the "Calcutta Line" in Asia. The Calcutta meeting has since become a lively source of controversy. At issue is whether it was there that the Communists received their "orders" from Moscow for unleashing the subsequent Communist agitation and insurrections in Indonesia, Malaya, Burma, and India (in Thailand, the Communists moved underground but lacked the strength for a coup; in Indochina, the Vietminh discarded its nationalist guise). There is no dispute, however, that the Calcutta meeting served as a transmission belt for the aggressive, belligerent new line. There is also no dispute that the new line jettisoned the posture of compromise and encouraged violence. However, it is doubtful that we shall ever learn what exactly transpired at Calcutta. But in view of the bloody sequel, the controversy over whether Calcutta was or was not the place where "orders" for revolt were circulated is largely academic.[1] Just how academic is illustrated clearly by the Indonesian events of 1948, when the Communists moved briskly from compromise and negotiation with the Dutch externally and the non-Communist parties internally to a new line of implacable aggression at home and abroad, culminating in the second Communist rebellion in Indonesia.

In the republic, meanwhile, the moderate parties had become increasingly apprehensive over Amir's Left-wing policies. The Masjumi, which had entered the cabinet in a display of national unity after the Dutch attack, was particularly disturbed by Amir's policy as Defense Minister of paring down the strength of irregular Islamic fighting organizations while promoting the development of the private armies of the Left, a policy which the Communists enthusiastically endorsed.

Against this background the Indonesians signed a new accord with the Dutch on January 17, 1948, the "Renville Agreement." Bearing the name of the American vessel aboard which it was signed, the agreement provided for a cease-fire and republican recognition of the imaginary Van Mook Line as the new Indo-Dutch perimeter. The republic had sacrificed its military position in return for Dutch acceptance of a dozen principles, including a free and impartial plebiscite to determine the future status of a sovereign Indonesia. Dr. Frank P. Graham, the able American delegate who did so much to repair the damage done by Foote, looked on the accord as opening the door to a political settlement by "ballots, not bullets." On the evening of January 17, Sukarno, who had always favored compromise and negotiation with the Dutch, perhaps out of lack of confidence in the republic's inherent strength, asked over Radio Jogjakarta: "If ideals can be achieved peacefully, why should we fight?"

The concessions set the stage for a cabinet crisis. The Masjumi moved to terminate Amir's administration and withdrew from the coalition. The Masjumi action was endorsed by Sjahrir, who, as in the days of the Japanese occupation, was working behind a screen. Sjahrir, already disturbed by the founding of the Cominform, felt that Moscow's increasing aggressiveness foreshadowed rising Communist pressure in the republic and a concomitant bipolarization of the republic into Communist and anti-Communist camps. Sjahrir considered it imperative that Amir be replaced as Premier. Sjahrir's candidate was Hatta, who until now had remained in the background, endorsing Sjahrir's program of democratization and establishing close relations with the Masjumi. A Hatta cabinet, Sjahrir reasoned, should be responsible to the President, not to the provisional parliament—to circumvent the Sajap Kiri's control of the KNIP and to render impotent any Communist agitation against Amir's successor. To agitate against a Presidential cabinet would mean agitating against Sukarno, a suicidal policy as long as the republic faced a Dutch threat, real or artificial. The PNI, meanwhile, sensing an opportunity to improve its position in a new cabinet, began attacking Amir for "capitulating" to the Dutch and entered the opposition. Amir's support was reduced to the Sajap Kiri—as was Sjahrir's after Linggadjati.

On January 23, Amir labored to reshuffle the cabinet and avert a crisis, but that night it became apparent that opposition to the Left was deeper than Renville. Amir resigned. The next day, the Sajap Kiri, demanding Amir's return, staged a demonstration in Jogjakarta. Aware of impending danger on the extreme Left, Sukarno acted; he appealed for calm and asked Hatta to form a cabinet—Sjahrir's formula.

The Soviet version of events in this period differs. Georgi Afrin, a Tass correspondent who had arrived the previous October to cover the U.N. negotiations, wrote in *Pravda* that Amir fell as the result of an intrigue between the Masjumi and the United States. Afrin averred that "with the help of backstage machinations, the Americans were able to secure the downfall of the government of Amir Sjarifuddin," which, he claimed, "had enjoyed the support of the Indonesian people."

In truth, Hatta had worked to compose a broad coalition, including participation of the Sajap Kiri, in a bid to neutralize its opposition and retain a façade of national unity against the Dutch. He offered the Sajap Kiri three portfolios, but on January 25, in a conference with Hatta, the Left demanded as many as a third of the posts, including the ministries of Defense and Home Affairs. Obviously, the Left wanted control over the armed forces, "the most important weapon of state power." [2] Hatta balked. On January 29, he formed the sixth cabinet of the republic, without the Left. For the first time, the Left was unrepresented in a republican government. Its hold on the revolution was loosening.

On January 31, on the eve of the Renville cease-fire order, the new cabinet was officially announced. The seventeen-man cabinet was dominated by the Center; the Masjumi and PNI each held four seats. Hatta was given Amir's former portfolio, becoming Premier and Minister of Defense. Supeno, the Minister of Reconstruction and Youth and a member of the Socialist Party, was the only leader of the Left to participate in the cabinet, and he did so as a private individual. Like Sjahrir, Supeno had become disenchanted with the Sajap Kiri's Communist drift. The Hatta cabinet, based on Sjahrir's strategy, was responsible to the President, not to the parliament—in a sense a return to 1945 and the first Sukarno cabinet. The irony of the situation was that in 1945, Sjahrir had been primarily responsible, though acting in good faith, for enlarging the Left's representation in the KNIP to guard against a fascist or national-Communist dictatorship under Sukarno. Now he was fighting the threat of a Communist dictatorship. Sjahrir's purpose then as now was to curb all manifestations of political extremism.

In 1955, at a time when the Communists were wooing Sukarno and the PNI, Aidit rewrote the history of the period, pointedly ignoring PNI participation in the Hatta cabinet. Aidit contended:

In essence, the sixth Indonesian cabinet was a Masjumi cabinet led by Moh. Hatta. From the time of its formation . . . this cabinet pursued a completely Masjumi policy and the Madiun Provocation [Communist revolt] was the most important implementation of this policy, i.e., the policy of rounding up and murdering Communists, the policy which the Masjumi leaders still pursue right up to this very day.[3]

The Sajap Kiri reacted sharply to the Hatta government. As expected, the Left went into the opposition. Unprepared for the Presidential stratagem, Amir directed his first blows at the "undemocratic" nature of the cabinet. The Sajap Kiri demanded a cabinet responsible to the KNIP. The fact that the Masjumi and PNI had reversed themselves and, after denouncing Renville, were now supporting the agreement convinced the Sajap Kiri that opposition to Renville was merely a gambit for toppling Amir. As for Amir, he was bitter. He felt that Sukarno, who had made no secret of his delight over Sjahrir's fall the preceding June and had strongly supported Amir for the Premiership over Masjumi objections, had betrayed him.

But the biggest blow to the Sajap Kiri was yet to come. On February 13, Sjahrir resigned from the Socialist Party and announced the formation of a new organization, the Partai Socialis Indonesia (PSI)—Socialist Party of Indonesia—with emphasis on the word "Indonesia." Officially, the split was generated as the result of Sjahrir's support of the Hatta cabinet in defiance of the party's opposition to the new coalition. But since his deposition by Amir and the extreme Left, Sjahrir had become increasingly alarmed at the growing Communist influence within the Socialist Party in particular and the Left in general. Sjahrir was convinced that Amir had "acted on instructions" to topple his government. Sjahrir was a democratic socialist who harbored no illusions about Leninism or Stalinism. He fiercely opposed totalitarianism in all its manifestations. His thinking ranged beyond the narrow confines of insular, isolated Indonesia. Sjahrir influenced not only his immediate followers, but students, intellectuals, political independents, and the liberals and moderates within the Masjumi and PNI. *Our Struggle*, his political manifesto, has remained, despite the post-1959 emphasis on Sukarno's *Political Manifesto* (currently state policy), the most eloquent exposition of the Indonesian ideal of an independent, democratic republic. In Sjahrir's view, as expressed in the platform of the PSI at its first congress in 1952, Indonesia's Communists were "political soldiers of the political army of Soviet Russia," executing "the tasks given to them by the command of that army." In Sjahrir's view, and in the view of those around him, "in the totalitarian state what is wanted of the people is only their obedience."

In splitting with Amir, Sjahrir recognized that Amir had become susceptible to Communist influence. In his view, Amir's political instability and ambition made him responsive to the Communist obsession with power. Sjahrir's intellectual appeal was immediately manifest. Three of the four Socialist deputies in the Working Committee, the pilot house of the revolution, bolted with him. They were Subadio Sastrosatomo, the able parliamentary tactician; Djohan Sjaharuzah, the underground organizer; and Sugondo Djojopuspito, destined to become a minister in the last cabinet of the republic. Of Sjahrir's aides, only Tan Ling Djie, who later admitted to being a Communist, refused to join the revolt of democratic socialists against Communist domination. More than half of the Socialist Party's council, including Sitorous, Sjahrir's intellectual twin, also joined Sjahrir. "Only the intellectuals joined Sjahrir," Amir taunted. "I have the masses." [4] Perhaps Communism did not succeed in misleading Indonesian intellectuals. But what constituted the "masses" to whom Amir referred? Peasants? No. Few peasants participated in politics, especially the politics of the Left. Only after 1952 did the Communists make a concerted drive to enlist support among the politically illiterate peasants, who constitute more than three-fourths of the Indonesian people. For the most part, the masses were urban or estate (suburban, if you will) workers, small traders, minor officials, and the armed adolescent gangs of the day: Indonesia's self-styled "proletariat."

Abroad, the Russians began applying the new line to Renville, branding it a product of the "imperialist, antidemocratic camp." On February 18, the Soviet delegate at Lake Success assailed the Renville agreement, which had been negotiated by Amir and the Left, as a "betrayal" of the Indonesian people. A week later, Soviet Deputy Foreign Minister Andrei A. Gromyko accused the United States of "strangling" the republic. The Soviet broadsides coincided with the opening of the Calcutta Conference. Two Indonesian delegates to the Communist-controlled meeting, Francisca Fangiday and Supeno (not to be confused with Minister Supeno), who had supported Renville only a month before, reversed their position and, echoing the Cominform line, denounced the agreement. A Prague summary of the conference reported:

> The prestige of Indonesia, won through two and a half years of heroic struggle against the Dutch, went up when the Indonesian delegate [*sic*] in unequivocal terms declared that Indonesian youth will continue the fight for final independence despite the truce, signed between the Indonesian and Dutch governments, under the pressure of the Three-Power Commission dominated by American imperialism.[5]

Reflecting the bellicose character of the line, the Calcutta Conference concluded that in Indonesia as elsewhere in Asia youth had to expose and fight the compromising policy of Right-wing leadership, and that ideas favoring compromise among any section of the youth must be rooted out.

At just about that time, Afrin, the Tass correspondent, returned from his first journey into the republic. Erik Werner of Agence France Presse jokingly asked him how he had liked Jogjakarta, the seat of revolution. Afrin was not amused. "Counterrevolution," he retorted. The republic, eulogized by the Cominform on the eve of Amir's fall, was rapidly losing Communist favor, if not flavor.

Inside the republic, the Communists dutifully reacted to the new line emanating from Lake Success, Calcutta, and Moscow. On February 26, Amir and Setiadjit, the former Vice Premier, attended a mass rally at Soerakarta, at which the Sajap Kiri was first buried and then resurrected as the Front Democrasi Rakjat (FDR) —the People's Democratic Front. Like its predecessor, the FDR was composed of the PKI, Amir's Socialists, Setiadjit's Labor, and Pesindo. The Communist-dominated labor federation (SOBSI) and the peasant front (BTI) endorsed the FDR program. The term "democratic" was judiciously employed to identify the new front with the "anti-imperialist, democratic camp." The Communists dominated the new organization as they had the Sajap Kiri. Two figures rapidly rising in the Indonesian hierarchy held key positions: Aidit, who had been nominated to the PKI's Central Committee at the Fourth Party Congress the year before and who directed the PKI's propaganda department, was named Secretary of the FDR's Executive Committee; and Njoto, who became head of its information section. At Jogjakarta, the consensus was that the Front had a membership of about 87,000.

Shortly thereafter, the FDR, tacking toward an aggressive line, denounced not only the Hatta government but also Renville and the policy of negotiation championed by the Indonesian Communists since 1945.

On February 26, the day the Democratic Front was created, the U.N. announced the completion of the withdrawal of republican forces from Dutch areas, under the provisions of the Renville truce. About 35,000 regular republican troops, largely the 3rd Division in West Java, had been evacuated from the guerrilla pockets behind the Dutch lines. The prestige of the republican army soared. Until then, it had been considered a disorganized, ill-trained, ill-equipped patchwork of terrorist fighting organizations. Tens of thousands of civilians, largely government officials and their families, accompanied the withdrawing forces. The influx of refugees taxed the republic's already meager food and medical supplies. In accordance with the Van Mook Line, the area of the republic had already been reduced. The truncated regions contained about 30 million people. As the Dutch blockade tightened in the coming months, preparatory to another assault, the economic situation within the republic became desperate.

The Dutch did not delay in tightening the drum. They were determined to isolate the republic and bring about its collapse. The Netherlands stalled on the implementation of Renville and prohibited a republican plebiscite committee from operating in Dutch-held areas, although the prospect of free elections was a vital provision of the Renville agreement. On March 9, 1948, by decree, the Dutch installed an interim federal government for the projected independent United States of Indonesia. The Dutch held nine of sixteen portfolios; hand-picked Indonesians held the other seven. In Indonesia, the conviction grew that the U.N. had neither the power nor the inclination to ensure implementation of the Renville agreement. Thus the republicans concluded, as did most observers, that the Dutch had no intention of peacefully abdicating power. The prospect, therefore, was for a renewal of Indo-Dutch hostilities sometime in the future. The FDR skillfully maneuvered to exploit the rising disillusionment. Its primary objective was to bring down Hatta. Amir, Setiadjit, and other Front leaders toured the republic urging unity but always managing to cause disruption. In a political probing action, the FDR instituted a series of small strikes in areas where Communist influence was strong, particularly in the Merapi-Merbabu mountain complex, between Jogjakarta and Soerakarta. The Pesindo provoked disorders at Soerakarta and Madiun. The FDR also moved to torpedo the resumption of U.N. negotiations.

With the departure of the U.S.S. "Renville" for China, where the situation was deteriorating, both the Dutch and Indonesians agreed to alternate the site of future deliberations every three weeks between Djakarta and Kaliurang, a hill station near Jogjakarta. On April 12, the talks shifted to Kaliurang for the first time. Five thousand demonstrators, organized by the FDR, met the U.N. truce train carrying 155 U.N., Australian, Belgian, American, Indonesian, and Dutch personnel. The unruly crowd spat on the Netherlands delegation and hurled epithets. The Dutch threatened to return to Djakarta, luggage unpacked. The Hatta government publicly apologized, and the U.N. prevailed on the Dutch to continue the deliberations. The Communists, hoping to disrupt the talks, had organized the incident. "No cabinet can be strong without the People's Democratic Front," Amir boasted later that week. "The time has come for a reshuffle." He also spoke vaguely of the "new democracies" emerging in Eastern Europe.

In the face of Dutch intransigence on the outside and pressure from the radical Left on the inside, Sukarno and Hatta were anxious to restore at least a semblance of unity. The government concurred with Amir's estimate of the situation. In April and May, the Hatta cabinet explored a reshuffle with the FDR. In an effort to improve the atmosphere, both sides agreed to celebrate jointly the fortieth anniversary of the founding of the nationalist movement on May 20, Budi Utomo Day.* Although it was the first time the republic celebrated the occasion, the date was to remain a significant one. (In 1952, the Communists employed May 20 as a springboard for the public launching of their return to a Right strategy; in 1960, Indonesia's democratic forces, banded in the Democratic League, issued a manifesto on May 20 to deplore Sukarno's authoritarian drift and the rise of Communist influence in the country.) On the occasion of the 1948 commemoration, the Masjumi, PNI, and FDR signed a joint statement of national unity. The statement called for a "united attitude, program, and action" to be carried out immediately. It urged that all differences among organizations and parties be avoided and all efforts directed toward close cooperation with the single aim of attaining a sovereign and free Indonesia in order to create a democratic society. The manifesto also stressed the need to consolidate the military and economic strength of the republic through the large-scale training of the army and the people. The emphasis on the duumvirate of the army and the people, which was to become a standard theme of the Communists in 1958, was designed at that time to thwart the army's ambitious demobilization program. The debacle in the face of the Dutch during the first military action renewed demands by the tactical staff for the creation of a small, tightly disciplined, mobile guerrilla organization. This entailed the reduction, or the absorption within the regular army, of as many as 200,000 irregulars, some of them mere armed gangs. The army's professional core, the "colonels," men like Simatupang (who was close to Sjahrir) and Nasution (who was close to Sukarno and Hatta) envisioned the establishment of a 60,000-man constabulary, approximating the size of the prewar Dutch colonial army. Such a force would be trained for policing operations in time of peace

* National Reawakening Day. Budi Utomo (Glorious or Pure Endeavor), founded in 1908, three years after Japan defeated Russia, was a cultural association with nationalist overtones, and now is recognized by Indonesians as the first stirring of the modern nationalist movement.

and for guerrilla tactics in time of war. Hatta favored this concept, and the "rationalization" plan became a prominent feature of the cabinet's program; but the scheme clearly jeopardized the existence of paramilitary fronts such as the Communist-dominated Pesindo.

Amir had favored the recruitment of an irregular armed militia in every village. The nucleus of his plan was a "people's army." Amir's views were backed by the President; Sukarno apparently was confident that he could control such an armed force through demagoguery. But Hatta and the "colonels" felt that the indiscriminate recruitment of irregulars diminished the influence and prestige of the regular army, contributed to an already serious problem of internal law and order, and, within the context of Indonesian society, where hostility between the secular Left and extreme Islam ran deep, sowed the seeds for civil war.

The May 20 pact confronted Hatta with the delicate task of reconciling these conflicting military views. But on May 26, five days before a scheduled conference between Hatta and the FDR to implement the manifesto by exploring a cabinet reorganization, Moscow detonated a political bomb. The Russians had ratified a diplomatic exchange with the republic. Radio Moscow announced:

> As a result of discussions taking place at Prague between the two governments, an agreement was concluded for the establishment of consular relations and an exchange of consuls between the Soviet Union and the Indonesian republic. The agreement that had been reached was ratified by an exchange of letters between the U.S.S.R. Ambassador to Prague, M. A. Silin, and Envoy Extraordinary and Minister Plenipotentiary of the Indonesian republic, Dr. Suripno.

In December, 1947, Sukarno had authorized Dr. Suripno, a member of the "student" group, who had been to Prague in July with Oey Gee Hwat, the SOBSI leader, as a delegate to the Youth Congress, to explore a diplomatic exchange with the Eastern European bloc. The authorization was made as the republic faced an impasse in the Renville talks and the possible renewal of Dutch hostilities. The republic was not merely courting Soviet support; Jogjakarta simultaneously was soliciting diplomatic and financial support from the West and, unable to secure aid on a government basis, concluded the "Fox agreement" at Havana.* According to Suripno, the Soviet consular treaty was initialed in January, but the republic ignored it, presumably because ratification would produce an unfavorable reaction in the United States and impair the Renville negotiations.

---

* Matthew Fox, an American and former motion-picture executive, largely financed the republic's activities at the U.N. in 1947–49.

The Moscow announcement stunned the republic. Jogjakarta suspected that the Soviet maneuver was double-edged, designed to strengthen the Front in its bargaining with Hatta and at the same time wreck the negotiations with the Dutch (since Renville prohibited the republic from extending foreign relations, and since the Dutch were already angered by Yemen's recognition of the republic the previous month). If this Indonesian analysis was correct, then the Russians had miscalculated. Instead of strengthening the political position of the FDR, the Soviet announcement weakened it. The Hatta government was embarrassed, then angered, by what it viewed as a transparent Soviet attempt to interfere in the republic's internal affairs. Islamic groups were outraged by what they interpreted as a maneuver to recognize a predominantly Moslem country as a counter weight to the Soviet recognition of Israel on May 17. As for its effect on the United States, the Soviet announcement was made while the GOC was at Kaliurang. The United States delegation was in a position to observe firsthand the republic's reaction. Few doubted at the time that if Washington had recognized the republic, there would have been rejoicing in the streets of Jogjakarta. But the United States was to continue a policy of vacillating between amity with the Netherlands and sympathy for the Indonesian revolutionists. A year was to pass before the United States, under the impact of China's collapse, recognized that a genuinely independent Indonesia was an asset to the non-Communist world in the struggle with the Communist world. It took the Dutch even longer to accept the validity of this fact.

The republic obviously was in no position openly to snub the Soviet Union by formal rejection of the treaty. The Indonesian "question" was likely to be reintroduced at the Security Council, and the republic would need all the votes it could muster. Premier Hatta announced that action on the treaty would be postponed, pending Suripno's return home for "consultations." "I do not know what really transpired at Prague," Hatta said.[6] Jogjakarta's rebuff of the Soviet good-will gesture incensed the FDR. It sought to go over the head of the Hatta government by appealing for a united front from below in support of the Suripno agreement. It claimed that Soviet Russia was a pioneer in the struggle against imperialism; that by calling home Dr. Suripno, the government had capitulated to Dutch colonialism. It appealed to the Indonesian people to support fully the step taken by the republic's representative in Czechoslovakia; and asked the people to urge the government to take a firm stand by extending the relations of the republic "with a state that was a defender and pioneer of independence, peace, and democracy, a great and powerful industrial state—Soviet Russia."

The tenor of the statement, its lavish praise of Stalin's Russia, shocked the Hatta coalition. On May 31, as agreed, Hatta and the FDR leaders gathered at Sukarno's residence to discuss a cabinet reshuffle. Negotiations collapsed, never to be resumed.

The republic's rejection of the Soviet overture was in the nature of a reprieve for United States policy-makers. But the State Department professionals, "European" in outlook and sensitive to the Dutch position, had already felt that Dr. Graham had impaired his usefulness in Indonesia by his open sympathy for the republic. As his replacement, the Department summoned Coert du Bois from retirement in Connecticut. Du Bois was an old friend of the Dutch; he had served as American Consul General at Batavia, from 1927 to 1930. Du Bois was astonished at receiving the assignment. He wrote the Department that he could not, with a clear conscience, accept the post, because of his Netherlands bias. The Department insisted. Du Bois took the hint and accepted.* On arrival in Indonesia, Du Bois made plain his distaste for the "illegal, Japanese puppet regime at Jogjakarta." But visits to the republic in the course of the negotiations made a deep impression on the sixty-six-year-old Du Bois, and he had the courage to reverse his position. He became convinced that the republic was a bona fide Indonesian creation and that the Dutch would never succeed in restoring their political position in the archipelago. By granting Indonesia independence, Du Bois reasoned, the Dutch would salvage by good will their legitimate economic and cultural interests in the Indies. He became an indefatigable champion of the republic. With a staff of able State Department officers—Charlton Ogburn, James Barco, and Philip Trezise—he drafted a plan for a peaceful settlement of the Indonesian dispute.† The plan was based primarily on free elections; in essence, the Du Bois proposals were a repetition of the Graham plebiscite formula. Thomas K. Critchley, the Australian delegate, gave Du Bois unqualified support, and the proposals became known as the Du Bois-Critchley Plan.

The republic enthusiastically accepted the plan in June to the consternation of the Communists, whose policy now was to sow discord between the republic and the Dutch, the republic and GOC

---

* Since Du Bois died on March 6, 1960, this story can now be told.
† Among other outstanding aides during this period were State Department officers Raymond Lisle and Edward Dow (on Cochran's delegation) and Professor William Brandeis, University of North Carolina (on Graham's delegation).

—particularly its American delegate. The Dutch rejected it out of hand and suspended negotiations. Netherlands pressure on Washington forced Du Bois' departure on June 23, ostensibly because of illness. That same day, the Committee cabled a report to the Security Council embodying the warning that the Dutch and Indonesians "are eyeing each other across the *status quo* line with reserve and suspicion." The Security Council was unconcerned, the United States indifferent. To all intents and purposes, negotiations under the aegis of the U.N. had terminated. A resumption of Dutch military action or the internal disintegration of the republic seemed likely.

Meanwhile, the collapse of cabinet negotiations between Hatta and the FDR had dangerously widened the breach between Communists and non-Communists in the republic. The deteriorating situation provided Tan Malaka and the intransigent radicals around him with an opportunity for recovery. Tan Malaka's supporters, aware of the new Cominform line, may have reasoned that by supporting Hatta they could secure Tan Malaka's release. Such a development might create a "revolutionary situation," which could be exploited in the name of a popular front. On June 6, 1948, a national Communist front, the Gerakan Revolusi Rakjat (GRR)—Revolutionary People's Movement—was formed. Its prime movers were Dr. Muwardi, Maruto Nitimihardjo—Tan Malaka's deputy in the KNIP—and Rustam Effendi, who had broken with the orthodox PKI on his return from Holland. In internal affairs, the GRR pursued policies approximating those of the FDR. Their point of departure was foreign affairs: The FDR urged an alliance with the Soviet bloc; the GRR favored nonalignment until independence was consolidated—after that, perhaps, an alliance with Moscow, but only on the basis of mutual respect and equality. The founding manifesto of the GRR spelled out its nationalist orientation: "As long as the sovereignty of the unitarian state of the Republic of Indonesia over the whole of Indonesia has not yet been recognized by the entire world, it is still impossible to play a role in international disturbances [the Cold War]."

The GRR, which was to become an important political factor after the abortive Communist revolt at Madiun, called on Hatta to take action against "destructive elements" in society, presumably the FDR, and "to set free immediately and to rehabilitate political prisoners who are victims of the negotiations," i.e., Tan Malaka and his co-conspirators in the plot to depose Sjahrir in 1946.

Thus, the mood of frustrated nationalism sweeping the republic served to stimulate the growth of both the orthodox and unorthodox Indonesian Communist movements. The Dutch were gradually tightening their economic blockade in an attempt to starve the republic into submission. Many Indonesians despaired of a peaceful settlement. The impression grew at Jogjakarta that the Dutch were preparing a second, decisive, action. This feeling gave rise to a desire to be done with negotiations. In this light, the militancy of the Communist fronts appeared more attractive to many Indonesians than the Hatta-Sjahrir policy of gradualism. The atmosphere abroad in this period was equally gloomy. The cleavage between Communists and non-Communists had become distinct. Elsewhere in Southeast Asia, the Communists were in open rebellion. The rift between Communists and national Communists was widening. Stalin and Tito were on the threshold of their titanic ideological struggle. The relationship between Russia and the West had worsened appreciably. The Berlin blockade was on. Above all, Chiang Kai-shek's China was on the brink of collapse.

The republic was intimately informed about conditions in Burma and Malaya. A clandestine air-courier service between Jogjakarta and Rangoon, manned by American free-lance pilots, was in operation, and the Malayan Communist Party was using Bagansiapiapi on the west coast of Sumatra as a base of operations. Indonesian intelligence had infiltrated the Malayan Party, (MCP), largely Chinese in composition. According to an Indonesian agent working in the MCP in 1948–50, the Communist strategy was to foment disorders in southern Asia as a diversionary action in support of the Communist offensive in China. It is likely, however, that this was the line used by the Communists to recruit Chinese in Malaya.

Thus, the FDR became the instrument for the implementation of the new, aggressive Party line in Indonesia, and the application of the new line served to deepen the crisis not only between the Indonesian Communists and non-Communists, but also between the PKI and Tan Malaka, the old adversaries.

8

Madiun

Alarmed by the Communist offensive abroad, particularly in nearby Malaya and Burma, Hatta pressed the "rationalization" of the armed forces. His immediate goals were the demobilization of regular army units suspected of having been infiltrated by Communists and the disbanding of the irregular fighting organizations of the Left. Because of their hardening line, the Communists soon found themselves in a serious plight. Fruition of the Hatta plan would leave the Left denuded of military power. The situation was particularly acute at Soerakarta, a stronghold of both the FDR and GRR. The city was a powder keg. The 4th Division, under the command of two Communists, Colonel Sutarto and his deputy, Lt. Colonel Suadi, was nominally in control. Both Sutarto and Suadi defied rationalization of the division. In July, Sutarto was assassinated. Suspicion centered on the GRR. But the official Communist view now is that Sutarto was murdered "because he was one of the high officers who did not agree to the so-called 'rationalization' of the Army which the Hatta cabinet wanted to carry out at that time. . . . If implemented, it would mean eliminating the people's elements [Communists] in the Army." [1]

Against this background of rising unrest within the armed forces, Suripno left Prague on June 21 for home and "consultations" with Hatta. He was accompanied by an Indonesian secretary by the name of Suparto whom he had acquired behind the Iron Curtain. On August 3, the pair left Rangoon for Bukittinggi, the republican capital of Sumatra, aboard a republican Dakota piloted by an American soldier of fortune. On arrival in Sumatra, Suripno gave an interview to the local "Voice of Free Indonesia" radio, in which he hailed Soviet ratification of the consular treaty as a diplomatic triumph and said Indonesia "need not expect too much from the Security Council." On August 10, Suripno and Suparto flew to Jogjakarta.

On arrival, according to John Coast, an Englishman in the employ of the Indonesian Foreign Office, Suripno "did not even pretend to behave as an official. . . . He regarded himself first as a member of [Amir] Sjarifuddin's People's Democratic Front. . . . He would cancel an appointment with his Foreign Minister [Hadji Agus Salim] in order to attend a small conference at Sjarifuddin's house." [2]

Jogjakarta was tense. Word spread that Suparto was in fact Musso, an architect of the abortive 1926 revolt, a member of the PKI Central Committee, the founder of the Illegal-PKI and, since 1936, an exile in Moscow. His melodramatic reappearance first aroused curiosity and then speculation. What was he like? What motivated his return? At their first meeting, Sukarno expressed the hope that Musso had returned to his homeland to assist in the struggle for independence. "Indeed, that is my task," Musso said. "I have come back to set things straight." [3] At Sukarno's urging, the GRR approached Musso and invited him to join their ranks; Rustam Effendi appealed to Musso not to permit himself to be "isolated from the people and the true popular leaders by the FDR." Musso rebuffed the invitation. Now fifty, he entertained other ideas. On August 17, the third anniversary of the founding of the republic, Musso, Amir, and Sukarno engaged publicly in a strained dialogue. Musso criticized the Hatta cabinet, denounced Renville, and called for creation of a strong national front and the speedy change of the present republican administration. Amir, in a spirit of self-indictment, said the republic had wavered in the struggle for independence. During the Japanese occupation Indonesia not only failed to build a national front, but "cooperated" with the Japanese—a veiled attack on Sukarno. Since 1945, the republic had pursued a policy of "cooperation" with the Dutch criticism of the Left and his own policies. "From now on," Amir concluded, "the revolution must be placed in the hands of revolutionary elements."

Sukarno replied to both. "Let us together defend this republic as our common property," he said.

Faced by army defiance at Soerakarta, rumors of impending disorders on the Left, and the seemingly prophetic return of Musso, Hatta marshaled support behind the government. "Titoism" by then had become synonymous with revisionist national Communism, as opposed to the submissiveness of orthodox Communists to Moscow. This, of course, was the essence of the long dispute between Musso, Alimin, and Sardjono on the one hand, and Tan Malaka on the other. Indeed, Tan Malaka was now being dubbed a Titoist, although it may have been more accurate to describe Tito as a "Tan Malakist." Hatta moved to exploit the situation. On August 17, the government granted amnesty to the leading figures in the Tan Malaka coup of 1946, among them Subardjo, Iwa, Sudarsono, Adam Malik, Mohammed Saleh, Pandu Wiguna, and Yamin. Yamin, received by Sukarno and Hatta, was informed that the Tan Malaka affair was "nearly solved." [4] On behalf of the released men, Yamin pledged: "We are ready to continue the struggle until the national revolution achieves its aim." Releasing Tan Malaka from confinement was apparently considered risky; he remained in jail. Obviously, Sukarno and Hatta were playing the game of the calico cat and the gingham dog: Orthodox and unorthodox Communists were to destroy each other.

Musso was not deterred. On August 20, at a Communist rally, he made his first public appearance. "I am Musso," he said. "I have come back to you." The tenor of his speech was belligerent. Musso's indictment of the Party and the republic, delivered in Marxist-Leninist terminology, constituted "merciless criticism." Musso declared, according to the August 23, 1948, issue of *Revolusioner*, the organ of Pesindo:

> The revolution has erred by emphasis on negotiation and compromise. . . . Sukarno and Hatta have done everything within their power to shift blame for the revolution's failure from themselves. Renville must be denounced and diplomatic relations with Soviet Russia ratified to offset Dutch and American pressures on the republic. Our nation must be led by the proletariat and not by the bourgeois elements, because the proletariat is the most revolutionary and the most anti-imperialist class. Errors must be corrected as soon as possible. The failure to create a national front was the weak point in the Indonesian struggle. A national front must be created to which individuals would subscribe irrespective of party affiliation. Thus the national front is not a convention of leaders, who are appointed by high authority, but started from below and rooted in society. A new cabinet must be formed, controlled by the most capable and experienced representatives of the national front.

In effect, Musso demanded a Communist-controlled national-front government. There was no doubt who would be the "most capable and experienced representatives of the national front." Non-Communists were to abdicate authority.

On August 25, his strategy was revealed. The Communist Party summoned an extraordinary conference, which "unanimously" endorsed Musso's detailed analysis of the contemporary Indonesian situation in a draft resolution—"The New Road for the Republic of Indonesia." In it, Musso assailed Sardjono and Alimin for minimizing the role of Communists in the revolution— the policy of concealment and infiltration pursued since Musso himself founded the Illegal-PKI. Musso declared that a national front was the solution for the Party's predicament. He conceded that it was still necessary for the Communist Party to cooperate with other parties, since "the Party of the working class cannot possibly complete the bourgeois democratic revolution on its own," perhaps a subconscious admission of the true situation in the republic. But Musso qualified this form of "cooperation" as being possible only through the national front, which the Communists would dominate. "Every Communist must be absolutely convinced that without a national front, victory will not be achieved," Musso said. Victory for whom? For Indonesia in the struggle against the Dutch, for the Party in the struggle for internal power, or for Russia on the global stage?

To enhance the role of Communists in the proposed national front, Musso demanded that "as quickly as possible, the three parties that recognize the principles of Marxism-Leninism, which are now associated in the FDR . . . should fuse into a single party of the working class" (i.e., Communists, Amir Socialists, and Labor). Finally, Musso indicated that he had no intention to defuse the crisis in the armed forces. His "New Road" resolution encouraged armed groups to defy Hatta's rationalization scheme. Lest he be misunderstood, Musso declared that above all, the army must be cleansed of reactionary and counterrevolutionary elements. Here Musso was employing the classic Communist tactic of equating anti-Communists with counterrevolutionaries.

We do not know, nor are we ever likely to know, the precise instructions Musso received before leaving Moscow. But Indonesia's Communists were apparently impressed by his credentials. With a frightening display of discipline, the FDR fell into line.

On August 27, Setiadjit fused his Labor Party with the PKI. On August 30, Amir's Socialists followed suit, issuing a statement explaining their action as an admission of "past errors": "The postwar policy of cooperation with the imperialists to fight the fascists should have been substituted, immediately after fascism was beaten, by a combined anti-imperialist policy under the leadership of the Communists."

Setiadjit's action shocked the republic; Amir's, while vindicating Sjahrir, stunned it. Yet the most remarkable developments were still ahead. On August 31, Amir disclosed that Musso had recruited him into the Illegal-PKI in 1935, and that Gerindo had been formed to "cloak Communist aspirations." [5] In fact, he said, the Gerindo was the PKI. He said that was the reason for his arrest by the Japanese. Nine days later, elaborating on his confession, Amir addressed a meeting of sugar workers and explained: "My policies in the past have been wrong. As a Communist, I should have been consistent. I should not have compromised with the enemy. In the future I shall not commit mistakes." [6] He confirmed that he had worked with Van der Plas and had received Dutch financial assistance to organize an underground against the Japanese in 1942, and that he accepted the money "because the Comintern had proposed to cooperate with the colonial powers in the struggle against fascism."

Whether Amir, his confession notwithstanding, had been a Communist has been disputed ever since. Most Indonesians still doubt it. Hatta felt Amir was vain and influenced by the flatteries of Setiadjit, Abdulmadjid, and Tan Ling Djie. Hatta also felt that Amir, converted to Christianity in his youth, "was too religious to be a Communist." Sjahrir agreed. He believed that Amir was a frustrated nationalist. The Dutch, sympathetic to Amir, advanced the theory that Amir had tried to save the Left from Musso's domination and sacrificed himself. Later, Van Mook wrote that Amir, "unbalanced and insanely ambitious . . . declared himself a Communist of old standing—which he was not." [7] Many felt Amir's decision reflected disillusionment with United States policy toward Indonesia. John Coast quoted Amir as saying when he went over to the Communists: "I am still a Left-wing Socialist, not a Communist. But I do not think the Americans have any intention of supporting a just solution [of the Indo-Dutch dispute]. The Russians are our only hope." [8] In any event, Amir's admission shocked the republic and provided new ammunition to the Tan Malaka revisionist Communists, who cited the admission as proof that the PKI had collaborated with the Dutch, that it was a foreign agent and dedicated to supranational goals.

In the face of these developments, Sukarno and Hatta maneuvered to exercise a restraining influence on the Communists by the prospect of free elections. On August 31, Sukarno signed a General Elections Act and promised early elections, but no date was set. The maneuver was lost in the excitement of the day. On September 1, the PKI "unanimously" elected Musso Party Chairman, replacing Sardjono, who, with Alimin, had guided the Party's destiny since 1946. That same day, a new Politburo was announced. The former Socialist Tan Ling Djie was elevated to the General Secretariat; Amir was awarded the Defense Secretariat;

Suripno, Foreign Affairs. Alimin and Sardjono were demoted to the Agitprop Secretariat headed by the twenty-eight-year-old Lukman. Aidit, then twenty-five, rose to the Labor Secretariat; Njoto, twenty-three, was appointed the Party's representative in the working committee of the KNIP. Musso was transfusing young blood into the hierarchy. Later, Aidit—like Musso a confirmed Stalinist—wrote that the new Politburo was an "important step toward saving the Indonesian revolution, which was then in danger, and the first important step toward building a Party of the Lenin and Stalin type." [9]

Thereafter, events in Indonesia moved rapidly. It was often the lot of the GOC to arrive in the republic at a moment of crisis. On September 2, the day after Musso gathered the reins of the PKI, the Committee arrived for a three-week stay at Kaliurang. The Communists, reverting to their tactics of the previous April, met the train at Jogakarta with a demonstration and demanded an end to negotiations with the Dutch. Although negotiations under the Committee had been stalled since the abortive Du Bois-Critchley plan in June, a new figure had arrived in August to reopen the deliberations—H. Merle Cochran, the new United States delegate—whose first foray into Asian affairs had been at Chungking during World War II. Almost immediately, he created the impression of a capable negotiator. He brought from Washington a new set of proposals based on the Renville agreement. The "Cochran proposals," as they were called, modified several features in the Graham and Du Bois-Critchley plans to which the Dutch had objected. Nevertheless, the Cochran proposals incorporated what the Dutch considered the most objectionable feature of all: elections. The Dutch position was that elections in a disorganized community such as the republic would generate agitation from which neither a clear expression of popular opinion nor a restoration of peace and order could be expected. In truth, the Dutch could not risk elections, since the republic would win handily. "When Mr. Cochran confirmed the position taken by his predecessor in this respect [elections], the implementation of the Renville principles became practically impossible," Van Mook later wrote.[10]

The day the GOC arrived at Jogjakarta, the Pesindo voted at Soerakarta to fuse with the reorganized PKI. The paramilitary front of the FDR had become the official fighting arm of the PKI. Pesindo's action closed the circle: All four groups within the FDR—Communists, Amir Socialists, Labor, and Pesindo—had merged under Musso's direction. In September, the SOBSI and BTI also climbed on Musso's bandwagon, or perhaps trundle cart would be a more accurate description. The SOBSI, which vigorously supported Linggadjati and Renville, convened a congress of its thirty-two affiliated trade unions claiming a membership of more than 1.25 million, and issued a manifesto that admitted "the error of the compromise policy with imperialists." The manifesto urged the creation of a national-front cabinet with SOBSI participation. The Communist-controlled front concluded ominously that it would actively fight for these resolutions and was prepared for all consequences.

Musso's steamroller tactics on the Left gave the PKI about 116 of the 413 seats in the appointed KNIP, and about 8 of 43 in the working committee; the exact figures were uncertain because of indecision among Left-wing independents. In any event, the Communists lacked sufficient votes for acquiring power by parliamentary means. Moreover, their powerhouse tactics had alarmed non-Communists and made them more determined than ever to resist a Communist take-over. But, if not by parliamentary means, what other road was there? There were persistent rumors, but no real evidence of an incipient Communist revolt. It was only after the Communist insurrection that the republic learned some of the details. A revolt had been planned for November. Unknown to the republic at the time, the FDR, apparently as early as July, had committed itself to acquiring power either by "parliamentary" or "nonparliamentary" means. The acquisition of power had become an end in itself. There could be no compromise. Communist world strategy was at stake, not the Indonesian Republic. It made no difference whether the republic was or was not encircled by hostile Dutch capitalist forces (to employ a Leninist image). It seems inconceivable that in Burma, Malaya, and the Philippines, much less Indonesia, the Communist insurrections simultaneously grew out of purely local conditions, in view of the sharply contrasting political situation in each country. The hard facts were that the republic was governed by a broad coalition, a cabinet composed of the Masjumi, the PNI, and Protestant and Catholic parties. The Left had been invited to participate, but had refused; and the non-Left parties were generally democratic in content, nationalist in orientation, and socialist in outlook. Indonesia's Communists, obedient to the Moscow line, their ideology undiluted, were oblivious to the prevailing situation.

The Communist strategy for acquiring power was outlined in a blueprint entitled "Stepping to the New Stage of Military Struggle." The plan was uncovered by republican authorities in the razzia that followed the Communist revolt. The Communists estimated that they controlled approximately 35 per cent of the republic's armed forces—about 100,000 men, largely irregulars. As it developed later, this was a miscalculation; at the height of the rebellion, the Communists had fewer than 40,000 men under arms. In any event, the Communists were determined to resist Hatta's rationalization program. To this end, they adopted a twofold strategy. The first phase, for the acquisition of power by "nonparliamentary" means, sought to

> accelerate the formation of the national front . . . The national front will stage a large-scale campaign for dissolving the present [Hatta] cabinet. . . . If the above-mentioned plan fails, large-scale demonstrations will be staged by those workers, peasants, army men, and other groups which can be persuaded to join us. . . . Large-scale demonstrations must be directly followed by a general strike and, if necessary, by forcible measures.

Failing in that, they would launch their second, "nonparliamentary" phase. This strategy would be executed by breaking "all relations with the government [to] continue our struggle under our own leadership either as rebellion or as a separate government." To prepare for this phase, the plan called for

1. Withdrawal of a part of our troops from the front lines facing the Dutch . . .

2. Removal of our troops to areas we consider as being strategic, and abandonment of those areas that can no longer be defended.

a. The Madiun area will be made the strongest guerrilla stronghold for the long-term struggle.

b. We must station at least five battalions in Madiun.

c. We will make Solo a "Wild West" in order to attract attention there.

3. Alongside the official armed forces we must now begin to establish a People's Army in the widest sense of the term. In a general sense, we will form these forces illegally.

a. In every subdistrict which we consider strategically situated and in which our influence is implanted, a group of sixty armed soldiers led by a commander will be stationed.

b. These sixty persons will be divided into smaller groups of six or ten and sent to the villages.

c. The general leadership in a subdistrict is in the hands of a committee representing the workers, peasants, and the commander of the sixty armed soldiers.

4. Our program for the second phase can be determined further according to the circumstances.[11]

There could be no misreading of Communist intentions, even without the blueprint. Yet despite the rush of events at the end of August, Hatta faced September with confidence. Hatta realized that the Masjumi and PNI, although not nearly as well organized as the PKI, still dominated the republic, and that Sukarno's charismatic appeal would muster wide secular and Islamic support in any showdown with the Communists. Thus the day Musso reorganized the PKI Politburo, Natsir, now the Minister of Information, served notice that the government could cope with any unrest emanating from the Left. The press of the center also encouraged resolution; the daily *Nasional*, for example, urged the government to "march forward and act firmly."

On September 2, Hatta appeared before the working committee of the KNIP in an appeal to the parties, including the Communists, not to permit the republic to become an "object of international political conflict." He chided the Communists, relatively mildly, for turning from "a champion of Linggadjati and Renville to opponents of the agreements." He warned that the republic would "discipline with an iron hand" any anarchic excesses manifesting themselves as "childhood ills of Indonesian democracy." The Masjumi and PNI sent messages of support; the army—General Sudirman and the "colonels"—reaffirmed loyalty.

At this point, the GRR sought to capitalize on Hatta's need for support by demanding the release of Tan Malaka from prison and the implementation of its June 6 program. The GRR declared that it was prepared to induce society to put aside all elements who in the past formed the champions of Linggadjati and Renville, whether in the parties, fighting organizations, government, army, police, labor, peasant, and youth organizations.

In effect, Tan Malaka declared that he alone could save the republic. The intransigent radicals around him were unblemished by compromise and negotiation with the Dutch. Certainly the PKI, by its own admission, was stained. For that matter, Tan Malaka was also prepared to "put aside" Sukarno and Hatta. The government ignored the GRR's appeal. But Jogjakarta soon reversed its position.

Musso, meanwhile, embarked on a tour of the republic to mobilize the Party for the approaching showdown. It was a fateful journey. He would never see Jogjakarta again. On September 7, he arrived at Soerakarta and conferred with leaders of the 4th Division. The next day, Musso arrived at Madiun, where he addressed a mass meeting. His address set the tone of his tour, betrayed the belligerence of the Zhdanov line, appealed for

Islamic support, and constituted his defense against accusations that he was a Moscow agent. He also sought to divide Sukarno from Hatta, attacking the Premier but not mentioning Sukarno by name. The PKI branch at Madiun gave Musso an ovation. The Internationale was played. Musso spoke haltingly in Bazaar Malay, the lingua franca of the islands, explaining: "Brothers, I originally intended to make this speech in Javanese, but owing to my twenty years absence, I have forgotten much of this language." The audience cheered. At the outset of his oration, Musso indulged in self-criticism, saying:

> The proclamation of independence has taken the wrong turning [with] the proletariat excluded altogether . . . although it is only the beginning of a national revolution, not a social and certainly not yet a Communist revolution. I admit that it has been the fault of the PKI that management [of the revolution] has fallen into the hands of the bourgeoisie.

Musso then assailed the republic's foreign policy of neutralism in the Cold War, the policy of Sjahrir, the "Right-wing Socialist." He went on:

> It is said that if we entertain relations with the Soviet Union, we are fighting for the Soviets. This is nonsense. . . . In 1926 . . . did we then, too, fight for Moscow? No, brothers, what Mr. Hatta has said . . . is not true. At present there are only two camps: the Soviet Union and those with colonies. . . . Can we maintain our neutrality in this controversy? Certainly not, brothers.

Reflecting the belligerence of the two-camp doctrine, Musso continued:

> Mr. Hatta as Premier thinks that the compromise proposals, made by America, point the road toward Indonesian freedom, but this is not true. By accepting these proposals, he leads our country toward a new colonialism. . . . If America did not back the Netherlands, the Dutch would have disappeared a long time ago. But now they are the tools of the Americans. . . . For three years, our government has licked the boots of the Americans; the result is the Americans support the Netherlanders [cheers]. . . . Are we able to oppose the Netherlanders? Just look at the Greek guerrillas [and] the people of Indochina. . . . Why then are we not able to do the same? It is our own fault. . . . We shall have to attack [the Dutch]. . . . If Islam really does not want to be suppressed by the infidels, the time has now come for a holy war [applause]. . . . They say we destroy religion, but we want to destroy the Netherlanders, not religion [applause].

Musso then attacked his critics.

> It is said that I am an agent from Moscow and that I have received
> instructions. These are lies. Our policy is not an instruction from
> Moscow, but is a natural consequence of the nature of our revolu-
> tion. . . .
>   Experience in Burma, China, etc., has convinced me that our
> revolution must be in the hands of the proletariat. . . . The Soviet
> Union is the leader of the world revolution, of which our revolu-
> tion forms a part. Consequently, we are led by the Soviet Union." [12]

As Musso spoke at Madiun, the SOBSI organized a campaign
designed to sow fear and suspicion within the republic and undercut GRR propaganda that the PKI had worked for the Dutch,
as Amir himself had conceded. SOBSI handbills warned that
"in the republic, a large number of secret Netherlands agents will
come into action at the moment the Dutch invade the republic"
and that the Hatta government employed "secret Dutch agents"
in the U.N. negotiations. The Communists were determined to
discredit Hatta. SOBSI followed up the attack by launching a
"Five-Anti" campaign against imperialism:

1. Anti-imperialism means the democratic right of liberty of
speech, of the press, of assembly, the right to hold demonstrations
and strikes.

2. Anti-imperialism implies no corruption.

3. Anti-imperialism implies home defense . . . the people are
armed.

4. Anti-imperialism means the denunciation of Linggadjati and
Renville.

5. Anti-imperialism means to substitute a responsible [parlia-
mentary] government, supported by the national front, for the
Hatta cabinet.[13]

As the Communist propaganda offensive gathered momentum,
the Communists did not ignore the area of negotiations. When
Musso and Amir embarked on the hinterland tour, several Communist leaders remained at Jogjakarta to explore the possibility of
inducing the Masjumi and PNI to form a national front, among
them Alimin, Sakirman, Tan Ling Djie, and Abdulmadjid. But
on September 11, the Masjumi formally rejected a PKI invitation
to form a national front, as did the PNI two days later. The parties
jointly staged a demonstration at Jogjakarta in support of the
Hatta government.

The Communists interpreted the demonstration as dashing the
hopes of obtaining power by parliamentary means. The PKI

called for the completion of "the people's defense," ostensibly to meet the threat of a renewal of Dutch action, but apparently a signal to Party members to prepare for the second, nonparliamentary phase of Musso's "New Road." That same day—only four days after Musso's military conference at Soerakarta—the 4th Division now under Lt. Colonel Suadi's command delivered an ultimatum to government forces in the city to surrender seven divisional officers "kidnaped" during Leftist disorders the week before. The abductions were believed to be the work of the GGR. But, significantly, the ultimatum was delivered to the government and not the GRR. The government forces, composed largely of the Mobile Brigade (Sjahrir's creation of 1946) and troops of the 3rd Division that had evacuated West Java under the terms of Renville, braced themselves. The GRR and the paramilitary Islamic front, Hizbullah, both supporting the government, also dug in. On September 13, the ultimatum expired. The Communists attacked. The Wild West phase had opened. The PKI forces consisted largely of troops of the 4th Division, a unit of Marines (ALRI), and Pesindo irregulars. During the action, Dr. Muwardi, a founder of the GRR, was taken prisoner by the Communists, tortured and executed; Sutarto's assassination had been avenged. "Fighting broke out in Solo," a United Press dispatch reported that day, "apparently following the refusal of the Masjumi and PNI to join the Communists in a popular front."

President Sukarno proclaimed martial law in the residency of Soerakarta, and the Army rushed reinforcements to the city. The fighting raged until September 17. The reinforcements broke the Communist offensive. The Communists had lost military control of the second-largest city of the republic. In truth, an undeclared civil war was already in progress. As the fighting developed in Soerakarta, two battalions of Communist militia occupied the villages of Ngawi and Ponorogo, on the outskirts of Madiun, and raised the red flag.

The republic interpreted the Communist actions as foreshadowing a full-scale civil war and acted accordingly. Sukarno appointed Colonel Gatot Subroto, then chief of the military police at Soerakarta and a man with a reputation for firmness, as military governor of the trouble zone. On September 15, General Sudirman issued an order describing the events at Soerakarta as a challenge to army authority and warning against "provocations." The GOC on receipt of field reports of a developing civil war, recalled all U.N. military observers from the republican territory.

On September 16, Hatta appeared again before the working committee of the KNIP. For the first time in the history of the republic, the government openly denounced the Communists. Hatta accused the PKI of pursuing a "suicidal policy for Indonesia." He said Musso sought to "drag the republic into a Soviet-American global conflict." The Premier said the republic endorsed Russia's anti-imperialist aims, but this did not imply that it was obliged to "simply follow the footsteps of Soviet Russia, whose history indicates a zigzag line in conformity with conditions she herself encounters . . . now turning Left, now Right. . . . The future of Indonesia does not rest with Soviet ideology." [14] He also announced the release of Tan Malaka and his youthful lieutenant, Sukarni, from jail. The national Communist leadership was at large for the first time in more than two years.

The release of Tan Malaka coincided with a heightening of Stalin's campaign of vilification against Tito, who was depicted as the epitome of diabolical nationalist tendencies within the Communist movement. It was a time of trials and purges in Eastern Europe. The attack on nationalism "in all its manifestations" that appeared in the September 8 issue of *Pravda* is typical of the writings of the period. The article branded nationalism as "the ideology of the bourgeoisie. . . . Marxism-Leninism cannot reconcile itself with nationalism, or with any nationalist deviation in the Communist parties; [Marxism-Leninism] must destroy nationalism in whatever form it arises."

In Indonesia, the "Calcutta line," as practiced by Musso in word and deed, had set in motion a chain of events he was unable to control, even had he wanted to do so. The losses sustained by the Communist forces at Soerakarta apparently panicked the Communist military leadership.

The failure to establish a national front by parliamentary means, and the posture of firmness adopted by Hatta, had placed the Communists in a difficult position. The PKI had misjudged the "frustrated nationalism" of the republic. "The unity meant by us did not materialize," Suripno wrote later. "Distrust [of Communists] ran too deep, obviously. This fact was very astonishing to me, who had just arrived." [15] Perhaps it was equally astonishing to Musso; we shall never know. The Communists, whose original strategy called for implementation of the second nonparliamentary phase in November, were at a crossroad. On the one hand, the Communists could launch a premature revolt in the hope of securing a land base, as they did at Yenan and were attempting in Burma (Pyinnanyi) and Malaya (Belum). From such a redoubt, they could broaden their area of control or, failing in that, confront the republic with the necessity of negotiating with a rival "independent" regime, the tactic employed by the Communists in China, Korea, Vietnam, and Laos. On the other hand, the Communists could temporize until Musso toured the republic and the preparations for revolt were completed. But then the revolutionary wave the Communists were hoping to generate would lose its momentum. The Communists had already unleashed provocative political attacks on the government. Retreat would be difficult, if not impossible and, of course, contrary to the Moscow line. The Communists had painted themselves into a corner. They had been swept away by the drama of Musso's return.

Confronted with the prospect of submission or armed action, the Communist fighting organizations, already defying Hatta's rationalization, chose action. In line with an earlier plan, Sumarsono (a Pesindo commander), Colonel Djokosujono, Lt. Colonel Sumantri, and Lt. Colonel Dachlan, local army commanders of Lt. Colonel Sungkono's 6th "Java Timur" Division, seized the initiative at Madiun.

At 3 A.M. on September 18, 1948, at Madiun, three pistol shots signalized the opening of the formal nonparliamentary phase of the Communist struggle for power. Armed detachments seized vital republican office buildings, including the headquarters of the Madiun Subterritorial Command, the police station, the bank, the post office, and the telephone exchange. In a fire fight with a loyalist unit, two republican officers were killed, four soldiers wounded. The coup was a success.

The red flag was raised at the city hall. Radio Madiun, in Communist hands, proclaimed:

> The hour of revolution has come! The republic is trying to deliver the Indonesian people into the hands of the Dutch. . . . The fascist collaborator Hatta tries to use the republic to suppress workers and peasants. The government consists of traitors.
>
> Madiun has risen! The revolution has begun! The people have disarmed the police and army. Workers and peasants have formed a new government. Arms will not be laid down until all of Indonesia will be liberated!

The rebels avoided a direct attack on Sukarno. The radio proclaimed the creation of a provisional administration; Colonel Djokusujono was appointed Military Governor, and Supardi, the Deputy Mayor of Madiun, Provisional Governor of the "liberated" area. The appointment papers were signed by the local leaders of the FDR. An 11 P.M.–5 A.M. curfew was imposed on the "liberated" region; the Communists appealed for support from "all people, especially the working class," and warned that anyone "disturbing the peace" would be severely punished.

That morning, the Communist standard flew in central-east Java at Purwodadi, Patjitan, Wirosari, Magetan, and in the surrounding villages. Musso and his entourage were at Purwodadi on the morning of September 18. How Musso reacted to the events at Madiun we do not know, nor are we ever likely to know. Musso doubtlessly was aware of the fighting provoked by the Communists at Soerakarta and of the piecemeal occupation of the villages in the area of Madiun in the days preceding the coup. Perhaps he believed the republic too weak to respond to the Communist challenge, perhaps he realized that the initiative was no longer in his hands and that he had no alternative but to support his field commanders. Musso and his entourage sped by armed convoy to Madiun, 22 miles southeast. He must have been impressed and confident. The territory traversed was Communist; red flags flew at every point along the road. The next move was up to the republic. Would it accept or ignore the challenge? Jogjakarta entertained no illusions about the future of the republic if it failed to act. At 10 P.M., in an address over Radio Jogjakarta, Sukarno rose to the occasion:

> Musso and his Communist Party staged a coup, seized power in Madiun, and established there a Soviet government under his leadership. . . . Musso's Communist Party is attempting to seize our beloved republic. . . . Anyone seizing Musso will serve the republic and anyone joining him is a traitor.
>
> I call on you . . . to make a choice . . . between following Musso and his Communist Party . . . or following Sukarno-Hatta, who, with God's help, will lead our Republic of Indonesia to independence.

The Sultan of Jogjakarta spoke next, charging that "Musso wants to destroy the republic." He was followed by General Sudirman, who announced the appointment of Colonel Sungkono as commander of East Java, with full power to restore the authority of the republic. Sukiman, the Masjumi leader, then Interior Minister, warned that in a Communist Indonesia Islam could not survive. The republic abandoned constitutional guarantees and began arresting Communists on a mass basis in an effort to crush the revolt. In Jogjakarta, 200 persons were imprisoned, including Tan Ling Djie, Alimin, Abdulmadjid, Sakirman, and Siauw Giok Tjan. Suripno eluded capture, escaping to Madiun that morning. Aidit, in Soerakarta, also fled. The offices of *Revolusioner, Suara Kota,* and other PKI journals were closed. The headquarters of SOBSI and BTI were "combed out." Military guards policed the streets. In other republican-held cities, similar brisk operations were conducted.

At 11:30 P.M., over Radio Madiun, Musso replied to Sukarno: "The people of Indonesia were asked by Sukarno to choose Sukarno or Musso. The people should answer back: Sukarno-Hatta, the slaves of the Japanese and Americans! Traitors must die!"

Then Musso launched a vicious attack on the *"romusha* dealer," Sukarno. The struggle was joined.

Premier Hatta summoned an emergency session of the working committee and told the deputies that the coup had been "long apparent" and was set in motion by the Communist demand for a national-front cabinet led by themselves. Hatta introduced an emergency bill empowering the President to take measures "outside the law" for a three-month period, retroactive to September 15. The working committee, with the FDR benches vacant, adopted the bill by a twenty-five to one vote; K. Werdojo, a "functional" labor representative, cast the negative ballot.

Sukarno placed communications, public utilities, and industries under the authority of the military forces. In effect, the republic was now governed by the army. That same day, September 19, Radio Moscow broadcast: "A people's government has been established in Madiun, and people's committees are being established in other major towns. This was a popular uprising against the government of the fascist Japanese Quislings, Sukarno and Hatta."

At Madiun, the revolution proceeded with dispatch. Radio Madiun outlined a program calling for the confiscation of all industrial enterprises, the creation of a people's militia, the establishment of people's security committees to dispense "justice," and the division of land under the slogan "Land for those who work it." The "feudal bourgeois" (republican) administration was replaced by a "people's administration." Hundreds of persons were imprisoned; many were tortured and still more shot. Islamic leaders were singled out for execution. There were signs of confusion, too. Radio Madiun and Radio Glorious Youth, the Pesindo station, referred to the new order variously as the "proletarian republic," "national-front government," and "people's republic."

On September 20, the Dutch Foreign Minister, D. U. Stikker, in Washington to head off the Cochran proposals, offered Hatta assistance in suppressing the insurrection. The republic's response was immediate. Hatta said: "We do not accept any [Dutch] proposal under any circumstance. . . . The Madiun revolt is an internal problem and we will use our own methods to suppress it." And the Ministry of Information added: "The persistent and malevolent agitation of the Dutch created favorable circumstances for the reception of Communism in the republic. This is the background of the coup in Madiun, which seems part of the Moscow plan in Southeast Asia."

That night, either in the hope of employing the Dutch offer as leverage for creation of a national front, or because they already realized that the revolt was premature, the Communists indicated misgivings. In a broadcast, Suripno saluted the Communist fighting organizations and said they were compelled to act because of the "anti-Communist attitude of the Hatta government." He said the events at Madiun were not so much a *coup d'état* as a "purge of reactionaries." Suripno said the Communists had not planned revolution, only unity (on Communist terms).

The republic was firm. "The republic," the government replied, "is at present taking steps to restore its legal authority and administration in this [Madiun] area. The entire population is asked to give its fullest support to the government for the sake of the well-being of the republic." On September 21, the army launched an east-west pincers movement against Madiun. Troops of the 3rd Division and the Mobile Brigade drove eastward from Soerakarta; troops of the 6th Division, westward from Kediri.

By September 22, it was obvious that a large part of the Communist organization was, to use Mao's phrase, a paper tiger. In Bantam, branches of the FDR disavowed the revolt. In Sumatra, the only disturbances were relatively minor clashes in Tapanuli, on the west coast, where some army officers sought to take advantage of the crisis to usurp power. Large sections of SOBSI and BTI defected and declared their loyalty to the republic. At Tjepu, the oil city, the workers opposed the Communists. That night, Radio Glorious Youth cited the organizational collapse and exhorted: "Stay on the offensive!" Amir spoke over Radio Madiun and echoed Suripno's line of moderation. He said that although he had accepted the challenge of the republic when it said the rebels would be destroyed, "the republic's constitution is our constitution, the republic's red-and-white flag, our flag." Perhaps the moral in Indonesia is that people can be led to the trough of Communism but cannot be made to drink. Had the Red Army not been there, perhaps, this might also have happened in Eastern Europe and Eastern Asia.

At Madiun, the Communists reshuffled their military command. Colonel Djokosujono, the Military Governor, assumed tactical duties, replacing Sumarsono. Command of the Communist armed forces had passed from the hands of the irregular partisans into those of a regular army officer. The colonel, perhaps less militant than the irregulars, appealed for a negotiated settlement. He invited republican commanders to Madiun for "peace talks" and stressed that they must avoid civil war and stand together against the Dutch. Supardi, the Communist civil governor, declared a state of martial law in the "liberated" areas because of the "tense situation." But at Jogjakarta, captured Communist documents revealed that the PKI had been preparing for a November coup and that the Madiun affair had been premature. The republic, in no mood for compromise, was determined to press its advantage.

On September 23, the republic announced that the two republican columns advancing on Madiun had dislodged insurgents from Magetan, 13 miles west of Madiun, and Ponorogo, 19 miles south of Madiun. Two days later Antara, the Indonesian news agency, reported "large-scale final operations" against Madiun. Now it was Supardi's turn to sue for peace. He declared that the national-front administration was not a Communist administration and that the Communists did not intend to overthrow the republic, the tactical line adopted by Suripno, Amir, and Djokosujono. The coup was only a "corrective measure," Supardi pleaded. Musso was silent. The Communists retreated to the outskirts of Madiun, which was now partly surrounded.

Yet on September 27, A. Multalid, the Communist district administrator for Madiun, sought to maintain the illusion of normality within the "liberated" territory. He appointed fifteen new officials, including a mayor for Madiun, five regents for Madiun, Magetan, Ngawi, Ponorogo, and Patjitan, and departmental heads for finance, labor, social affairs, economic affairs, agriculture, and cultural affairs; significantly, perhaps, none for defense or foreign affairs. A decree was issued abolishing income taxes as "not in accordance with a democratic state." Private property was confiscated. Citizens were ordered to register gold, jewelry, and money; no person was permitted more than 500 rupiahs in currency. Radio Madiun also adopted a new line: "The national front does not intend to establish a Soviet or Communist regime. The local people's government forms part of the republic." The inference was that the Communist administration was a local government and did not intend to usurp the authority of the central government. But it was too late. On the night of September 28–29, Musso, his aides, and a hard core of about 3,000 Communist troops fled the city. The Communist regime at Madiun had collapsed.

Republican troops occupying the city on September 30 found the situation chaotic. The retreating Communists had applied the scorched-earth policy. Bridges, rail facilities, and major buildings were dynamited, telephone lines slashed, and many prisoners executed. That day, President Sukarno incorporated the districts of Soerakarta, Semarang, Patih, and Madiun into a single military zone and appointed Colonel Gatot Subroto, who had broken the Communist "Wild West" at Soerakarta, as Military Governor.

What followed is best described as a will-o'-the-wisp guerrilla campaign, with the government forces either mopping up isolated Communist "pockets" or in hot pursuit of the main elements and the leadership. In this situation the Communists had recourse to two sanctuaries, both predicated on the widely held assumption at the time that the Dutch would resume hostilities against the republic in the near future. Their obvious refuge was in the mountains dotting central-east Java: Willis, Lud, Kawi, Lawu. If the guerrillas secured footholds in the mountain complex, they could wage a war of attrition almost indefinitely, or simply lie low and await the impending Dutch offensive. If the Dutch attacked, the Communists could exploit the assault for a return to republican respectability under the cloak of a popular front against the common Dutch foe. The second sanctuary, paradoxically, was behind the Dutch demarcation lines. The presence of evacuees in the larger Dutch-occupied cities was commonplace. The Communists could cross into the Dutch-held areas, posing as refugees and re-form themselves in the Dutch rear. The republicans acted to meet both strategies. In the drive against Madiun, the army had sent patrols into the mountain areas. Few Communist bands found sanctuary in the foothills. Many headed for the Dutch positions. Sufficient numbers escaped from the republic over the *status quo* line for the republic to ask the Dutch to return any they captured. The Dutch, according to the Soerakarta *Merdeka*, rejected the request.

On October 31, a republican patrol ran into a fire fight with insurgents near Sumandang, south of Madiun. Two Communists were slain. At the hospital in nearby Ponorogo, 15 miles south of Madiun, a body was identified as that of Musso. Photographs confirmed the identification. Musso was dead—eighty-nine days after his return from almost twenty years of exile in Moscow. The body was publicly cremated. Thousands witnessed the rites.

Throughout November, the will-o'-the-wisp campaign continued. On November 29, Colonel Djokosujono, the Communist military commander, Maruto Darusman, Sardjono, and Francisca Fangiday were seized in a village between Purwodadi and the Indo-Dutch demarcation line near Demak. They were traveling in the direction of the Dutch positions. Djokosujono told his captors that the group had been disconnected from the main elements led by Amir and that they did not intend to flee into Dutch-occupied territory. The Communist field commander said he hoped to contact and re-form dispersed Communist units in the Djapara-Rembang area. Republican troops on the *status quo* line, 5 miles distant, were alerted. Two days later, Amir, Suripno, Harjono, and 800 Communist troops were encircled in a swampland. Although many were armed, they were in disarray and surrendered without resistance. Many suffered from dysentery and edema. Amir denied that the force intended to cross into the Dutch areas. He said he planned to return to Soerakarta and Jogjakarta in the guise of a trader. That week, about 1,500 Communists, more than half of them unarmed, were taken prisoner. The suspicion was that they had cached their arms for future use.

On December 4, a gaunt, limping, bearded, heavily guarded Amir arrived by rail at Jogjakarta. En route, he had read a volume of Shakespeare. A large, unusually quiet, crowd gathered to see the former Premier of the republic. Three days later, the government officially proclaimed the end of the rebellion. Thirty-five thousand rebels and rebel sympathizers were in detention camps; thousands had been slain; the Communist leadership had been almost completely liquidated—either imprisoned or killed. Only three major Communists eluded capture: Setiadjit, who suffered from tuberculosis and may have died in the field; and Wikana and Sumarsono, the youth leaders. So did several then minor Party functionaries, among them Aidit. Indonesia had crushed an internal armed Communist bid for power without assistance from the outside, specifically from the West. At that critical hour the republic stood alone. Indeed, it was blockaded by Western land, sea, and air power. The republic was without Western military advisers, without the presence of large Western embassy staffs, without Western programs of economic or technical assistance and without the presence of Western information services. In a sense, the republic was without the elements of Western influence that have often compromised leaders in underdeveloped countries in their struggle against internal Communist machinations. The Communist bid for power in Indonesia, generated from within, was met and defeated from within.

Why had the Communist revolt failed? Obviously the Communists had misjudged the situation and overestimated their popular support. George McTurnan Kahin, a leading American scholar on Indonesia, who was in Jogjakarta during the Madiun period making a study of government and politics under the auspices of The Johns Hopkins University, drew these conclusions in the November 17, 1948, issue of *Far Eastern Survey:*

> [The Communist's] Western-educated leaders . . . clearly failed to understand the strength and character of Indonesian nationalism and in particular the loyalty of the people to Sukarno and Hatta. What the Communists mistook for support of their movement was for the most part nothing more than a general resentment arising from difficult economic conditions and thwarted nationalistic hopes. Such sentiments led many people to back the Communists in their demands for a stronger government policy toward the Dutch. . . . Most Indonesians were, however, by no means prepared to follow it [the Communist Party] in an effort to overthrow a government and leadership that had become the very symbols of their own nationalism.

And Suripno, in his candid memoirs, written in prison, provides this insight into the failure of the Communists at Madiun:

> The most important factor causing our defeat was the very deficient support of the population. Outside the city of Madiun, where the people's support could be called good, the support was very slight, and in some instances the villagers were even rallied to capture us. Does this mean that our political platform is wrong? Of course not! We are still convinced that our policy and our political platform are right. Our fault was that we did not carry out our political platform properly.

Could the Madiun revolt have been avoided? Suripno wrote: "The question cannot be easily answered. . . . The prevailing circumstances compelled us to consider the affair a *fait accompli.* We all felt cornered so that we had to act in solidarity with our comrades at Madiun. . . . There were many other factors which caused our defeat." Among them he listed the failure to establish a national front; the people's distrust of the Communists; the insufficient time to indoctrinate sympathizers; the lack of organization and ideological conviction among irregular military groups; "the excesses estranging us from the people's sympathy"; finally, the government's superior military force. As for excesses, Suripno wrote:

> The most regrettable thing in connection with the Madiun affair was the killing and other atrocities which happened in some places. We did not feel responsible for these happenings. . . . When we were in Bandara about mid-October, a Council of Justice was set up under my chairmanship, which had primarily the task to investigate and try members of our People's Army who broke army discipline. . . . The Council of Justice was also asked advice about

people arrested by our Army. It was a great pity our organization was less perfect and that we were continually pursued, so that this council would not be asked its advice about prisoners [executed by Communists].

Above all, Suripno wrote: "The lesson we learned, a very precious one, although very hard, was that *the people did not support us.*" (Italics added.)

The lesson has been conveniently forgotten by the Communists. In creating their myth of a Madiun provocation, Aidit explained in 1955 that the Communists were "defeated in the fight because we had really no intention of waging war on the government." And the official Party history went on to explain further:

It was said that in Madiun the Communists had carried out a seizure of power and that they established a soviet state. On the basis of this lie, the government called on its entire apparatus to hunt down, arrest, and murder members and sympathizers of the PKI. Thus, the second white terror broke out, a duplicate of the white terror of the Dutch government in 1926–27. . . . In such a situation, there was nothing else for the Communists to do but to take up arms and defend themselves with all their might against the white terror which was then raging. . . . The "Madiun Affair" had made the PKI cadres and members more vigilant and more militant.[16]

9

Chaos in the Field

The suppression of Musso's rebellion did not ease the internal Communist and external Dutch pressures on the Hatta cabinet. The republic had emerged intact from the showdown with the PKI. Republican prestige was at a high in the archipelago, Asia, and the West. The republic had demonstrated national unity at a time of crisis and had proved its ability to maintain order. But the Communist revolt was a costly affair. Communist scorched-earth tactics had disrupted communications; the plight of refugees had worsened; many villages had been gutted. The economic situation was chaotic.

The leadership on the Left was shattered. The political chaos was dramatized by the disavowal of Musso at the time of Madiun by a large segment of the FDR. Only two figures of stature were in a position to fill the void on the Left—Sjahrir and Tan Malaka —and Sjahrir was clearly at a disadvantage in such a competition. Although a gradualist and intellectually incapable of demagoguery, he conceded that in an impoverished, illiterate land, demagoguery was a feature of political life. Even if Sjahrir had accepted the challenge of the Left, it is doubtful whether he could approach, much less equal, the charismatic appeal of Tan Malaka, whose image was rivaled only by that of Sukarno. Thus, in the wake of the abortive Communist coup at Madiun, Tan Malaka, the revisionist Communist, emerged by default as the leader of the extreme Left. An uncompromising defender of the August 17 proclamation and an aggressive opponent of compromise, Tan Malaka was a Marxist-Leninist whose radical nationalism was unquestioned. Thwarted in earlier attempts to gain control of the republic, he set about to recoup his losses.

At the outset, Tan Malaka adopted Musso's strategy. Musso had telescoped the FDR into a single Communist organization. Tan Malaka likewise fused the main elements of the GRR into a single party, the Murba, a word he had coined and defined as "proletariat." On October 3, 1948, the constituent groups of the GRR announced plans to merge on November 7, the thirty-first anniversary of the Russian Revolution, as if to symbolize Leninist orthodoxy. Sukarni, Tan Malaka's heir, was elected chairman of the Murba.

Like the Communist Party, the Murba was based on the Leninist concept of "democratic centralism." Like the Communists, the Murba declared implacable opposition to the trinity of "fascism, capitalism, and imperialism." The terms were never clearly defined. Murba yearned to "return to '45"—to the revolutionary spirit of August 17, 1945. In two respects, however, the structure of the Murba contrasted with Musso's PKI. Unlike Musso, who had assumed direct control of the PKI, Tan Malaka remained officially aloof of the Murba. He held no official position in the Party and was content to influence the situation from the sidelines. This, of course, was the tactic employed by Sukarno, who refrained from affiliation with any party. And unlike Musso, who absorbed the Communist militia into the Party, Tan Malaka kept his military and political organizations separate. Irregular fighting organizations such as the Bambu Runtjing (Bamboo Spears) and the Barisan Banteng, affiliates of the GRR, did not fuse with the Murba. Although committed to Tan Malaka's leadership, they retained their identity. Tan Malaka, anxious to influence the regular army, may have reasoned that bringing the irregulars into the Murba would only serve to antagonize the army and dilute Murba's political appeal.

The revival of Tan Malaka's fortunes coincided with a resumption of the deadlocked negotiations between the Dutch and the republic, ostensibly under the protecting influence of the GOC, but in truth under the aegis of the United States. The suppression of the Communist rebellion had produced a favorable reaction in the United States and the feeling of the American delegation, the outcome at Madiun not withstanding, was that a prolongation of the Indo-Dutch conflict would only serve to push more and more legitimate nationalists into the Soviet embrace.

But negotiations foundered almost immediately, not on the principle of free elections that undermined the Graham and Du Bois efforts, but on the question of Dutch control of the republican armed forces during the interim period leading to the federalized U.S.I.—the issue that wrecked Linggadjati. Hatta, however, as Sjahrir before him, labored for an accommodation with the West. On November 11, in the course of informal discussions with a Netherlands ministerial mission, Hatta handed the Dutch a secret *aide-mémoire* implying republican recognition of Dutch sovereignty in the interim period. A member of the republican delegation leaked the contents to Tan Malaka, who promptly exploited it in his campaign to stir opposition to the Hatta government. Tan Malaka circulated the *aide-mémoire* in the army and denounced Hatta as an "appeaser" who would "betray" the army to the Dutch. The attack found a mark among many army officers who, obviously, were not disposed to place themselves under the Dutch Army high command, even briefly; indeed, the army suspected the Dutch demand was a ruse aimed at destroying the republic. Tan Malaka's propaganda also impressed the radical wing of the PNI, led by Mangunsarkoro, a Marxist pamphleteer who had broken with Sjahrir in 1945 over the compromising policy of negotiation. On November 29, at Kaliurang, Mangunsarkoro urged Hatta to abandon informal talks with the Dutch. He implied that the PNI and a large part of the army shared this view. Hatta contended, however, that the *aide-mémoire* had been deliberately distorted and that his object was solely to get the negotiations off dead center. The Masjumi and Sjahrir's PSI rallied around Hatta. As evidence of good faith, Hatta "clarified" his position in a fresh round of talks with the Dutch. He maintained that the republic's suppression of the Communist revolt was ample evidence of the ability of the Indonesian army to put down internal disorders arising in the interim period, and that Dutch forces could not suppress such disorders because the Netherlands forces would not have the support of the people. The Dutch, however, were unimpressed and took the view that Hatta was retreating on his *aide-mémoire* in the face of rising extremist pressure in the republic.

The incident of the *aide-mémoire*, meanwhile, heightened suspicions that Tan Malaka, in seeking to create unrest in the army, was plotting another coup. In the light of the government's experience with the FDR, Hatta was in no mood to temporize. The government moved to isolate Tan Malaka. On December 1, *Murba*, the Party's newspaper at Soerakarta, was banned. The government revoked the broadcasting license of the GRR's private radio station. Dr. Tjoa Sik Ien, a Leftist of Chinese origin on the republican delegation, suspected of having provided Tan Malaka with the *aide-mémoire*, was dismissed from government service.

The unorthodox Communists had outlived their usefulness in disposing of the orthodox Communist threat. But the government measures alerted Tan Malaka. He hurried his plans. The Murba, together with the familiar group of intransigent radicals that participated in the abortive 1946 coup, announced plans to convoke a "People's Congress" at Jogjakarta on Christmas Eve. The suspicion was that the Congress would be the starting point for a massive "people's campaign" against the government—the tried Communist stratagem of united front from below. Rumors spread that Tan Malaka had enlisted Mangunsarkoro's support for the withdrawal of the PNI from the cabinet with the purpose of inducing a cabinet crisis. The suspicion was so strong that on December 10, the conservative wing of the PNI, led by Wongsonegoro, broke with the Party and formed the Greater Indonesian Party (PIR) in support of Hatta. Five days later, Hatta summoned the sponsors of the People's Congress to a meeting to ascertain their objectives. Abikusno, the spokesman of the group—a PSII leader and key participant in the 1946 coup—assured the Premier that the Congress sought only to "create understanding between the government and the masses." This smacked of Tan Malaka's strategy in forming the Persatuan to bring down Sjahrir. That night, determined to nip the coup, Hatta authorized Colonel Nasution, a rising Sumatran army officer, to make preparations for disarming Tan Malaka's fighting organizations.

As these developments unfolded, the focus in Indonesia shifted from internal affairs to the conflict with the Dutch. On December 11, the Dutch unilaterally suspended negotiations on the Cochran proposals. Jogjakarta interpreted the Dutch maneuver as "a warning that the Netherlands would resume last year's police action." [1] The feeling, however, was that the arrival of the GOC at Jogjakarta on December 16 for its regular three-week stay in the republic would deter an overt Dutch move at that time. But on December 16, the Dutch army reported 330 incidents along the *status quo* line, the highest number since the Renville truce. If the report was correct, the military situation was indeed deteriorating; if the report was manufactured, the Dutch were laying the groundwork for "preventive war." The republic contributed to the war of nerves by ordering large-scale field maneuvers for December 19.

Hatta strove desperately to avert a settlement by arms, convinced that the struggle would be prolonged, that the Dutch would not succeed in restoring their political power, and that the outcome would be chaos. The republic warned the Dutch that in the event of attack, the 30,000 Communists and fellow travelers in the detention camps would be released. [2] Surely the West, in a struggle for survival with the Communist world, could not morally or politically countenance strengthening the Communist position in Indonesia. Hatta also appealed for U.N. "arbitration" of the dispute; but the non-Communist world ignored the plea. The Netherlands rejected arbitration, characterizing the appeal as informal and personal, citing past experience that Hatta did not always speak for the republic (a reference to the scandal of the November *aide-mémoire*).

On December 17, the Dutch handed the republic an eighteen-hour ultimatum demanding recognition of Dutch sovereignty and concomitant Dutch control of the republican armed forces during the interim period. Cochran flew to Batavia and warned the Dutch that the United States would not countenance negotiation by ultimatum. The Dutch ignored Cochran. At 11:30 P.M., December 18, 1949, the Dutch renounced the Renville truce and resumed "freedom of action." Cochran was not permitted to transmit the note of renunciation to Jogjakarta; the Dutch had severed communications with the republic. As it developed, the republican leadership learned of the Dutch decision from a United Press dispatch filed from Batavia that night and transmitted in a Manila newscast at about 4:00 A.M. One hour later, Dutch paratroopers descended on Jogjakarta. The second blitzkrieg was on. The republic, battered by the Communists in September, was buffeted by the West in December.

The catastrophic consequences of the Dutch action cannot be understood solely within the framework of Indonesia. Indeed, it is impossible to appraise the aftermath without an understanding of the international temper at that time. China was about to fall to the Communists. While the Dutch spearheads crossed Java, the Chinese Red Army shelled Peking's outskirts and harassed Nanking's communications. Only a week before the Dutch action, the *Kedulatan Rakjat*, a Jogjakarta newspaper, criticized the West, particularly the United States: "In the long run, the U.S. is bound to face the reality that continuously siding with the Dutch will not pay dividends—China is a good example." In China, of course, it was too late; in Indonesia, it was not. At Bandung, the capital of the Dutch "puppet state of West Java," a constituent state in the projected U.S.I., *Pikiran Rakjat* reflected:

> Communist victories in China must serve as a stimulus to [Western] reactionary elements to alter their political course in order to strengthen the power of democracy in stemming the Communist tide. The Communist peril can only be coped with if the democracies, including the Dutch, recognize the sovereignty of the Indo-

nesians, enabling the latter to fight side by side with them to counter the Red tide. The current confusion in this country affords an opportunity for Communism to spread its influence.

The Dutch attack was a sacrificial propaganda offering to Moscow. The Dutch thus vindicated the Communist thesis that the world was divided into two camps and that the opponents of Western colonialism had no alternative but to side with the democratic, anti-imperialist camp led by the Soviet Union. The Dutch dealt the West a hard blow throughout the Afro-Asian world and made a mockery of the Western contention that colonialism was in its death throes. Above all, the Dutch seriously weakened the moral posture of the non-Communist world, the most powerful weapon in democracy's arsenal in the contest with the Communist world. The West's folly, of course, would be perpetuated in Indochina, and later repeated in Algeria and Angola.

In Indonesia the Dutch had obviously blundered. Their military action played directly into the hands of the extremists. From the ashes of colonial war, the Communist phoenix would rise anew. For a critical moment, the Dutch nearly succeeded in replacing the moderate leadership of Hatta (and Sjahrir) with that of Tan Malaka. The fact is that the Dutch army, well equipped, trained, and commanded, had fewer than 100,000 front-line effectives and in terms of sheer numbers was incapable of occupying an overcrowded area of 50 million people, short, perhaps, of an outright compaign of terror, for which the Dutch were temperamentally unsuited. By seizing Jogjakarta and overrunning Java within a fortnight, the regular Indonesian army and the ubiquitous irregulars had attained complete mobility. There were no front lines; guerrillas moved at will from area to area. The modest forces of the Dutch were thinned along the main roads. The rice fields and mountains, the heartland of Indonesia, were beyond their control. Thus the Dutch created a military power vacuum in the countryside that could give rise to chaos if the regular Indonesian army proved incapable of controlling the irregular bands. The Dutch attack set the stage for a new power struggle in Indonesia between non-Communists and Communists. On January 19, Colonel Simatupang, chief of the army general staff, a devout Christian and a Sumatran, sent from "somewhere in Java" a memorandum to Cochran and the committee that assessed the situation thusly: "I personally consider the Dutch effort to solve the Indonesian problem by force of arms a crime, since their army is not strong enough to force a quick settlement, so that the end result is chaos of long standing."

On December 19, at 10:00 A.M., as Dutch paratroopers surrounded Jogjakarta, the cabinet held an emergency session. The full details of the session are still unknown. Simatupang and the government urged Sukarno to evacuate with the army into the hills and lead the guerrilla campaign. Sukarno had always boasted that one day he would play such a role. Once again a moment of truth arrived for Sukarno. Once again he hesitated. The situation was acutely embarrassing; obviously the government could not evacuate and abandon the President to the Dutch, or even give the appearance of having done so. Hatta then arrived from his overnight stay at Kaliurang with the U.N. He proposed that the government keep close to the U.N. committee. In the face of outraged world opinion, the Dutch would be compelled to resume negotiations. The cabinet concurred; it was a face-saving device. Sukarno's personal prestige among those present suffered grievously. As it developed, the decision to surrender to the Dutch was wise, for it left them no course but to resume political negotiations. However, there is reason to believe that the capture and survival of Sukarno and the government was fortuitous.

Although the evidence is circumstantial, it appears that Captain R. P. Westerling, the notorious "pacifier" of the Southern Celebes, was on a special mission that morning in Jogjakarta to eliminate the republican leadership. In *Challenge to Terror*, Westerling's autobiography, the captain quotes General Spoor, the Dutch army commander, as informing him on November 11: " 'You are going to lead an important mission.' It turned out that the role of my unit was to be to take Jogjakarta and imprison the members of the republican government." [3]

Westerling said he informed General Spoor that he would accept the mission on condition that Sukarno and the others would be tried for collaboration with the Japanese. Spoor said he would not accept conditions; the captain thereupon said he was "resigning" from the army. It seems inconceivable that the Dutch would permit Westerling, a seasoned soldier, to "resign" on the eve of a military action. The plausible inference is that Westerling went on the mission, but not in an official capacity, and that his objective was the liquidation of the republican government. There is reason to believe that he was delayed en route by a fire fight with Sukarno's Ambonese and Menadonese guards. In any event, Sukarno and the government succeeded in safely surrendering to the regular Dutch army. Prior to their surrender, the cabinet formally named Sjafruddin Prawiranegara, the Masjumi Finance Minister and Sundanese leader then touring Sumatra, as head of an "Emergency Government of the Republic of Indonesia in Sumatra with full power to act as the Government of the Republic of Indonesia." Sjafruddin, a man of great integrity and courage, had played a critical role in arranging local cease-fires between republican and Allied forces in West Java in 1945–46. (By an unkind twist of history, Sjafruddin, in 1958, was to return to his guerrilla haunts on Sumatra to lead a revolt against rising Communist influence on Java and against Sukarno's increasing authoritarianism.) The cabinet also established a Commissariat of the Central Emergency Governor for Java, including five ministers who had evacuated Jogjakarta with the army: two representatives of the Masjumi; one of the PSI; one, PNI; and one of the Catholic party.

What effect did the Dutch blitzkrieg have on the orthodox and unorthodox Communists during that fateful December? As Hatta had forewarned the West, the gates to the detention camps were opened and the Communist rank and file released. But despite hostility toward the Dutch, the republic was not inclined to provide the Communist leadership with the opportunity for a new attempt to seize power. A different fate awaited the Communist hierarchy.

At Soerakarta, Colonel Subroto, acting on instructions from Jogjakarta, ordered the execution of the prominent Communists under his jurisdiction. At 11:30 P.M. on December 19, near Karangangjar, north of Soerakarta, a common grave was dug for Amir, Suripno, Sardjono, Darusman, Harjono, Oey Gee Hwat, Sukarno (Pesindo), Lt. Colonel Djokosujono, Katamhadi, Ronomarsono, and Mangku—the last three minor figures at Madiun. All were shot; Amir, first. Alimin later grimly jested that their burial ground was a "Cominform grave." [4] At Magelang, Colonel Bambang Sugeng dispatched forty-one other prominent Communists, among them Suprodjo, who, as a member of Setiadjit's Labor Party, had held the portfolio of social affairs in the Amir cabinet. Duch troops occupied Magelang that night and found the bodies at the local prison. The hastily evacuating Indonesian army lacked the opportunity for burial. At Jogjakarta, in the confusion of the Dutch parachute attack, Alimin, Tan Ling Djie, and Abdulmadjid escaped.

Thus, within twenty-four hours, the leadership situation in Indonesia had altered radically. Sukarno and Hatta were in Dutch captivity; the Communist command was largely liquidated. This development was an open invitation to Tan Malaka, who, having eluded the Dutch encirclement of Jogjakarta, had fled to Kediri. On December 21, the day Dutch columns drove into Soerakarta, Radio Kediri announced the arrival of Tan Malaka, "the father of the republic, who will lead the people to complete independence." Tan Malaka had taken political control of the Indonesian revolution. At 7:30 P.M. that day, Tan Malaka vowed over Radio Kediri: "I shall lead the fight against the Dutch to the bitter end." He assailed Hatta, Sjahrir, and the orthodox Communists, whose policy of appeasement, he said, had invited the imperialist on-slaught. The broadcast was poorly monitored at Djakarta, but Tan Malaka apparently avoided attacking Sukarno directly. Tan Malaka proclaimed a seven-point program of resistance. He called on the people to:

1. Annul Linggadjati, Renville, and the Hatta *aide-mémoire.*
2. Root out the puppet states (created by the Dutch in occupied territory).
3. Recapture every patch of ground occupied by the enemy.
4. Confiscate all foreign property.
5. Annihilate "fifth columnists" (presumably orthodox Communists).
6. Reject negotiations not based on complete independence as proclaimed on August 17, 1945.
7. Unify all parties and fighting organizations; maintain the people's army.

His stature soared. He was the only major political leader to have escaped the Dutch and broadcast to the people with a powerful transmitter.

Meanwhile the United States, morally outraged, summoned an emergency meeting of the Security Council. It was not until December 24 that enough votes were mustered to pass a resolution urging both parties to cease fire and the Dutch to release the political prisoners. Russia and the Ukraine, anxious to recoup lost prestige in Indonesia, abstained because the American-cosponsored resolution did not go far enough. By weak, clandestine radio and by courier, from "somewhere in Sumatra," Sjafruddin instructed the republican delegation to reject any resolution short of a return to the *status quo ante bellum.* The Security Council acted, as is often the case at the U.N., without knowledge of the real situation, in this instance, on Java. At Djakarta, the Dutch branded the resolution "unrealistic" and pointed out that compliance with the cease-fire would leave the republic reduced to the area between Madiun and Kediri—now controlled by Tan Malaka! For the first time, the Dutch appeared apprehensive about the political consequences of their action in terms of the effect on the internal struggle for power within the Indonesian nationalist movement. Dutch columns raced for Kediri. The city fell on Christmas Day. But Tan Malaka again eluded the Dutch.

By New Year's Day, the Dutch had succeeded in occupying the

whole of Java and a large part of republican Sumatra. The Dutch were never to capture Sjafruddin and the emergency governor, nor did they attempt to occupy the northern tip of Sumatra (Atjeh), an Islamic stronghold. The Dutch sweep offended the sensibilities of the non-Communist world. The United States, under whose auspices negotiations were resumed in good faith, felt it had been deceived by the Netherlands. On December 22, the State Department suspended Marshall Plan assistance to Indonesia as a display of displeasure. But it was a half-hearted gesture. Only $60 million had been allocated to the Indies, compared to about a half billion dollars in loans and grants to the Netherlands. In Congress there were demands for sterner action—the severance of all aid to the Dutch. The demands intensified as the Dutch persisted in defying the Security Council.

In January, the international situation darkened as Peking and Tientsin fell to the Chinese Communists. Dean Acheson replaced the ailing George Marshall as Secretary of State, and the United States brought new pressure to bear on the Netherlands. On January 28, with France and the Communist bloc abstaining, the Security Council passed a resolution framed largely by the United States. The resolution urged the Dutch and Indonesians to cease fire and resume negotiations with a view to transferring Dutch sovereignty over the archipelago to the Indonesians by July 1, 1950. The resolution requested the Dutch, in the furtherance of this aim, to release the political prisoners and facilitate their return to Jogjakarta. The GOC, empowered only to mediate, was transformed into the Indonesian Commission, with powers to arbitrate—the formula Hatta had proposed on the eve of the Dutch attack. The Dutch, having survived the power politics of Europe for centuries, were not slow to acknowledge that the Netherlands was not France and that Indonesia was not Indochina. The resolution produced a cabinet crisis in Holland and a change in Netherlands policy. In part under the pressure of the United States—generated largely by the collapse of China—and in part in the realization that the Indonesian guerrilla war would be protracted, the Dutch reversed their position. On April 14, the Indonesians and Dutch resumed negotiations at Djakarta under the chairmanship of Cochran. Mohammed Rum was chairman of the republican delegation; Dr. H. J. Van Roijen of the Netherlands delegation. "It is not for us to find fault," Cochran told both parties, "but to find a solution." On Bangka, Cochran gave Sukarno and Hatta personal assurances on behalf of the United States that Washington was committed to the establishment of a sovereign Indonesia. Van Roijen conducted the Dutch retreat with professional aplomb. On May 7 (with more than half of China now Communist) both sides agreed to implement the cease-fire and other provisions in the January 28 resolution. Perhaps the Netherlands now realized that a non-Communist Indonesia, like a non-Communist Netherlands, could survive only in a non-Communist world, and that in view of this common denominator an independent Indonesia was in their national self-interest. However diverse the ideas and interests of the Dutch and Indonesians may be, they were treading the same non-Communist path. At stake was the future of the non-Communist world. The big question now was whether the guerrillas on Sumatra and Java would accept the Rum-Van Roijen accord. But first, what of Tan Malaka and the orthodox Communists?

As the Dutch reconquered Java, their lines stretched to the vanishing point. Large cities such as Jogjakarta, Soerakarta, Magelang, Madiun, Kediri, and Blitar became Dutch islands in an Indonesian sea. On the arterial roads, the Dutch constructed fortifications fashioned from stone, hewn trees, and barbed wire. The outposts were often dependent on passing armored convoys for supplies. Troops rarely left the confines of these strongholds except for patrol activity. As dusk settled, the Dutch returned to the protection of the redoubts. In effect, the Dutch were conducting a sand-bagged occupation of the republic, particularly in Central-East Java. In many regions there was chaos, as Simatupang had prophesied.

In West Java, the area evacuated under the Renville terms, the returning republican forces met surprising resistance from Moslem extremists led by S. M. Kartosuwirjo, who, accusing the republic of abandoning West Java to the Dutch in 1948, had remained with 5,000 irregulars from the Japanese-sponsored Hizbullah and Sabillah in the mountains of West Java to protect the population against the occupying infidel.[5] As early as November, 1947, following the republic's compliance with the Security Council's cease-fire order, Kartosuwirjo established a Council for the Defense of Islam. The signing of the Renville accord and the subsequent withdrawal of republican troops from the "pockets" confirmed Kartosuwirjo's suspicions of republican betrayal, and on May 5, 1948, at Tjimendji he proclaimed the formation of an interim Darul Islam (State of Islam) cabinet composed of ten ministers, with himself as imam (chief). In a strict sense, all Moslems are dedicated to the creation of a Darul Islam. The ultra-orthodox interpret this as a pro-forma state governed by Islamic law, the modernists as a state where Islam may be practiced and developed free from harassment.

Kartosuwirjo's checkered career was guided by two constants: a fundamentalist's approach to Islam and enmity for the Dutch. During World War I, he was expelled from the Batavia Medical School for nationalist activity; in 1926, he participated in the Communist revolt; and in the 1930's he trained propagators of the faith at the Suffah Institute, which he had founded. During the Japanese occupation he became a political power, converted the institute into a training center for Hizbullah and Sabillah auxiliaries, and became the Masjumi Commissioner for West Java. In 1946–47, he resisted Amir's efforts to "rationalize" Islamic paramilitary organizations. When republic troops withdrew from West Java under the terms of Renville, Kartosuwirjo fell heir to the area along the southern coast.

Kartosuwirjo rejected the Rum-Van Roijen accord as a "sell-out," and when the cease-fire went into effect on Java on August 7, 1949, preparatory to the withdrawal of all Dutch forces from Indonesia, Kartosuwirjo proclaimed the birth of the Negara Islam Indonesia, the Islamic State of Indonesia. In the course of time it devolved into a terrorist movement. Later, in November, 1949, on the eve of the transfer of sovereignty, Dutch and republican forces joined in a combined clearing action against the Darul Islam in the Cheribon and Tasikmalaja areas. Kartosuwirjo became convinced more than ever that the republic had betrayed the August revolution.

Except in East Java, where Tan Malaka's influence was strong, direction of the guerrilla campaign rested with local army commands. The army, theoretically at least, was responsible to Sjafruddin on Sumatra and the Commissariat on Java. The conception of guerrilla war as advocated by the Communists when Amir was defense minister was ignored. Amir's idea had been based on the indiscriminate arming of a "people's army" and the creation of coordinating committees on a village level in which leaders of political fronts, the irregular fighting organizations, and the regular army would share authority. It was a complicated device, apparently designed to curb the authority of the army while assuring the Communists of a voice in directing the resistance at the village level. It was a subtle political form of infiltration of future governments. Aidit later described Amir's concept of guerrilla warfare as Chinese Communist in origin.[6] As Nasution explained the republican strategy, however, the resistance was carried out by "an effective division of labor between the army and the people, not according to the conception of Amir Sjarifuddin, i.e., by arming the people. There was no command by council or coordinating body; all command was vested in the army." [7] Thus the army was the principal authority of the republic between the attack on December 19, 1948, and the restoration of Sukarno and Hatta, at Jogjakarta on July 6, 1949, under the terms of the Security Council resolution. The most serious internal political threat to the army in this period was from the extreme Left, particularly between the period of the January 28 U.N. resolution and the conclusion of the May 7 Rum-Van Roijen agreement. In that period, with the orthodox Communists largely devoid of leadership and the Party disorganized, the revisionist national Communists bitterly fought for power.

The PKI played an insignificant role in the second military action. The orthodox Communists were mistrusted and feared in the villages. Stories about atrocities at Madiun had been widely circulated. Ideologically, however, the Dutch attack created a favorable climate for a united front against the common enemy, and the PKI attempted to exploit this atmosphere. At the outset of the Dutch onslaught, the PKI encountered little difficulty in fitting their aggressive line to the militant republican posture of unrelenting struggle against the Dutch. Indeed, the republican and Communist positions dovetailed. A PKI leaflet circulated in Jogjakarta in late January declared: "We Indonesians . . . must not fight one another lest we bring back the Dutch—on the contrary, we must wage a joint guerrilla fight against them. . . . Long live the Republic of Indonesia! Long live anticolonial unity!" But in March, when it became apparent that the republic was seriously entertaining a resumption of talks with the Dutch under the terms of the January 28 resolution, the PKI was in a predicament. The problem of the Communists was to retain the myth of a national front while opposing a republican policy of negotiation with the imperialists. Consequently, the Communists adopted a tortuous reasoning process to justify continuing the struggle without compromise. The PKI did so by first rejecting the January 28 ceasefire resolution. Then the Communists argued that if Jogjakarta was restored, the *status quo ante* should obtain in the liberated republican territory. The Communists concluded on the note that the imperialists would never countenance a transfer of sovereignty to the republic and that, therefore, the only road was armed struggle. A PKI leaflet, circulated in Jogjakarta during this period but bearing a Kediri imprint, perhaps to confuse both the Dutch and

the republican armies as to the location of the Communist headquarters, illustrates this line. The leaflet only indirectly referred
to Madiun, reaffirming Musso's New Road as PKI policy—perhaps
to imply that Musso's analysis of the Indonesian situation within
the framework of the two-camp thesis had been correct. The leaflet
declared:

> In the month of August, 1948, the PKI corrected its mistakes in
> the field of political organization. . . . At the present moment,
> the PKI still adheres to those corrections. . . . [Thus] the direct
> aim of the PKI is to establish a republic of Indonesia free from for-
> eign political and military domination. . . . Therefore, the PKI
> categorically rejects the Security Council's resolution. . . . But in
> case the return of the republican government to Jogjakarta becomes
> a reality, we must make use of the occasion . . . to rectify the
> political mistakes made in the past. The return of the republican
> government to Jogjakarta must be used to maintain the . . . con-
> stitution of our republic. . . . In short, the democratic rights of
> the people must be guaranteed.
>
> One thing can be established, however, namely Dutch imperialism
> and its supporters [America, Britain, etc.] will not let the republican
> government change its policy. Dutch imperialism will not let the
> republican governmennt [achieve] full sovereignty over the whole of
> Indonesia. We are convinced that Dutch imperialism will always
> avail itself of its armed might to force the Indonesian nation to ac-
> cept a "union relationship." . . . That is why we must continue
> our guerrilla warfare against the Dutch army concurrently with seiz-
> ing the opportunity of the possibility of the republican government's
> return to Jogjakarta to change its incorrect policy to a consistent
> anti-imperialistic policy. . . . Therefore, the PKI invites and calls
> on the whole Indonesian nation to continue guerrilla warfare until
> the Dutch army leaves Indonesian soil.

Despite the glowing statements about armed struggle and guerrilla war, the Communists, significantly perhaps, avoided direct
military participation in the military campaign, confining themselves primarily to pamphleteering. Of course, they had not recovered from the losses inflicted on them at Madiun. In some areas,
however, the PKI succeeded in recovering weapons cached during
the Madiun rebellion and organized small armed groups. These
groups skirted clashes with the Dutch and, perhaps uncertain of
their reception, also avoided contact with the regular republican
army.

This was at a time when the international Communist apparatus was exhorting Indonesia to intensify its armed struggle
against the Dutch. For example, the February 15, 1949, issue of

the Cominform journal *For a Lasting Peace, for a People's Democracy!* carried the following declaration:

> The people of Indonesia are now paying heavily for the division in the ranks of the national liberation movement—a division caused by the reactionary, feudal, bourgeois clique. But the people are not defeated. They are rallying around the Communist Party and are continuing their struggle for freedom and independence.

The journal described the Madiun revolt as an "American intrigue" and, confidently surveying the world situation, said: "All roads lead to Communism." And on March 21, the San Francisco office of the Associated Press monitored a Chinese Communist broadcast urging the Indonesians to follow Mao's example by concentrating first on the creation of a "proletarian-led revolutionary army," then waging guerrilla warfare in the hinterland while preparing to capture the cities. The Chinese Communists, in accordance with the Moscow line, assailed the captive Sukarno and Hatta as reactionaries who "pursued anti-Communist and anti-popular policies at home and refused to establish friendly relations . . . with the Soviet Union."

Under the cloak of guerrilla warfare, however, several small, armed Communist groups sought to even some domestic scores. There were clashes between Communist and national Communist groups, and Communist and Masjumi groups, notably the Hizbullah. The Communists also apparently sought to track down individual opponents. On March 28, Sukiman, a member of the Commissariat, surrendered to the Dutch under Communist pressure.[8] There is a parallel to this situation. The republican leaders apparently preferred surrender to the Dutch to surrender to a domestic foe; the Communists felt similarly after Madiun. But the paramount fear of the Communists in this period was the ascendancy of Tan Malaka. The PKI appeared concerned that the Murba would replace the PKI in a national front against the Dutch. On April 5, 1949, a PKI leaflet issued by the Agitprop Section of the PKI Central Committee, "somewhere" on Java hinted at this concern:

> Reactionary and counterrevolutionary cliques are now busily engaged in planting feelings of hatred and distrust of the FDR . . . now resisting colonial assaults. People of Indonesia! Do not allow yourselves to be played off one against the other by these reactionary and counterrevolutionary cliques. Do not allow them to control the members of the FDR, Masjumi, PNI, and other parties who still prove themselves to be anticolonial fighters. Preserve the unity of the unfinished struggle. . . .

Long live the republic of Indonesia and its people!
Long live the PNI and Masjumi, the FDR and the other anti-colonial organizations! Long live national unity against foreign conquest!

Significantly, the united front envisioned by the Communists excluded the Murba and the GRR. Nor was the PKI alone in expressing concern over the growing influence of Tan Malaka. The Dutch and the republican armies were equally disturbed by the growing stature of Tan Malaka. A master propagandist, Tan Malaka was in the unique position of being able simultaneously to lash Sukarno-Hatta-Sjahrir, the PKI, the Dutch, and the Americans. The propaganda was crude but convincing. A March 25, 1949, summation of the Murba line by a republican guerrilla is illuminating. Tan Malaka fulminated:

> Where are Sukarno and Hatta? Living in nice houses, dining lavishly in Bangka as the guests of the Dutch, while we guerrillas starve in the mountains. Sukarno and Hatta are far away. They will never return. . . . Look at the situation around us. Aided by secret Communist agents like Amir, and by the Hatta policy of compromise, the Dutch have attacked us. Look at the arms used by the Dutch. The Dutch are poor. Where do they get their arms? From the Americans. Their tanks, airplanes, and jeeps are made by the Americans.

Tan Malaka's propaganda was well received—as the Dutch conceded. In the January 31 budgetary debates in the Netherlands Parliament, the Dutch Government acknowledged that it could not gauge how long the guerrilla campaign would last and confirmed that Tan Malaka had proclaimed himself the leader of the resistance. In Batavia, *Keng Po*, Indonesia's most reliable newspaper, operated by Sino-Indonesians, reported on March 26. "We may draw the conclusion that Tan Malaka's influence has increased rapidly. There are now groups, including the intelligentsia, who dream of a " 'Free Red Indonesia' [Maeda's dream also] without Sukarno-Hatta. . . . This not only threatens the nationalist movement, but also Dutch interests here and other anti-Communist groups."

Tan Malaka's usurpation of authority, the effectiveness of his propaganda, the belief that his plan to depose the constituted republican authority had been wrecked solely by the Dutch offensive, generated demands within the army that his influence be curtailed. Colonel Nasution, implementing the order Hatta gave him shortly before the Dutch attack to mop up all elements attempting to annihilate the government, instituted the necessary measures.

The disarming of Tan Malaka fighting units began soon after January 28, when it became clear that Tan Malaka would balk at implementing the Security Council resolution. By the end of February, Tan Malaka was denouncing both Hatta and Nasution for preparing to betray the republic by accepting the January 28 resolution. Tan Malaka continued to avoid a direct attack on Sukarno, although he was soon to change his tactics. Tan Malaka at that time was in an uneasy alliance with Major General Sungkono's 4th Division in East Java and hoped to perpetuate the fiction that he did not oppose the President as the symbol of the republic, only the government of the republic. A Tan Malaka leaflet dated February, 1949, declared:

> The Armed Forces Staff, led by [Colonels] Nasution, Djatikusumo, Bambang Sugeng, etc., has resumed disarming units of the people that are not officially in the TNI. Concurrently, they have issued orders for further action against groups that might disagree with the contents of the Security Council's [January 28] resolution. People of Indonesia! The demise of the republic will be aggravated if Hatta and Nasution are given the opportunity to come to power again and repeat their compromising policies. . . . For the sake of the state and the people, continue the guerrilla warfare as long as there are Dutch troops in our country.
>
> Reject every informal and clandestine diplomacy. . . . Resist imperialism, resist the enticements of the diplomacy of capitalist-imperialists. Long live the republic! Long live our guerrillas, the Masjumi, the FDR, the PNI, PSII, MURBA, and PSI! They all live for freedom forever and victory!

Tan Malaka's inclusion of the Communists (FDR) and Sjahrir Socialists in his popular front attested to his confidence in the effectiveness of his appeal on the rank and file of all parties. His tactic, therefore, was a combination of the united from above and the united front from below. But the increasing belligerence of Tan Malaka's line, coupled with Colonel Nasution's standing order for a house cleaning of armed groups in opposition to Sukarno-Hatta strained Tan Malaka's alliance with Sungkono. The breaking point became apparent in March, when a brigade of the 4th Division, led by Major Sabarudin, who had won honors in the fight against the orthodox Communists at Madiun, defected to Tan Malaka. Shortly thereafter, Tan Malaka was arrested near Blitar. A clash ensued between the brigade and the division; Sabarudin's force was eliminated. On April 16, a Sungkono aide ordered Tan Malaka's execution. Tan Malaka, "the father of the republic," was dead. As is the case in so many other movements in history, the influence of the national Communists waned with his death, and, despite its broad social base, seemed to dissipate with the passing of its founder. Yet in 1958, the fortunes of the nationalist Communists revived with the rise of Sukarno's "guided democracy."

Thus the Left fared badly during the second action. Much of the orthodox and unorthodox Communist leadership was liquidated; the PKI's military role in the guerrilla war was undistinguished. Aidit's history of the PKI devotes only three sentences to the second guerrilla campaign:

> During the war against the Dutch, from the end of 1948 to the beginning of 1949, PKI cadres and members including those that had been released or who had escaped from the Hatta government prisons, courageously took part in defending the republic of Indonesia in the most advanced outposts. This fact opened the eyes of the people to the falseness of the slanders the reactionaries had leveled at the PKI during the "Madiun Affair." The PKI's stubborn resistance to the Dutch army raised the prestige of its policy in the eyes of the people, and this made it quite impossible for the government to outlaw the PKI.[9]

10

The Left Modified

With both orthodox and revisionist Communist forces in disarray, the Masjumi and Nationalist parties on May 28, 1949, endorsed the accord negotiated over a three-week period by Rum and Van Roijen. Like Sukarno and Hatta, the parties had little choice in the matter. The alternative to negotiations was a prolongation of the guerrilla war and the prospect that extremist factions would regroup their decimated forces and make another attempt at the forcible seizure of the leadership of the revolution. They reasoned, too, that in view of the continuing guerrilla struggle, the inflamed state of world opinion, the revolutionary tide sweeping Asia, and United States irritation with The Hague, the pressure for a political settlement was on the Dutch. On June 14, with misgivings, Sjafruddin's emergency government approved the Rum-Van Roijen accord. A cease-fire was proclaimed in the Jogjakarta residency four days later, and the Dutch army began evacuating the area in compliance with the Security Council's resolution. On July 6, Sukarno and Hatta boarded a U.S. Air Force plane and flew from confinement on Bangka to freedom at Jogjakarta. The restoration of the republican government marked the beginning of the end of the Indonesian war of independence.

At Jogjakarta, Sukarno felt constrained to explain his surrender to the Dutch, a decision that angered many intellectuals, particularly in the emergency government and the army high command, where he was assailed for cowardice. On August 3, in his first public speech, Sukarno defended his action on the ground that he had been guided by the conviction that the dispute with the Netherlands could never be resolved by force. He did not amplify his defense but claimed that the government decision to surrender was a "unanimous" decision, a claim that was open to serious question.

The diminishing influence of the Left was glaringly demonstrated the next day. Sukarno installed his third Presidential cabinet, dominated by the resistance leaders of the Center, with Hatta as Premier. Sjafruddin, in recognition of his leadership of the republic at the darkest moment of the revolution, was elevated to the Vice Premiership. The critical post of Minister of Defense went to the Sultan of Jogjakarta, whose palace had been a center of underground resistance during the second Dutch action. Sjahrir's Socialists were invited to participate in the new government, but they, hopeful of capturing the splintered, leaderless, and largely disillusioned Left, balked and announced opposition to the Rum-Van Roijen accord. Opposition to the agreement was the prevailing sentiment in Indonesia at that time. Conditioned by Dutch procrastination and intransigence in the past and the bitterness of the second military struggle, few Indonesians believed that the Dutch were prepared to withdraw from Indonesia. This disbelief persisted until the eve of the transfer of sovereignty. "In view of the fact that their prosperity mainly depends on this rich colony of theirs, and also in view of their actions since August 17, 1945, it is hardly conceivable that the Dutch would be willing to hand over their colony unconditionally," *Nasional*, a Jogjakarta daily, said as late as October 16.

The irrational radical nationalists of the extreme Left seized on the Rum-Van Roijen agreement to agitate against the government. The most publicized effort was the convocation of a guerrilla congress by Mohammed Djoni, a radical, unorthodox Communist who had opposed the PKI's postwar "policy of appeasement." In 1947, he broke with the PKI and formed a splinter group, the Red Communist Party (PKIM) in protest against Linggadjati; "Red" denoted aggressiveness. Djoni had led a turbulent life. He was placed in "protective custody" at the time of Madiun and imprisoned by the Dutch during the second military action. Djoni scheduled the congress for September 17 at Prambanan "because of Prambanan's historical significance," [1] an allusion to the PKI conference there in 1925 that drafted plans for the 1926 revolt. Although it was extremely doubtful that Djoni commanded respect, much less a following, the program of his congress reflected the overwhelming feeling of the irregulars. It called for:

1. Mass withdrawal of Netherlands troops from the whole of Indonesia by December 31, 1949;

2. Rejection of the government's "rationalization" program for the armed forces.

The crux of Djoni's appeal was opposition to the rationalization of the armed forces. But having repressed Musso's and Tan Malaka's defiance of rationalization, the republic was not disposed to treat Djoni lightly. The Sultan of Jogjakarta ordered the congress disbanded; Djoni was arrested. Now in his sixties, he retired from political life.

The atmosphere of the period was also illustrated in the armed opposition of fighting organizations allied to the late Tan Malaka. In East Java, remnant Tan Malaka groups attacked the Dutch in violation of the armistice proclaimed August 7 in accordance with the Rum-Van Roijen agreement. In September and October, as political negotiations leading to a transfer of sovereignty progressed at The Hague, the incidents mushroomed, particularly in the Blitar area, where Tan Malaka had been executed. On October 29, the republican army announced that it would undertake "disciplinary measures" for the purpose of "liquidating irresponsible elements" in East Java. The clearing action proved successful. But that same month, fresh disturbances erupted in the Bantam residency, on the western tip of Java. Again the incidents were provoked by Tan Malaka sympathizers. The prime mover was Chaerul Saleh, who had announced the formation of a "people's army" on October 14, 1949, to continue the struggle against "the Sukarno-Hatta compromise policy." A manifesto of the new people's army urged a return to the spirit of '45 and declared:

> The climax of resistance and rebellion came when the Indonesian people forced their will upon two leaders, Sukarno and Hatta, on August 15, 1945, and entrusted them with notifying the Indonesian people of independence. . . . The Indonesian people can no longer be entrusted to leaders who are weak. [We] therefore proclaim the establishment of a people's army. . . . This army will not lay down its arms until the desires of the Indonesian people have been realized.

The Saleh group embarked on a reign of terror. It was not until February 16, 1950, that Saleh was apprehended and his organization dispersed. But he was destined to play a prominent role in Sukarno's guided democracy a decade later.

Other seemingly insignificant extremist groups flourished in this period. Typical of the demagoguery on which they hoped to base political ascendancy was a "news bulletin" circulated regularly in Central Java by the Defenders of the Proclamation, a Tan Malaka group in league with Islamic extremists. The gist of these bulletins was that the proposed federal Republic of the United States of Indonesia (R.U.S.I.) was a Western creation designed to camouflage operations against China. A July 25, 1949, bulletin alleged: "In Surabaya, four large ships with American troops and war materials have arrived for resistance against China. . . . The withdrawal of Dutch troops to Europe is only for the defense of Berlin. . . . The R.U.S.I. is absolutely false. Do not allow yourselves to be deceived. . . . Do not deviate from the principles of August 17, 1945." The charge was nonsensical, but the theme of deviation from the original proclamation of independence was to develop into a resounding slogan—Return to '45—as the political, economic, and social problems of independent Indonesia multiplied. By the standards of responsible Indonesians, these irrational ultranationalist groups constitute the lunatic fringe and do not warrant attention. Perhaps, but in an impressionable country of illiterate, impoverished people, haunted by the fear of foreign encroachment, frustrated in achieving the lofty ideals of the revolution, these elements furnish grist for the demagogue's mill. In point of fact, these irrational groups have exercised an invisible veto power over the constructive efforts of responsible Indonesian leaders to put the country's house in order. They have generated demands for incoherent radical measures, not for the purpose of reform, but solely with a view to avenging past injustices and as a means of acquiring or maintaining power. These elements are largely responsible for the recent chaos in Indonesia; Sukarno has exploited them in implementing his guided democracy.

The restoration of the republic at Jogjakarta posed a delicate internal political problem with regard to the Communists. Should the past be buried and the Communists permitted to operate freely, or should the Communist Party be outlawed because of its role at Madiun? The issue was debated for two months. The Communists, uncertain of the outcome, remained in the background. At this point, of course, only a few Communist leaders were in republican custody. It was not until December 5 that the Dutch revealed that they would transfer about 400 Communists, many of whom were apprehended at the demarcation line after the Madiun debacle, to the new R.U.S.I.

Ultimately, the republic decided on a policy of leniency. The decision not to outlaw the PKI was based on several considerations. The PKI leadership was decimated. The Communists no longer constituted a serious political challenge. The government felt itself in a better position to control overt than covert PKI activity. There was a Lincolnesque spirit, now that the war was concluded, of charity for all, a desire to rebuild the republic on a democratic base, and, among the wishful thinkers, a belief that the Communists would reform. Inferiority complexes were also at work. The desire for equality with the Netherlands had to be complete. If the Communists could operate freely in Dutch society, why not in Indonesia? Did the Westerners think they were the only people who knew how to deal with Communists or who were safe from the Communist virus? An ingenious Communist argument, transmitted through fellow travelers such as Dr. Buntaran Martoatmodjo, was that to suppress a political party that did not violate the law was not only undemocratic but meant siding with one bloc in the Cold War. Finally, there was a disposition, particularly in the PNI, to look on the Communists as allies in neutralizing the dominant position of Dutch capital in an independent Indonesia. Justice Minister Susanto Tirtoprodjo (PNI) hinted at this on September 4, 1949, observing that those present at Madiun would not be molested "providing they cause no trouble," and adding cryptically: "Even their cooperation is needed to face the dangers from without." The Dutch financial stake in Indonesia at the transfer of sovereignty would be an estimated $2 billion. The Dutch would continue to own and operate almost all of Indonesia's interisland shipping, banking, trade companies, and estates. The Communists, some Indonesians naïvely reasoned, could be used to neutralize Dutch economic influence. Whatever the basic consideration, on September 7, 1949, at Jogjakarta, the cabinet approved the policy of leniency. The republic came to rue the day. A government announcement said that members of existing social, economic, or political organizations involved in the Madiun *coup d'état* were free to continue their activities as long as there were no criminal cases against them that constitutionally would deprive them of their rights, and that government policy toward government employees will be based on loyalty to the maintenance of the country's sovereignty.

The republic, democratic in form and content during the revolution, was encouraging opposition but demanding loyal opposition. Its Communist policy was administered amidst confusion. Communists, transferred from Dutch to republican detention, were released in haphazard fashion. On December 31, the PKI complained self-righteously that the republic was not living up to its democratic ideals and that many Communists were still imprisoned. (But by the end of 1950, the Communists had regained freedom of movement.)

Three days later, on September 10, Alimin, thought dead by many, emerged from seclusion. Interviewed "at an unnamed place near Jogjakarta" by a correspondent of *Sin Po*, the pro-Communist Sino-Indonesian daily, Alimin adopted a cautious line. He implicitly repudiated Musso. He denied that the PKI had provoked the Madiun revolt. He blamed unnamed individuals who had joined the Party. Thus, he reasoned, the government should not repress the Party; the Party was not responsible, individuals were. Alimin expressed regret, however, that the republic had acted "rashly" and "imprudently" at Madiun and therefore permitted itself to become an "imperialist-capitalist" tool to destroy national unity. Alimin emphasized that the PKI would continue to strive for national unity. He tactfully rebuked the Sukarno-Hatta leadership. It had become clear, Alimin said, that Indonesia's victory was due not only to the strength of the republic but to the weakness of the Dutch. As for the Rum-Van Roijen agreement and the resumption of negotiations, Alimin said the PKI would not bear responsibility for the outcome. "If the People's Democratic Front were still as of old," Alimin said, "it would surely hold mass demonstrations to protest against the round-table conference." Alimin confirmed the execution of Amir and other Communist leaders, stating that between 2,000 and 3,000 members of the FDR had disappeared. The Sino-Indonesian correspondent reported that Alimin's "face clearly radiated joy" when he conveyed his greetings and congratulations to Mao Tse-tung and the new People's Republic of China.

The ideological problem confronting Alimin, who had assumed titular leadership of the PKI now that Musso, Sardjono, and Amir were dead, was complicated. Although the Left strategy and the two-camp doctrine prevailed as the international line, the PKI was obviously in no position to continue the armed struggle. Up to the restoration of Jogjakarta in July, the PKI could cling to the Party line and call for armed conflict. But when the round-table conference at The Hague materialized and an independent Indonesia seemed imminent, the PKI was compelled to modify its stand. Party discipline prevented an outright change of line. Alimin, influenced by his experience in China, solved the dilemma by adoption of a flexible, modified Left line. Outwardly belligerent and aggressive, the new strategy continued to direct fire at feudalism, imperialism, and capitalism, but sought to distinguish between foreign and domestic capitalists—as the Sarekat Islam had earlier—on the ground that the national bourgeoisie was oppressed by foreign imperialism and could therefore join in the struggle against imperialism. Such a strategy is applicable in a "semicolony," that is, in a country in which foreign capital "dominates" the economy. This is the description Mao applied to China and that the PKI was to apply to independent Indonesia. Ostensibly first employed by Mao in China, this strategy gave rise to the four-class coalition composed of peasants, workers, intellectuals, and the national bourgeoisie. In such a coalition, the Communists are prepared to enter an alliance with national capitalists. Thus the four-class bloc exploits the apprehensions of weak domestic capitalists and appeals to their sense of nationalism. The strategy appeals to the national bourgeoisie, a small but influential minority in an impoverished country, by offering them, in this instance, a role in a future Communist state. This modified Left strategy, which has been termed "neo-Maoist," [2] is designed to fit the conditions in underdeveloped countries.

Thus, on October 7, in the knowledge that The Hague talks were drawing to a close and that an independent Indonesia was in the offing, Alimin poured the foundation for the new line, i.e., that a sovereign Indonesia was, in reality, a "semicolony," and that the national bourgeoisie, petty bourgeoisie, peasants, and workers should form a national front against the compradore bourgeoisie (national capitalists whose economic interests coincided with those of foreign capitalists) and foreign imperialists. A statement by the PKI Politburo noted that the Communists did not oppose capitalism per se:

> The following [condition] should be fulfilled if the R.U.S.I. is not to become a semicolonized state. . . . All foreign enterprises managed by the republic of Indonesia during the time it controlled the administration should be defended against foreign proprietors. The PKI is not out to eliminate capitalism; it only wants to check its development. For this purpose, the state should be controlled by the people.

Barely a month later, on November 2, 1949, the round-table conference at The Hague, convened in accordance with the Rum-Van Roijen accord, ended in agreement. A free Indonesia was born. The conference, which had begun on August 23, moved relatively quickly and smoothly considering the abyss of mistrust on both sides. Article 1 of the round-table agreement stated:

> The kingdom of the Netherlands unconditionally and irrevocably transfers complete sovereignty over Indonesia to the Republic of the United States of Indonesia and thereby recognizes said Republic of the United States of Indonesia as an independent and sovereign state. . . . The transfer of sovereignty shall take place at the latest on December 30, 1949.

The pace of the negotiations had been set by the deterioration in international affairs and by the knowledge that a deadlock would foreshadow a renewal of hostilities to the peril of both parties. During the conference, the Chinese Communist offensive had rolled on and the Soviet Union had exploded its first nuclear device. Aware of the consequences of prolonged guerrilla war, the United States had exercised its influence for a peaceful settlement of the Indonesian dispute. "The United States Government is doing everything to eliminate the possibility of a resumption of hostilities," Jacob Beam, the United States Consul General in Indonesia declared in October, after a visit to Jogjakarta. The United States position at The Hague was delicate. The North Atlantic Treaty Organization had come into force earlier that year, and Washington's ties with Holland were now stronger than ever in the long history of close relations between the two nations.

At the conference, the only dispute of serious political consequences centered on the status of West Irian—the western half of New Guinea—the second-largest island in the world and an integral part of the former N.E.I. The dispute was to have a profound effect on Indonesian-Dutch relations and on the course of events in independent Indonesia.

West Irian, an area of 154,000 square miles, three times as large as Java and twelve times as large as Holland, constituted 22 per cent of the former Dutch Indies empire. The territory, covered by impenetrable jungle, contained about 700,000 people, whose cultural development has been described as largely late Stone Age, perhaps 5,000 B.C. About 262,000 of these tribal peoples were under regular Netherlands administration; the Dutch claimed to be in "periodic contact" with only about 129,000. For so remote a place, New Guinea has had a lively political history. Since the beginning of recorded time, the petty rajas of East Indonesia, such as the Raja of Goa, have laid claim not only to the island but to nearby Australia as well. In the fifteenth century, Spain and Portugal contested for its possession. Control later passed into the hands of the Dutch and Germans. At Versailles, the German colony of East New Guinea was transferred to Australia as a League of Nations mandate. During World War II, the Australians and Americans broke the Japanese South Pacific offensive on New Guinea in some of the bloodiest fighting of the war.

As early as 1946, during the first phase of the Indo-Dutch deliberations, the status of West Irian loomed as a source of contention. At that time, in the heated atmosphere of the period, many Indies-born Dutch looked to the island as a possible sanctuary for themselves and some 200,000 Indo-Europeans. It seems curious in the light of later developments that, in 1949, the republican delegation at The Hague offered no strenuous objection when the Dutch broached the question of excluding West Irian from the immediate transfer of sovereignty. Protests, however, came from the federalist delegation, composed of representatives of the Dutch-sponsored puppet states in the occupied territories. Some of the federalists, collaborators of the Dutch during the revolution, doubtlessly desired to demonstrate their nationalist fervor; others felt betrayed by the Dutch and, accordingly, assumed extremist anti-Dutch positions; still others were genuinely alarmed at the prospect of lingering Dutch power in the East. Whatever the case, the federalists, not the republicans, vigorously campaigned for inclusion of the region in the transfer of sovereignty.

In Indonesia, the overwhelming majority of Dutch business interests were disturbed by the prospect of Dutch retention of Irian. They favored an unconditional transfer of sovereignty. They argued that omission of the area would only provide the Communists and other extremists with a political anti-Dutch club. They contended that in view of the Dutch economic stake in Indonesia, Irian was not worth the risk. Moreover, they stressed that Irian was a financial as well as political liability. The outgoing cabinet of the Indies government unanimously advised The Hague to include the area in the transfer. But extreme nationalist opposition in the Dutch parliament (as intransigent as ultranationalist opinion in Indonesia) was formidable—the First Chamber, for example, ratified The Hague accord by a margin of only one vote. Netherlands Premier Willem Drees (Labor) was therefore compelled to press for the exclusion of Irian from the transfer of sovereignty as a sop to nationalist opposition. The Indonesians were impatient for a main settlement. Both sides agreed to leave the issue unsettled. Article 2 of the transfer agreement stated:

With regard to the residency of New Guinea it is decided . . . in view of the fact that it has not yet been possible to reconcile the views of the parties on New Guinea, which remain, therefore, in dispute . . . that the *status quo* of the residency of New Guinea shall be maintained with the stipulation that within a year from the date of transfer of sovereignty . . . the question of the political status of New Guinea be determined through negotiations between the Republic of the United States of Indonesia and the kingdom of the Netherlands.

In Indonesia, the omission of Irian brought some adverse criticism, but, for the moment at least, there were no serious political repercussions. The consensus among the Indonesians was that as soon as the transfer was completed and the dust had settled, at most within a year, the Netherlands would relinquish the disputed territory. Of what value could it possibly be to the Netherlands? But the dust did not settle.

The apparently successful outcome of The Hague deliberations, particularly the constructive role played by the United States, dashed Communist hopes and aspirations. The Hague settlement had closed another chapter in the West's colonial relations with Asia and simultaneously broadened the world coalition of independent, non-Communist nations. The settlement worked clearly in the Indonesian and Western interests and against the Communists. The international Communist movement railed against the accord. On October 31, with success at The Hague imminent, *Krasnaya zvezda* (*Red Star*), the Soviet army organ, scathingly denounced the accord as flouting the interests of the Indonesian people. Accusing Premier Hatta of pursuing a "policy of treason," the paper charged: "Fearing the anger of his people, this cowardly Quisling Hatta is endeavoring to make his people believe that he is resisting the demands of his masters with all his strength. However, the activities of this renegade will not prevent the Indonesian people from intensifying their struggle."

In November, the international Communist propaganda offensive intensified. In New York, the *Daily Worker* declared: "One of the shabbiest and most shocking examples of how colonial peoples are cheated of their independence is now being celebrated at The Hague. The contrast between the New China and the new Indonesia tells the story. In this sell-out, the State Department has had a heavy share." In Moscow, the *New Times* denounced The Hague accord as "imperialist aggression" and reported that the Indonesians were intensifying the struggle for independence. In the Security Council, Soviet Russia twice vetoed resolutions commending the work of the Indonesian Commission in resolving the dispute. On December 12, the Ukrainian delegate charged the round-table agreement with having restored Indonesia to "old colonial rule" and claimed that "wide democratic circles" were already resisting the agreement, involving the Dutch and Hatta governments in armed clashes. Moscow apparently referred to the disruptive militant activities of the remnant Tan Malaka forces. Interestingly, after the transfer of sovereignty, the PKI began to woo the Murba and attempted to form an alliance. In a resolution that obviously had no chance of adoption, the Soviet bloc called for the creation of a new United Nations Commission, composed of the eleven Security Council powers, with a view to reaching a new Indonesian settlement. But this proposal was defeated. Nobody—Indonesia least of all—was anxious to wreck The Hague pact and give Moscow a voice in a new settlement. On December

31, *Pravda* continued the campaign of vilification, reprinting a PKI broadside "unmasking" the "deal" among the Dutch, Americans, and the "Hatta clique." *Pravda* quoted the PKI as declaring that the transfer agreement fastened a yoke around the neck of the Indonesian people. But while Stalin had suffered a rout in Indonesia, the Communist bloc had closed the year in Asia on the credit side of the ledger: Chiang Kai-shek had fled to Taiwan on December 7.

In Indonesia, meanwhile, the Communists continued to develop the modified Left line that Indonesia had entered a "semicolonial" phase. They lost little time in exploiting the Irian dispute. As early as November 16, 1949, a member of the PKI Politburo who desired anonymity (probably Alimin) declared in an interview with P. I. Aneta, the Netherlands-Indonesian news agency, "somewhere outside the town of Jogjakarta," that Irian was proof that the Dutch had reneged on their promise of an "unconditional" grant of complete independence. The PKI leader said: "Because of this [Irian], the fight for freedom starts anew with the formation of the Republic of the United States of Indonesia."

On December 11, four days before the KNIP ratified the terms of the Hague settlement, the PKI Politburo drafted a program designed to overcome the "heavy burden" imposed on Indonesia under the terms of the agreement. The program sounded the call for "national unity against imperialism [the West]," and "national unity against . . . semi-imperialism [the neutralists]." In line with the two-camp doctrine, the Communists deplored neutralism as immoral; the PKI program urged the new Indonesia to "cooperate with the anti-imperialist nations," i.e., the Communist camp. The program also called for the elimination of the colonial aspects of the economy, but it was vague on details. It urged "democratization" of the government by guarantees of "unrestricted democratic rights," including freedom of the press, assembly, the right to demonstrate and to strike—rights already set forth in the R.U.S.I. constitution adopted at The Hague on October 27. As expected, the program also raised the delicate issue of rationalization of the armed forces. But the PKI tacked significantly. The Communists recognized that with the war of independence at an end, the days of armed irregulars had also drawn to a close. The PKI now directed its appeal to the regular republican army and proposed that the "anticolonial army units" be indivisibly incorporated into the new R.U.S.I. army, which was to include units of the old Netherlands East Indies army. The PKI, for the first time since Madiun, appeared as a champion of the republican regular armed forces that had crushed the Communists.

The Communist program attracted little attention and less response. Preparations were advanced for the momentous transfer of power over the archipelago.

On December 10, the first republican troops entered Djakarta to take over responsibility for law and order. Four days later, at Jogjakarta, after a heated debate, the republican parliament ratified The Hague accord by a vote of 226 to 62, with 31 abstentions. The Masjumi and PNI backed The Hague agreement; Sjahrir's Socialists abstained. The extreme Left, composed of Communists and intransigent radicals, voted against the settlement. The dissent emanating from the Left-wing splinter groups was equally loud. The Murba denounced the transfer as "the fruit of a compromise policy."

That night, representatives of the republic and the fifteen Dutch-created federalist states signed the new constitution of the R.U.S.I., which incorporated twenty-six basic rights and was drafted largely at The Hague conference. Article 33 of the bill of rights—if enforced—provided a simple check on political extremism. It stated: "No provision of this section may be interpreted as implying for any public authority, group, or person any right to engage in any activity or perform any act aiming at the destruction of any right and freedom set forth herein."

On December 16, a National Preparatory Committee composed of republican and federalist delegates unanimously elected Sukarno the first President of the new state. Four days later, the first cabinet of the R.U.S.I. was formed. The composition of the new government had a familiar ring. Hatta held the portfolios of Premier and Foreign Minister (Sjahrir had refused the latter post); the Sultan of Jogjakarta was Minister of Defense; Sjafruddin, Minister of Finance. Three federalists were in the cabinet. The government issued a seven-point program. Point Six called for a "peaceful solution of the Irian problem within one year."

The moment was at hand for the transfer of power to Indonesia. On December 27, 1949, an overcast, drizzly day, Indonesia emerged from the fires of political revolution as an independent sovereign state. The Dutch tricolor was lowered at Djakarta and the Indonesian red-and-white flag raised. A relatively small crowd, perhaps fewer than 10,000 of the city's more than 2 million people, witnessed the historic moment. Djakarta had a ghostly appearance. Streets were empty, shops closed. Uncertain about the future, the Dutch, Indo-European, and Chinese minorities that dominated the life of the city locked their doors and drew their shutters. The delegates of fifteen nations attended the transfer ceremonies; the Soviet bloc was conspicuously absent. The following day Djakarta stirred. Sukarno arrived from Jogjakarta; cheering Indonesians mobbed the 4-mile route between the airfield and the palace. It was his first appearance at Djakarta since 1946. Sukarno received a thunderous ovation. The transfer had been completed without incident. By the end of the week, Djakarta bustled with activity. The minority groups, relieved by the absence of violence, were elated; the Indonesians jubilant. Indonesia was free.

But the Communist view of these events differs. The Fifth Plenum of the Central Committee of the PKI, held at Djakarta in July, 1957, averred that the round-table agreement fixed Indonesia's status as semicolonial, that the so-called transfer of sovereignty was aimed at creating the illusion among the Indonesian people that Indonesia had been granted complete independence, but that in fact the Hatta government restored Dutch imperialist power over Indonesia's economy.

11

The Chinese Question

The role of Indonesia's 3 million Chinese[1] in the turbulent years before independence bears indirectly on the development of the Communist movement and requires elaboration. During the 1940's, the Chinese minority was wracked by fear. Tension between the Indonesians and Chinese was largely generated by religious, economic, nationalist, and, to some degree, racial factors. During the Japanese occupation and the Indonesian revolution, these tensions intensified.

Japan had pursued an ambivalent policy toward the overseas Chinese in Indonesia, assiduously cultivating a Wang Ching Wei movement on the one hand and encouraging anti-Chinese sentiment on the other. The Japanese considered the Chinese largely as an Allied fifth column and treated them accordingly. When the Japanese capitulated and the republic was proclaimed, the Indonesians on the other hand adopted a conciliatory attitude toward the Chinese. A Chinese flag outside a dwelling assured its occupants of protection.[2] China, of course, had emerged from the war a victorious power and Indonesia was in need of support from abroad; moreover, many Indonesians believed that the Allies intended to prosecute both the Japanese and their Indonesian collaborators for war crimes.

But with the arrival of the Allies, tension between the Indonesians and Chinese flared up once more. The British failure to arrest "collaborating nationalists" and disarm the Japanese-sponsored Indonesian military organizations emboldened Indonesian extremists. As clashes erupted, first between the Indonesians and the British, then between the Indonesians and the Dutch, the Chinese found themselves in a no man's land between the contending factions. As the Indonesians withdrew before the superior arms of the foreigner, armed bands often relieved their frustration by exacting revenge on the unarmed foreigner in their midst—the Chinese. The republic deplored these excesses, but it was not until the initialing of Linggadjati that terrorism against the Chinese abated. No sooner had the tension eased, however, than the first Dutch military action generated new anti-Chinese outbursts. In forward areas, murder, arson, and looting in Chinese districts preceded the Dutch thrust into the republican interior. Once again, anti-Chinese feeling subsided when a cease-fire was effected. Thus, in a conflict between Indonesians and a third party, it appeared that the Chinese were likely to suffer grievously —an assessment confirmed at Madiun.

The Communist rebellion was a family affair in which Indonesians of Chinese racial origin were to be found on both sides. The Chinese emerged relatively unscathed. The Federation of Chinese Associations (Chung Hua Tsung Hui), the most powerful of the Chinese organizations, was committed to the republic. The Federation considered Madiun part of the broad Communist strategy for Asia and therefore an extension of the Chinese civil war. The PKI hierarchy included many well-known Chinese-Indonesians of *peranakan* and *totok** origin, including Tan Ling Djie and Oey Gee Hwat. It is not inconceivable that, like their comrades in Malaya, they considered the 1948 Communist disorders in Southeast Asia a diversionary action in support of Mao's mainland offensive. But, significantly, in this internecine conflict, the Chinese emerged relatively unscathed.

Perhaps the most difficult period of the adjustment for the Chinese came during the Dutch occupation of the whole of Java the following year, when the Chinese were subjected to pressure from the Dutch within the towns to cooperate, and pressure from the guerrillas without not to do so. The Indonesians felt that most Chinese were inclined toward collaboration, that they traditionally had a closer affinity with Europeans than Indonesians. A leaflet, found in a letter box of the Federation in occupied Jogjakarta on February 4, 1949, reflected the anti-Chinese sentiment of the period: "We declare hostility against your race. Though you pretend to be neutral, you idolize the Dutch dogs, who shall certainly be driven from Indonesia before long. . . . Then we shall clear you from our sacred Fatherland. Coward race, learn

* Local born and foreign born, respectively.

to swim so you may escape to your country in the northern seas."

Relations between the Indonesians and Chinese were further roiled that year by Mao's triumph on the mainland. The overwhelming majority of Chinese in Indonesia were apolitical. Motivated by fear, opportunism, or honest conviction, they were inclined to accept Peking and protect family and trade connections with the mainland. They viewed Communist ascendancy in China with misgivings, but were inwardly relieved that the protracted civil war had come to an end. A united, powerful China, many reasoned, would protect overseas Chinese interests; Communist ideology was not at issue. To the small hard-core Communist faction in Indonesia, Mao's victory presaged a Communist sweep in Asia. This group reasoned that membership in the PKI served the interests of "two motherlands." Later, many young Chinese subscribed to this theory, entered the PKI, and entrenched themselves within the Party apparatus. There was yet a third faction in the Chinese community. Close to the Sjahrir Socialists, this group felt that the future of Indonesia's Chinese lay with the new Indonesia, with assimilation. They desired to be done with both Nationalist and Communist interference from overseas; in particular, they felt it suicidal for overseas Chinese to propagate Communism, since the Chinese middle classes would be among the first victims of an Indonesian social and economic revolution.

On October 10, 1949, the Double Ten anniversary of the Wuchang uprising that had influenced the growth of Indonesian nationalism in 1911, these currents collided. In the still Dutch-occupied urban areas, where the Communist flag was prohibited,* the Chinese protested by flying no flag on this Chinese holiday. This silent protest was indicative of the direction toward which most Chinese leaned. In liberated Jogjakarta, the Nationalist Consul, New Shiu Chung, gave a reception at which locally recruited Chinese artists declined to perform unless the Kuomintang colors were replaced by the Communist flag. A compromise was reached: Only the red-and-white Indonesian flag would be displayed. The protest was not lost on Sukarno, who, appearing in mufti for the first time since 1945, attended the reception. Thus, on the eve of independence, Indonesia was increasingly troubled by the question of the future of the Chinese minority, a question, as we shall observe later, complicated by the issue of double citizenship. As *Pedoman*, the Socialist daily, observed that October: "Not until now has the Chinese Revolution become a problem."

* The Netherlands recognized Peking on March 27, 1950.

And, as if to dramatize the possibilities, the Cominform journal on October 7, 1949, said:

> Unquestionably, the victory of the Chinese Revolution will inspire the peoples of the colonial and dependent countries to intensify the national liberation struggle. . . . Indonesia . . . and other countries of the East—defined by Stalin as the heavy reserves and the main hinterland of world imperialism—have either already become centers of struggle for their freedom and national independence or have matured as reserves of the revolution. The People's Republic of China will be their loyal friend and reliable bulwark in the struggle against imperialism.

12

Crossroad

The new Indonesia was almost immediately engulfed by armed disturbances, disorders that provided the Communists with a breathing spell in which to collect their dispersed forces and reorganize the Party's high command for the postindependence struggle for power. Independence had removed a major roadblock from their path to power. Now a more formidable barrier appeared on the horizon: the determination of Indonesia's leadership to maintain a genuinely independent Indonesia.

Within a month after the transfer of sovereignty, Captain Westerling reappeared at the head of a patch-quilt force that included demobilized Dutch colonial soldiers who felt they had no future in an independent Indonesia, Darul Islam elements anxious to exploit unrest in the new state, and other malcontents. With fewer than 2,000 men Westerling seized Bandung. The Dutch were stunned, then appalled, by Westerling's escapade and denounced the conduct of "ambitious and irresponsible elements" who were irreparably damaging relations with the new Indonesia. The Dutch army forced Westerling to yield Bandung and flee Indonesia. Later it developed that the Bandung adventure was the prelude in an elaborate plot to kidnap the cabinet on January 26 and seize power.

The intransigent radicals of the revolution—now the ultranationalists of free Indonesia—their nationalist thirst unquenched by the transfer of power, together with the Communists, still pursuing a Left strategy, fanned the Westerling incident to incite anti-Dutch and anti-Western sentiment. New disorders encouraged the extremists. Small groups of former Dutch colonial troops raised revolts against the new government on Sulawesi and Ambon, where a "Republic of the South Moluccas" was proclaimed.

The postindependence wave of disorders intensified the popular demand for the dissolution of the R.U.S.I. Most Indonesians felt that federalization was the price of sovereignty. The overwhelming sentiment in Indonesia was for the re-creation of a unitarian republic as envisioned at the outbreak of the revolution in 1945: a return to '45. There was little doubt, viewed dispassionately, that the federal structure of the R.U.S.I., embodying a bicameral legislature and patterned on a judicious blending of the attributes of the parliamentary and presidential systems, was ideally suited to the far-flung islands, each with a different culture, language, history, and economy, but sharing the same intense desire for unity through diversity.

Federalism, however, as observed earlier, was identified with the postwar Dutch strategy of Balkanizing the archipelago: a crude attempt to divide and rule. What the Indonesians failed to appreciate in the passion of the period was that the Dutch had not created the conditions for federalism but had simply sought to exploit the insular make-up of Indonesia to retain some semblance of "indirect" rule. Indeed, the postwar Dutch policy of federalism contrasted sharply with the prewar Dutch policy of imposing by arms a highly centralized government on the diverse islands. But federalism bore a "Made in Holland" imprint and was in disrepute. The R.U.S.I. was unable and unwilling to withstand the surge for a unitarian republic. The fifteen Dutch-installed states of the R.U.S.I. crumbled like tenpins, and authority was transferred either to the R.U.S.I. at Djakarta or the sixteenth "state," the original republic, at Jogjakarta. On August 15, 1950, Sukarno formally dissolved the federation and proclaimed a new Indonesian republic. The revolution had triumphed; the proclamation of independence had been fulfilled—except for the inclusion of West Irian into the republic, and that was due by the end of the year.

The armed disorders and the demise of the R.U.S.I. occurred as the PKI, which strongly favored a unitarian state, underwent a reorganization. In February, Alimin, who had assumed the chairmanship of the Politburo, the position formerly occupied by Musso, arrived at Djakarta. Alimin remained in seclusion, still uncertain about the government's policy toward the PKI despite official assurances given on February 4, 1950, that "the Communist Party is not forbidden—in principle, Indonesia is a democratic state in which all parties may function, including the Communists, providing they observe law and order," [1] the Sjahrir policy of 1945.

The PKI, its hierarchy fragmented, was reduced to a few thousand stalwarts, a seasoned core that had survived Madiun and the second Dutch military action. Alimin's strategy was to abandon the policy of a mass movement and rebuild the Party on a narrow base in defiance of Musso's New Road. Alimin reverted to pre-Musso tactics. Seeking to minimize the presence of the PKI in independent Indonesia, he concentrated on the development of labor, youth, and women's fronts. He also sought to maintain the fiction of the old Socialist and Labor parties. But he had not established complete control over the Party; his leadership was contested by young Turks. Thus, while Alimin was proceeding cautiously, the SOBSI embarked on an aggressive labor offensive attuned to the prevailing Left strategy emanating from Moscow. The SOBSI campaign was directed by Njono, a young firebrand who had emerged as the successor to the late Harjono.

The situation within Indonesia was ripe for militant labor agitation. During the revolution the workers had been led to believe that independence meant utopia. In the colonial period the labor movement had been shackled. Independence lifted the lid on the boiling labor cauldron; the contents bubbled over. In the first month of independence there were seventeen major strikes. The next month there were twice as many. Njono, in the field with the only organized labor federation, maneuvered to exploit the prevailing sentiment. The government did not consider the first strike wave a threat; indeed, there was satisfaction in some quarters that foreign economic influence was being effectively neutralized. True, the West might control the new nation's sources of capital and technical know-how, but Indonesia controlled labor. Under Njono's leadership, however, labor unrest assumed alarming proportions—even for the government. By mid-August, Indonesia's seaports and estates were semiparalyzed. By December 31, almost 8 million man-hours had been dissipated in strike actions, and the resultant loss of production and foreign exchange was considerable. The economic strength of Indonesia was being sapped. The government realized that the Communists were deliberately wrecking the economy. Hatta appealed to the workers in March to avoid becoming "the tool of provocateurs seeking chaos and disorder." He said that there was nothing so dangerous after independence as the misuse of authority, and that the people had not been fighting and making sacrifices for forty years for that. But as the labor crisis deepened, the R.U.S.I. displayed weakness through inaction. To the Communists, the government seemed paralyzed. Then, on June 25, 1950, the SOBSI had a new and urgent incentive to sustain the labor crisis: war in

Korea. Indonesia's commodities had become strategic war materials; the strike actions multiplied.

Hatta, meanwhile, struggled not only with demands for constitutional changes, armed disorders, and labor unrest, but also with problems involving Moscow and Peking.

In line with the then-prevailing line, Russia and China pursued an unrelenting campaign of abuse toward a free Indonesia, describing the "Sukarno-Hatta clique" as "the running dogs of imperialism" and "the agents of American imperialism." Relations between Djakarta and the Communist bloc were further complicated by residual issues, such as the Suripno affair and Madiun. Nonetheless, the Russians made the best of an unpromising situation. On January 26, 1950, the Soviet Union recognized the R.U.S.I., and on February 21, Hatta dispatched a mission to Moscow headed by L. N. Palar, the Indonesian representative at the U.N., for the purpose of negotiating a diplomatic exchange. Surprisingly, the "Trotskyite" Yamin was included in the delegation. The mission arrived at Moscow on April 30, in time to witness a huge military parade in Red Square on May Day; in Indonesia that same day, the PKI organized a demonstration at which posters read: "Sukarno-Hatta: Parasites of the People." At the Kremlin, the Palar mission was icily received. It was obvious that the Russians were not interested in an exchange. Palar departed on May 8. Not until 1954, after the Kremlin had shifted to a Right strategy, did the Russians establish an embassy at Djakarta.

Hatta had gambled that by establishing friendly relations with Russia, domestic Communist opposition would ease. Palar implied as much on April 18, when he told newsmen that Soviet recognition of the R.U.S.I. had already lessened the antagonism of the Communists toward the government. The establishment of a Russian embassy at Djakarta, he said, would "improve things further." It was wishful thinking. Communist pressure on Djakarta had not eased; on the contrary.

As for China, Djakarta's policy had been foreshadowed by the action of the Dutch the month before in recognizing the Chinese People's Republic. On February 4, Hatta announced that Indonesia was prepared to recognize Peking provided the Chinese first recognized Indonesia, since Mao's regime had been established earlier. Peking consented three weeks later. Indonesia's headlong rush into relations with China was motivated, as was the case with Russia, largely by domestic considerations. Djakarta sought to steal the thunder of the Left and, in this instance, resolve tensions within the Chinese community as Alimin, on February 20, launched a drive for a "democratic, progressive front" whose common denominator was recognition of Peking. The Left line, Peking's diatribes against Sukarno, and Moscow's reluctance to open an embassy at Djakarta notwithstanding, the Chinese moved swiftly to implement the Hatta-Chou accord. No doubt Peking was motivated by a desire to give support and direction to the Chinese community. The first Chinese ambassador, accompanied by a staff of sixty-four, including personal servants, arrived in August. Peking's choice of envoy shocked Djakarta. He was Wang Jen-shu, a former Medan school teacher and member of the PKI who had been expelled by the Dutch for Communist activities. His return to Indonesia as a high official of the Chinese government disturbed many Indonesians; it was reminiscent of the return of prewar Japanese to Indonesia as members of the invading Imperial army in 1942. The ambassador and his staff dressed in drab uniforms and gave an impression of discipline and militarism that ran counter to Indonesia's mood. Although Wang spoke fluent Indonesian, he annoyed many Indonesians by insisting on speaking Chinese and employing an interpreter. Wang's appointment and behavior reflected poor judgment on the part of Peking.

It is doubtful if Indonesia seriously considered the profound effects of Chinese recognition. Thus in the rapid sweep of events following the transfer of sovereignty, Indonesia, intentionally or unintentionally, embarked on a course at variance with that of her neighbors. Indonesia was the only independent power in Southeast Asia with a *substantial* Chinese minority to recognize the Peking regime.

But the most serious international problem confronting Hatta in 1950 was Korea. Early in the revolution, Sjahrir had fathered an independent foreign policy of nonalignment in the Cold War. The policy of neutralism was, he felt, a historical necessity, justified by Indonesia's past experience. The Indonesian national struggle had been against alien, i.e., Western, domination. As an independent nation, Indonesia, for psychological reasons, could not adjust to an alliance with the West. For that matter neither could Indonesia align herself with Soviet Russia, although it could be argued that Moscow had championed the cause of Indonesian independence for a generation and was engaged in a decisive struggle with Indonesia's former overlords. But Indonesia's democratic leadership was cognizant of Moscow's neocolonialism. Moreover, there was little doubt that the history of the national movement was also a register of the struggle between Communists and non-Communists for the leadership of a free Indonesia. Thus, viewed internally, nonalignment was designed to rob the extreme

Left of a Cold War issue; neutralism, it was hoped, would give Indonesia the domestic peace necessary to develop and draw abreast of Japan, China, and India, the three powers likely to contend for influence in Asia. Of course, the PKI's presence in the domestic arena would be difficult to reconcile with neutralism. The fact that Indonesians avoided discussing this aspect of the Communist problem was not only proof that the problem was recognized, but also that Indonesian intellectuals had failed to develop a reasonable answer to the dilemma of professing nonalignment abroad while permitting the PKI, a tentacle of Soviet power, to play an active role in Indonesia's internal affairs.

On June 25, Indonesian nonalignment was put to a test. The Communists invaded South Korea, a ward of the U.N. Would Indonesia act in concert with the non-Communist world to halt the aggressor? Apparently not. Five days later, the government declared in a communiqué:

> The so-called civil war in Korea is first and foremost [a] matter concerning the two big powers in the Cold War. . . . It would be premature and useless for the Indonesian Government . . . to take up a position. . . . Indonesia obtained its independence *de jure* six months ago and now faces great internal problems requiring solution at short notice. The Indonesian Government, though watching developments in Korea very closely and attentively, is of the opinion that its most urgent task at present is to cope with domestic problems.

The stress on "domestic problems" was an added incentive to the PKI to intensify unrest and keep Indonesia uncommitted in the Korean War. Indonesia's failure to endorse the U.N. course in Korea was disappointing. But Indonesia herself had been the victim of Dutch aggression in 1947 and 1948, and neither the United States nor the U.N. had rallied to fight the aggressor. U.N. intervention in Korea stirred Indonesian resentment and reaffirmed Djakarta's neutralist convictions. Yet Korea had implications beyond the East-West conflict. At stake was the right of either power bloc to employ aggressive tactics and war as instruments of national policy in a world of nuclear weapons. At stake was the right of either side to carry arms against the U.N.

These Cold War developments, however, were overshadowed by the crisis on Irian, a crisis that would profoundly influence the course of events in Indonesia and the development of the Communist movement. Irian was to destroy the working relationship between Sukarno and Hatta, bar cooperation between Sukarno and the rational moderates, and drive the President to the Left in search of extremist, radical nationalist, and Communist support. Unappreciated by many at the time was a significant Sukarno-Hatta exchange that set the stage for the rupture to come.

On January 2, 1950, at a palace reception, Sukarno publicly vowed: "Before the cock crows on the first sunrise of the new year, West Irian will be incorporated into independent Indonesia. . . . For this we must remain united."

The following day, Hatta returned from the Independence Day ceremonies at The Hague. Unaware of Sukarno's vow, Hatta was asked at the airport about Irian. Hatta replied: "There are many more important questions than Irian. . . . The problems of the people's welfare and prosperity are much more important at this time than the question of Irian." [2]

The lines were being imperceptively drawn. To complicate an already delicate situation, a third vested interest—Australia—also entered the picture.

During the Indonesian revolution, Australia had befriended the republic. Canberra's Labour government had viewed the collapse of Dutch anti-Japanese resistance in 1942 with disquiet. The Indonesians had welcomed the Japanese as liberators from Western domination. The Australian government conjectured that, given an independent Indonesia, the Indonesians would have something to fight for and that a sovereign Indonesia would constitute Australia's northern shield. But on the eve of Indonesian independence, the political climate in Australia radically altered. At home, the Liberal-Country parties coalition ousted the Labour government. Abroad, the Communists completed their conquest of China. These developments strengthened the hand of the conservatives, who favored the *status quo* in New Guinea, contending that an unstable Indonesia in control of West Irian would jeopardize Australian security. The new Minister for External Affairs, Percy Claude Spender, en route to Colombo for a Commonwealth conference, stopped over at Djakarta to review the Australian position. Spender arrived on January 3, and within two days had drained the store of good will that Australia had accumulated during the Indonesian revolution. At a news conference, Spender described New Guinea as "vital to our defense," splashed cold water on Indonesia's claim, and, baited by the nettled press, conceded that Australia was "anxious" to welcome former Dutch soldiers who wanted to settle in Australia, but implied that the invitation did not extend to Eurasians and Indonesians. "There can be no compromise with Australia's so-called 'white policy,'" Spender said, "because of the very economic nature of that policy." Actually, the conservatives executed that policy with greater awareness of human relations than the Labour government had done. In any event, his remarks produced an instantaneous adverse reaction.

The PNI expressed "astonishment" at Australia's position and issued a statement emphasizing that Indonesia's claim to West Irian was not based on race but on the fact that the disputed area was formerly part of the Netherlands East Indies: "We have not claimed the Australian half of Irian, British Borneo, Portuguese Timor, or Malaya, all of which are racially one." The PNI warned that there would be no peace in the archipelago until the Dutch transferred their power over Irian. The feeling was that the PNI spoke for Sukarno. The intransigent radicals reacted more sharply. Yamin, returning to prominence, laid claim on January 30 to the whole of the archipelago and urged the government to initiate talks with Australia on the question of East Irian as well as with the Dutch on the problem of West Irian. Yamin envisioned—apparently under Indonesian control—a powerful Malayasian federation embracing Indonesia, Malaya, the Philippines and the residual European holdings in the archipelago (Portuguese Timor, British North Borneo, etc.). Such a union, he argued, would neutralize the influence of India, China, and Japan and give the Malayasian peoples a stronger voice in international affairs. Thereafter, Yamin became a leading exponent of Indonesian expansionism.

The developing friction between Australia and Indonesia coincided with the first conference of the newly established Netherlands-Indonesian Union, a loose arrangement that had been set up under the Hague accord. The conference proceeded amicably. "It appears that the issue of Irian is the only one that causes friction," Hatta said. "The sooner the issue is removed from the agenda, the closer and the stronger will be the basis of cooperation between both nations." [3] Both parties agreed to continue to seek a solution. It was felt at Djakarta that the Dutch, in view of their economic position in Indonesia, would surely relinquish the jungle territory. The logic of history dictated that one day Indonesia would control West Irian, the last Dutch possession in the archipelago.

In the months that followed, Sukarno campaigned vigorously for Irian. On August 17, 1950, two days after the re-formation of the unitarian Republic of Indonesia, Sukarno made an impassioned public plea for the disputed area: "Irian is not a trifling question. . . . Part of our country is still colonized by the Dutch. . . . Once again I declare: We will not stop fighting, we will continue fighting, we will keep on fighting whatever may come, until Irian has been returned to our fold." Because the Moluccas, west of Irian, were then the center of disturbances by pro-Dutch elements,

Sukarno and many Indonesians believed that Indonesia would not be secure as long as the Dutch retained a potentially strong base in the archipelago.

At this juncture, the new unitarian republic was proclaimed. Hatta, who had held the Premiership since Renville, stepped aside. The desire in Djakarta was to start anew. On August 22, Sukarno asked Natsir, as the chairman of the Masjumi, the largest party, to form a government. Fifteen days later, Natsir succeeded in framing a coalition dominated by an informal Masjumi-PSI alliance. It was expected that the Masjumi would neutralize the appeal of the extremist Darul Islam while the Sjahrir Socialists neutralized the Left. The strategy had three flaws: Natsir's reformist interpretation of Islam was suspect among orthodox religious scholars; Sjahrir's party lacked a mass following and was clearly at a disadvantage in combating Communist demagoguery with appeals for reason and moderation; and, lastly, the PNI, was excluded from the club. The PNI had declined to participate in the cabinet because it was "too socialist-minded"; since most Indonesian parties are basically "socialist," the PNI reference was obviously to Sjahrir's influence. The seemingly endless struggle in Indonesia between Sjahrir's democratic socialism and Sukarno's authoritarianism—submerged during the struggle against the Dutch in 1947, the Communists in 1948, and the Dutch again in 1949—was coming to the surface in an independent Indonesia.

Sjahrir had expected PNI influence to wane after independence. He reasoned that the Masjumi was held together by the ideology of Islam, the Socialists by an economic objective. The *raison d'être* of the PNI—independence—had been fulfilled. But Sjahrir misjudged the latent xenophobic content in Indonesian nationalism. As long as Indonesia remained a have-not power nursing grievances against the colonial past, nationalism would offer a broad emotional appeal, particularly against the West and the Chinese, whose commercial presence in Indonesia was manifest. Then there was Irian. And finally, being the country's largest secular party, the PNI was to assume the role of defender of the secular republic against proponents of an Islamic state.

The most urgent problems inherited by Natsir were labor unrest and Irian. In September, when Natsir came to power, the situation in the seaports was chaotic. Even Alimin shed his caution; the PKI, apparently looking for an issue, announced plans to commemorate the "Madiun provocation" by the reburial of the eleven Communist leaders executed near Soerakarta. The government prohibited their disinterment. The PKI replied by calling for demonstrations on November 19, 1950, to protest the ban. That morning, determined to forestall incidents, Natsir authorized the army to detain persons suspected of inciting disorders for political reasons. The military raided the PKI headquarters at Djakarta; *Bintang Merah* (*Red Star*), the Party's theorectical journal, was confiscated. A thirty-hour curfew was imposed on the capital. Raids were conducted at Medan, Surabaya, and Semarang. In Central Java and North Sumatra, leaders of the SARBUPRI (Estate Workers Union), the largest group within the SOBSI, were arrested. Natsir's brisk action served notice on the Communists that the cabinet was prepared to take measures against any group that sought to undermine governmental authority. The impetus of the strike wave was momentarily arrested.

But while Natsir was responding to the Communist challenge, he was being engulfed by the issue of Irian, an issue that was to provide the Communists with a strong weapon in bringing about the weakening of an independent Indonesia.

Negotiations with the Dutch had collapsed. In Holland as well, Irian had become an emotional, irrational issue. Dutch intransigence on Irian coincided with a hardening of the Australian position. Canberra's view was conditioned by Communist aggression in Korea and Tibet, Communist consolidation on the Chinese mainland, and Communist unrest in Malaya and Indonesia. Spender, in The Hague, alluded to Yamin's expansionist claims and told newsmen that if the Indonesian claim to West Irian was conceded, "It would be only a matter of time, no matter how genuine the assurances to the contrary, when the claim will be pushed further so as to include the trust territory of Australian New Guinea." But at the heart of the Australian position, Spender implied, was Communist ascendancy on the Asian mainland and the PKI revival in Indonesia: "Experience has shown Australia how strategically vital to Australian defense is the maintenance of New Guinea. One cannot disregard the ever-increasing Communist pressure in Asia. Communism has not yet gained a foothold in Australian New Guinea. Australia is determined in so far as it can to ensure that it will not." [4] Seen in this light, Natsir's anti-Communist razzia of September may have been motivated in part by a desire to demonstrate to Australia that Indonesia was determined to resist Communist subversion. The United States at this time was, of course, pressed by all parties to the dispute. Washington struck a neutralist posture, thereby offending everyone, particularly the Indonesians who felt neutralism endorsed the *status quo*. When the negotiations between Indonesia and the Dutch collapsed, the United States earned the displeasure of The

Hague by dispatching a note to both sides on January 8 urging a resumption of talks. The Communists, of course, charged that the Dutch and Australians were acting as agents of the United States; in December, *Sovetskii flot* (*Red Fleet*), the Soviet naval journal, alleged that the United States desired a naval base at Hollandia, the Irian beachhead of World War II.

On December 11, in a last-minute appeal to resolve the dispute amicably, the republic offered the Dutch "special" economic rights in Irian in exchange for the territory. It was a generous offer. The Dutch rejected it on the specious grounds that the Papuans must have "the right of self-determination." To Indonesians, this smacked of the white man's burden. On December 27, the day set by The Hague agreement for a final disposition of Irian, talks were suspended.

Natsir was under pressure to take a stand. Sukarno not only had staked his prestige on the issue, but in August had proclaimed Indonesia's freedom of action if the Dutch did not surrender Irian. The atmosphere in Djakarta was charged. Ultranationalist groups, joined by the Communists, staged rallies and demonstrations in support of Irian. On December 28, the government warned that it would not countenance "threats, instigations, and intimidations" in the campaign for Irian. But on December 31, Sukarno delivered a bitter speech hinting violence and drastic action against the Dutch if The Hague did not yield. Obviously, the government was speaking with two voices. A showdown between Sukarno and the cabinet was in the offing.

On January 5, at a cabinet meeting attended by Sukarno and Hatta, Sukarno delivered a moving plea for stern action against the Dutch. If necessary, Sukarno said, the republic should confiscate Dutch properties and expel the Dutch from Indonesia. Sukarno asked for a vote of confidence. Natsir trembled with anger. He asserted that he had not become Premier to make war, that Sukarno did not understand the implications of his request. Natsir said he prayed to God never again to see men, women, and children—Dutch or others—confined in concentration camps. The reference to the Japanese occupation hit home. Sukarno flushed. Natsir declared: "I will hear no more." The cabinet rejected Sukarno's demand; only two ministers supported Sukarno, both aged nationalist leaders—Wongsonegoro, Minister of Justice, and Pandji Suroso, Minister of Labor.

The breach between Sukarno and Natsir was never mended. Natsir realized that Sukarno was obsessed by Irian, and Sukarno, on the other hand, thereafter considered Natsir as "Sjahrir-minded." As a consequence of the cabinet showdown, the government curbed Sukarno's speech-making and sought to relegate him to the role of a figurehead, a part he was emotionally incapable of playing. In the 210-member parliament,* formed by a merger of the KNIP and the parliaments of the former Dutch-sponsored federal states, Natsir was also challenged on Irian. In response, on January 3, he set a tone of responsibility and moderation. He committed Indonesia to fight for the national claim on Irian in a peaceful way. Appealing to Dutch reason, Natsir cautioned The Hague that the failure to settle Irian would inevitably lead to a reappraisal of Indo-Dutch relations, implying a threat to Dutch commercial interests in Indonesia. The opposition PNI and PKI were dissatisfied by Natsir's "gradualism." The PNI submitted a motion demanding annulment of the Netherlands-Indonesian Union. The government succeeded in avoiding defeat, but more than half of the house abstained. The Communists joined the PNI in supporting the motion, a hint of things to come. The Communists exploited Irian in the interest of increasing Indonesian-Western friction. But the Communists were hampered by adherence to the two-camp doctrine and the unremitting attacks of Moscow and Peking on the "Sukarno-Hatta clique."

The rising tension over Irian in early 1951 served to obscure the intense struggle for power taking place within the PKI between the aging Alimin and the youthful Aidit.

When Alimin assumed the direction of the Politburo in 1949, filling the vacuum left by the death of Musso, he did so largely by default and on the basis of seniority. Amir and Sardjono were also dead; Setiadjit had disappeared and was probably dead; the youthful "Bolshevik" leaders like Aidit were missing. But among the PKI's younger elements, Alimin—admittedly the titular leader of the Party and respected by the rank and file—was mistrusted. When Musso returned from Moscow, he had demoted and replaced Alimin, apparently on Stalin's orders. Alimin's name was synonymous with the failure of the 1926 revolt. Although there was no proof, it was whispered that Alimin opposed the 1948 *Putsch*. In his interviews late in 1949, Alimin had implied criticism of Musso's leadership and, in the process, cast doubt on the infallibility of Stalin. Alimin was also an admirer of Mao Tse-tung, a "Yenan man." Worse, Alimin had sought to soften the Party's

---

* By June 3, 1953, the divisions in the unelected parliament, had become reasonably stable: Masjumi, forty seats; PNI, thirty-eight; PIR, seventeen; PSI, fifteen; PKI, sixteen; Democrats (Federalists), thirteen; PRN (a minor nationalist group), eight; Catholic Party, nine; NU, eight; Labor Party (non-Communist), six; PSII, four; Parkindo (Protestant), five; Parindra (a minor nationalist group), five; Murba, four; SOBSI, three; SKI (a minor nationalist group), five; BTI, three; Progressive Faction (crypto-PKI), eight; Independents, sixteen.

strident Left strategy. For example, his first lieutenant, Tan Ling Djie, was actively trying to revive the Socialist Party in defiance of Musso's New Road resolution demanding that all Marxist-Leninist parties fuse with the PKI. Alimin also disagreed with Njono over the handling of the strikes. The younger elements in control of SOBSI chided Alimin for "deterioration of ideology." In 1950, *Bintang Merah*, controlled by the youth faction, accused Alimin of stifling "criticism and self-criticism" within the Party. The leadership struggle within the PKI was sharpened by the relatively rapid recovery made by the Communists in the first year of independence. On December 27, 1949, the remnant Party leadership was in hiding, the Party itself disorganized. Although the PKI later claimed 7,910 members, it was doubtful if it had half that many.

With independence, SOBSI, which by its own admission had fewer than 200,000 members, became the largest Communist front. But within a year after the transfer of sovereignty, its ranks swelled to more than 1 million, due largely to its militancy and the disappointment of the workers that their living conditions had not improved overnight. While Njono energetically rebuilt SOBSI, Wikana, the former Pesindo and Illegal-PKI youth leader, reconstructed a youth front, the Pemuda Rakjat (People's Youth). The new organization was affiliated with the World Federation of Democratic Youth (WFDY), whose first vice president was Alexander N. Shelepin. Shelepin was to succeed General Ivan A. Serov, the man who put down the Hungarian rebellion, as head of the Soviet security forces. There were other signs of a Communist revival. Between 1950 and 1951, the circulation of *Bintang Merah* climbed from 3,000, to 10,000. On February 1, 1951, the PKI also acquired control over the Chinese-owned *Harian Rakjat (People's Daily)* and converted it into a Party paper under the editorship of Siauw Giok Tjhan and Go Hauw Gie, both of Chinese origin.[5]

It was becoming increasingly obvious that the PKI's coffers were bulging and that local Chinese were playing an important role in Party affairs. The Chinese had become a primary source of funds and technical know-how for the PKI. Chinese clerks handled the Party's bookkeeping and other adminstrative chores. As Mao consolidated his victory in China, the Chinese community in Indonesia contributed lavishly to the PKI: some voluntarily out of conviction, or as insurance against the future, or to protect relatives on the distant mainland; others, out of fear of reprisals or to protect business interests in Indonesia. Invariably, Indonesian workers in Chinese employ were enrolled in SOBSI unions. Naturally, the Chinese were aware that in an Indonesian social or economic revolution the Chinese, the backbone of the Indonesian middle class, would suffer. But confronted with the reality of a Communist China and the haunting specter of a Communist Indonesia, cognizant of the hostility of most Indonesians toward them, the Chinese had little choice but to contribute to the PKI. After all, had not Djakarta encouraged Peking's recognition?

Whatever the case, the Communists were making a rapid recovery. In 1950, Aidit had returned to Indonesia in the company of M. H. Lukman, who, like Aidit, was Sumatra-born. Lukman was a second-generation Communist with a Left-deviationist background. His father, a *hadji*, had been active in the Sarekat Islam and, later, the Sarekat Rakjat. In 1929, the Dutch exiled the Lukmans to West Irian, where the father was classified as "irreconcilable." In 1938, Lukman bid his parents farewell and departed for Java, where he was variously employed and subjected to PID surveillance. In 1942, he joined the Menteng 31 student group, met Aidit, and participated in the Sukarno Hatta kidnapping. During the *bersiap* period he was imprisoned by the Japanese for terrorist activities—as was Aidit—but escaped. For a brief period he was identified with Jussuf. When the Party denounced Jussuf as a Left deviationist, Lukman returned to the "correct" path under Sardjono's guidance. In 1948, Sardjono named him a candidate member of the Central Committee; when Musso reorganized the Party, Lukman became a member of the Committee.

Lukman had fled abroad with Aidit at the time of Madiun. The consensus was that both men had spent 1948–50 in the Soviet bloc. According to Aidit, however, they slipped out of Indonesia early in 1949, during the confusion of the second Dutch military action, and worked as kitchen helpers aboard a Chinese ship. "I left Indonesia," Aidit has said, "because I was eager to learn about the world." [6] In 1950, after visiting Vietnam, Singapore, "and other places," the pair re-entered Indonesia as stowaways on a Dutch vessel. Aidit was arrested by Indonesian authorities, and, "after a few days," Suwirjo, the PNI Mayor of Djakarta, intervened and ordered his release.

On January 7, 1951, the Party summoned a plenary session of the Central Committee at which Aidit thrust Alimin aside and assumed control of the Politburo. Lukman and Njoto in particular backed Aidit in his power play. With their assistance, Aidit "corrected the political and organizational mistakes made by the Central Committee." [7] Aidit's disclaimer notwithstanding, it is not inconceivable that he took over the direction of the Politburo from Alimin on Stalin's orders after a visit to Moscow. Perhaps, in view of the rising red star over China, Moscow wanted to ensure PKI fidelity by the appointment of a youthful, dedicated Stalinist. We can only speculate. But the Party has since called the Aidit-Alimin rivalry the victory of the proletarian ideology and policy over non-proletarian ideology and policy. Thus the Aidit faction was depicted as the champion of "proletarian ideology," that is, loyalty to Moscow, while Alimin was ostensibly "independent minded." Doubtless, another ingredient in the rivalry was the element of men honoring the rising rather than the setting sun. Still, Alimin was to attempt comebacks in 1956 and 1961; on both occasions, Khrushchev, like Stalin before him, was to back Aidit.

On assuming control, Aidit launched a program to strengthen the membership's ideological moorings. He encouraged "theoretical discussion" within the confines of Lenin's *gotong rojong* concept of "freedom of discussions, unity in action" and pruned Party ranks by mixing "internal democracy with criticism and self-criticism." Aidit's critics were given the choice between confession or expulsion. Tan Ling Djie, for example, was ordered to abandon his plan to revitalize the Socialist Party.

Under Aidit, the PKI also opened an intensive propaganda campaign to erase the stigma of treason acquired at Madiun. Aidit employed the "big lie" technique, enlarging on the theme emanating from Moscow that the Communists were "provoked" at Madiun by Sukarno and Hatta in league with American imperialism. The PKI issued a White Paper based on a series of articles appearing in *Red Star*, which presented the PKI as the victim of the "White terror."* Aidit, as Alimin before him, also worked to organize a united front. The PKI concentrated on joining forces with the Murba (whose influence was waning), the Sjahrir Socialists (now in the government), and radical Communist splinter groups like ACOMA,[8] particularly on issues such as Irian, Korea, Indochina, and the recognition of Peking. However, Aidit, like Alimin, made little headway; the PKI was mistrusted on the Left. Aidit, of course, was also aware of a community of interest with the PNI on specific issues. Both the PKI and PNI resented the "intellectualism" of Sjahrir's Socialists and feared the strength of Islam. Both the PKI and PNI favored extremist action on Irian, e.g., the wholesale liquidation of Dutch economic interests in the country. In Parliament, the PNI and PKI often joined forces. But the PKI was in no position to take advantage of the situation. The Communists were the voluntary captives of the Left strategy. Moscow continued to assail Sukarno and an independent Indonesia. So did the PKI. In a pamphlet written during this period, *Karl Marx's Struggle and Teachings*, Aidit said: "In Indonesia, too, there are treacherous imposters, people like Sjahrir, Tan Malaka, Darsono,

* The paper, entitled *Buku Putih Tentang Peristiwa Madiun* was issued by the PKI Central Committee in 1953, and withdrawn from circulation by order of the government that same year.

Sukarno, and Hatta. They are social-imperialists who claim to be socialists but who are really nothing less than cunning, rotten-to-the-core imperialist tools." * The PKI, loyal to Moscow, was always prepared to sacrifice itself on the altar of the international line.

Aidit's triumph over Alimin, in January, 1951, signaled an intensification of the SOBSI campaign of strikes and disorders. Open looting, encouraged by the Communists, converted Medan and Surabaya into nightmare ports. The murder of European planters on estates became as commonplace in Indonesia as it had been in Malaya, but amidst so many other crises, this received little public notice. The abetting of unrest in Indonesia by the Communists was not an isolated tactic. It was part of the broader campaign of disorders promoted by the Communists in the non-Communist world in support of the Chinese offensive in Korea. It would be a grave miscalculation to consider PKI activities in Indonesia as divorced from the mainstream of world affairs.

By early February, an estimated 500,000 estate workers were on strike. The Communist strategy was to paralyze the plantations at a time when the Korean war boom in raw materials was at a peak. After considerable vacillation, Natsir moved to restrain the Communists. He did so reluctantly. Natsir knew that it was not a question of rank-and-file workers being Communists; the majority were illiterate, unaware that they were expendable pawns in a bigger game.

On February 13, 1951, Natsir issued Military Decree No. 1, which prohibited strikes in "vital" industries. Virtually the entire economy was deemed "vital." Natsir also moved to curtail the activities of armed bands in the Merapi-Merbabu complex in Central Java, which the government believed had been converted into a training ground for Communist guerrillas. The next day Natsir sent the Sultan of Jogjakarta, now the Vice Premier, to the mountainous region to combat the disturbances. But the marauders continued their activities until late 1952, when the Communist line began to shift. Finally, on February 28, Natsir announced a ceiling of 4,000 a year on Chinese immigration. Indonesia was not inclined to provide the PKI with unlimited sources of revenue.

Thus, although Natsir resigned in March, primarily because of his showdown with Sukarno on Irian, the republic was beginning to react to the Communist challenge.

---

* In an interview with Pedoman on November 30, 1954, Aidit denied ever having attacked Sukarno. "I have gone through the 1950–51 Party statements, and I did not find a single statement saying that 'President Sukarno has sold out Indonesia, etc,'" Aidit said, whereupon Pedoman reprinted the above-quoted extract from *Karl Marx.*

13

The August Razzia

The removal of Natsir, the Moslem moderate and reformer, was clearly in the Communists' interest. It was also, coincidentally, in Sukarno's interest. It developed that Natsir's survival of his clash with Sukarno over Irian was short-lived as Sukarno maneuvered behind Natsir's back to induce the two opportunistic PIR ministers to resign and force the cabinet into crisis on March 20. But to the dismay of the Communists, Sukarno, in pressing for a new government responsive to his will, preferably a Nationalist-dominated coalition, on April 26 settled for a return to the old Masjumi-Nationalist formula. Dr. Sukiman, the leader of the Masjumi's conservative wing and an implacable foe of the Communists, emerged as Premier. The new coalition, which included six minor factions, excluded the Sjahrir Socialists. The government's composition, a curious mixture of conservative and radical nationalist opinion bound together by personal loyalty to Sukarno, was disconcerting. Inevitably, whenever loyalty to Sukarno was at issue, familiar faces linked with the PNI and Tan Malaka past turned up, in this instance, Subardjo as Foreign Minister and as a member of the Masjumi and Yamin as Justice Minister and unaffiliated independent. The army, influenced by Sjahrir's PSI, protested against Subardjo's and Yamin's presence in the government and was appeased by the appointment of an ineffectual defense minister, R. A. Sewaka of the PIR, which now held three cabinet portfolios.

At the outset, the cabinet was hobbled by the unpopularity of Sukiman, although he was the first Javanese Premier in a predominantly Javanese country. Sukiman's unpopularity, particularly in intellectual circles, stemmed from his conservatism, association with the Islamic proprietary class, and advocacy of close ties with the West. Yet his program was similar to that of the liberal Natsir. Sukiman called for continued clear and drastic measures to secure peace and order and, Sukarno's influence notwithstanding, urged a moderate policy of negotiation with the Dutch on Irian. Sukarno himself conceded on May 13 that on the whole, the government's program was similar to that of Natsir. But Sukarno, an astute tactician, having failed to secure support at home for extremist measures against the Dutch, was preparing to flirt with the United States on Irian. This was not perceived at Djakarta, despite Sukiman's known American bias. If anything, the "conservative" government displayed a "radical" bent.

In May, Sukiman was embroiled with the United States at the U.N., where Washington pressed for an embargo on the shipment of strategic war materials to China. As the world's leading rubber producer, Indonesia viewed the embargo with misgivings, Korea notwithstanding. "Indonesia," Subardjo declared, "should be permitted to sell her raw material to everyone, even to the devil." On May 18, the U.N. passed the embargo and Indonesia announced its compliance. Then, in June, the cabinet was shaken by Yamin, who released 950 political detainees, including former Tan Malaka adherents, without securing cabinet approval. His action caused a sensation, particularly the release of gang leaders such as Chaerul Saleh. Sukiman rode out the storm by accepting Yamin's resignation on June 15 and by dispatching Saleh to Switzerland as a "student."

The activities of the intransigent radicals in the cabinet, coupled by the spread of the Darul Islam movement into southern Sulawesi and Kalimantan, encouraged Aidit. In June, SOBSI, in defiance of the strike ban, launched new strikes tied to demands for Lebaran (Islamic New Year) bonuses. By the end of June, SOBSI had paralyzed Indonesia's airways, bus lines, shipping companies, sugar mills, oil installations, and estates. Significantly, the bulk of these enterprises were foreign-owned. Clearly, the PKI labor offensive had a threefold purpose: to fan Islamic and labor unrest, generate hostility toward foreign capital, and wreck the economy.

In July, as strikes and armed disturbances increased, the foreign policy of the Sukiman government moved in the direction of the United States. On July 25, the government announced that Indonesia would participate in the San Francisco conference on the Japanese peace treaty, which the Soviet bloc and Asian neutralists were boycotting. And relations between Djakarta and Peking cooled appreciably when Sukiman blocked the arrival of fifty additional members for the Chinese Embassy. Sukiman was convinced that the Embassy was promoting disorders through the PKI. Then, on August 5, a band of 150 armed men raided a police post at Tandjong Priok, Djakarta's port. Eleven persons were killed. In the ensuing action, several SOBSI leaders were arrested. The next day, at Bogor, south of Djakarta, a hand grenade was tossed into a crowd, wounding eighty-six persons. On August 8, the cabinet threatened to take action against groups disturbing the peace. The Left was unmoved. Two days later, the Communists announced plans to observe August 17 independently of the government. Sukiman responded by banning unauthorized public celebrations. But the PKI, already defying the government's strike ban, indicated that it would defy the cabinet's prohibition as well. Sukiman was alarmed. On August 11, he ordered the army and police to curb disorders in East Sumatra's estate belt. More than 600 persons, mostly members of the PKI, BTI, SARBUPRI, and SOBSI, were arrested. The Communists protested the government's "undemocratic" action. But the next day peace returned to troubled East Sumatra. Medan's authorities were impressed. The rapid restoration of law and order reflected in part traditional Indonesian respect for authority, especially among the Javanese who constituted the bulk of the East Sumatran estate workers. Sukiman was also impressed. On August 15, the government launched large-scale security raids in the capital. Fifteen members of parliament, mostly PKI members, were arrested; PKI and SOBSI headquarters were raided. Six high Communist officials in the Labor Ministry were placed in custody. The editors of the pro-Communist *Sin Po* were detained. The PKI panicked. Alimin sought sanctuary in the Chinese Embassy, deepening suspicions that the Chinese had a hand in the disorders, possibly as a diversionary action related to Korea. Aidit disappeared. Later, the PKI conceded that the August round-up

> was a heavy test for our Party, because this happened when the Politburo, elected on January 15, 1951, had been at work only six months in consolidating the Party, when the Party was not yet firmly related to the masses, especially to the peasant masses. . . . Some members . . . were panic-stricken at the outset of the August roundup, recalling the cruelties of the reactionaries in the "Madiun Affair," which they thought might be repeated in August.[1]

On August 16, a sixteenth member of parliament was arrested, the Communist deputy Sarwono. Three days later, the security raids reached into the Javanese hinterland. More than 200 persons were detained in Eastern Java, 50 at Madiun alone, and more than 50 in Western Java. Many were prominent pro-Peking Chinese, others were members of the PKI or SOBSI. By the end of August, the government held more than 2,000 political prisoners, including Pardede, Sidik Kertapati, K. Werdojo, Sakirman, Siauw Giok Tjan, Tan Ling Djie, Tjugito, Djaetun, Sarwono and, Muchfaruddin. "Our Party," Aidit later explained, "was compelled to work under emergency conditions [underground] for about one year."

On August 17, Sukarno backed Sukiman's play, declaring that the government was determined to destroy armed bands "with or without an ideology, whether Leftist or Rightist, whether 'red' [Communist] or 'green' [Islamic]." Government harassment of the extremist Left intensified. On November 12, the police again raided PKI headquarters in Jakarta. The next day, Go Hauw Gie, an editor of *Harian Rakjat*, was arrested. That same week, police in East Java detained several leaders of the SBG (Sugar Workers Union), a SOBSI affiliate. At Surabaya, the police banned an issue of the *New Times*, a Communist publication, featuring a cover photograph of Musso. By the end of the month, the number of detainees had reached 15,000, half as many as after Madiun.

The razzia also had the effect of temporarily stiffling Communist propaganda about Korea. The government curtailed the activities of the Indonesian World Peace Council, which was busy gathering 2 million signatures for the Stockholm peace petition. The Communists, of course, had actively supported the Communist war in Korea, establishing numerous fronts for the promotion of "Indonesian solidarity with the Korean people in the struggle against American imperialism." Indeed, for a time germ warfare was the dominant PKI propaganda theme. The Communist imagination was unrestrainedly fertile. As an example of the kind of propaganda disseminated among the credulous during the Korean conflict was the report in *Harian Rakjat* that

> ten thousand *glatik* paddy-birds [a bird as common as the sparrow] have been sent to Holland by the steamer "Tarakan." . . . It is striking the way Europe is interested in these birds. . . . Some people believe that the glatik birds have some connection with U.S. germ warfare. Some time ago it was reported that American laboratories in West Germany were cultivating germs for hostile purposes. It is also known that in the Korean War the Americans use glatik birds to spread infectious germs. Some scientists think if these diseased, germ-bearing birds are set free, they will fly back to their places of origin in the tropics. The government should give this matter due attention! [2]

Fantastic? Perhaps. But the fact that the Communists employ such propaganda attests to the nature of the society in which they expected such patently absurd charges to find a mark.

Sukiman's firmness against the irresponsible but not irrational PKI had an electrifying impact on the country. With Aidit and Alimin in hiding, and second- and third-rank Communists imprisoned, the strike wave ebbed. However, the favorable impact of the government's security sweep on Indonesia's Chinese community had not been foreseen. The burst of enthusiasm for the People's Republic had waned among the Chinese. What had promised to be a new order in China was simply the old order with a new label; the mainland was as oppressed as ever. China's participation in the Korean War also dampened the ardor of overseas Chinese for Peking, as did Sukiman's cold war against the Chinese Embassy. Many Chinese now shifted to a "third-force" position and moved to disengage themselves from Communist influence. Sukiman's refusal to permit the Embassy to enlarge its staff was interpreted as a straw in the wind and was received with relief in Glodok, Djakarta's Chinese quarter. The Chinese shift was reflected on May Day, 1952, when scarcely any Chinese Communist flag was to be seen in Glodok. This was quite unlike May Day in the first year of Indonesian independence, when almost every Chinese building displayed the Communist banner. Now, portraits of Sun Yat-sen replaced those of Mao or Chiang in the windows of Chinese shops. The Chinese had slipped into nonalignment. In part, fear had helped to accelerate the shift. In the wake of the August razzia, Sukarno, speaking at Surabaya on November 10, 1951, chilled the Chinese with a warning that

> the difference between the poor and rich [in Indonesia] goes hand in hand with racial discrimination. The rich here are the foreigners, the rich here [are] of foreign nationality. The hatred for the rich, who have harmed the people, turns into a hatred for the foreigner, who has prejudiced the people's interests. Here [in Indonesia] social controversies can very easily become racial controversy. . . . Unfortunately . . . there are some elements among the above-mentioned groups [of foreigners] who always and continually propagate Communism or social revolution! They are not aware of the fact that, if a social revolution starts in this country, it will immediately become a racial revolution. And their own countrymen will be the first victims of the revolution. . . . They forget the Kudus affair some decades ago. They forget the tragedy of Tangerang, of Mauk, Kebumen, etc. They are playing with fire, which, if it spreads, will burn to coal the bodies of many of their countrymen in this country.

Although Sukarno did not identify the "foreign group" by name, his pointed references to past Chinese massacres were sufficiently clear. On November 13, *Keng Po*, the dispassionate, responsible Sino-Indonesian daily, felt impelled to "repudiate the general opinion in Indonesia that it is the Chinese who are behind Communist propaganda in this country. . . . The PKI has been in existence much longer than the Chinese Communist Party. It is a fact that the Communist ideology in Indonesia has come from Europe, not from China."

And *Sin Po*, significantly, in view of the tension that later developed between Djakarta and Peking in 1959–60, warned: "We should carefully read his [Sukarno's] speech and keep it deeply in mind."

Following the roundup, Sukiman instituted a series of emergency laws designed to stabilize labor. On September 17, the government rescinded Natsir's ban on strikes, which had been widely criticized as undemocratic, and promulgated Emergency Law No. 16, which prescribed a system of compulsory mediation and arbitration for the settlement of labor disputes. On November 18, the government issued Information Regulation No. 264, prohibiting government workers from criticizing the government, a ruling aimed at neutralizing SOBSI influence in civil-service unions.

Despite the success of the August razzia, Sukiman's mishandling of the security sweep, in which even anti-Communist critics of the government were arrested, coupled by the temporary arbitrary detention of hundreds of persons, soon mitigated the effects of the raids. There was considerable criticism in the press over the mishandling of the operation. The Sjahrir Socialists and the liberal wings of both the Masjumi and PNI accused the government of trampling on civil rights. On October 29, Sukiman appeared before parliament to defend his actions and to stifle the growing criticism. He disclosed that the August sweep was ordered after the government uncovered evidence of a movement aimed at the violent overthrow of the republic. Sukiman told parliament that the conspirators planned the assassination of Sukarno, Hatta, and the cabinet. "The government interpreted the incidents [at Tandjong Priok, and Bogor] as deeds of terrorism and intimidation," the Premier said. "There was no denying that the movement at Priok was under extremist Leftist influence, several [participants] were leaders of a certain political party and a trade union." Although the government avoided pinning a Red label on the affair, Sukiman left little doubt that his reference was to the PKI and SOBSI. There was evidence, too, he said, that the Darul Islam, Westerling, and Tan Malakists had had a hand in the affair. Sukiman said the divergent groups shared a common interest: the destruction of the republic. Sukiman said the government decided to act following the demands by the Communists to celebrate

August 17 separately. He said there was fear the maneuver fore-shadowed the creation of a new Left-wing front. "These events recalled the developments before Madiun," Sukiman said. "The government was compelled to avert another tragedy." It appears, then, that the government was as preoccupied by thoughts of Madiun on the eve of the razzia as the Communists were when the razzia was initiated.

As for the arrest of non-Communist leaders during the raids, the Premier conceded that the government had erred. "We admit some mistakes were made in the execution of the order," Sukiman said. "This is the inevitable consequence of a state of emergency. Indonesia is a young country. Its organization and experience are far from perfect." Sukiman reaffirmed his dedication to legal proc-esses and denied that the government sought to stifle the opposi-tion or settle private feuds by the arbitrary use of state power.

Parliament was impressed. Sukiman received an ovation. The suggestion of humility in his exposition subdued the deputies. "Sukiman's position seems stronger than before," *Keng Po* ob-served. On November 1, a PSI draft motion expressing dissatisfac-tion with the government reply was defeated ninety-one to twenty-one. The Sjahrir Socialists, to their discomfort, found themselves aligned with the PKI on the motion.

However, when the government failed to prosecute the detain-ees, the PKI made political capital of the razzia. Aidit contended:

> Conscious of the danger which threatened from the revolutionary people's movement and from the PKI, which was in a process of growth, seeing that the "Madiun Provocation" had not "killed" the revolutionary movement and the PKI, the foreign imperialists and the domestic reactionaries became infuriated and drew up a new plan to smash the PKI. This time, it was not with a provocation in Solo or Madiun, but with an "attack" on a police post in Tand-jung Priok, which the Sukiman government claimed to be a "Com-munist attack." About 2000 Communists and other progressives were arrested and put in jail. But under the pressure of the people, they were all released after having been in prison for many months with-out it being possible to bring a single person up before a court. Fail-ure of the August razzia was an indication that the revolutionary movement in Indonesia had been rebuilt and that it had strength.[3]

True, Sukiman's failure to bring the detainees to trial dimin-ished the luster of the security sweep, although the consensus was that his forceful action had immeasurably improved the security and labor situations in the ports, larger cities, and estates, and had reduced tension in the capital. A reason for Sukiman's failure to press the legal case against the detainees was that no sooner had the razzia ended in November than the cabinet was confronted with a crisis that toppled the government. For the Communists, Sukiman's departure was beyond their wildest expectation. Within the framework of the Cold War, Sukiman's defeat over the question of American aid merits detailed attention.

On October 10, 1951, in the midst of the Korean War, the 82nd U.S. Congress passed the Mutual Security Act of 1951. One of the purposes of the MSA was the streamlining of the aid program by the administrative consolidation of the Mutual Defense Act of 1949, the Economic Cooperation Act of 1948, and the Act for International Development. The MSA, which was adopted after considerable debate, declared that the "purpose of this Act is to maintain the security and to promote the foreign policy of the United States by authorizing military, economic, and technical assistance to friendly countries to strengthen the mutual security and individual and collective defenses of the free world."

Under Section 511(B), the Act authorized the President to furnish economic and technical assistance abroad, and under Section 511(A), to disburse military as well as economic and technical assistance, provided the recipient power contributed "to the development and maintenance of its own defensive strength and the defensive strength of the free world."

In Indonesia, as elsewhere in the neutralist Afro-Asian world, the phrase "free world" offended sensibilities. To many Asians, the arbitrary division of the world into "free" and "Communist" areas is the American counterpart of the Communist "anti-imperialist" and "capitalist" world division. In the Afro-Asian world, the term "Communist world" is self-explanatory; "free world" is meaningless, without justification in either theory or fact. Were the colonies of Africa and Asia "free"? What about Irian? To many Asians, the free world is a part of the world dominated by the West, i.e., Caucasoid, capitalist, and Christian. Asked to make a choice between the free and the Communist worlds, Indonesia stood aloof, nonaligned, and independent. Had the choice for the new nations been expressed in specific terms, for example, as a choice between representative government, transcending race, religion, and economic system on the one hand, and totalitarianism, whether Communist or Fascist, on the other, Indonesia could not afford to remain neutral—nor could any other emergent Afro-Asian state.

The success of the Marshall Plan in Western Europe, which was technically capable of absorbing massive assistance, prompted Washington to embark on a similar program for Asia. The United

States indiscriminately made a similar assumption about the new states, despite their diverse political, economic, cultural, and religious backgrounds and temperaments. The United States failed to appreciate the starkly different psychological climate in neutralist Asia as compared to that in the committed West. In large areas of decolonized Asia, the motives of the United States had become suspect. As expressed by *Indonesia Raya*, which was influenced by the army and the Sjahrir Socialists, "The word 'security' in MSA is unwise because it creates suspicions in recipient countries." And in an illuminating commentary, the Djakarta *Star* said: "The majority of the people fail to understand why white people are being so sympathetic."

Washington's insensitivity to the climate of opinion in the neutralist world was compounded by failure to appreciate that aid is of value only when it is wanted, when the recipient either dwells on the frontiers of the armed Communist colossi or has embarked on a bold program of economic and social reform with a view to making democratic processes work. Indonesia was not yet in either category.

At that time H. Merle Cochran, the former delegate on the U.N. Commission, was the U.S. Ambassador to Indonesia. He presented his credentials on December 30, 1949, three days after the transfer of power.

At a news conference held that day, Ambassador Cochran disclosed that discussions with the new government for a $100 million export-import loan had begun; significantly, the term used was "loan," not "grant," the political euphemism for a gift. Cochran emphasized that the United States would not press Indonesia.

> We are not taking much initiative. We are outlining the necessary requirements for a loan. We are leaving it up to Indonesia to make the approach, but are illustrating the type of projects we are willing to finance, such as promoting rice production, the rehabilitation of highways, harbors, etc. We want the Indonesians to assess their needs carefully. If we can help along these lines, it will really be constructive.[4]

In March, 1950, the loan was approved. Then, in August, in the face of deteriorating security, Cochran negotiated an arms accord. The United States provided Indonesia with about $5 million worth of small arms for "Sjahrir's" Mobile Brigade, the best-disciplined, best-equipped, and best-trained force in the country.

Conservative by nature, Cochran moved cautiously. His object was to avoid the impression of United States pressure on Indonesia. Partly in the furtherance of this goal, Cochran maintained the Embassy in the faded quarters of the old Consulate-General building. (The United States now has an ostentatious structure in the heart of Djakarta, a city of slums.) He vetoed suggestions that the Embassy acquire a weekend retreat in the mountains on the ground that travel into the hills risked an incident with bands. (The United States now maintains a mountain retreat.) He also favored a small mission. (Later, American ambassadors, unable to dam the flow of personnel from Washington, found themselves increasingly occupied with problems of housing, dependents, commissaries, and motor pools.) Cochran also took a dim view of the United States Information Service and discouraged its activities; later, at least two directors of the local USIS recommended closing operations in Indonesia. (Since then, the United States has enlarged the scope of USIS activity.) [5]

Cochran was also personally unpopular. Almost inaccessible, he lived alone in an austerely furnished mansion. He entertained infrequently, and his press relations were poor, a serious flaw since the press in the Afro-Asian world often constitutes "popular opinion," and, more often than not, if unfettered—as it was in Indonesia—it is the opposition. Cochran's diplomatic position was unique. His personal relationship with both Sukarno and Hatta predated Madiun.

Only against this background is it possible to comprehend Cochran's vigorous opposition to the grants-in-aid program. There was another factor. In the West, notably because of the Marshall Plan, the American assistance program was identified with stability and progress, and, on the whole, it was a success. In East Asia in 1951, the American aid program was identified with failures—the Nationalists in China, the French in Indochina, and the Dutch in Indonesia. American economic aid, initiated in Indonesia as part of the Marshall Plan in 1948, was administered by the Dutch. The republic, of course, did not participate; Dutch policy at the time was to blockade the republic into submission. Although the United States had stopped assistance to Indonesia after the second Dutch military action, in November, 1949, at the conclusion of The Hague agreement, the ECA program was resumed.

This was the setting when R. Allen Griffin arrived in Indonesia in April, 1950, to head an aid mission. He "urgently" recommended an assistance program for Indonesia. An aid agreement authorizing a "gift" of $8 million was signed with Natsir on October 16. In early December, 1951, Griffin again went to Indonesia. Despite the vigorous opposition of Cochran, who urged the termination of MSA funds at the end of the fiscal year, Griffin plumped for continued grants-in-aid. On December 9, at a news conference to which American newsmen were not invited—perhaps to avoid embarrassing questions—Griffin announced that he would propose to Washington an extension of the $8-million aid program. At that time, Indonesia had accumulated $400 million in gold and securities in the United States, twice the amount on hand at the transfer of sovereignty. Indonesia had also built up a trade surplus of $89 million for the year as a result of the Korean War boom.

Cochran was instructed by Washington to proceed with the MSA program. On January 4, after preliminary talks with Subardjo, Cochran sent a note to the Foreign Minister requesting a reply in four days, the deadline publicly set by Congress for acceptance of aid funds. The following day, Subardjo replied, opting for military aid under Section 511(A), "in order to facilitate the availability of equipment needed by the Indonesian Government for the maintenance of internal security," as Acting Secretary of State James Webb later expressed it. Subardjo apparently felt that MSA aid in no way prejudiced Indonesia's independence and that Indonesia would not be bound closer to the United States than before. After all, Indonesia had accepted both economic and military assistance from the United States in the past. As it developed, however, Subardjo acted without the knowledge of the cabinet, the Foreign Minister, or the Defense Minister; he did, however, have the approval of Sukarno. It is difficult to assess Subardjo's motivation, other than personal opportunism, unless Sukarno was hopeful of attracting American support on Irian. Subardjo had flitted from peak to peak in Indonesian politics, identifying himself with the Communists in the early prewar period, the Japanese during the occupation, the Tan Malaka revisionist Communists during the revolution, and the Masjumi after independence. He was Sukarno's choice for Foreign Minister in 1945 and again in 1951. Now he was in the role of befriending the United States.

In late January, a United States Army colonel approached the Defense Ministry to initiate discussions on military assistance. The ministry, dominated by the Sjahrir Socialists, Sukiman's bitter domestic foe, was perplexed; so was the colonel. On February 5, *Abadi*, which reflected Natsir's policies, reported rumors of a "secret" agreement under whose terms Indonesia had abandoned its independent foreign policy. The ministries of Foreign Affairs and Information denied the existence of such an agreement; an inquiry began. The political fallout was immediate. The Socialist opposition press, sensing an opportunity to bring down Sukiman, launched a massive campaign against American aid. It became the object of gibes: "American aid means aid America!" "MSA stands for the Mutual Suspicion Act!" On February 8, in an angry session, the cabinet questioned Subardjo, the first time that MSA was discussed at the cabinet level. Sukiman sought escape. The government dispatched Cochran a note seeking clarification of the term "free world" and suggesting that perhaps it meant free and sovereign countries. But the political opposition sensed its advantage. Three days later, the PIR Defense Minister called for Subardjo's resignation; it was apparent that the Sjahrir group controlling the Defense Ministry had put Sewaka up to it. The opposition was using the PIR against Sukiman in the same fashion that Sukarno had used the PIR against Natsir. Subardjo, in a letter to Sukiman, offered to resign. The next day, however, the cabinet floundered. The Masjumi announced that it could not assume responsibility for American aid. Four days later the PNI followed suit. Clearly, Subardjo was discredited, and Cochran along with him. Washington had misjudged the depth of the neutralist sentiment in Indonesia and the depth of the opposition to Sukiman. Washington had erred at a time when a friendly government was in power and the Communists suppressed. The fall of the Sukiman government and the involvement of the United States in the crisis was to provide the PKI with new opportunities.

The United States executed a diplomatic retreat. On February 19, Cochran replied to the cabinet's note of February 8. The United States agreed to modify Section 511(A) to make it read "the defensive strength of the free and sovereign countries." Clutching this reed, Sukiman worked to avert collapse. On February 20, the cabinet accepted Subardjo's offer to resign. But the next day the Masjumi, influenced by Natsir, declared the cabinet's position untenable. Sukarno acknowledged the spectrum of opinion aligned against Sukiman and made no serious effort to save the cabinet. The policy of flirting with the United States was unlikely to produce results on Irian, and this, after all, was the strategic objective. On February 8, as the MSA crisis was developing, Australia urged that the question of Irian be relegated to the "icebox." And on the eve of the cabinet's resignation, the Netherlands dashed hopes for an early settlement by a constitutional provision making the disputed territory an inviolable part of the Netherlands Kingdom, thereby further complicating, if not aggravating, an already difficult situation. Sukarno, tacking on Irian, altered his westward course and now pressed for the "internationalization" of the dispute through the U.N.; if that course failed, Sukarno could turn to the Communists for support.

On February 23, 1951, Sukiman resigned. The Mutual Security Act, designed "to maintain the security and to promote the foreign policy of the United States" and "to strengthen the . . . collective defense of the free world," had precipitated a cabinet crisis in what was potentially the leading power in Southeast Asia. The departure of Sukiman was an unexpected bonus for the Communists, although it must be emphasized that Indonesian opposition to American aid was almost unanimous and that the influence of the Communists, then underground, was negligible.

Indeed, the absence of PKI activity at the time had encouraged Indonesia's intellectual, non-Communist left, principally those around Sjahrir, to rain blows on Sukiman's pro-Sukarno coalition. In point of fact, on the eve of Sukiman's resignation the PKI was reshaping its strategy and tactics to suit the new line promulgated by Stalin. The cabinet's fall played into Aidit's hands by facilitating a *volte face*. As for the United States, the MSA crisis put Washington in the awkward position of appearing prepared to compromise a friendly nation of 80 million people for $8 million. What made the crisis a particular tragedy for the non-Communist world was that the form of government and the general political direction of Indonesia in this period was democratic and anti-Communist.

14

Stalin Veers Right

The crisis arising out of the issue of United States aid, and the subsequent fall of the Sukiman coalition, coincided with the second shift in the postwar line of the international Communist movement.

In the years of the Left strategy, the international Communist movement had made impressive gains. Eastern Europe was absorbed, as was most of eastern Asia, in an arc extending from northern Korea through China into northern Indochina. But the Left strategy had run its course. Resistance to the Communist offensive was stiffening in the non-Communist world, notably in the West. The West had broken the Berlin blockade, turned back the Communists in Greece, and quelled Communist disorders in France and Italy. Confronted by the Soviet threat, NATO had been forged, drawing a line from Norway to Turkey and challenging the Soviet Union to cross it. Stalin's bluff was called. Neither Russia nor the West could risk a major war in a nuclear age. Stalin, moreover, was confronted with a revolution of "rising expectations" within his own borders as Russia, in 1950–51, moved into a stage of sustained economic growth. Finally, in eastern Asia, the Communists were checkmated. Their hopes of absorbing the whole of Korea had dissolved. Japan had become a link in the non-Communist world's defensive chain. The Chinese Nationalists had consolidated their position on Taiwan. In southern Asia, the Communist-inspired disturbances in India and the open Communist revolts in Burma, Malaya, the Philippines, and Indonesia, had misfired. Only in Indochina, where the French, with a distorted sense of grandeur, engaged doggedly in a hopeless colonial war, was the Communist position promising. Obviously, the Communists had reached another turning point.

Stalin may have been either exhausted, or anxious to consolidate his postwar territorial acquisitions, or he may have been concerned over Western economic recovery, political unity, and military resurgence, or, perhaps, he merely sensed new opportunities by assuming a posture of reasonableness. He may have realized —indeed, he probably did—that to continue the Left strategy would ultimately lead to a nuclear war from which no nation in possession of nuclear weapons would emerge intact. A lessening of tension, the deceptive tactics of the Right strategy, might succeed in generating disunity in the West. Also, the Right strategy held a broad nationalist appeal. In Indonesia, for example, Sukarno was vilified when the Left strategy prevailed. A shift to the Right would put local Communists in a position of exploiting rising nationalist sentiment in the emerging Afro-Asian world.

In 1951, whatever the motivation, Stalin prepared the way for a return to the Right strategy. A hint of this was contained in an interview of Stalin with himself that appeared in *Pravda* of February 16, 1951. In it, he modified Lenin's theory of the inevitability of war by saying that "at least at the present time [war] cannot be considered inevitable."

Apparently in an effort to force a military settlement in Korea before the line shifted, the Chinese launched what became their last major drive in the Korean War. The second spring offensive, as the thrust was called, collapsed on May 22. The following month Jacob Malik, the Soviet delegate to the U.N., sounded the call for a Korean truce. Although armistice negotiations were not concluded until 1953, large-scale fighting in Korea had come to an end.

With the precision of ballet dancers, the sections of the international Communist movement whirled from the Left to the Right. In India, on September 17, 1951, the Communist Party challenged Nehru to ease his pressure on domestic Communists. In return, the Indian Communist Party pledged to abandon terrorism and employ constitutional means in contesting for power. In Malaya, on October 1, 1951, the Communist Party issued a directive calling for a change in tactics and the progressive diminution of the shooting war. The directive called for the unity of all classes and races (Malay, Chinese, and Indian) against Western imperialism. The new line stretched into Indonesia in January, 1952, and was publicly enunciated on May 23 of that year.

It is beyond any doubt that the Right strategy was formally launched at the Nineteenth Congress of the Bolshevik Party, held

October 5–14, 1952. There Stalin himself laid down the new line of cooperation with nationalist movements, collaboration with non-Communists, and the abandonment of the two-camp Zhdanov thesis with its emphasis on discouraging compromise and encouraging violence. The sectarianism of the Left gave way to the opportunism of the Right. According to the official Soviet account of the proceedings, the Congress

> opened in the Grand Hall of the Kremlin Palace in Moscow on October 5. In the hall were the Congress delegates . . . and representatives of foreign Communist and Workers' Parties [including the PKI]. At 7 P.M., the delegates warmly applauded the appearance on the tribune of Comrade Stalin and his loyal colleagues [including Khrushchev]. All rose to their feet and waves of cheering resounded through the hall: "Hurrah for Comrade Stalin," "Hurrah for the great Stalin," "Long live Comrade Stalin," "Hurrah for our own, beloved Stalin." [1]

For nine days, the representatives of fifty-eight Communist parties sang paeans to Stalin as the "beloved, brilliant leader of all progressive mankind," and developed the disarmingly friendly new line of peaceful coexistence. The delegates called for a united front in the West against United States imperialism and a united front in the Afro-Asian world against Western imperialism. The United States was to be isolated. Specifically, the non-Communist world was accused of having bartered independence for American aid, an interesting line for the PKI in view of Sukiman's debacle.

The keynote, delivered by Georgi Malenkov, one of the four secretaries of the Central Committee of the CPSU and a trusted lieutenant of Stalin, cited Indonesia as a country suffering from "protracted imperialist oppression" and "rapacious exploitation" by the imperialist West. Such countries, Malenkov averred, had abandoned their independence and had become American lackeys. But, he continued, in Indonesia and elsewhere, there were "genuine peace-loving democratic forces" determined to follow an "independent, peaceful policy" that would lead to "a way out of the impasse into which they have been driven by the U.S. dictators."

On October 14, at the last session of the Congress, Stalin mapped the road ahead. The official summary described the session as "impressive and unforgettable." Accompanied by "his closest colleagues," including Khrushchev, Stalin appeared on the rostrum to affix his seal on the Right strategy. Nationalism, excoriated and denounced by the Cominform as the "ideology of the bourgeoisie" and the "enemy of Marxism," was redeemed. Stalin authorized the international Communist movement to assume the mantle of nationalism:

> Formerly, the bourgeoisie was considered the head of the nation, it championed the rights and independence of the nation, placing them "above everything." Now, not a trace remains of the "national principle." Now, the bourgeoisie sells the rights and independence of the nation for dollars. The banner of national independence and national sovereignty has been thrown overboard. There is no doubt that you, representatives of the Communist and democratic parties, will have to pick up that banner and carry it forward if you wish to be patriots of your country, if you wish to become the leading force of the nation. There is no one else to pick it up. [Tumultuous applause]. That is how matters stand at present. . . .
>
> Long live peace among the nations! [Prolonged applause]. Down with warmongers! [All rise. Tumultuous, prolonged applause growing into ovation. Cries: "Long live Comrade Stalin," "Hurrah for Comrade Stalin," "Long live Comrade Stalin, great leader of the working people of the world," "Hurrah for the great Stalin," "Long live peace among the nations!" Cries: "Hurrah!"] [2]

In short order, the Nineteenth Congress specifically called for a nuclear-test ban, disarmament, and the nurturing of nationalism. Only the "summit" was missing. Stalin applied that crowning touch on Christmas Day, 1952, when he expressed his willingness to meet with President-elect Eisenhower. As the international Communist movement glided from the Left to the Right, the Cold War was transformed into a cold peace.

In assessing Communist intentions and capabilities, it is well to remember that the inauguration of the era of peaceful coexistence predates Stalin's death. The Right strategy was inaugurated in 1951, accelerated in 1952, and elaborated upon by Stalin's successors, first Malenkov and then Khrushchev. Thus, when Moscow responded affirmatively to President Eisenhower's April 16, 1953, appeal to the post-Stalin Russia for *rapprochement* by deeds— "an Austrian treaty . . . an honorable armistice in Korea . . . Indochina, and Malaya"—and Prime Minister Churchill's May 11 proposal for a confrontation at the "summit," Moscow merely carried on where Stalin had left off. In 1953, the Korean armistice was signed. In 1954, the Indochina war ended. In 1955, the first "peaceful coexistence" summit meeting was held.

In Indonesia, the Left years had been hard on the Communist movement. In rapid succession, the PKI had been led by Sardjono, Musso, Alimin, and Aidit; it had lost ground in the Indonesian revolution; it had the label "traitor" pinned to it at Madiun. It was Aidit's task, in Stalin's words, to pick up the banner of nationalism if the PKI was to become the leading force in Indonesia. The PKI and its apologists ascribed the Party shift in Indonesia to Sukiman's fall and the formation of a new and "progressive" government under Wilopo, not to the change in the international Communist line. These were the same groups who argued that the Madiun rebellion was generated by internal pressures, not the Zhdanov line.

Aidit not only executed a dramatic reversal in the PKI line in early 1952, he also employed the shift as a cloak to purge the Party hierarchy of lingering opposition to his rule, notably of Alimin and Tan Ling Djie, who had been premature exponents of a Rightist strategy. The new PKI posture profoundly influenced the future course of events in Indonesia. PKI identification with nationalism injected a new factor into the Indonesian political scene, widened the schism between political moderates and extremists, between Sukarno and Hatta and the powerful groups around them. As a result of the new Communist line, Irian was drawn into the East-West arena. By espousing nationalism (Sukarno), the PKI succeeded in destroying the post-independence opportunities of the Sjahrir Socialists to develop the non-Communist Left. The developing Right strategy set the PKI off on a new road, to borrow Musso's phrase. The ultimate PKI goal—power—remained unchanged, however. But theirs was not the bourgeois concept of power renewed by consent and restrained by intricate parliamentary checks and balances; it was the Leninist vista of absolute, unlimited power.

In Asia, the new Right strategy was to bear the richest fruit in Indonesia. In neutralist India, Cambodia, and Burma, where sentiment was anti-anti-Communist, in noncommitted Malaya and in committed Thailand, the Philippines, and Pakistan, the local Communist movements made little headway under the new strategy. In Indonesia, where the primary leadership—under Sukarno—espoused militant nationalism, the Indonesian Communist Party was able to register impressive advances.

15

The Turn in the Road

The main point of departure for the PKI shift from Left to Right was at the Party's National Conference in January, 1952, *before* the MSA crisis evolved. At that conference, Aidit uncoiled the guidelines of the new strategy: the formation of a "united national front, including the national bourgeoisie," the liquidation of the Darul Islam, and the development of a Communist mass movement. The objectives interlocked.

By Aidit's definition, the "national bourgeoisie" was composed of business interests "oppressed by foreign capitalism and domestic feudalism" and, therefore, "anti-imperialist and anti-feudal—in this respect one of the revolutionary forces."[1] Aidit made it plain that he referred to the PNI by defining the "compradore bourgeoisie" as the "big bourgeoisie serving the interests of the big foreign capitalists" and led by the Masjumi. These characterizations, with little basis in fact, laid the theoretical foundations for Party action. In truth, the class origins of the leadership of both the Masjumi and PNI were strikingly similar. But Aidit required a "Marxist-Leninist thesis" as window-dressing for his new line. One of the basic intellectual appeals of Communism, after all, is its ability to present pseudo-scientific analyses and a concomitant sense of inevitability for courses guided by circumstances rather than by fixed principles.

At this stage the Communists regarded the Masjumi as "the main enemy." Thus, Aidit found it necessary to distinguish between the bourgeoisie in the PNI and in the Masjumi and to emphasize the need for the eradication of the "fascist" Darul Islam. The Communist objective was to isolate the Masjumi by identifying it with "imperialism" and with extremist, theocratic Islam—the term "theocratic" being employed loosely, since Islam is devoid of a clerical hierarchy, although it does not provide for a separation of church and state. Aidit obviously hoped to capitalize on the instinctive fear of the secular PNI. Quite understandably, the PNI had become increasingly alarmed by the expansionist tendencies of the Darul Islam, which had spread from West-Central Java into South Sulawesi. Aidit's tactics apparently found a mark, for that same month Natsir, in an effort to ease PNI concern, denounced the Darul Islam and observed that "no one should be so foolish as to weave Stalinism and democratic socialism on the same loom, although both are based on Marxism. It is just as foolish and dangerous to compare the Masjumi with the Darul Islam."

In developing a mass movement, a hallmark of Aiditism,* Aidit explained that the task of "accentuating the formation of a national united front" could only be achieved by an expansion of the Party membership. With the members the Party had at the time, it was "impossible to execute such far-reaching duties" as developing a united front with the PNI and isolating the Masjumi. Accordingly, the conference resolved to expand its membership by 100,000 within 6 months. Aidit hinted at the obvious: that the PKI's adherence to a nationalist line and the abandonment of the truculence of the Left strategy would facilitiate the Party's growth. In Aidit's words, "the decrease in sectarianism would encourage many people to join the Party." [1] Thus the conference concluded that "it was important to eliminate sectarianism . . . and adventurousness from the Party [the Left strategy]." [2]
Musso and the 1948 line were repudiated.
It is interesting to speculate whether Moscow participated directly in the promulgation of the new line. In December, 1951, as Aidit executed his *volte face*, a Soviet emissary, Tass's Vassilev Outchav, arrived at Djakarta. Outchav's arrival generated considerable interest. His visa had been issued at The Hague, but he landed without the foreknowledge of the ministries of Foreign Affairs or Information. He rarely attended news conferences. His return to Moscow aroused even greater interest. He departed on July 31, 1953, three weeks after Beria was deposed. What aroused speculation was not merely Beria, however. That week, a cabinet was formed based largely on an alliance of the PNI and PKI. The

* The term "Aiditism" was coined by Van der Kroef (see "Communism in Indonesia," *Problems of Communism*, November–December, 1958) to describe the *ad hoc* adjustment of the PKI line to Indonesian developments.

Masjumi was isolated. Whatever the case, as the National Conference adjourned, the political scene in Indonesia was rent by the MSA issue and the resignation of Sukiman. The PKI professed to believe that Sukiman resigned "under the continuous pressure of the democratic people's movement [PKI], as the national bourgeoisie [PNI] inclined more and more to the Left, and as a result of the contradictions within the domestic ruling clique.[3]

Out of the debris of Sukiman's collapse, on April 1, 1952, emerged a Masjumi-PSI coalition in the Natsir tradition—but with one important difference: PNI participation. Both Sjahrir and Natsir recognized that a government without the Nationalists could not survive for long. Indeed, at the head of the cabinet was Wilopo, the first Nationalist Party Premier in the history of the republic.

Sukarno was cool to the new government; Wilopo represented the PNI's small liberal wing and was suspected of "Sjahrir-mindedness." But Sukiman's debacle had pushed Sukarno into the background. Although he tried, Sukarno was unable to prevent the formation of the moderate Wilopo coalition. Many Indonesian intellectuals again wistfully interpreted the composition of the cabinet as evidence that Sukarno was in eclipse and that the emotional revolutionary nationalist tide in Indonesia was receding.

In the course of forming the cabinet, a deep rift developed within the Masjumi. The orthodox Nahadatual Ulama faction within the Islamic "corporation" withdrew in April. Composed largely of religious scholars and teachers, it declined to support Wilopo. The ostensible reason was the NU's failure to receive the portfolio of religion, its preserve since the revolution. Natsir refused to endorse K. H. A. Wachid Hasjim as Minister of Religion, the post Hasjim had occupied in the Hatta, Natsir, and Sukiman cabinets. The reformist Masjumi leadership had grown disenchanted with NU corruption; the proverbial last straw was an unpublicized scandal involving Hasjim and the misuse of funds in connection with a pilgrimage to Mecca. At the time, the split between Natsir and Hasjim, a powerful East Java figure who had served in the revolution as General Sudirman's personal religious adviser, was overshadowed by other events. Like the PIR, the NU became a free agent, often allied to the highest bidder. The religious scholars were prepared to cooperate with any group, including the PKI, provided its religious sensibilities were not offended and its financial demands met. The Communists were elated by the schism. The PKI assiduously avoided criticism of either Islam or the NU, but reviled the mundane Masjumi.

As Wilopo came into office, the economy was strained. Korean truce negotiations had deflated the boom in raw materials; Indonesian production was still below prewar Dutch levels; and the population was expanding at a rate of 800,000 annually. In 1941, the last "peaceful" year in Indonesia, the Dutch had imported 81,604 tons of rice, as compared to almost 600,000 tons, in 1952. Even so, the daily Indonesian diet in 1952 contained only 1,712 caloric units, as compared to 2,121 in India. On April 27, 1952, in one of his rare utterances on the economic and social challenges confronting postwar Indonesia, Sukarno predicted that by 1960 the population would be 88 million, an increase of 8 million. "If we do not increase our production of rice, Indonesia will have to live on 1,500 caloric units a day by that time," he said. "This will mean famine." Although Indonesia has become the world's largest importer of rice, 1960 passed without famine. Its urban population survived largely on rice supplied by the West and the Soviet bloc.

Wilopo was ideally suited to guide Indonesia from empty nationalist slogans towards responsibility. He combined the qualities of the average Javanese: unhurried, unambitious, sensitive, reflective, and tolerant to the point of submissiveness. He had served as Labor Minister with Hatta and as Economic Minister with Sukiman. Wilopo set the tone of his administration in an interview that appeared in *The Christian Science Monitor* in May:

A strong and stable Indonesia from within is our big contribution not only to our own welfare but to world peace as well. . . . Indonesia must direct all her efforts toward the solution of home affairs. I cannot emphasize this point too often. Foreign policy is secondary. . . . MSA is not the most important aspect in the good relations between the United States and Indonesia. . . . The issue has become magnified out of proportion. [As for Communism] we do not consider Communism in Indonesia a problem today. . . . The Indonesian people find little appeal in Communism. On the contrary, their way of life actively opposes it. The overwhelming majority of the people in this country are non-Communist and would combat any attempts to impose Communist ideology on them.

But the Communists were changing their appeal. The fall of Sukiman had provided Aidit with an incentive to accelerate the development of a nationalist line. On April 22, the PKI startled Djakarta with the announcement that the Communists would support Wilopo. For the first time since Amir, the PKI was supporting a government. The Communists were quick to demonstrate their good faith. On April 30, SOBSI suspended all strike actions "in keeping with SOBSI's decision to support the Wilopo cabinet." The period of SOBSI-inspired labor unrest was at an end. In conformity with the Right strategy, the PKI moved to form a national front. Alimin, cast by Aidit in the role of icebreaker, approached the elder statesman of the Masjumi, Hadji Agus Salim, much to Salim's amusement. It was the first time they had spoken to each other since the 1920's. Salim rejected Alimin's overtures. So did the PSI. But when the Communists approached Sidik Djojosukarto, the PNI leader, they struck a responsive chord. Sidik had strongly opposed PNI participation in a cabinet dominated by what he considered clerical (Masjumi) and anational (PSI) elements. Sidik believed that in the event of a general election, an alliance with the Left was not only feasible but also essential. He accepted the invitation of the PKI and sixty-two other organizations, many of them Communist fronts, to join in a "unity-of-attitude" program to commemorate Budi Utomo Day on May 20. This is where Amir's FDR had left off in 1948. A joint statement, prepared by a seven-man committee including three known Communists (Tjugito, Susanto, and Utarjo) who had played a key role in the FDR—and one radical nationalist (Sabilal Rasad), pledged the signatories to "implement democracy in all fields of life" and to collaborate in the struggle for Irian. Sukarno, smarting under four years of Communist abuse, was distressed by Sidik's action, and confounded by Alimin's appearance at a Budi Utomo fete at the palace. It was the first time a Communist Party leader had attended a Presidential reception since Madiun. That week, however, Sukarno—unimpressed—persuaded the parliamentary faction, led by Manai Sophian, to boycott a meeting of parties that had signed the joint statement.

Sukarno's action notwithstanding, the rhythm of the Communist transition to a nationalist line accelerated. On May 23, the thirty-second anniversary of the PKI's founding, the Right strategy was publicly proclaimed at the Gedung Kesenian, Djakarta's prewar "opera house." * At a plenary session, Aidit called for a national front in all areas of Indonesian life and pledged that the Communists would not "interfere in the internal problems of other parties." Alimin then addressed the meeting and voiced the slogans "Long live Sukarno! Long live the PKI!" The audience gasped, unprepared. With Aidit's visible encouragement, Alimin repeated the catch phrases. There was a pause, followed by shouts

---

* At that time, PKI headquarters were at 18 Djalan Lontar IX. On August 19, 1954, the PKI, being affluent, moved into new and impressive quarters at 81 Kramat Raya. Aidit claimed that the Party financed the new building by selling 400,000 picture postcards to Party members and sympathizers. (See *Harian Rakjat*, August 20, 1954.)

from the delegates of "Long Live Sukarno! Long Live the PKI!"
The demonstration, in Communist language, was tempestuous.
The new line was launched.

Indonesia's leadership was quick to sense the implications.
Janus' other face was a principal topic of conversation among the
"elite" of the Masjumi, PNI, and PSI. On May 28, Sukarno, Hatta,
cabinet ministers, and the chiefs of the armed forces witnessed
naval games from the destroyer "Gadja Mada." The question
asked was what impact the Communist shift would have on
domestic affairs. Some Indonesian leaders already viewed the future
with misgivings; the object of their concern was Sukarno, whose
field of operation had been enlarged by the Communist appeal to
bourgeois nationalist leadership. Indeed, the day before, Pedoman
had alluded to the Communist shift as a "tactical maneuver
designed to give Sukarno the impression that the Party has earnest
intentions [of unity]." But the Communist maneuver was not
tactical; it was strategic.

The turn in the Communist road was accompanied by intense
Party activity. PKI functionaries toured the countryside in July and
August explaining the Right strategy. As a display of honorable
intention the Communists, for the first time since Madiun, offered
to participate in government-sponsored independence-day activities. In Djakarta, the PKI almost captured the August 17 festivi-
ties by assuming the chairmanship of the arrangements committee
on July 14. How the Communists engineered this minor coup
has never been satisfactorily explained. But the Masjumi protested
and five days later organized a "Committee to Defend Proclamation Day." Supardi, the PKI committee chairman, graciously
stepped aside and said the Communists had no intention of creating dissension. The PKI issued a statement on July 22 calling for
unity and expressing "regret" that controversy between "Communists and non-Communists, between nationalists and Moslems,
should mar independence day." The incident was the first conflict
between the PKI and Masjumi since the advent of the new line.

Within the Communist movement, the Right strategy was
vigorously applied. On September 27, at Djakarta, representatives
of thirty-one SOBSI and four non-SOBSI trade unions, claiming
2.5 million members, held a conference at which the new line was
adopted. Njono described Indonesia as a "semicolonial" country
where not only workers and peasants but "national capitalists" as
well were being suppressed by "monopolistic imperialists," and
declared that, therefore, the Indonesian revolution should not be
a social but a "national" revolution. Accordingly, SOBSI approved
a new constitution in which phrases such as "socialism," "people's

democracy," and "class struggle" were eliminated. Other fronts, for example, Pemuda Rakjat, took similar measures. Clearly, the Communists were preparing to court bourgeois nationalism at all levels of Indonesian society.

Abroad, too, the PKI became increasingly active, dispatching delegates to the WFDY Festival, the WFTU congress at Vienna, and the Asian and Pacific Peace Conference at Peking. The conferences, of course, were part of an elaborate global Communist program to implement the Right strategy. Each departing Indonesian delegation announced it would raise the Irian issue abroad. Aidit was skillfully maneuvering for Sukarno's attention.

In general, the PKI's shift from Left to Right went smoothly, although it was jarred by isolated "sectarian" manifestations. On April 30, a SOBSI union at Semarang balked at a strike settlement. Sakirman, a labor leader and also caucus leader in parliament, visited Semarang to explain the new line and resolve the dispute. In Soerakarta, at a May 23 anniversary meeting of the PKI, the police removed a portrait of Musso from the dais and replaced it with a photograph of Sukarno, thereby arousing the ire of the delegates, who shouted: "Long live Musso!" at a time when they should have yelled "Long live Sukarno!" Peking also crossed signals with the PKI. On May 3, the *Chang Chiang Jih Pao* of Hankow, in a May Day article perhaps not intended for distribution outside China, cited continuing guerrilla activity in Indonesia and claimed the disturbances were "under the leadership of the Communist Party." Actually, in this period, the activities of Communist armed bands in the Merapi-Merbabu complex in Central Java were diminishing in conformity with the new line.

Not that the PKI was enthusiastic about the prospect of supporting a Masjumi-PSI-PNI coalition. On May 15, in parliament, Sakirman described the Wilopo program as "far from satisfactory," and on June 5, in an effort to develop a foreign issue—Wilopo's program subordinated foreign affairs to domestic issues—the Communist caucus proposed a special session of parliament to consider the American role in Irian. But on June 19, the PKI joined the government parties in giving Wilopo an "opportunity to work."

Although the Communists appeared to be rapidly closing the gap between "international proletarianism" and bourgeois nationalism, Sukarno remained indifferent. On July 16, President Elpidio Quirino of the Philippines arrived on a state visit. Sukarno, of course, was soliciting support on Irian; Quirino was hopeful of rousing Indonesian interest in a Pacific pact directed against Chinese expansionism. The Communists were disturbed by the prospect of a Quirino-Sukarno accommodation. The PKI accused

Quirino of trying to "drag Indonesia into imperialist America's defense plans," and Communist deputies boycotted Quirino's appearance before parliament on July 17. That week, the SBG launched the first major SOBSI strike action since the new line, a warning to the government to maintain an "independent" foreign policy if it valued labor peace. Communist apprehension was unnecessary. Quirino failed to impress Djakarta. At a July 25 press conference, he brushed aside Irian, saying: "That's your problem, not mine." [4] Sukarno was convinced more than ever that flirting with the anti-Communist bloc on Irian was fruitless. But the following month, the PKI had new cause for alarm as Indonesia tacitly recognized the existence of "two Chinas." On August 15, rice arrived from Taiwan aboard a Chinese Nationalist vessel; 200 Sino-Indonesian children, waving Kuomintang flags, welcomed the ship. Peking protested; the PKI denounced the "unfriendly" act.

The arrival of Nationalist rice coincided with a tightening of the belt at home. Luxury imports were slashed; political patronage curbed; government expenditures trimmed. The Socialist Finance Minister, Sumitro Djojohadikusmo, conceded that the government was trying to do the "impossible." The austerity campaign severely affected the armed forces. The defense budget of 2.8 billion rupiahs, accounting for about a third of the national budget, was halved. The army proposed to meet the challenge by reducing its strength from 200,000 to 120,000. Since 1950, Simatupang, now a major general and chairman of the joint chiefs of staff, and Colonel Nasution, now the army chief of staff, had labored to develop a relatively compact, mobile armed force to replace the amorphous regulars and irregulars of the revolution. But the question was which 80,000 were to be demobilized. Those slated for discharge by January 1 included many irregulars of jingo and collaborating nationalist stripe. The army's political composition was to be re-cast, apparently at Sukarno's expense. Several partisan officers balked; one, Colonel Bambeng Supeno, complained directly to the President and was suspended by the army.

The issue landed in parliament; the debate dissolved into a power struggle between the forces that had been contesting for mastery of the republic since 1945. Aligned in one camp were Hatta, the Sjahrir Socialists, the Masjumi, and the PNI's Wilopo wing; in the other, Sukarno, the PNI, and the intransigent radicals of the revolution. The PKI always seemed to hold a balance of power. In 1945, they had backed Sjahrir; now, Sukarno. The Communists were anxious to destroy Sjahrir's influence in the armed forces, a dominant theme in the debate. (Sjahrir, Sima-tupang, and Ali Budiardjo, the Defense Ministry's able secretary general, were related by marriage.) But the PKI proceeded cautiously. The Communists feared that a crisis would open the way for the return, with Sukarno's encouragement, of a Masjumi-PNI cabinet of the Sukiman flavor.

During the debates, several motions were tabled, among them one instigated by Sukarno and introduced by Sophian. It called for changes in the Defense Ministry and high command. The motion passed on October 16, on the strength of a coalition composed of the PNI (in deference to Sukarno and out of hatred for Sjahrir), the PIR (which sensed another cabinet crisis), the NU (which sought to remove Christian influence from the army), and the PKI. Aidit had abandoned caution when he realized that Sukarno called the play. For the PKI, it was an incredibly for-tuitous development. The Masjumi and PSI were momentarily isolated from the mainstream, an objective of the Right strategy. The development inaugurated a period of parliamentary coopera-tion between the nationalists and the Communists. A cabinet crisis was imminent.

But the following morning the regime, not the cabinet, faced a crisis. There are as many versions of the affair as there were participants. Essentially, the "October 17 Affair" was the confluence of three main currents in the army. First, there was a Simatupang faction that resented the interference of the unelected parliament in army affairs and demanded the dissolution of parliament and general elections. This faction opposed a coup, considering it a dangerous precedent for the orderly constitutional development of the new republic. A Nasution faction, however, considered In-donesia not yet ready for parliamentary democracy, favored the dissolution of parliament ("a coffee house") and the parties ("pri-vate clubs"), and proposed that Sukarno run the country with army support. Both Simatupang and Nasution sensed the nature of the shifting Communist line and were also anxious to check-mate the PKI early in the "nationalist" charade. A third army faction was composed of partisan officers loyal to Sukarno who despised "Western" democracy, suspected Simatupang's "Sjahrir-mindedness," and mistrusted Nasution's Bonapartism. As for Sukarno, he vacillated. For a time he went along with Nasution but withdrew support when he suspected a "Sjahrir plot." Sukarno wanted power, but not responsibility nor opposition, no matter how loyal. He dreaded elections. He considered them divisive and feared an Islamic sweep that would destroy the secular republic.

On the morning of October 17, 1952, army vehicles deposited

about 300 demonstrators before parliament. The "demonstrators" carried banners demanding dissolution of parliament and speedy elections, ransacked the house, and marched on Sukarno's palace. Sukarno awaited them; loudspeakers were already installed on the palace lawn. The crowd assembled in orderly fashion at the palace gate. Sukarno told them: "The sentiment for elections is the sentiment of Djakarta. We must hear the voices in the regions. You do not want me to be a dictator. If I dissolve parliament I would become a dictator. I do not want to be a dictator." The throng dispersed at his command. However, while Sukarno was speaking, armored cars surrounded the palace. Simatupang and Nasution had apparently found a common cause. They demanded an audience with the President; Hatta and Wilopo were summoned. It was immediately evident that the intrigues had produced so fine a balance of power that the situation was in a state of suspended animation. Sukarno wept, and in a passionate appeal for national unity, always his trump card, prevailed on the participants to depart in honor and peace. As the meeting progressed, a detachment whose allegiance was undetermined trained field pieces on the palace. It was a moment of defiance Sukarno would never forget. It impressed on him the need to wrest control of the armed forces from "Sjahrir-minded" groups.

Wild rumors of a coup swept Indonesia; the people instinctively rallied behind the President. Sukarno capitalized on the confusion. With the aid of Lt. Colonel Zulkifli Lubis, the ambitious head of the army intelligence bureau, he dispatched couriers to outlying divisions. Partisan junior officers in the 5th (East Java), 7th (East Indonesia), and 2nd (South Sumatra) divisions bloodlessly deposed their commanding officers—appointed by Simatupang and Nasution—and reaffirmed their loyalty to the President. Elsewhere the army, including the two most powerful divisions— the 1st (North Sumatra), commanded by Colonel Simbolon, and the 3rd (West Java), commanded by Colonel Kawilarang— was either neutral or loyal to Simatupang. The 3rd Division controlled the capital and its approaches. Simbolon and Kawilarang, like Simatupang, were Christians, enjoyed the support of the Masjumi and PSI, and were confirmed anti-Communists.

Thereafter events moved swiftly. Nasution resigned on December 5; the Sultan of Jogjakarta, the Defense Minister, on January 1. The parties had successfully avoided a cabinet crisis. The government survived. So did parliament. But the damage caused by the events of October 17 was irreparable. Yet the bluffed coup, for that is really what it was, had one salutary effect. It accelerated the program for general elections. In November, Masjumi Interior Minister Rum ordered the printing of 50 million registration ballots. On April 1, 1953, parliament passed Indonesia's first electoral law. But not until 1955, under a "Sjahrir-minded" cabinet, were elections actually held. As for the affair itself, Wilopo observed on October 20 that "this is not the first time our democracy is confronted by a severe trial." He reaffirmed Indonesia's dedication to "democratic principles as the basis of our lives."

The Communists played no part in the affair other than to support the Sophian motion in parliament. But the episode provided the PKI with the opportunity to discredit the PSI and rally to the defense of Sukarno. In Communist literature, October 17 was described as "the attempted coup of the Rightist Socialists [Simatupang] and militarists [Nasution]." [5] Under the protective cover of nationalism, the PKI sought to gain an advantage. On October 24, the thousandth day after General Sudirman's death, which was observed by Islamic rites, the PKI sent Mrs. Sudirman a telegram of condolence. General Sudirman, togther with Simatupang and Nasution, had mapped the military campaign against the Communists at Madiun. By paying respect to his memory, the Communists, in one swoop, were courting nationalism, the army, and, of course, the orthodox NU faction. On November 8, the PKI announced that on Hero's Day, Sudirman and Tjipto Mangunkusmo, a nationalist leader who had died in 1943, would be admitted into the Marxist-Leninist pantheon of "heroes of the working class." PKI branches were instructed to display their portraits alongside those of Marx, Engels, Lenin, Stalin, Mao, and Musso. No doubt, when the appropriate hour arrived, the PKI would claim Sukarno as a hero.

At this juncture, perhaps to avoid being implicated in the aftermath of the bluffed coup—there was still fear of a civil war or an army seizure of power—Aidit and Njoto flew to Holland on November 15 to attend a congress of the Netherlands Communist Party. At a reception at Party headquarters on the eve of their departure, pictures of Aidit and Sudirman were prominently exhibited. The Dutch, however, refused Aidit and Njoto a permit to land.* Rebuffed, they disappeared behind the Iron Curtain. On Christmas Eve they were reported in Prague.

In Indonesia, meanwhile, the Communists apparently felt in

---

* This coincided with the arrest (on November 24) and subsequent expulsion from Holland as suspected Communist agents of Go Gien Tjwan, Amsterdam director of Antara, and Sunito, the Chairman of the Perhumpinan Indonesia. On returning home, Go assumed financial direction of Antara; Sunito settled in Surabaya. Implausibly, perhaps, many Indonesians regard Sunito, who served in the Dutch socialist underground during World War II, as a leading Marxist-Leninist theoretician although he apparently holds no official position in the PKI.

an increasingly strong position. On December 15, the government appealed to all parties to refrain from inflammatory statements that would obstruct the efforts to resolve the October 17 events peacefully. But on December 28, the PKI intensified its propaganda. The attack was directed by Lukman, who was running the Party in Aidit's absence and was widely thought to harbor "sectarian" sentiments. The PKI assailed the "Right-wing Socialists under Sjahrir's leadership" as those responsible for the bluffed coup and called for the dismissal of the Sultan, Budiardjo, and Simatupang. The Communists anticipated their resignations and sought credit for their subsequent departures. Thus, it required no clairvoyance to observe that "the Communists saw in the [Sophian] motion the beginning of an Army rift and played their hand accordingly in the hopes that the split would run its natural course and erupt into civil war," and that "one of the significant aspects of the crisis was the complete Communist support of partisan commanders against the Chiefs of Staff and Defense Ministry." [6] Indeed, as events later proved, October 17 was a signpost that pointed to civil war. The affair became an almost insurmountable barrier to future cooperation between the Masjumi and PNI, between Hatta and Sukarno. October 17 widened the abyss between rational and irrational forces in Indonesia and thereby abetted the Communist campaign for a "united front with the participation of the national bourgeoisie"—an alliance between the PNI and PKI.

During the Japanese occupation, Tokyo had encouraged landless Indonesians to squat on the cleared lands of idle estates and replace money crops with food crops. In 1952, Wilopo pressed a program of land reform, reviving a government offer of bulldozed homesteads if the squatters vacated foreign-leased properties. The government hoped to open virgin land for development while encouraging the rehabilitation of revenue-yielding estates. By March, 1953, about 20,000 out of 50,000 squatter families in East Sumatra had been peacefully resettled. At Tandjong Morawa, on the outskirts of Medan, however, a group of Chinese squatters resisted efforts to displace them. The government sought their land for an agricultural experimental station. For eight months, the squatters obstructed the attempts by the *gadjah kuning* (the yellow elephants) to plough the area, which the Chinese had named "Peace Village." Then, on March 16, 1953, the tractors returned with sixty policemen. Each side accused the other of a provocation; five Chinese and one Indonesian were slain, and sixteen persons wounded. Among the dead was a schoolteacher who had been a member of a local Chinese association organized by Wang Jen Shu before Wang became Peking's Ambassador to Indonesia. The only reporter on the scene was a *Harian Rakjat* correspondent. In Djakarta, the impression was that the incident had been Communist-inspired, that the uneducated squatters were the victims of professional agitators. So strong was the impression that on March 21 *Keng Po* felt compelled to caution the PKI and its Chinese followers that they "played with fire." Jusuf Adjitorop, the PKI leader in East Sumatra, denied PKI complicity. Nevertheless, SOBSI and the BTI demanded that Wilopo suspend the land-reform program and protect squatter interests.

In April, the Communists intensified their campaign. The offensive coincided with the solidification of the nationalist line. On May Day, for the first time, no portraits of Lenin, Stalin, or Mao were displayed. How far the Communists had traveled along the nationalist road is indicated by the fact that the keynote address on Budi Utomo Day (May 20) was delivered by Sakirman over Radio Indonesia—only a year after the line had altered. The Communist resurgence reflected many factors: the exploitation of the credulous; the naïveté of many Indonesians about Communist strategy and tactics; overconfidence that the PNI would be able to dispose of the Communists at the proper moment. In part, too, the Communist revival stemmed from a defeatist attitude among the Hattas, Sjahrirs, Natsirs, and Wilopos. In a nation of illiterates, how can demagoguery be defeated by moderation? Then, too, there was a tendency not to take the Communists seriously; 1926 and 1948 had demonstrated that the PKI danger was more apparent than real. Both Sukarno and Hatta doubted that in a showdown comparable to Madiun, the PKI could mobilize 1 per cent of its following. There were other factors: a disposition on the part of secular non-Communists to cooperate with the Communists in neutralizing the influence of Islam; a revolutionary current in Indonesia society generated by widespread dissatisfaction with the results of independence, particularly among the emerging middle class which formed the backbone of the Communist movement—a class, to employ a Leninist image, "growing wild." There was also a disposition to use the PKI as a lever against foreign capital, as a demonstration of independence from Western influence.

On May 14, Aidit and Njoto returned from their five-month sojourn behind the Iron Curtain. Aidit received a tumultuous Party welcome at the airport. That evening, he served notice on the "sectarians" within the Party that if they expected a change in PKI policy on his return from Moscow—a sub-conscious admission of Kremlin influence on the Party's policies—they were "quite mistaken." [7] Indeed, Aidit declared, the Right strategy must be pressed with vigor. "It is the responsibility of each member of the Party not only to be a good Communist, but also a good nationalist," he said.

At the PKI's thirty-third anniversary celebration Aidit and Njoto reaffirmed the line and related their experiences in the Communist world. They eulogized "the great, mighty, and noble Stalin," and told how they formed part of the guard of honor at Stalin's bier. Njoto described Stalin as a beloved great teacher who had won the affection of millions of people throughout the world. As for Aidit, he stressed the need for the Party to improve organization and discipline; in particular, he criticized Party members who resented singing the Indonesian national anthem or saluting the national flag. Aidit said: "The red-white banner is our revolutionary flag, which should be defended to the last. The same goes for Indonesia Raya, the national anthem of the Indonesian people and hence also of the Communists. And who would protect and defend the beloved flag and national anthem if not the Communists?" [8]

Aidit also appeared anxious to intensify the campaign against Hatta, branding him a "Japanese puppet" and collaborator of the "Right-wing Socialists" and "compradore Masjumi." Obviously, Aidit sensed the developing fissure between Hatta and Sukarno stemming from October 17 and moved to widen it.

And on that same May 23, only nine days after Aidit returned from Moscow, Sidik Kertapati, a parliamentary fellow traveler and member of the Communist-infiltrated Indonesian Peasants Association (SAKTI), tendered, in effect, a motion of no-confidence in the cabinet's Sumatran land reform program. The PNI faction in parliament, now firmly controlled by Sukarno and Sidik, announced their support of the Kertapati motion. Wilopo had reached the end of a tortuous journey. On June 2, 1953, he resigned the Premiership rather than face the humiliation of his own party voting him down. The following day, Wilopo publicly ascribed the cause of the government's fall to Tandjong Morawa. Kertapati boasted that "there was no doubt" that his motion had toppled Wilopo. As for the motion, it never came to a vote in parliament; Wilopo's successor carried on the same program. Tandjong Morawa notwithstanding, the real cause for Wilopo's fall was October 17 and the strengthening, with Sukarno's encouragement, of the PNI–PKI alliance. Indeed, the Masjumi assailed the Nationalists for "cooperating more with the opposition than with the government parties." In a rejoinder, the PNI declared that in a democratic state "every political ideology" should participate in determining policy. The PNI expressed its preparedness to "cooperate with any group of any ideology." The Communists rejoiced. "The next government should be more progressive than Wilopo's," *Harian Rakjat* forecast on June 5. "It is possible to form such a government as the balance of forces now favors the people and democracy," i.e., the PKI.

Among Communist theoreticians there has been disagreement over whether it was the "reactionary" Masjumi or the pressure of the "democratic forces" that toppled Wilopo. On June 4, Radio Moscow suggested that it was the former. The Soviet version was that before parliament could discuss Tandjong Morawa, "the Masjumi executive decided to break off its collaboration with the PNI. In this way, parliament was kept from examining this issue of prime public interest. It was the break-up of this two-party coalition that forced Premier Wilopo to resign."

But two years later, Aidit explained that "because of the anti-people's measures carried out by the Masjumi and PSI ministers, the entire democratic forces, including the PNI itself, brought about the downfall of the Wilopo cabinet." [9]

In any event, for Aidit, who—like Sukarno—was paring the opposition layer by layer, the fall of the constructive, moderate Wilopo was a memorable event.

16

Bourgeois Alliance

The demise of Wilopo, with Sukarno applying leverage against him through the informal Nationalist-Communist alliance, terminated a relatively responsible era in the republic's history and afforded the Communist machine its most promising prospect since 1945. In the first *windu* following the proclamation, from Sjahrir's deposition of Sukarno in 1945 to Wilopo, Indonesia had been governed largely by constructive, moderate, and progressive men. Now a new mood, carefully nurtured by Sukarno and the intransigent radicals around him, emerged. The leadership of Indonesia passed into the hands of politically unprincipled men of radically divergent views united by a strong desire for power. They sought power without responsibility; they believed in collective responsibility. The first Ali Sastroamidjojo cabinet—governing from July 30, 1953, to July 24, 1955—provided them with opportunities. In this period, arid, excessive nationalism became the dominant Indonesian theme. It fed not only on mounting frustrations at home but also on the deepening colonial crisis abroad.

Western influence in Asia was approaching a perigee. The Korean truce in 1953 was widely interpreted in Asia as a defeat for the West without parallel since Japan's victory over Russia in that very same arena at the turn of the century. Sukarno was deeply impressed by what he considered a Chinese victory. "How could the Chinese *win* a stalemate against America's superior arms?" asked Sukarno privately. "Was it because of superior ideology?" Sukarno was not alone in questioning the meaning of Korea. "Korea was the first war that we failed to win," wrote Gen-

eral James M. Gavin. "Was it also the symptom of our decline?" [1]
There were many reasons for the failure in Korea, above all, the
disinclination on the part of the American people to assume the
sacrifices and burdens implicit in the defense of the non-Communist world. The situation in Asia, in the vital interest of the
whole of the non-Communist world, demanded that the Chinese
Communist aggressor be returned to his point of entry. Neither
the Truman nor Eisenhower administrations, nor America's allies,
nor the neutralists, were prepared to do so; on the contrary, in the
United States—the arsenal of the non-Communist world—the
policy of both the Democratic and Republican administrations
was to end the war at the least immediate cost to the United
States. The end of the Korean War marked the beginning of the
decline in the relative strength of the non-Communist world vis-à-
vis the Communist bloc, an issue that came to haunt and trouble
America in the 1960 Presidential campaign.

If there was controversy about Korea in 1953, there should have
been none about Indochina, where the French repeated the folly
of the Dutch in Indonesia. False pride, and intransigence born of
that pride, led to an impossible situation. French hunger for
grandeur misled Paris into expending her strength in a hopeless
war that played into the hands of the Communists in Asia and of
extremists of the Right and Left at home. The situation in Indochina was incontrovertible. In the spring of 1954, Dien Bien Phu,
the gateway to Laos, fell to the Communists. The French position
in Indochina collapsed. Nor was it only the West that retreated
before the Communists. The neutralists also retreated. That same
spring, Peking's military absorption of historically peaceful and
autonomous Tibet, the umbrella of the Buddhist world, was
sealed at New Delhi on April 29 by the Chou-Nehru accord, a
pact known as the Five Principles of Peaceful Coexistence:

1. mutual respect for each other's territorial integrity
2. nonaggression
3. noninterference in each other's internal affairs
4. equality and mutual benefit
5. peaceful coexistence.

It is noteworthy that the principles failed to provide for the
explicit settlement of disputes by peaceful negotiation, for the
right of collective defense, or for the right of self-determination.
The accord was little more than a nonaggression pact between a
militarily strong and militarily weak power—with all that implies.
It was dictated by Peking. In retrospect, it was the Dien Bien Phu
of Asian neutralism. Within five years, the Chinese traversed the

Himalayas and occupied 12,000 miles of Indian territory, crushed a people's revolt in Tibet, and extended Communist influence into Nepal, Bhutan, and Sikkim.

In 1954, the psychological impact of rising Communist and falling non-Communist strength in Asia ran deep. In Indonesia, Premier Ali observed in July that the balance of power in the world seemed to be shifting to new positions. This shift was not lost on the nonaligned camp. This, then, was the nature of the crisis in Asia—and the non-Communist world—as the Communists lifted high the banners of nationalism. Only against this background is it perhaps possible to appreciate the import of the post-1951 Moscow line and its impact in Indonesia.

Wilopo's resignation led to a record fifty-eight-day cabinet crisis. The question was whether the Nationalists would leap from the PKI's back or hang on for a long ride. The Communists pushed for a government without the Masjumi and PSI; so had Sukarno since October 17, and the Communists knew it. The PKI put irresistible pressure on the PNI. The PKI described a Masjumi-PSI-PNI coalition as "out of fashion"; demanded prosecution of the PSI "organizers of the anti-Sukarno *Putsch*" (October 17); and implied that Hatta was implicated and, therefore, unfit for the Premiership. The Communists called for a "united-front government comprising all democratic parties and organizations" and assailed the Masjumi and Sjahrir forces as "undemocratic."

The PKI organized demonstrations against the Darul Islam, raising the specter of a theocratic state and subtly drawing the PNI into a popular front to preserve the secular republic. The PKI employed the Darul Islam as a wedge in an abortive effort to open legal channels for the procurement of arms. In a line traceable to the late Amir, the PKI urged the creation of a "people's militia" to fight Islamic extremism and cajoled the PNI into cosponsoring an open letter to Sukarno proposing that "public security organizations be established to render assistance to the state's power instruments in crushing the Darul Islam." [2]

The line was echoed by Tass, which, on July 22, reported a growing struggle between "progressive" and "reactionary" forces in Indonesia. It was also played back at rallies in which the All-Indonesia Association of Former Strugglers (PERBEPSI) served as the principal energumen. For the Communists, PERBEPSI filled the vacuum created by the destruction of the Pesindo at Madiun. At its second congress, held on October 20, 1953, PERBEPSI claimed 205,704 members and 194 branches, conceding that 60 per cent of the membership had "no permanent source of in-

come." [3] The consensus, however, was that PERBEPSI strength
was half that figure and that it was drawn chiefly from the Pemuda
Rakjat.

The agitation by the Communists and their satellite organizations generated the fiction of a spontaneous demand for a national-front government by what passed in Indonesia as "popular opinion." The Communist strategy was transparent. As early as June,
Keng Po had warned against the formation of a cabinet without
the Masjumi or PKI but with PKI support in parliament. "By such
tactics," wrote editor Injo Beng Goat, "the PKI will be able to
isolate the Masjumi and other anti-Communist parties." And the
following month, John H. Ritman, the editor of *Nieuwsgier*, Djakarta's influential Dutch daily, observed:

> The pattern everywhere is quite the same; the people enthusiastically demonstrate against the Darul Islam, but incidentally also
> against the Masjumi and PSI, which actually have nothing to do
> with the Islamic-tinged outlaw gangs, and even against the Vice-President. . . . A widening of the gap between the PNI and Masjumi and an intensification of the current tensions would be useful
> to the Communists.

During those months, terrorism on Java deepened. The Jogjakarta-Bandung express was derailed June 22; eleven persons were
killed. A guerrilla band raided Garut, West Java, on July 13; three
were slain. An armed gang held up a bus south of Djakarta. Invariably, official reports ascribed the incidents to "bandits." The
consensus was that the terrorism was the handiwork of the Darul
Islam. But there was also evidence of a revival of activity by intransigent, Tan Malaka-oriented groups such as Chaerul Saleh's
"people's army" and the remnant Bamboo Spears. In any event,
the attacks fueled the Communist campaign.

As the crisis lengthened, it become clear that a Masjumi-PNI
coalition was indeed out of fashion. In July, Sukarno assured this by
manipulating the cabinet formateur's instructions without Hatta's
agreement. As a consequence, there emerged on July 30 a PNI-NU
coalition government with Communist support in parliament. The
Masjumi and PSI were in the opposition. The new cabinet was
led by Dr. Ali Sastroamidjojo, a veteran PNI leader and Indonesian Ambassador to the United States. The religious scholars,
who occupied eleven seats in parliament, held five portfolios, causing the Masjumi paper, *Abadi*, to observe that this was a maneuver
to create the impression that the Islamic community had not been
thrust aside. But how could the orthodox NU justify participation
in a cabinet so "Leftist" that the Masjumi was in the opposition?
In part, the answer was that any group could purchase the support

of the NU. The religious teachers were also inclined to underestimate the Communist threat. They conceded that the PKI was probably the fourth-largest party, but held that compared to Islam "this was not very impressive." [4] In acknowledging Communist influence on the cabinet, the NU also held that "we should not forget that in the Communist Party are true patriots who also sacrificed much in the struggle for independence." The religious scholars rationalized participation in a government dependent on Communist support on nationalist, not religious, grounds.

Whatever the case, the composition of the cabinet was disquieting. Nine ministers had controversial backgrounds, among them: Iwa Kusumasumantri, Minister of Defense, Progressive faction* and an adviser to the Indonesian Marhaen Association (Permai), an irrational Marxist splinter group (*Pemandangan*, a PSII-orientated paper which wavered in support of the cabinet, observed: "Even though Iwa is not a member of the PKI, he is the champion of the PKI in the cabinet."); Mohammed Yamin, Minister of Education and Culture—an unaffiliated independent, who played a prominent role in Tan Malaka's 1946 coup; Abikusno Tjokrosujoso, Minister of Communications, PSII, also involved in the 1946 coup; Dr. Sunario, Minister of Foreign Affairs, PNI, signer of the Stockholm Peace Appeal; Djody Gondokusumo, Minister of Justice, the National People's Party (PRN), a minor nationalist faction (Djody had attended the Budapest World Peace Conference); Dr. F. L. Tobing, Minister of Information—a member of the Indonesian Sovereignty Association (SKI), another nationalist splinter, at whose September 27, 1953, congress the PKI's faults, if any, were described as the result of shortcomings among Communists rather than with the Party's Marxist-Leninist tenets; Dr. Ong Eng Djie, Minister of Finance—a PNI member of Chinese extraction who was Vice Finance Minister in Amir's cabinet and had been a member of the FDR; Siradjudin Abbas, Minister of State Welfare—a representative of PERTI and signer of the Stockholm Peace Appeal who later attended the Peking World Peace

* The Progressive faction was organized by Luat Siregar on March 1, 1952, and included Abduljahat, Krissubanu, Moh. Padang, I. R. Lobo, and Iwa. Siregar and Abduljahat have since died and are interred in the PKI's "Heroes' Cemetery" at Djakarta. Krissubanu, together with Wikana, was active in the Illegal-PKI and, later, the Pesindo. Iwa and Padang hold prominent posts in Sukarno's "guided democracy." When Siregar died (February 5, 1954), the PKI claimed his parliamentary seat, an indication that the PKI continues to practice Sneevliet's "bloc within" tactics, thus generating suspicion among Indonesians about the credentials of such "independents" as Sidik Kertapati (SAKTI), K. Werdojo (Permai, now Partindo), Siauw Giok Tjan (then SKI), and Iwa himself.

Conference; Sardjarwo, Minister of Agriculture—a BTI leader and the cabinet's only direct link with the PKI.*

In the West, most of these men would probably be regarded as fellow travelers; but in Indonesia, where politics is primarily the politics of the Left, they belonged chiefly to the irrational, radical nationalist fringe, guided by intense hostility toward the West for past wrongs. By supporting Communist positions on international issues, they felt that they were continuing the struggle against the West. Ali's presence as Premier camouflaged the nature of the cabinet, at least abroad. He was in Washington when the government was formed. Ali, who prided himself on being a statesman, had no illusions about the Communists, but like Sidik, his mentor, he believed the Nationalists were making use of the PKI. Indeed, in view of Ali's Washington background and his advocacy of private capital investment in Indonesia, the Communists entertained misgivings about him. He was considered a "bourgeois nationalist" and therefore unreliable. In July, as Ali arrived at Djakarta for consultations, Radio Moscow claimed: "The feeling becomes stronger after Ali Sastroamidjojo, the Ambassador at Washington, arrived suddenly in Djakarta that a foreign power is attempting to violate Indonesia's sovereign right to determine its fate and to form a government if it so desires." [5]

Moscow reassured its listeners, however, that "although its program tends at times to be confusing, the PNI nevertheless is defending the vital interests of the Indonesian people." But when the cabinet was formed, Moscow selected a new record as the PKI greeted Ali's premiership as a triumph for "progressive and democratic forces" over "reactionary and fascist groups." [6] Actually, the pursuit of a non-Communist policy at home coupled with a pro-Communist policy abroad characterized the Ali cabinet. As for the PKI, it had little choice but to support Ali; the alternative would have been a government with Masjumi participation.

The sharpest reaction to the cabinet came from Atjeh, on the northern tip of Sumatra, a warlike Islamic redoubt. Whereas the Communists welcomed Ali with "joy and happiness," [7] the Atjehnese rose in rebellion under the leadership of Tengku Daud Bereuh, the former revolutionary governor of the region. Daud proclaimed a State of Islam (Darul Islam) on September 20 in protest against the formation of a "pro-Communist and anti-Islam" government. In this manner the Darul Islam movement spread to a fourth island. Since Kartosuwirjo's proclamation in 1949, Kahar Muzzakhar had proclaimed a Darul Islam in the

* The PKI mistrusted him. In June, 1958, Sardjorwo joined the PNI.

South Celebes and Ibnu Hadjar in South Kalimantan. These revolts were uncoordinated and over the years deteriorated largely into terrorist movements. But the revolt in Atjeh enjoyed popular support and the dissidents quickly established control of the hinterland, confining government forces to towns and arterial roads. It was the old Indonesian-Dutch fighting pattern all over again. The rebellion had many motives, but its overriding political character was manifested by the rebels' abduction and murder of PKI, PNI, and PERTI members.[8]

The Atjehnese revolt dramatized the threat of Islamic extremism to the secular republic and confirmed Sidik's earlier conviction that "the Darul Islam constitutes a more dangerous threat to the state at present than the Communists."[9] Sidik was determined more than ever to thwart a Masjumi victory at the polls, which, he reasoned, would lead to the formation of an Islamic republic. Only by an alliance with the Communists, he believed, could the PNI hope to neutralize Islamic strength at the polls. Sidik believed that the Masjumi-NU schism had cost the Masjumi about half its strength. Sidik's strategy, therefore, was to widen the breach between the Masjumi and NU while simultaneously using the Communists to maintain a PNI-dominated government until the elections. Playing with Aidit was risky, but Sidik was confident. Thus he instructed PNI branches to "establish close relations with the PKI and cooperate closely with the NU. I am confident you will carry out this task tactfully."[10]

On September 10, in the wake of the Atjeh rebellion, the parliament voted 122 to 34, with 26 abstentions, to provide Ali's government with the "opportunity to carry out its program." It is perhaps significant that the Masjumi and Catholics were alone in the original opposition. The PSI abstained; Sjahrir doubted that the parliamentary system could afford a prolongation of the crisis. Thus it appeared that Ali was correct in maintaining that the cabinet was not dependent on the Communists for support. But by December 15, 1954, parliament had rejected a Masjumi motion of no confidence in the government by a 115 to 92 vote, with 6 abstentions. For its majority of 23, the cabinet required 17 Communists, 3 SOBSI, 2 BTI, and at least 1 of the 8 votes it received from the crypto-Communist Progressives, the faction of Defense Minister Iwa.

Firmly entrenched in power, the cabinet pursued an authoritarian-nationalist program. "Patriotism" was invoked to stifle the spirited Indonesian press, which had attained freedom of dissent for the first time during the revolution. The cabinet held that the main task of a "national" press was not to reflect but to "guide" society.[11] By 1960, the pretense of a free press was abandoned and only officially licensed papers were permitted. On January 7, 1961, *Pedoman*, the last of the opposition dailies, was silenced in the name of "guided democracy."

The central government seeded the administration with Javanese, PNI-oriented officials. In the "outer islands," the policy of Javanization gave rise to restlessness. Within three months of Ali's investiture, the Masjumi felt constrained to reproach Ali for pursuing a personnel policy which was "based exclusively on the party system and violating the legal security of civil service officials in general." [12] Ali's cabinet also introduced measures for the surveillance of foreigners, presumably Dutch and Chinese, but affecting Indonesians as well.[13] Indonesians offering hospitality to foreigners were instructed to report to the police within twenty-four hours the arrival of foreign visitors. Another measure empowered the Justice Ministry to detain suspected aliens for one year for investigation; the parliamentary opposition protested these measures, observing that in the colonial period officials were empowered to hold aliens for only twenty days. Despite the ominous implications of these controls, most Indonesians viewed them lightly as part of the government's "war of nerves." Sophisticated Indonesians felt that the measures were only for show, since the state apparatus was too inefficient to implement such decrees. The majority of Indonesians were convinced that what was apparent was not real, that Indonesian politics would always remain a shadow play in which nobody would be injured. Did the PKI feel that way too? "Now you're dragging in the Cold War," a cabinet minister said in reply. In any event, the statutes were on the books and only awaited enforcement by a future government.

In this period, too, recurring crises weakened the money economy in the seaports, the inland towns, and the estate belts—the main areas of PKI strength. In the isolated rural areas, where a barter economy prevailed and life was at the subsistence level, the growing economic dislocation was slow to take effect. But as shortages of consumers' goods developed—soap, matches, kerosene, etc.—smuggling, black-marketing, and hoarding became commonplace. The phrase *bawah medja* (under the table) also was heard increasingly after 1953 as corruption within and outside the government assumed massive proportions and seriously undermined the moral authority of the government. In July, 1954, the PIR threatened a cabinet crisis over an "unfair" division of import-export licenses, and *Sumber*, an army newspaper, warned as early as April 27, 1954, that "the name of the nationalist movement will be stained" if corrupt practices continue unchecked among groups "who consider themselves so powerful that they openly pursue courses reminiscent of the Kuomintang and King Farouk." Even the Communists were troubled. On November 30, 1954, Aidit criticized growing bureaucratic corruption. It was clear that in supporting the government, the Communists incurred grave liabilities.

The PKI abetted deterioration in Indonesia in many ways. Ali, for example, struggled to arrest a decline in production by proposing to increase the working day from seven to eight hours. SOBSI assailed the proposals as "capitalist exploitation." But when a delegation returned from Moscow and reported that some Soviet workers put in a nine-hour day, SOBSI hailed the "vitality" of "socialist society."

During this interlude, the Communists benefited enormously as the rift between Sukarno and Hatta moved into the open for the first time. Hatta, disturbed by Sukarno's preoccupation with Dutch windmills while ignoring domestic problems, publicly declared that the fight for West Irian will be unsuccessful if based only on slogans. The Indonesian people, he said, must show that they are capable of developing the country, thus proving to the world that they are able to exploit the natural resources at their disposal for the welfare of the people and the country.

Sukarno was unmoved; only through Irian, he felt, could national unity be consolidated and the far-flung islands welded together. But what after Irian? The schism within the duumvirate widened appreciably. By the end of 1954, Hatta announced that he would resign. Actually, the breaking point in their relationship had come in the summer, when Sukarno took a second wife (his fourth marriage). While plural marriage is permitted under Islam, the practice is frowned on by modern religious leaders. Sukarno's action generated widespread disapproval, especially among the educated classes. Until then, the President's licentious private life had not been public knowledge; now, however, it attracted national and international attention. The Communists were embarrassed; *Sin Po* defended the President in circuitous fashion. "Mr. Sukarno seldom has a rendezvous with his new wife," *Sin Po* said. "He only visits her once a month—and stays a week." Hatta was determined to dissociate himself from this sordid business.

Hatta was also troubled by the growing political irresponsibility of Sukarno and the PNI. The President accused the opposition of "treason" when it sought to bring down the cabinet by parliamentary means and declared that if Indonesia was "leaning"— an allusion to the Cold War—it was "leaning toward the side that opposed colonialism." Sukarno was discarding his traditional domestic political impartiality. Sidik also opened a wide-ranging campaign to discredit the opposition. He charged that "imperialist nationals" had infiltrated the government, that "rows on rows of imperialist forces are ready to colonize Indonesia again," and that there was not only "foreign imperialism but also national imperialism, which assumes various forms and which we must all oppose." The effort to discredit the Masjumi and Sjahrir Socialists in particular was enthusiastically endorsed by the PKI.

The creation of a bristling nationalist atmosphere in Indonesia at a time when Communist power was expanding on the Asian mainland led inevitably to repressive measures against the Dutch minority and an intensification of the Irian issue. The pre-cabinet PNI-PKI drive against the Darul Islam acquired new dimensions. The Darul Islam was employed not only to blacken the Masjumi but also the Dutch and, by association, the West. Sukarno accused the Darul Islam of seeking the support of a "Cold War bloc" and charged that Dutch nationals had conspired with Kartosuwirjo. In truth, however, the Dutch had sought to avoid entanglement in Indonesia's domestic politics in the hope of maintaining their economic position; Dutch business interests were critical of The Hague's retention of Irian. Nevertheless, a wave of Dutch arrests followed. By February, 1954, thirty-two Dutch nationals were being detained, some on charges of abetting the Darul Islam and some on no charges at all. The wave of arrests was followed by a note to The Hague in March, 1954, proposing negotiations on Irian and the Netherlands-Indonesian Union. The note coincided with the opening of the struggle for Dien Bien Phu, the convocation of the Geneva conference on Indochina, and the first meeting of the Colombo powers (Indonesia, Burma, Pakistan, India, and Ceylon). Ali, sensitive to Cold War pressures, was determined to "internationalize" the New Guinea issue and felt this was "the appropriate time for action."

Indonesia's note to Holland came at a time when Djakarta had its first envoys at Peking and Moscow. Mononutu, the former PNI Information Minister, had arrived in Peking in January, and in March, Dr. Subandrio, a former Socialist who had left his party after the Sjahrir-Amir rupture, arrived in Moscow. Subandrio received immediate assurances from Foreign Minister Molotov of Soviet support on Irian. In Peking, Mononutu received similar assurances from Foreign Minister Chou En-lai. "We believe," Chou told Mononutu, "that every power has the right to claim friendly frontiers."

The Dutch, meanwhile, agreed to discuss dissolution of the

Union but balked on Irian. In August, after fifty days of negotiations at The Hague, both parties agreed on the dissolution of the Netherlands Indonesian Union and the abrogation of the Union's statute.

The 1949 effort by the Dutch to salvage their position in Indonesia by the creation of a commonwealth along British lines had ended. The Dutch failed to realize that the British Commonwealth was founded on good will and voluntary association. The new Hague accord—the details of which were still to be worked out—provided Ali with a propaganda triumph at home. "I regard this as one of the biggest achievements of my year-old government," Ali said. And *Nieuwsgier* commented: "Nobody will question its passing because it has always been a false symbol. The effect of its abrogation is primarily psychological in character."

Although the PKI approved the agreement, the Communists reacted like the dog robbed of a bone. "Only fools can be satisfied with the mere annulment of the Union," *Harian Rakjat* said, demanding liquidation of the Dutch economic position in Indonesia. And Buntaran Martoatmodjo (Progressive) criticized the Dutch for acting more in the Western interest than the Dutch national interest by accepting the Union's dissolution.(!) Obviously, abrogation of the Union was a notable example of disengagement between the West and radical nationalism.

But the biggest bone of contention between the Dutch and Indonesia, between Indonesia and the West, remained—Irian. Sukarno had been building a slow fire under Irian. He never failed to fan the embers on his endless tours of the islands. "I have been described as an 'agitator' over the Irian question," he declared. "I shall inscribe that on my breast in letters of gold. This epithet of 'agitator' I accept [with] honor."

But having failed to secure Irian by wooing the West during the Sukiman period, Sukarno now turned to the U.N. for assistance.

Indonesia's international position appeared favorable. Djakarta enjoyed the support of the Communist and emerging Afro-Asian blocs. But there was uneasiness in Indonesia. Past Indonesian experience with the U.N. demonstrated that it was little more than a Cold War arena. There was fear that Irian would become an East-West issue serving Moscow at the expense of Djakarta. But on August 17, the die was cast. Sukarno announced that the dispute would be submitted to the world organization. Significantly, perhaps, the President discarded six pages of prepared text that day devoted to the deteriorating economic situation. The following evening, the Communists organized an Irian Liberation rally in front of the palace.

In September, Foreign Minister Sunario emplaned for New York as a crowd of about 200 representing, they claimed, 35 nationalist and Communist organizations, wished him well. In a joint statement, they accused "reactionary elements" at home of hampering the Irian liberation campaign. The absence of opposition party signatures pointed to the "reactionaries." It was a tactic of deception; the Masjumi and PSI, for example, learned of the statement only after it had been released.

In Indonesia the consensus was that the General Assembly would pass a mild resolution and that the "victory" would bolster the chronically shaky Ali cabinet.

On December 10, to the surprise of almost everyone, the General Assembly, by a thirty-four to twenty-one vote with four abstentions—three short of the necessary two-thirds majority—rejected the operational paragraph of a resolution urging both parties to "find a solution in conformity with the principles of the charter of the United Nations." Indonesia was stunned. Sukarno, at a PNI congress at Bandung—where "victory" at the U.N. was to be celebrated—denounced the Assembly's action and in fury called for the development at home of "power, power, and once more, power." Sidik warned that Indonesia would continue to strive for a peaceful solution of the dispute, but, if this becomes impossible, it would, if necessary, use force. For the PKI, the Assembly's action was an unanticipated bonus. On December 12, Aidit declared: "It is again clear that America and other states are wielding great power in the United Nations. As a result, no concrete decision could be taken on a *peaceful* solution of the issue of colonial oppression in West Irian."—(Italics added.)

On the intransigent radical Left, the failure at the U.N. generated new demands for an end to the policy of appeasement. The same voices that had opposed the Linggadjati, Renville, and Hague accords were heard anew. On December 15, the late Tan Malaka's Murba—like Sjahrir's Socialists now a minor party but exercising disproportionately large influence—cited the U.N. reversal as the "umpteenth failure in the history of weak diplomacy based on compromise." Murba said the government should declare the Netherlands an aggressor, that it should sever diplomatic relations between Indonesia and Holland, confiscate Dutch property, appoint a military governor to West Irian, and unilaterally abrogate all agreements with the Netherlands. That same day, a small group known as the "1945 Generation" gathered at the home of Djakarta's Mayor Sudiro (PNI) for their "first reunion." This was part of the group that had participated in the kidnaping of Sukarno and Hatta in 1945, had played a prominent role in the period of the *bersiap* terror, was implicated in the Tan Malaka *Putsch* in 1946, and had been in armed opposition to the Round Table settlement in 1949. The chairman of the meeting was A.M. Hanafi, an irrational radical nationalist and adopted son of Sukarno. There was unanimous agreement at the meeting that a revival of the "Spirit of '45" was a prerequisite for the attainment of Irian. The meeting had been encouraged by Sukarno. After 1957, the Murba program was to be implemented and control of Indonesia passed largely into the hands of the Generation of '45. For orthodox and unorthodox Communists alike, this was a historic occasion.

The United States, pursuing its neutralist policy had, of course, abstained when the General Assembly voted on the Irian question in 1954. In the view of a former American Embassy official, the failure of Washington to exercise leadership reflected "a totally unimaginative lack of policy which, let alone not preparing for eventualities, tries to ignore their very existence." [14] The Dutch, of course, were morally wrong to impose their rule on West New Guinea, and intelligent Westerners knew it. It would have served Dutch interests, and those of the whole non-Communist world, if the United States had forced a solution of the Irian issue as it had on the question of Indonesian independence in its final stages. It was clear that a Western policy of intransigence on Irian would ultimately drive Sukarno into the arms of the West's principal adversary. But in defense of the United States and the West it should be noted that supporting Indonesia's claim to Irian in 1954 was inopportune. It would have meant enhancing the position of a basically corrupt, extremist, nationalist government whose retention of power was predicated on Communist support. The time for a transfer of Irian to Indonesia was with a Hatta, Natsir, or Wilopo in power. Thus, the failure of Western policy in Indonesia lay in not providing the moderate, constructive and progressive forces in Indonesia the support they needed to hold rein on Sukarno, the extremist radical nationalists, and the Communists.

Sukarno turned to the world body three more times for aid and comfort between 1955–57. Spurned each time, and encouraged by the Communists and radical nationalists, Djakarta in 1957 drove the Dutch from Indonesia in a fit of desperation and frustration. In 1961, with the acceleration of Soviet arms shipments, Indonesia prepared for the forcible seizure of Irian and, in the process, enhanced the Communist position on Java.

17

Aidtisim

In the atmosphere of the Ali cabinet, the Indonesian Communists engineered a spectacular revival, establishing the Communist "presence" in post-independent Indonesia. This happened a mere seven years after Madiun and two after Sukiman's razzia. In Aidit's words, the PKI had become an "important national force which neither friend nor foe can ignore." [1]

The PKI recovered at a time when the Communist parties of Burma, Malaya, the Philippines, and Thailand, desperately attempting to pursue a Right strategy, were proscribed and Communist activity in India circumscribed. Indeed, nowhere in non-Communist Asia did the Communists masquerade so successfully in nationalist guise—and accordingly enjoy so free a hand—as in Indonesia.

It may also be added that nowhere in non-Communist Asia was the national leadership as irresponsible or unaware as in Indonesia.

As interpreted by Aidit, a cabinet without Masjumi and Sjahrir Socialists was a triumph of the Right strategy and evidence that a mass party could influence the course of events outside the government. "The formation of the Ali government," Aidit held, "teaches that a mass movement is not only capable of realizing economic demands and immediate political demands but also teaches that with a mass movement changes of policy can be realized, that with a mass movement a somewhat progressive [pro-Communist] government can be formed." [2]

The unpredictable winds of history were blowing in Aidit's direction, at least momentarily. Not only could he claim the cabinet as a personal victory, but its formation coincided with the struggle over Stalinist succession in Moscow and the liquidation of Beria on July 10 as a "bourgeois degenerate" and "agent of international imperialism." Purges in Moscow have always provided Communist parties with a cover for settling intra-Party feuds. Following Beria's arrest, the Chinese, Korean, and Japanese parties conducted purges. Aidit was not inclined to miss the opportunity. "The liquidation of Beria," he said, "should be a reminder to national as well as international popular movements." Aidit, whose leadership credentials were traceable to his return from Stalin's bier, now moved to exploit the advent of Ali and the demise of Beria to consolidate his control over the Party apparatus. At a plenary meeting of the Central Committee, October 6–9, 1953, the old PKI leadership was purged, a new hierarchy "elected," and a stamp of approval affixed to Aidit's "Road to a People's Democracy." Aidit's "Road" was designed to lead the PKI from the dead end into which the Party had been driven by Musso in the period of the Left strategy.

The first hint of purge was Aidit's announcement on October 9 that Tan Ling Djie had been expelled from the Central Committee for "subjectivism, legalism, and liquidationism." Tan was given until the convocation of a Fifth Party Congress the following March to "proletarianize his ideology," i.e., subscribe to Aidit's "Road." In a tactic reminiscent of Stalin in 1928, Aidit used the Tan affair to elevate himself into the position of sole arbiter of disputes within the Party. Henceforth, Aidit alone would judge who was guilty of "Right-wing" or "Left-wing" opportunism. In the ideological sphere, the malady of Tan Ling-djieism was condemned in a plenum resolution as reflecting both "dogmatic and empirical trends in the Party which caused the Party to make Rightist and 'Leftist' [sic] mistakes which seriously damaged the growth of the revolutionary movement." [3]

In Marxist-Leninist cant, as a "dogmatist," Tan was a theorist who isolated himself from the masses; as an "empiricist," Tan labored unguided by theory. Clearly, Tan Ling-djieism was the embodiment of all evil. In point of fact, Tan's heresy was his advocacy, with Alimin's connivance, of a policy of attaining power "legally" by the development of militant labor unions and peasant organizations, by resorting to strikes, and by waging an intense parliamentary struggle. Tan favored a return to the tactics of the popular front, the development of a small cadre party, and the tactics of concealment and infiltration. Tan regarded the unsophisticated masses as unreliable and scoffed at Aidit's faith in a mass movement. Thus Tan's condemnation for "subjectivism" referred to his personal opposition to Aidit's program; "legalism," to his emphasis on a parliamentary struggle; and "liquidationism," to his advocacy of a small hard-core party as opposed to a mass-based party.

Doctrinally, Tan and Aidit occupied the same ground—Mao's "four-class bloc," now standard Moscow-Peking fare in the underdeveloped Afro-Asian world. Their point of departure was tactical. Aidit favored a mass movement, depreciated parliamentary struggle, and advocated operating not only aboveground but also in the foreground. Aidit eschewed a "legal" path because the "history of the struggle for national independence by the Indonesian people . . . as well as in other countries has shown that parliamentary struggle is not sufficient in order to be successful in forming a people's democratic government.[4]

No, it was "not sufficient." Without exception, Communist rule was imposed and maintained by arms in the Communist world; in Mao's words: "Every Communist must grasp the truth: political power grows out of the barrel of the gun." But although the PKI may de-emphasize parliament as an arena of struggle, Aidit advised the Party to "take the most active part" in the mechanics of the parliamentary system. Still, if parliamentary struggle is "not sufficient," what is the way out for the PKI? Revolution? Doubtlessly a reckless venture would obliterate the gains made since 1952; moreover, such tactics were obviated by the nature of the Right strategy. Then how? "The way out," Aidit said, "is by changing the balance of power between the imperialists, landlord class, and compradore bourgeois on the one side [the rulers], and the strength of the people on the other side [the ruled]. The way out is by agitation, mobilization, and organization of the masses. . . . A mass movement is capable of causing a *change of policy*. [Aidit's italics.] The formation of the Ali Sastroamidjojo government is evidence of this."

Agitation, mobilization, and the organization of the masses, then, is the core of "Aiditism." In an impoverished country of credulous masses, what method is better than demagoguery? Encased in the theory of the four-class bloc, Aidit's program held forth the promise of utopia once the Communists achieved power. All the ingredients of Mao's "New Democracy" were there.[5] In an Indonesian people's democracy, the peasants would be provided free land and the right of tenure. The properties of rich and middle-class peasants would be protected; only "feudal" tracts and foreign estates would be seized. National capitalists would be protected against foreign competition; only the holdings of foreign capitalists would be expropriated. Workers would enjoy the right of collective bargaining and the right to form trade unions; all debts would be canceled. Intellectuals would be provided with un-limited opportunities. Civil liberties would flourish, etc. A dispassionate appraisal of the Communist record in lands where they have acquired absolute power—and nowhere have they succeeded without "the barrel of a gun"—reveals that the Communist program is clearly a fabrication designed to snare the gullible, unsuspecting, and frustrated. Tragically, today the Communist appeal appears as effective in the underdeveloped world as it was in the West yesterday. The West may be in the winter of its experience with Communism, but for Asia it is only summer, and in Africa it is barely spring.

The commotion in political circles accompanying Tan's demotion mounted on October 10 with the disclosure that Alimin had been shunted from the Party's Politburo to the Central Committee for "reasons of health." To many Indonesians, Alimin had been Aidit's real target, but the young Turk was compelled to treat the elder statesman with circumspection in view of his lingering prestige among the rank and file. However, now the purge acquired a new coloration. Tan was of Chinese racial extraction; Alimin had studied at Yenan and had introduced Maoist doctrine into Indonesia. Was the purge a manifestation of a broader conflict between Moscow and Peking? In November there was greater speculation; Siauw Giok Tjhan resigned from the editorship of the Party daily, *Harian Rakjat*. Within a year, however, Siauw reappeared as a leader of a powerful Chinese organization, Badan Permusjawaratan Kewarganegaraan Indonesia (BAPERKI)—the Consultative Body on Indonesian Citizenship—suggesting a reappraisal of the "Chinese withdrawal" from the Party. Although it was never clearly determined, the impression thereafter was that the purge of Chinese was superficial and may have been designed to dissociate the PKI from the Chinese minority in the face of the rising nationalist sentiment generated by the PKI-PNI alliance. It is also conceivable that the purge was designed in part to provide Communists of Chinese racial origin with the opportunity to capture the leadership of the Chinese community, which, at that time, was already planning to enter a future general election as a distinct ethnic minority. This interpretation was strengthened the following year, after the Party's Fifth Congress. At that time, the PKI launched an intensive pro-Chinese educational campaign. The Party sought to impress on the country the view that Indonesians of Chinese ethnic origin formed a "national potential" in the struggle against "imperialism and foreign capital." Indonesians of Chinese ancestry, it was said, should therefore be protected by the government in the competition against "foreign capital."

In any event, the purge of Chinese gave rise to an impression of controversy within the PKI over the question of Moscow or Peking leadership of the international movement.* This was premature, if not misleading. Assuredly, a Chinese faction existed within the Party. Aidit himself, in his draft program, confirmed its existence. But the coordination, if not subordination, of PKI policies to either Moscow or Peking at this time was only indirectly, if at all, related to the debate.

The Indonesian Communists, since the founding of the Party by the Dutch, had looked toward Moscow for guidance and inspiration. In the early 1950's it appeared unlikely that the Party would alter its orientation. Neither the so-called Moscow nor Peking faction, for strategic reasons, seemed inclined to accept the idea of Peking overlordship. Russia, as viewed from Indonesia, was a distant power; China, a nearby giant. Aidit referred to China in his program as "our big neighbor." Obviously, an Indonesian people's democracy would enjoy a greater degree of "independence" by leaning toward Moscow rather than Peking at some future date and by employing the Kremlin for leverage against China and the Chinese. In this context, looking in the direction of Moscow could be interpreted as a manifestation of the PKI's "nationalist orientation." Yet there was real controversy between "Moscow" and "Peking" factions. Five years later, the dispute was to assume serious proportions, and by the spring of 1962, the PKI appeared to be caught in the middle of the Moscow-Peking conflict over strategy in the nuclear-missile age.

What, then, was the nature of the controversy incubating in 1953? At its heart was the question of how far to go in the alliance with bourgeois nationalism in the person of Sukarno. The Moscow faction, led by Aidit, was conscious of the potential dangers of identifying the Party with the President. But Aidit considered this the price for a short cut to power. It was also the price of "proletarian internationalism," i.e., fidelity to Moscow's Right strategy. The Peking faction, then loyal to Moscow on international policy and influenced by Lukman and, to a lesser degree, Sudisman, advocated a collision course with the corrupt, demoralized, and inefficient nationalist regimes that administered Indonesia from 1953 onward. In sum, the Aidit faction regarded Sukarno as another Sun Yat-sen; the Lukman faction, as another Chiang Kai-shek. However, whether, in the final analysis, this Peking faction could con-

* The author pleads guilty to premature optimism over the possibilites of a Moscow-Peking rift as viewed from Indonesia. See his dispatches to *The Christian Science Monitor*, November 7, 1953, and April 8, 1954, and to *The New York Times*, March 23, 1954.

tinue to divorce internal from external policies was doubtful. A PKI deviation from the international line, even if only internally, could be construed as a desire for a larger degree of independence from Soviet direction. Yet the Peking faction within the PKI, at least until December, 1961, when the PKI criticized Moscow's denunciation of Albania, believed it could both have and eat its cake, that is, pursue an independent line at home while following the Moscow line abroad. But by late 1961, as the dispute between Moscow and Peking intensified, the Left-wing of the PKI found it increasingly difficult to support Khrushchev's Right strategy abroad. Moreover, Khrushchev's gradual transformation of the monolithic unity of the Communist bloc into a seemingly flexible commonwealth (in part dictated by the necessity to dissociate a nuclear Russia from the possible adventures of a non-nuclear ally, China) served still further to encourage divisive tendencies within the PKI (and other out-of-power Communist parties).

Perhaps with a view to avoiding an ideological dispute within the Party, Aidit, as early as late 1953, was defending himself against the Left not in theoretical or ideological terms (this came only in 1959) but in strategic terms. By doing so he attested to his long-run nationalist outlook, the "nationalism" of the Left faction notwithstanding. Thus Aidit observed that

> some Party members, after studying the experience of the Chinese revolution are of the opinion that because it is more important to stir the peasants so that they may join the struggle, all the Communists must leave the city and work among the peasants. This conclusion is, of course, wrong. Firstly, it must be noted that the Chinese Communists never neglected work among the laborers; on the contrary, they stress the importance of working in the cities, especially when they carry on guerrilla war outside the cities. Secondly, there are specific differences in geography and political development between Indonesia and China that must be noted.[6]

Although Aidit avoids cataloguing the "specific differences" between China and Indonesia, some are obvious. Indonesia, for example, is an archipelago; China is largely a single land mass. China, moreover, possesses extensively populated tracts, mountains, and forests far from towns and lines of communication and Indonesia, particularly Java, the PKI citadel, does not. What is perhaps decisive is that China, unlike Indonesia, possessed an "active sanctuary," the friendly rear contiguous to a Communist country where Communist guerrillas could train, rest, and be refurbished. Russia served as Mao's "active sanctuary" after he began his Long March in October, 1934. The Communists in Korea, Vietnam, and Laos have also enjoyed "active sanctuaries." There were other differences. Mao had a Red Army; at Madiun, the Indonesian Communist forces were shattered. Only the year before, with the creation of PERBEPSI, did the PKI make its first serious effort to reassemble a paramilitary front. Unlike China, too, the PKI is confronted with an organized and potent religious force, Islam, whose extremist orthodox wing has already been in the field as guerrillas. In the colonial era, Islam had been a rallying point against Western encroachment. As manifested by the revolt in Atjeh, Islam was now developing into a rallying point against Communism.

Four years later, at a fifth plenum, confronted with growing demands by the Peking faction to abandon the Right strategy at home for a more aggressive line against Sukarno, Aidit put the issue squarely before the Party membership in geopolitical terms. The PKI's position was "difficult," Aidit said, because "Indonesia has no frontiers with a country already completely liberated from imperialist power." [7]

In effect, Aidit implied that the PKI could not wage an armed struggle for power because the Party lacked an "active sanctuary." On that and subsequent occasions, Aidit would therefore conclude that for this and other reasons, it is "all the more necessary for the Indonesian revolutionaries to take their own course in bringing the Indonesian revolution to completion." That course is set forth in Aidit's Road—the "agitation, organization, and mobilization of the masses."

Thus the purge of Tan and Alimin was unrelated to the Moscow-Peking controversy over Communist-bloc leadership. In the Plenum's election of a new hierarchy, therefore, it was not surprising that the Peking faction, loyal to both Moscow and Aidit, retained a large voice. At that time, with Stalin's passing, "collective leadership" was the catch phrase in the Communist world. In the struggle for Stalin's mantle, the interlude of uncertainty prior to Khrushchev's victory was euphemistically portrayed in those terms and sanctified as a "Leninist principle." The PKI of course parroted the line; Aidit went so far as to declare that the "characteristics of the Party can only be preserved if Party members and cadres are loyal to . . . collective leadership."

As applied to Indonesia, control of the Party in 1954 passed into the collective hands of a trio composed of Aidit, then thirty years of age; Lukman, thirty-four; and Njoto, twenty-nine. Njoto, like Lukman, was a "second-generation" Communist; his father, Rustandar Sosrohartono, an East Javanese Party official, had been arrested by the Dutch in 1947 and died in jail on April 10, 1948. During the Japanese occupation, Njoto had worked in the anti-

Japanese underground in Surabaya and, in 1945, had established a Party branch at Besuki, East Java. In 1947, Sardjono named Njoto to the KNIP and later he became chairman of the PKI caucus in the working committee. In June, 1948, Njoto was appointed to the Politburo as a candidate member. Musso apparently recognized in him the Stalinist qualities of leadership and elevated him to full membership in the reorganized Party hierarchy.

At the plenum meeting, Aidit was "unanimously elected" as Secretary General; Lukman, First Deputy Secretary General; and Njoto, Second Deputy Secretary General. A hint of Lukman's Left or Peking background—within the Indonesian context—was provided in the official biographies issued after the session. Njoto was described as abiding "by the Leninist-Stalinist wing of the Party, which is led by Comrade Aidit." Perhaps it was an oversight, but nothing was said of which wing Lukman abided by.

18

Toward a Mass Movement

The Fifth Party Congress, held March 14–21, 1954, at which the decisions of the plenum were rubber-stamped, was an event of historic importance in the Communist world. The Australian and Dutch parties sent emissaries; international fronts such as the WFTU and IUS sent representatives; an East German trade delegation arrived; so did Georgi Afrin of Tass, who had left Indonesia in 1948, after the formation of the FDR. A Party presidium handled the Congress' housekeeping arrangements. The presidium, intended as a display of Party unity, consisted of Alimin as a representative of the 1926 rebellion; Achmad Sumadi of the 1935 Illegal-PKI; Aidit, the 1942 anti-Japanese underground; Njoto, the 1945 August Revolution; and K. Supit, the 1948 "New Road" group. Malenkov and Mao were nominated honorary members, apparently in an attempt to silence rumors of a Moscow-Peking rift. This demonstration of supranationalism was defended by Aidit on the ground that "these [foreign] leaders have done much to help the struggle of the Indonesian people to defend democracy and crush world imperialism." But whispers of a Moscow-Peking schism persisted as the Congress concluded with an outdoor rally at which portraits of Malenkov and Aidit were displayed behind the speakers' rostrum, whereas Mao's picture was relegated to the wings with those of Marx, Engels, Lenin, Stalin, and Musso. Here, certainly, was additional proof, if any was necessary, of the Party's Moscow orientation.

During the Congress, the Tan-Alimin purge deepened. Tan, having failed to "proletarianize" his ideology, was expelled from the Party; Alimin was expelled from the Central Committee but was permitted to retain his Party membership. Lesser figures were demoted; Aidit succeeded Ngadiman, a Tan Ling Djie aide, as a PKI deputy in parliament. A new table of power emerged in the PKI:

Secretariat

D. N. Aidit, Secretary General
M. H. Lukman, First Deputy Secretary General
Njoto, Second Deputy Secretary General

Politburo	*Central Committee*	
Aidit	Achmad Sumadi	Njoto
Lukman	J. Adjitorop	Nurah Nursuhud
Njoto	Aidit	P. Pardede
Sudisman	Bachtaruddin	Sakirman
Sakirman	Djokosudjono	Sudisman
	Lukman	K. Supit
	M. Zaelani	

Central Committee
Candidate Members

A. Z. Anwar
Anwar Kadir
Siswojo

The new team moved to exploit the favorable climate of the Ali cabinet for the "agitation, mobilization, and organization of the masses." Aidit moved his first pawn on the eve of the October plenum. On September 17, the Communists, employing militant, Sukarnophile, and anti-Dutch slogans, assumed formal control of the 200,000-member BTI, the largest peasant front in Indonesia. A BTI "national congress" voted to fuse the organization with the Indonesian Peasant Organization (RTI), the official peasant arm of the PKI, but to retain the name BTI. Until then, the BTI had been jointly administered by the PKI and PSI, their last link since the Amir-Sjahrir rupture. With the PKI in control, Sjahrir's followers bolted, taking a quarter of the membership into a rival Indonesian Peasant Movement, the GTI. Sadjarwo, Ali's Minister of Agriculture, remained in the reorganized BTI. For Aidit, the Sjahrir withdrawal was another victory. *Sikap*, Sjahrir's magazine, explained the Socialist retreat by asserting that the "non-Communist members of the BTI could do nothing to check the spread of Communist influence. In fact, their presence within the BTI served the Communists' purpose, because they acted as a front to attract public support."

The Communist move was the first of several in which the PKI, in quest of a mass movement, asserted control over organizations that had long been under their influence, including the Pemuda Rakjat, GERWANI,* and SOBSI. For example, SOBSI's Njono publicly applied for PKI membership because "I have come to see the light [after] a study of the decisions of the Fifth National Congress." [1] Njono insisted, however, that SOBSI was "a truly independent mass movement."

The consolidation of Communist control over youth, labor, women, and peasant organizations was accompanied by a seemingly endless series of rallies: "Anticolonial," "International Solidarity," and "International Women's" days, ad infinitum. Dotting the calendar with special events assured the Party of uninterrupted activity through the year. Compared to other Indonesian parties, there was never a dull moment for the PKI rank and file. Communists always found a cause to defend, a protest to raise, a barricade to mount.

Under Aidit, the Communists also labored to erase the stigma of Madiun and create the impression of being a "genuinely" Indonesian party. Aidit was confronted with an awesome task, and although the Communists enjoyed considerable success, the Party never quite was able to remove the suspicion that it was a secret, conspiratorial organization dominated from abroad. Aidit declared that the "Communists would always defend the red-and-white." He endorsed the Pantjasila, the five pillars of the secular republic formulated by Sukarno in June, 1945 (belief in God, nationalism, humanism, democracy, and social justice); condescendingly absolved the PNI for its alleged complicity in the "assassination of PKI leaders at Madiun"; and developed the line that "at the moment there are no Indonesians who want to think and believe any longer that the Madiun provocation, which was responsible for the loss of so many lives, was engineered by Communists." The latter theme was developed within the context that colonialism—i.e., the West—not Communism, was the main enemy of Indonesia. On occasion Aidit's enthusiasm ran away with him; for example, in a momentary slip that generated sharp press criticism, he observed that the August Revolution had been "only a general rehearsal for the real show, which is still to come." And in another blunder, on December 7, 1954, in a speech commemorating the thirty-seventh anniversary of the Bolshevik Revolution, he claimed that "without the October Revolution, there would have been no

* The Indonesian Women's Movement, formerly the All-Indonesia Women's Movement (GERWIS), founded in 1950 by Mrs. Suwarti, a PKI member of parliament. Aidit's wife, Tanti, who studied medicine at Moscow, is a prominent leader of GERWANI, which claims no political affiliation.

revolution in China, no revolution in Eastern Europe, and no revolution in August, 1945."

In his Road, Aidit skirted a question then troubling Communist movements in other newly independent countries. Was the "imperialist" enemy in the "semicolonial" countries the former colonial power that continued to exercise cultural and economic influence in its former colony, or was it the United States, the *bête noir* of Moscow and Peking? Aidit apparently interpreted Soviet and Chinese hostility toward the United States as a manifestation of nationalism under the Right strategy. Thus, he concluded, the main enemy of the Indonesian people was Dutch imperialism, in view of its great influence in different fields, especially in the field of economy. That is why, he continued, the united national front must be directed primarily to the liquidation of the Dutch imperialists, not the liquidation of all foreign imperialists simultaneously.

Aidit, of course, was in an enviable position; he could link American and Dutch "imperialism" through Irian and develop a line that would later justify massive Soviet military assistance to Indonesia without jeopardizing Indonesia's "independent" foreign policy. In Aidit's words: "If the Dutch continue in power in West Irian, it means that a pistol is constantly being aimed at the Indonesian republic. . . . If the United States and other imperialists give arms to the colonial Dutch and their Indonesian agents [i.e., the Darul Islam], our fighting must be directed against all imperialists." [2]

Otherwise, Aidit's international Road unwaveringly followed the Moscow line. The foreign-affairs section of his program was lifted from Malenkov's speech before the Supreme Soviet delivered in August, 1953, a month after the arrest of Beria. Thus Aidit paraphrased Malenkov in assailing the "reactionary, imperialist forces whose cowardly acts and crimes became clear when United States imperialist agents like Tito of Yugoslavia, Rajk in Hungary, Slansky in Czechoslovakia, Gomulka in Poland, and Kostov in Bulgaria carried out their dirty tasks. Lately, the biggest of all U.S. agents, namely Beria, was unmasked, and so were all his tools. But everywhere these wanton imperialist activities are frustrated and liquidated." [3]

"World peace," on Moscow's terms, became the PKI's basic foreign line; "foreign" issues developed by the Party ran the gamut from appeals to Washington to commute the death sentences of the Rosenberg atomic spies, to demonstrations against the James Mason film "Desert Fox" (which was denounced for popularizing

German militarism), to attacks on the "imperialistic" reintroduction of Coca-Cola in August, 1954 (*Harian Rakjat* darkly hinted that the soft drink was a "political as well as commercial venture").

Perhaps the most elaborately staged front activity of the period was an International Peace Congress at Djakarta in January, 1954, sponsored by the Indonesian Peace Committee, which had collected 3 million signatures on a Stockholm Peace petition. The Congress' leading participants were Professors Prijono (University of Indonesia) and Ir. Purbodiningrat (Gadja Mada University). A galaxy of foreign Communists attended; later Prijono boasted that when Sukarno received them at the palace on January 30, it was the first time "peace delegates had been received by a head of state outside the Iron Curtain [*sic*]." A conference report by Prijono on the alleged use of germ warfare by the U.N. in Korea won him a Stalin Peace Prize later that year. Prijono was fairly typical of the unstable, opportunistic personalities attracted to the "wave of the future" in this period. He had been prominent as a "collaborating nationalist" and had unsuccessfully urged the Japanese to decree Javanese as Indonesia's official language. During the revolution he attained popularity with an ingenious satire on Sukarno patterned on Burroughs' *Tarzan and the Apes*. In 1950, he was identified with the Indonesian Peace Committee—at a time when Communist propaganda was Sukarnophobe. Two years later he emerged as a Sukarnophile.

As the tempo of Communist activity accelerated, so did demands by the educated classes for elections. Rightly or not, however, there was growing doubt that fair elections would ever be held by an Ali cabinet. On November 28, 1954, for example, Sukarno installed a Central Indonesian Elections Committee (PPI), composed only of government-supporting parties. The government was also fabricating the line that the opposition, in league with "foreign countries," plotted to overthrow Ali and block a general election. But the most disturbing development had occurred the previous June, when the PPI released an official list of parties and symbols, sanctioning the use of the hammer and sickle as the symbol of the "PKI and those without a party." Indonesian credulity was strained. "This makes a 'Communist' even of the President and Vice President, who are nonparty," the *Medan Mestika* observed. But several political "independents" rallied behind the PPI, declaring their preparedness to campaign under the hammer and sickle, among them Mrs. Salawati Daud (GERWANI); Dr. Tjokronegoro (BTI); Professor Purbodiningrat;

Henk Guntung, a painter and member of the Indonesian Artists'
League (LEKRA), a PKI cultural front; Hendra Gunawan, a
sculptor in LEKRA; and other prominent fellow travelers.

The crudity of the maneuver, however, jarred even NU sensibilities. In a note to the cabinet in July, reaffirmed at their
twentieth congress at Surabaya in September, the religious scholars
threatened a cabinet crisis unless the hammer and sickle was removed as the symbol of "nonparty independents." Eventually the
cabinet—with PKI approval—bowed to the pressure of the orthodox Moslems, and on January 22, 1955, the PPI, and NU signed
a pact deleting the phrase from beneath the Communist emblem.
The damage had been done, however; incredible as it may seem,
in many simple minds the hammer and sickle became a symbol
for persons unaffiliated with any party. For the Communists, of
course, it was imperative to maintain the cabinet and the atmosphere it engendered; especially in view of the line adopted by
Aidit at the Central Committee's second plenary session, November 8–10, 1954, that "our people are influenced by three political
trends—the Communist trend, the Nationalist trend, and the
Islamic trend." In a barb aimed at the Peking or Left faction
within the Party, Aidit added: "Apart from the Communist trend,
which has glorious and heroic revolutionary traditions, the Nationalist and Islamic trends also have traditions. . . . For this reason,
it is wrong for Communists to refuse to cooperate with all Nationalist and Islamic parties and leaders." But, significantly, he
also noted: "It is an undeniable fact that there are more points of
agreement between the Communist masses and the Nationalist
and Islamic masses than there are between their leaders."

Thus Aidit placated the Peking group by acknowledging that
the "united front from above" was a short-term tactic whereas a
"united front from below" remained the long-term strategy. In
any event, as the PKI-NU crisis passed, the Ali government appeared indestructible. From within, the PNI-NU coalition was
stronger than ever; from without, the cabinet enjoyed the un-
flagging support of Sukarno and the Communists. Moreover, with
the convocation of the Afro-Asian Conference at Bandung, April
18–24, 1955, over which Ali presided as host, the government's
prestige soared.

The twenty-nine countries at Bandung represented one quarter
of the earth's land mass and nearly two-third's of the earth's population. Much has been written about Bandung and its meaning,
but little about the political, economic, and social deterioration
in Indonesia at that time.[4] It is doubtful if the participants had
more than a passing acquaintance with Indonesian conditions.

But despite Bandung's apparent success, the conclave was too weak to sustain the Ali coalition. Three months later, the cabinet collapsed under the pressure of the army whose influence had been growing since October 17.

Since 1953, Iwa had pursued policies as Defense Minister that had won Communist approval. He endorsed PERBEPSI's plan for "volunteer battalions" (which the cabinet later rejected);* reorganized the Defense Ministry without army approval; pushed through Defense Act No. 29, which provided for a "people's defense" (PERBEPSI described the measure as "firmly establishing the tradition of a people's defense"); sanctioned a National Security Congress for the purpose of raising paramilitary battalions to ensure that the elections were "conducted in a peaceful and free manner" (the cabinet balked under army pressure, and Iwa denied that the thought of using the Congress to raise volunteer battalions "had ever occurred to me"; and abolished Simatupang's post of chairman of the joint chiefs of staff (Sukarno was delighted with the removal of the last higher officer involved in the October 17 affair).

Iwa was involved in other scandals, the most sensational that of May 11, 1954, when the army arrested Sidik Kertapati on the charge of serving as an underground leader of the Tan Malaka-oriented Bambu Runtjing, which had terrorized West Java since revolutionary days. The surrender of 1,500 Bambu Runtjing guerrillas the month before had implicated Kertapati, whose faction in parliament—the Progressives—was the same as Iwa's. Although severely shaken, the cabinet survived the affair on the strength of the PNI-NU-PKI collaboration.

But these Iwa controversies had the effect of restoring a semblance of unity within the army, and on February 5, 1955, the army leadership signed a "Charter of Unity" at Jogjakarta that presumably ended pro- and anti-Sukarno rifts within the high command. With Bandung approaching, tension eased for a while. But no sooner had Bandung concluded than Iwa resumed the offensive. On May 11, 1955, he accepted the resignation of the army chief of staff, Colonel Bambang Sugeng; his deputy, Colonel Lubis, became acting chief of staff. But neither Sukarno nor Iwa trusted Lubis, who had played a vital pro-Sukarno role on October 17, and passed over him, appointing Colonel Bambang Utoyo as Sugeng's successor. The army, on Lubis' orders, boycotted Utoyo's investiture at the palace on June 27. When the army band failed

* Supardi, the chairman of PERBEPSI, was one of Iwa's principal unofficial advisers.

to appear at the ceremonies, a band from Djakarta's fire department was hastily summoned to play the national anthem. The performance was ludicrous. The diplomatic corps witnessed the incident. Sukarno, Iwa, and Ali were humiliated. Ali then tried to rescue the cabinet by jettisoning Iwa on July 13. But the army demanded Ali's resignation as well. On July 18, Sukarno saved face by flying to Mecca on a holy pilgrimage. Six days later, Ali returned his mandate to Hatta. The political pendulum in Indonesia was swinging. Hatta and Natsir had been "Sjahrir-minded"; Sukiman, "Sukarno-minded"; Wilopo, "Sjahrir-minded"; and Ali, "Sukarno-minded." Now a new "Sjahrir-minded" coalition came to power, the last (at this writing in 1962) of Indonesia's responsible, moderate, constructive, and progressive governments.

Ali's resignation jarred the Communists. Aidit claimed that a "holy alliance" of Western "imperialists and domestic reactionaries" had conspired to bring about the downfall of the Ali Sastroamidjojo government in order to wreck the general elections or at least to prevent them from being held under the Ali Sastroamidjojo government which was supported by the people (Communists). Aidit also cited Ali's resignation as proof that the parliamentary form of struggle is "not sufficient" in the struggle for power and that the PKI must intensify the program of "agitating, organizing, and mobilizing the masses" in pursuit of a "people's democracy." In Aidit's view, Ali fell not because of the balance of votes in parliament, but because of a factor outside parliament, the armed forces. "This is a lesson for us," Aidit said, "because it teaches us that when they are hard-pressed and fear the development of the people's movement, the reactionaries, without the slightest shame, cast aside the banners of bourgeois democracy."

19

Compradore Rule

In Djakarta and the outer islands the mood was for change—and the Communists sensed it. Sukarno also detected the discontent on his return from Mecca and absented himself from the capital. Thus it was Hatta who appointed the *formateur* and approved the installation, on August 11, 1955, of a coalition headed by Burhanuddin Harahap, the Sumatran who had led the Masjumi faction in parliament since 1951. The Harahap cabinet, based on the Masjumi-Socialist alliance, included the opportunistic NU but excluded both the Nationalists and Communists. With the advent of a "compradore bourgeoisie" government (to use Aidit's terminology), a fresh breeze stirred Indonesia. Harahap's program de-emphasized foreign affairs and concentrated on domestic issues: "the restoration of the moral authority of the government," curbs on inflation and corruption, the holding of a general election. The new sense of national purpose was reflected in this commentary by Radio Indonesia on August 19: "Each of us is asking himself: 'How much longer will this depressing state of affairs go on? When is it going to end?' Many of us even ask: 'Is this the fruit of independence promised us by our leaders?'"

Harahap labored to put an end to the "depressing state of affairs." The army affair was resolved by the promotion of Colonel Nasution to the rank of major general on November 3 and his reinstatement four days later as army chief of staff. Ali's Economic and Justice ministers, and a score of lesser officials, were arraigned on charges of corruption. Stringent economic measures were initiated. Sumitro, holding the finance portfolio he had held in the Wilopo cabinet, was given free rein. Again he tightened the belt; by November 30, the state deficit of 3.5 billion rupiahs, inherited from the Ali government, had been halved.

Doubtlessly, the most important achievement of the Harahap administration was the holding of the oft-postponed elections, now scheduled for September 29 (parliament) and December 15 (constituent assembly). Whether Ali would have held to the schedule is uncertain. Within the new cabinet there were already demands for postponement, pending an inquiry into Ali's preparations for the elections. But Harahap vetoed the suggestions; like Hatta and Sjahrir, he felt there had been enough procrastination and that the deteriorating situation warranted risk. He was also confident of a Masjumi sweep. Harahap moved with daring. On August 22, for example, the cabinet promulgated an emergency act enlarging the PPI to insure Masjumi-PSI representation. Sukarno signed the measure only on September 18, eleven days before the election.

Harahap's pace caused Aidit to recast the Communist line. Considering the virulent content of Communist propaganda attacks on the Masjumi and PSI, the PKI's criticism of the new cabinet was relatively mild. The prevailing Right strategy, of course, necessitated support of any cabinet, however distasteful; moreover, the Communists were anxious to avoid offending the NU in order to develop the thesis that the three main currents in Indonesia were "nationalism, Islam, and Marxism." On August 19, therefore, the PKI Central Committee announced its support of the government, describing the composition of the new cabinet as similar to that of the previous government and characterizing the Harahap program as a "formal victory" for the parties that supported Ali. Aidit went so far as to assert that the cabinet's "Sjahrir-mindedness" did not detract from the merits of certain ministers of the cabinet who belonged to the parties that formerly supported the Ali Sastroamidjojo government and showed good will.

But the Communists also developed the line that Harahap was "not interested" in elections and was making great efforts to postpone them. When elections verged on reality, Aidit reversed himself and contended that the pressure of "democratic forces" had compelled Harahap to implement the Ali schedule.[1]

Among the parties preparing for elections, the PKI was the best financed, best organized and oldest in the field. Although Aidit disparaged the parliamentary form of struggle in 1954, the electoral campaign had served as a pretext for the "agitation, mobilization, and organization of the masses." Now, however, that elections were imminent, the Communist organizational drive of the preceding two years proved prescient.

In the six weeks remaining before the balloting, the Communists intensified their effort "to rouse the masses." As the electoral campaign progressed, it became patently clear that the parties employing moderation and restraint, notably the Masjumi and PSI, were at a serious disadvantage in competing against those exciting the population with ultranationalist slogans, particularly the PNI and PKI. Indeed, in many respects, the techniques employed by the PKI were reminiscent of those developed in the recruiting campaign of 1925–26. In addition to the promise of free land to the landless peasants—the most attractive lure—the Party also strove to identify itself with local issues. On Bali, the PKI endorsed cockfighting, a favorite pastime.[2] In estate areas (on Java and Sumatra), the Communists appealed to emotions with slogans such as "Drive out the Dutch." Everywhere the Party pledged to support Sukarno for the Presidency, an obvious effort to develop a link between the Party and the palace. In the villages, the Communists pitched their campaign at the lowest level. The Communists spread rumors that Masjumi agents were poisoning village wells and then provided guards to "protect" the wells.[3] The Communists concocted the story that "Irian" was a daughter of Sukarno whom the Dutch had abducted and that only if the people voted Communist would she be returned.[4]

For the benefit of the literate population, the Communists revised their long-range objective. On June 24, a month before Ali resigned and elections were certain, the Politburo already felt it expedient to replace the goal of a people's democracy as enunciated at the Fifth Party Congress, with the more modest aim of a "national-coalition" government. Aidit apparently regarded the elections as introducing an intermediary stage preparatory to the realization of a people's democracy.

During the campaign, the PKI incontrovertibly was the most affluent party. The Communists chartered buses to transport the people to rallies; provided free entertainment and soft drinks at meetings; distributed kites to children in the villages and straw hats to dockworkers (both emblazoned with the hammer and sickle); and plastered the most remote areas with PKI posters. The campaign was conservatively estimated to have cost the Communists 200 million rupiahs—a sum raised at Party bazaars, "donations" from the Chinese, voluntary and otherwise, and by "contributions" from the Soviet and Chinese embassies.

As in 1926, the Communists were sensitive to band-wagon psychology. Especially in the villages, the possession of a membership card of any party had become a symbol of status. The Communists sought to capitalize on this sentiment by the indiscriminate distribution of such cards. In addition to the regular Party membership for votaries and candidate membership for novitiates, the PKI created a third category, *anggota-pentijinta,* literally "lover member." [5] By the end of 1955, Aidit could claim a Party membership of 1 million. The Party was rapidly developing into a mass movement. But the political depth and reliability of such a movement was open to serious question.

Indonesia's first general election was unmarred by serious incidents. On Java it bore the character of a mystic ritual. There were 257 seats at stake, 43,104,464 registered voters, and 37,875,299 ballots cast. Although official results were not released until March, the outcome was known immediately. Indonesia was stunned. Four major parties emerged:

Parties	Number of votes	Percentage of total	Number of seats	Provisional seats in parliament
PNI	8,434,653	22.3	57	42
Masjumi	7,903,886	20.9	57	44
NU	6,955,141	18.4	45	8
PKI	6,176,914	16.4	39	17
Others	8,404,705	22.0	59	122

The Socialists attracted 753,191 votes (2 per cent of the total) and won 5 seats, compared to 14 in the provisional parliament; Murba, 199,588 (.5 per cent), winning 2 seats, compared to 4 in the provisional parliament. The army, which was polled separately, was an unknown quantity. The returns were never released, but there were persistent reports that the PKI polled more than one-fourth of the votes. What is known about the army, however, is that in 1954 a group of army officers, including Nasution, organized the League of Upholders of Indonesian Independence (IPKI). This moderate grouping received 541,306 ballots (1.4 per cent of the total votes) and won 4 seats in parliament. Interestingly, almost the entire IPKI vote was cast in West Java, a non-Javanese area.*

An analysis of the voting showed that PNI-PKI-NU strength was largely Javanese, whereas Masjumi influence was relatively evenly distributed among the islands. In a broad sense, the Masjumi had emerged as the representative of the outer islands. Significantly, had the NU and PSII not withdrawn from the Islamic "corporation," the Masjumi would have accounted for 42.2

---

* According to census figures released on December 28, 1961, West Java has a population of 20,426,000, of which perhaps three-fourths are Sundanese, the remainder largely Bantamese. Central and East Java have a Javanese population of 42,307,000. The total population of Indonesia was given as 95,889,000.

per cent of the vote. Even so, the prospect for establishing an Islamic republic would have been remote; more than half the vote was "secularist," and the constitution would require a two-thirds majority for adoption—assuming the distribution of strength in the constituent assembly corresponded to that in parliament. Sjahrir had fared badly; disastrously as compared to the Communists. Murba's showing must have disturbed Tan Malaka's ghost. Nonetheless, because of their influence in intellectual circles, the PSI and Murba would continue to exercise disproportionate influence.

As for the Communists, it seemed clear that Islam confronted the PKI with a formidable obstacle in the peaceful realization of its long-term goal. Moreover, as shown by the following table, the Communist virus infected primarily Java and Javanese conclaves in Djakarta, South and East Sumatra. Indonesian Communism was largely a Javanese phenomenon:

Regions	PKI vote	Percentage of total vote
East Java	2,299,602	23.2
Central Java	2,326,108	25.8
West Java	755,634	10.8
Greater Djakarta	96,363	12.0
South Sumatra	176,900	12.1
Central Sumatra	90,513	5.8
North and East Sumatra	258,875	10.8
West Kalimantan	8,526	1.8
South Kalimantan	17,210	2.2
East Kalimantan	8,209	4.8
North and Central Sulawesi	33,204	4.4
South and Southeast Sulawesi	17,831	1.6
Maluku	4,792	1.4
East Nusatenggara	5,008	0.5
West Nusatenggara	66,067	5.3

Another interesting feature was that the four major parties accounted for 90 per cent of the vote and occupied 198 seats in parliament. The remaining 59 seats were apportioned among 24 other parties, none of whom possessed more than 8 seats. The election had buried more than a score of parties and organizations. The prospect was that as the electoral process matured, the number of parties would continue to diminish. Transcending other considerations, Indonesia had taken another long stride toward the ultimate ideal of an independent, democratic republic. Indonesian prestige abroad soared; more important, for a nation suffering from an acute inferiority complex, a legacy of colonial rule, the election provided the nation with a justifiable throb of self-respect.

Aidit interpreted the Communist showing barely seven years after Madiun as a spectacular recovery. He perceived the possibility of another PNI-NU coalition with PKI support in parliament, perhaps even a popular front regime. However, in an analysis of the election in *Harian Rakjat* on October 11, Aidit displayed greater interest in a coalition. In a second Ali cabinet, he probably reasoned, the Communists would continue to enjoy a free hand in building a mass movement yet avoid the hazards of responsibility. Thus in proposing a national-coalition government, Aidit was careful to emphasize his desire for "a coalition *led* by the PNI-NU, with the participation of the Masjumi and PKI." In the realization that the Masjumi would decline to sit in a cabinet with the PKI, Aidit further proposed that the "compradore bourgeoisie" cooperate with the PKI in the struggle against the main enemy, i.e., "the remnant forces of Dutch colonialism in the economic, political, educational, and cultural fields." Aidit was breaking ideological ground in Indonesia and preparing the creation of a "five-class bloc."

But Aidit misjudged the situation. The Communist showing at the polls, confirming the rapid growth of the movement since 1952, had disquieted the PNI and NU. They had opened a Pandora's box. Now they desired to close it. The PNI belatedly recognized the existence of a special relationship between Moscow and the PKI. Mangunsarkoro, the successor to the late Sidik, cautioned that a cabinet with PKI participation would endanger Indonesia's independent foreign policy. *Merdeka*, Ali's mirror, described the PNI as a middle-of-the-road party and proposed a *rapprochement* with the Masjumi. For its part, the Masjumi, unsettled by the election results, was amenable. But Sukarno, like the Communists, entertained other ideas. Sukarno was also elated by the outcome of the balloting, particularly Sjahrir's debacle. Since the "June 27 Affair," Sukarno had remained in the background; now he returned to prominence. In the seventy-seven days preceding the election of a constituent assembly, Sukarno injected a harsh new note of excessive nationalism into the campaign. With Sjahrir eliminated, Sukarno sensed a fresh kill: the Masjumi.

The President opened his campaign at Surabaya on November 14 with the claim of having uncovered two "plots" to destroy the republic, both ostensibly Western in origin: one aimed at wrecking the country by "sabotaging the bureaucracy and stimulating corruption" (by implication authored by the Dutch who "controlled" the economy); the other, by "making the republic sign foreign treaties whose disadvantages would not be known until later" (MSA and the Masjumi). The government denied knowledge of the "plots" and the progovernment press challenged Sukarno to produce the evidence. He never did. Instead, five days later, he broadened the charge to include an attack on "Western" democracy for allegedly creating an abyss between rich and poor. Sukarno then proposed a vaguely conceived "planned democracy" to bridge that abyss.[6] Sukarno apparently feared the sapping of his power through the electoral process. He was determined to destroy the parliamentary system at its infancy. Harahap struggled to restrain the President, but Sukarno was contemptuous of a lame-duck administration that had been "repudiated" at the polls; in point of fact, however, the Harahap coalition commanded a majority in the new parliament.

On December 15, Indonesia returned to the polls to elect a constituent assembly. The impact of Sukarno's charges had a telling effect, as these figures show:

Parties	Number of votes received	Number of seats
PNI	9,070,218	119
Masjumi	7,789,619	12
NU	6,989,333	91
PKI	6,232,512	80
Others	11,627,544	66

Harahap's time was limited; over PNI and PKI objections, he announced his intention to hold office until the organization of a new parliament in March.* In a desperate effort to undercut Sukarno and the radical nationalists, he reopened negotiations with the Dutch on unsettled issues. Indonesia's moderate leadership realized that the continued presence of the Dutch in West Irian provided Sukarno, the PKI, and the intransigent radicals with a devastating weapon; if ever there was a moment to transfer Irian to a responsible government, however demissionary, now was that moment. A resolution of the Irian dispute would immeasurably strengthen the Masjumi position in the bargaining over a new cabinet. As Hatta later eloquently expressed it:

> The claim to West Irian is a national claim backed by every Indonesian party without exception; but the most demanding voice, apart from that of President Sukarno himself, is that of the Communist

---

* On November 15, 1955, Harahap won parliamentary approval by a vote of 135 to 2, with 2 abstentions. The PNI, PKI, SOBSI, SKI, and BTI boycotted the session.

Party of Indonesia. By putting itself in the vanguard of those demanding realization of this national ideal [complete independence], the Communist Party of Indonesia is able to capture the imagination of an ever-growing section of the population. The West Irian question thus represents a tragedy. . . . Indeed, till the question of West Irian is settled, Indonesian politics will be more irrational than rational.[7]

On December 12, 1955, negotiations opened at The Hague in the face of strong criticism from Sukarno, the PKI, and the PNI. The Dutch consented to the talks providing the Irian question was not raised; nonetheless, Irian was the main issue. That same month, the tenth General Assembly shelved the Irian question and passed a resolution calling for a "fruitful" settlement of Indo-Dutch differences. Harahap had gambled on Dutch appreciation of the delicate nature of Indonesia's internal political situation. But the Dutch proved as imperceptive and obstinate as ever. Now they revived the issue of the right of Papuans to self-determination. The Dutch moral position was weak; prior to 1949, they had never acknowledged Indonesia's right to self-determination. Negotiations collapsed on February 11, 1956. Once again, the Netherlanders proved insensitive to the situation in their former colony. Five years later, having been expelled from the archipelago, the Dutch engaged in complicated diplomatic stratagems at the U.N. in an effort to withdraw from Irian while saving face.

Harahap sought to extract something of value in his last month in office by unilaterally abrogating the Netherlands-Indonesian Union, then still under negotiation. But Sukarno was not inclined to permit the Masjumi a "nationalist" conquest and refused to sign the decree until the formation of a new government. Sukarno, of course, anticipated either a national-front government of the big four or a PNI-NU coalition with PKI support, or, in any event, a government amenable to his influence. For Sukarno—and the Communists—there was time enough for the Dutch.

20

Spiritual Crisis

The Communist conception of a national coalition appealed to Sukarno, and shortly after the elections he proposed a national-front government composed of the PNI, Masjumi, NU, and PKI. "Who ever heard of a three-legged horse?" Sukarno asked. He developed the thesis that only by cooperation of the three main forces—nationalism, Islam, and Marxism—could the "national revolution be consummated."

As Sukarno toured the hinterland delivering his message, Communist throngs turned out to chant: "We want a four-legged horse." Sukarno professed to believe that the organized sentiment of one party reflected the popular will of the people. Lukman again directed the impressive PKI campaign in the absence of Aidit, who had been summoned to Moscow to attend the Twentieth Congress of the Soviet Communist Party, the scene of Khrushchev's de-Stalinization speech. Thus as Sukarno pressed for the inclusion of the PKI in a national-front government, the PKI's First Secretary was abroad attending a "foreign" Party congress. Sukarno ignored the incongruity of the situation.

The President had instructed the PNI, as the largest party, to form a "four-legged" government. But the PNI balked. The Nationalists were disturbed by the Communist showing at the polls. Impressed by its own strength, obtained largely by identification with Sukarno, the PNI was also in the mood for greater independence from Sukarno. On March 16, formateur Ali Sastroamidjojo resisted Sukarno by forming a PNI-Masjumi-NU coalition without the Communists. For four days the President delayed approval of Ali's cabinet, but relented when the NU and the Masjumi refused to sit at the same table with the PKI.

The Communists were also bitter over the composition of the second Ali cabinet; Lukman publicly called it "disappointing." But as with Harahap, the PKI, hewing a Right line, had little choice but to support Ali. On April 9, the Communists consoled themselves with the claim that Ali's program was a "complete rejection" of Harahap's program and worthy of support. Only the year before the Communists had characterized the Harahap program as a "formal victory" for the first Ali cabinet.

From the beginning, Ali was overwhelmed by psychological obstacles; unfairly, perhaps, he had become a symbol of inefficient, corrupt government. A cabinet crisis developed almost immediately: a flight of Chinese and Dutch capital; a new wave of regional unrest; and renewed tension in the army. The "outer islands" looked on Ali as an advocate of highly centralized rule from Java; in the provinces, charges of "Javanese domination" were increasingly heard. By October 29, Sukarno himself felt constrained to warn that "racial and regional" sentiment endangered national unity. The unrest in the non-Javanese islands had assumed serious proportions following Hatta's July 23 decision to resign the Vice Presidency with the convocation of the constituent assembly. Rightly or not, the "outer islands" considered Hatta their protector on Java. The Masjumi warned: Hatta's decision cannot be detached "from the feeling of dissatisfaction among the people in the regions." [1] Hatta's decision to resign was another retreat in a long line of retreats by Indonesia's democratic, moderate leadership.

Restiveness in the regions was accompanied by rising tension in the army. The colonels who had deposed Ali the previous year considered his return as Premier and Defense Minister as intolerable. An army faction, influenced by the ambitious Colonel Lubis, schemed against Ali. Its intrigues matured on August 13, when a group of officers arrested Foreign Minister Roeslan Abdul Gani, an able PNI theoretician and confidant of Sukarno, on charges of corruption as he prepared to leave for the Suez conference at London. (He was convicted and fined on April 17, 1957.) The arrest was intended to force Ali's resignation, but the plan was thwarted when Nasution intervened and ordered his release. Lubis went into hiding and radically revised the conspiracy plans; he no longer intrigued against the Ali cabinet but the very system of government. He plotted for a dissolution of the cabinet, parties, and parliament; the elimination of Nasution; and the creation of a military junta with Sukarno as figurehead. Even Lubis appeared loath to remove Sukarno. Indonesia could neither live with or without him. Lubis' intrigue collapsed in November largely as the result of a counterrevolt by junior officers loyal to Sukarno, if not Nasution.[2] Although his plot was fluid, Lubis originally had planned the coup in Sukarno's absence.

The United States had been understandably disturbed by Sukarno's performance during the elections and felt a visit to Washington would clear the air. But an invitation to Sukarno at this juncture was questionable. Although under Soviet pressure personal diplomacy has come increasingly into vogue, it is of doubtful value in dealing with politically unstable countries; inevitably, personal diplomacy is entwined in domestic affairs. In the case of Sukarno, a visit to the United States would be interpreted in Djakarta as an endorsement by Washington; moreover, Sukarno was certain to raise Irian, and the Eisenhower Administration, like its predecessor, was committed to a neutralist posture since—in Secretary of State Dulles' words—"it serves the general cause of [American] friendship [for Indonesia and the Netherlands] for the United States to take an impartial and neutral position." [3]

In any event, on March 12, 1956, Dulles visited Indonesia and with Ambassador Cumming's encouragement invited Sukarno to Washington. Sukarno was delighted. So were the Russians who —judged by their reaction—sensed Sukarno's drift and realized that a visit to Moscow had been precluded by Indonesia's "independent" foreign policy. Now Sukarno enjoyed freedom of movement. On April 9, Moscow reacted by openly inviting the President to the Soviet Union. Six days later, in the spirit of nonalignment, the cabinet simultaneously approved the Moscow and Washington visits. "My trip abroad," Sukarno said on May 14, as he departed for Washington, "is not for pleasure, but in the interests of the people and the nation."

Sukarno's tour of the United States, which lasted from May 16 to May 26, was triumphant, as was to be expected. Sukarno's personal relations with Americans had always been good. He liked Americans for their informality, boyish enthusiasm, and political naïveté. The Americans in turn liked Sukarno's personal charm, warmth, and candor. The Eisenhower-Sukarno talks, however, were inconclusive. "The [Irian] situation, I would say, was left much as it was before the visit," Dulles told newsmen on May 23. But four days later, Radio Indonesia, for home consumption, reported that Sukarno had "clearly brought home to the Americans the unlawful occupation of West Irian by the Netherlands," and that "this should serve as an inspiration in the preservation of national unity." Sukarno's tour carried him to Canada, Italy, West Germany, and Switzerland; on July 3, he returned to Djakarta. It had been Sukarno's first experience in the open societies of the West. What were his impressions? Sukarno was noncommittal. "Significantly," reported Ronald Stead, the correspondent of *The Christian Science Monitor*, on August 6, "he [foreign minister Roeslan Abdul Gani] explained that, despite the value of President Sukarno's Western tour, a correct assessment of the success of Indonesia's foreign policy could be obtained only after Mr. Sukarno visited the Soviet [bloc.]"

On his return, Sukarno found Indonesia strained by mounting internal crises—unrest in the army, Hatta's imminent resignation, economic decline, and dissatisfaction throughout the country. A responsible leader may have felt inclined to remain at home; not so Sukarno, who apparently viewed the Soviet visit as an integral part of his domestic program. In his annual August 17 address, Sukarno shunned domestic issues; his only comment on the "August 13 Affair" four days earlier was that it was "unnational and antirevolution" and lowered Indonesian prestige abroad. The burden of his speech dealt with Egypt, which had just nationalized the Suez Canal Company, an action Aidit cited as a "model for Indonesia in facing the Dutch capitalists and their agents in this country." *

Sukarno's guest of honor on the occasion of Indonesia's eleventh anniversary of independence was Soong Ching-ling (Madame Sun Yat-sen). Mme. Sun influenced Sukarno as perhaps no other foreigner ever had, implanting the thesis that the difference between the bourgeois democracies and the Communist world was that in the former the people were moving from freedom of expression to freedom from want, whereas in the latter the situation was reversed. Sukarno made wide use of this thesis in subsequent speeches, causing Natsir to observe dryly that the order of priority—freedom from want to freedom of expression— "means a return to the colonial period."

On August 26, Sukarno departed on a second wave of visits: Austria, Yugoslavia, Czechoslovakia, Russia, Outer Mongolia, and China. In the Communist world he was lavishly entertained as only a push-button state can. Fifty-one days later, Sukarno returned home, impressed by what he had seen behind the Iron Curtain, particularly in China. On October 28, he launched a series of allocutions on his experiences abroad and their application to Indonesia's domestic problems. His first broadside was fair warning

---

* As a sequel to Nasser's action, Djakarta repudiated $1.07 billion in debts to the Netherlands arising out of The Hague accord.

of what was to come. His target was the Hatta-Sjahrir program of democratization, which he described as the root cause of Indonesia's deterioration. "We made one big mistake in November, 1945: advocating the establishment of parties," he said. "Now we reap the bitter fruit." The solution? Sukarno said he "dreamed" that the party leaders conferred and agreed to "bury all parties." Two days later, he explained: "I come back from my visit to Soviet Russia, Yugoslavia, Czechoslovakia, Mongolia, and the Chinese People's Republic [conspicuously omitting Austria] with a tremendous sense of amazement." Although the reference to Yugoslavia was probably cold comfort to Moscow and the PKI, Sukarno enthusiastically related that under Communism, people "work like ants" building a new society, "especially in the Chinese People's Republic." Sukarno confessed that the Communist system bore a resemblance to his own conception of government. Now, he said, "I no longer dream. . . . I propose that the leaders of the people confer and decide to bury all parties." Sukarno added: "The democracy I would like to have for Indonesia is not the liberal democracy of Western Europe. . . . What I would like to have for Indonesia is a guided democracy . . . but still a democracy . . . especially if we want to construct in the way I saw in the Chinese People's Republic."

The concept of "guided democracy" was launched—"misguided" Hatta later labeled it.[4] Did Sukarno propose the dissolution of parliament? The constituent assembly? The party press? Sukarno was vague. On November 10, he presided at the opening of the constituent assembly and merely introduced the transitional device commonly employed to justify dictatorship. He observed that at least *"for the time being,* our democracy must be a guided democracy."* (Italics added.) Four days later, at a rally held in Djakarta, Sukarno returned to the Chinese theme. "I feel fortunate to be a comrade, indeed, a brother of Mme. Sun," he said. "I feel fortunate to have been able to shake hands with Chairman Mao Tse-tung as a brother, a friend, a comrade." At Soerakarta, Sukarno reassured his audience that when he extolled the ant-like organization of the Chinese mainland "I do not have in mind the *romushas*. No, not at all. . . . What awed me when I was in the Chinese People's Republic was how construction was going full tilt by use of the people's energy . . . not through regimentation but through the people's consciousness." * All he wanted, he told

---

* Sukarno's enthusiasm was unbounded. On August 27, 1957, he told a student rally in Ambon that "only" China under Communism "can serve as a good example for Indonesia." He said: "For example, it was very well known in the past . . . you could see flies everywhere [in China]. But when I visited the Chinese People's Republic, I did not see any flies."

a Bandung rally, was "a democracy that is not imported . . . a *national democracy.*" (Italics added.) He pledged that "Bapak [father] had no intention of violating our provisional constitution." At Bogor he called on Indonesia to "turn back, turn back and rediscover our Indonesian democracy, not a democracy imported from The Hague." By a twist of irony, Sukarno's perorations on guided democracy coincided with Lubis' plot to overthrow the government and establish a junta rule. Thus both worked at cross-purposes toward the same goal: the destruction of Indonesia's developing parliamentary system. In this objective they were joined by the Communists.

There is poignant tragedy in relating this sequence of events. Sukarno's appeal for guided democracy so that Indonesia could construct along the lines of the Iron Curtain countries cannot be treated in Indonesian isolation. Sukarno aired his concept as the Communist system was shaken by its deepest spiritual crisis. In point of fact, Sukarno visited the Communist world only six months after Khrushchev had unmasked Stalin for his "monstrous crimes," "abuse of power," and his self-glorification as the "Great Leader." Sukarno toured restless Eastern Europe two months after tanks put down rioting in Poznan, Poland. Sukarno launched his guided democracy as the Hungarians rose against the repressive Communist system and peasant rebellion flared in Communist North Vietnam.

Khrushchev's repudiation of Stalin shook the PKI. Under the cloak of de-Stalinization, Alimin made an abortive effort to wrest control of the Party from Aidit. On March 25, 1956, "on the basis of information I had obtained from some comrades," Alimin distributed a circular in the Party criticizing PKI "clique rule" (Alimin apparently sensed that de-Stalinization signalized the end of "collective leadership" in Russia); accused Aidit of "Right opportunism" (support of the national bourgeoisie led by Sukarno); and charged him with "violating Leninist principles" (a handy club in any event).[5] Soon thereafter, however, Alimin realized that he had erred, that Khrushchev's behavior at Moscow was motivated by the need to ease tensions at home and in Eastern Europe, that "Stalinism" in Asia was unaffected, and that the Right strategy would prevail.

With Aidit still abroad—he had been conferring for two months in Peking en route from Moscow to Djakarta—it was Lukman's task to reprimand Alimin. He did so on May 7, declaring that since "the international and domestic situation have never been so favorable" for the PKI and the international movement, the Party must "oppose incessantly any inclination toward a split within its ranks." Three days later, "as a loyal Party member," Alimin recanted, withdrawing his criticism. Then on July 4, with Aidit home, the Central Committee formally repudiated Alimin, denouncing him for attempting to "revive Left-wing opportunism in the Party" and "open the door for provocations which, at this very time, are being actively prepared by reactionaries," apparently a reference to rumors of a Lubis coup. There again Alimin miscalculated. On August 1, he resigned from the Party because of "old age and poor health." But an Alimin outside the Party, commanding a personal following, could prove more subversive to Aidit and Party unity than an Alimin working from within. Two days later Aidit summoned an extraordinary press conference at which he and Alimin denied that the aging Party leader had any intention of resigning. As Aidit explained, the disciplinary action against Alimin had "only the character of a warning." Their performance had an authentic Marxist-Leninist ring. In 1951, when the Left strategy prevailed, Aidit ousted Alimin as a "Rightist." Denuded of obscurantist terminology, it was simply a duel for personal power. Now, when the Right strategy prevailed, Alimin was the "Leftist," Aidit the "Rightist."

Alimin had also erred in attacking Aidit as his stature within the Party and the international movement soared. This was confirmed at a fourth plenary meeting of the Central Committee, July 31–August 3, at which Aidit delivered a report on the Twentieth Congress and on his conversations with Khrushchev and Mao. On de-Stalinization Aidit interestingly assumed the position later adopted by Peking: Stalin committed excesses, but the man, not the system of "democratic centralism" was at fault; it followed, therefore, that it was not necessary to "correct" the system. Stalin continued to be revered by the PKI for his contributions to the New Order; his portraits, for example, were not removed from PKI buildings.[6]

Aidit's position had also been strengthened at the Twentieth Party Congress, the first to be held since Stalin's death. There, Khrushchev reaffirmed the Right line adopted by Stalin at the Nineteenth Congress—"peaceful coexistence," the refutation of Lenin's premise that war was inevitable, etc. Khrushchev, however, contributed an orginal theory to Marxism-Leninism, which may have been influenced in part by the Communist showing at the polls in countries like Indonesia, but more likely was a response to fundamental changes in the world arena: the emergence of Communism from the confines of one country ("the principal feature of our epoch," Khrushchev said); the recognition that in the nuclear age there is no alternative to Cold War other than "devastation" (Khrushchev's word); and the tacit acknowledgment that the Communists had spent their revolutionary momentum in some areas. With respect to the last, Khrushchev held out the prospect that the Communists could acquire power by peaceful means, by the creation of a popular front that could achieve "a firm majority in parliament." Khrushchev was imprecise. He limited this method to "highly developed capitalist countries and former colonies." He warned, however, that in countries where capitalism remained strong, "the serious resistance of reactionary forces is inevitable." There the transition to a Communist order would proceed amid conditions of "acute class revolutionary struggle." In any event, Khrushchev had raised the prospect of acquiring power by parliamentary means—an innovation in the violent world of Marxism-Leninism. In Indonesia, this was a thesis that strengthened Aidit's position (Tan Ling-djieism notwithstanding). Since the elections, Aidit has reappraised the parliamentary form of struggle and now considered it a practicable path to power.

Aidit had no sooner returned from Moscow and set the PKI house in order than Indonesia was shaken by the events in Hungary and Egypt. Tragically, the Anglo-French-Israeli misadventure in Suez served to detract from Hungary, providing the Communists and their sympathizers in the Afro-Asian world with a psychological sanctuary; indeed, Hungary may well have been lost on an Egyptian beachhead. In a costly sense, however, Hungary and Suez also provided a classic exercise in Indonesia's independent foreign policy.

Throughout the epic Hungarian struggle for freedom, Sukarno maintained silence while denouncing Suez; but not so the majority of the Indonesian parties and newspapers Sukarno would have preferred to bury. The Masjumi, NU, Sjahrir Socialists, Christians, independent intellectuals, and a myriad of organizations condemned both Hungary and Egypt and called for the immediate withdrawal of foreign troops from the two areas. The PNI and lesser nationalist parties, applying the double standard that was to become increasingly fashionable among radical nationalists in the emerging Afro-Asian world, vigorously condemned Suez but softened their criticism of Hungary. The Communists, of course, and their fellow travelers defended Soviet intervention in Hungary as "assisting in the suppression of a revolt against a people's democracy" while denouncing "imperialist intervention" in Egypt. Then, on November 1, Hungary abrogated the Warsaw Pact and proclaimed an "independent" foreign policy. Officially, however,

Djakarta continued to remain silent—notwithstanding a joint Soviet-Indonesian communiqué, signed at Moscow on September 26, at the conclusion of Sukarno's visit, that expressly condemned military pacts. Finally, on November 5, unable to resist the outcry of world and domestic opinion, the Indonesian government expressed official "regret" over Soviet intervention in Hungary. It was not until November 17 that Indonesia called for the withdrawal of Russian troops from Hungary—three days after Premier Ali had been pressured at New Delhi into signing a joint communiqué of the Colombo powers calling for the evacuation of foreign forces from both Egypt and Hungary.

In this atmosphere, the opposition to Sukarno's guided democracy crystallized. On November 30, Hatta resigned the Vice Presidency, and in a series of articles sharply criticized Sukarno's proposed dictatorship. Shortly thereafter, the country was wracked by bloodless military revolts in the "outer islands." On December 20, Lt. Colonel Achmad Hussein, the military commander in Central Sumatra, seized control of the provincial civil administration because of "the growing dissatisfaction and disillusionment of the people of Central Sumatra." He named a joint civil-military council to administer the territory. Two days later, Simbolon in North Sumatra declared that his province "no longer recognizes the present cabinet," and on December 24, Lt. Colonel Barlian followed suit in South Sumatra. In each instance, the dissidents pledged loyalty to the republic, appealed for the return of Hatta to office, and called for a larger degree of regional autonomy. Federalism, they felt, would provide a self-enforcing check and balance on Sukarno's—and Java's—authoritarian drift.

On December 28, the political character of the revolt was dramatized when Simbolon's deputy, Lt. Colonel Djamin Gintings, armed SOBSI, PERBEPSI, and SARBUPRI branches, composed largely of migrant Javanese estate workers, and re-established Djakarta's authority in a lightning countercoup. Like the unfolding bellows of a camera, the political character of Gintings' countercoup became evident a year later, when he in turn thwarted an effort by the Communist fronts to assume control of his command.

The Communists in 1957, of course, recognized great pith and moment in the Sumatra revolt. On December 24, the Politburo denounced the Sumatra rebels as "fascist" and proposed a united front against their "undemocratic and illegal action." The Communist satellite organizations joined the chorus. Then, on January 10, 1958, the Masjumi, which morally supported the revolts, withdrew from the government and, in anticipation of a crisis, proposed Hatta as Premier. The Communists were elated. Aidit boasted that

the Masjumi withdrawal had strengthened the cabinet. He knew
that the opportunistic, Java-centric parties in the cabinet—notably
the PNI and NU—would seek to retain power at any cost. He was
correct. The NU refused to follow the Masjumi example, and the
following day the PNI declared its intention to maintain the cabinet by a return to the formula of the first Ali cabinet—a PNI-NU
coalition with PKI support in parliament. The PNI said it entertained no intention of inviting Communists into the cabinet,
but that "support from the Communist Party will certainly be accepted." Aidit was not inclined to enter the government, anyway;
as long as the situation continued to develop along favorable lines
he was as content as during the first Ali cabinet to remain on the
sidelines without responsibility for the ensuing disorder. Ali's decision to maintain the cabinet had the unfortunate effect of intensifying anti-Javanese sentiment in the outer islands. As viewed
from Sumatra, the PNI-NU-PKI were primarily Javanese parties.[7]

By now Sukarno's divisive concept of guided democracy had
become the eye of a national storm. "Western parliamentary
democracy, to be successful, requires a certain amount of literacy
and a certain degree of prosperity," Sukarno declared. He observed
that Indonesia possessed neither and that "to save democracy I
must find a way out from the experiment." As for the burial of
parties, Sukarno said: "I do not mean to bury democracy." He
observed also that the Dutch, like most colonial powers, had instituted a highly centralized regime, but he denied that this was
his intention. Sukarno conceded that "there is no escape for Indonesia from a system of local autonomy," but that the adjustment
required "time and complex preparations." Sukarno claimed that
his intention was a return to traditional village values: *gotong
royong, mufakat,* and *musjawarah.* By returning to the past,
Sukarno hoped to escape the present and the future. His argument
was disingenuous. These values were practical on a village level
but hardly at the national level in a populous, modern state. In
many respects, throughout history representative government has
been distilled from such universal values found in hardship societies. The fact remains that democracy can and does work in the
developed and underdeveloped worlds wherever and whenever
there is responsible leadership and a disposition on the part of the
leadership to make it work.

On the basis of Sukarno's dissertation, Natsir and other Indonesian critics concluded that Sukarno intended to replace the parliamentary system with a "democracy without opposition." In Natsir's view the "level of education and the standard of living of the
people of Indonesia is . . . not a decisive factor whether we can

practise a system of so-called Western parliamentary democracy or not. . . . In Russia and Yugoslavia, the level of education and the standard of living is higher and yet those countries are living under a system of dictatorship." [8]

He cited neighboring countries where the standard of living was as low as that of Indonesia and where representative government worked, i.e., Malaya, the Philippines, and others. The Moslem leader emphasized that the quintessence of democracy "is freedom to state your opinion" and that there could be no distinction between "Western," "Oriental," or "Indonesian" democracy. "Democracy is one, and the only distinction you can make is whether you have democracy or you do not have it," Natsir said.

During the debate, the PKI organized rallies in vigorous support of Sukarno. The Tan Malaka-oriented Generation of '45, the intransigent radicals of the old revolution, also warmly endorsed the President's concept. On January 30, the Generation of '45 met formally for the third time at Mayor Sudiro's house and named Chaerul Saleh as their general chairman. The group was destined to serve as the dynamo of a political machine that Sukarno would belatedly seek to fashion in his own name.

Until now, Sukarno's conception was vague. Then, on February 22, assailing "imported Western" democracy as inconsistent with the spirit of the Indonesian people, Sukarno proposed the formation of a *gotong royong* cabinet and the creation of a national council composed of "functional" groups—labor, youth, peasants, intellectuals, national entrepreneurs, the Generation of '45 *— which, he said, "I shall lead" and which "will proffer advice to the cabinet, whether requested or not." All he sought, Sukarno said, was that "all members of our family sit at the same dining table," a proposal that prompted one commentator to observe that the Communists were political cannibals and that given the opportunity they would devour everybody at the table, including Sukarno.[9] With the participation of all the parties in the cabinet and the national council as functional groups, Sukarno naïvely contended that "the opposition would be eliminated." Sukarno defended the inclusion of Communists in the government by asking: "Can we ignore a party that won 6 million votes in the general election?" With his formula, Sukarno told the nation, "I offer you national peace."

Sukarno had drastically modified his original concept of guided democracy in the face of opposition from his principal supporters, the PNI and PKI, both of whom were disquieted by the prospect

* The Generation was officially recognized as a functional group on April 1, 1959.

of a burial of their parties and the interment of parliament and press. Aidit, in his first criticism of the President since launching the Right strategy, had cautioned that the PKI would oppose such "drastic measures." Thus, in the modified version of guided democracy, neither the parties, parliament, nor press would be entombed —yet. Sukarno assured his backers: "It is with clear and resolute statement that I say I shall not dissolve parliament. Parliament must carry on. The present parliament is the outcome of the people's choice through election."

The revision notwithstanding, the reaction against the plan was heated. Hatta and Sjahrir foresaw the destruction of democracy in Indonesia but were powerless to prevent it; only Natsir, who had a mass organization, was in a position to resist. Hatta called on Sukarno to assume the responsibility of office and form a Presidential cabinet responsible to parliament, but his was a useless try. Sukarno, intolerant of criticism, no matter how constructive, would not assume responsibility unless he possessed absolute power. Hatta asked Sukarno how he could propose bringing the PKI into the government when "the history of the past thirty years" demonstrated that the Communists were "prepared to sacrifice Indonesian interests, even independence itself [in the] realization of their ideals." [10] What, asked Hatta, would Sukarno do if the parties that had polled more than three times the votes of the Communists refused to sit in a cabinet with Communists? To force a popular-front government, Hatta warned, would sharpen controversies and move the nation further away from national peace. The Masjumi and NU endorsed Hatta's appraisal; the PNI wavered.

In the outer islands there was another explosion. On March 2, Lt. Colonel H. N. Ventje Sumual, the military commander in East Indonesia (the islands east of Java and Kalimantan), assumed control of the civil administration in four provinces: Sulawesi, Maluku (the Moluccas), Nusatenggara (Lesser Sundas), and West Irian (a "paper" province). Sumual was quoted as "preferring to cooperate with American imperialists rather than Communists." [11] The "revolt" reduced the central government's area of control to Java, Madura, Kalimantan, and East Sumatra.

The Communists assailed Sumual as a fascist and branded Hatta the *auctor intellectualis* of a separatist movement designed to thwart Sukarno's conception. From the outset, the Communists had unreservedly endorsed Sukarno's revised plan for guided democracy. Forewarned of the plan's contents, Aidit described the Sukarno conception on February 18 as "exactly what has been longed for by the entire Indonesian people." Aidit claimed that the scheme directed a hard blow against "imperialism, particu-

larly Dutch imperialism." Four days later, in the Party's first official
reaction, the Politburo described Sukarno's blueprint as "a new
weapon in the struggle to complete the August 17, 1945, revolution"—once again appealing to ultranationalism. The PKI had
additional cause for satisfaction on February 28, when the twelfth
General Assembly rejected a resolution calling for a "good offices
commission" to assist the Indonesians and the Dutch resolve the
Irian dispute; the vote was forty to twenty-five, with thirteen abstentions—again short of a two-thirds majority. The Soviet bloc
supported the resolution.

Aidit now demonstrated that a mass movement can influence
events outside parliament—and that the Communists had developed an efficient and extensive apparatus. Communist sound
trucks drove through Djakarta exhorting the people to support
Sukarno's conception. Public buildings, embassies, churches, hotels,
and foreign-owned stores (mostly Chinese), were painted with
PKI slogans extolling guided democracy. Communist youth squads,
not unlike the Black Shirts or Hitler Youth, roamed the streets.
When students at the University of Indonesia protested the de-
facing of their buildings, a Communist gang fired a Sten gun in
the air. The situation appeared to grow uncontrollable. On March
11, Nasution acted. He banned the brush-and-bucket campaign.
The PKI, careful to avoid an open collision with the army and
anxious to demonstrate they were behind the Government, complied.

Ali's position was untenable, and on March 13 he resigned.
Sukarno immediately proclaimed a state of war and siege and appointed the PNI chairman, Suwirijo, as formateur, with instructions to implement the "nation-saving device." Suwirijo's effort
collapsed when the Masjumi and NU declined to sit at the same
table with the PKI. The Masjumi pressed for Hatta; the PKI
countered with threats of a general strike if the new cabinet included the Masjumi but excluded the Communists. Suwirijo returned his mandate. In a bizarre maneuver, Sukarno, as President
and commander-in-chief of the armed forces, appointed "Citizen
Sukarno" as formateur. On April 9, Citizen Sukarno reported success to President Sukarno. Sukarno described the republic's seventeenth cabinet as a "emergency extraparliamentary cabinet of ex-
perts" and appointed a colorless careerist, Djuanda Kartawidjaja,
a nonparty independent who had served in numerous governments,
as Premier. Again Sukarno avoided the Premiership. Again he displayed tactical brilliance. His *gotong royong* cabinet was built
around the PNI and NU, and included fellow travelers but no
direct representative of the PKI. Sadjarwo (BTI) was named Min-

ister of Agriculture; Prijono, Minister of Education. Oddly, perhaps, the cabinet was a "three-legged horse." Sukarno appointed only one Masjumi minister, and he was immediately suspended from the party. Perhaps the most significant development was the inclusion, for the first time, of the Generation of '45 in the government. Saleh was named Minister of Veteran Affairs; Hanafi, Minister for the Mobilization of the People's Energy and Development. The Generation group had neither a seat in parliament nor a party in the real meaning of the word. The Communists were distressed by the stirring of the Tan Malaka movement and, worse, the implication that Sukarno had licensed the Generation to develop a national front under his guidance. The February, 1959, issue *Review of Indonesia*, a monthly journal of the PKI's Central Committee, edited by Bintang Suradi, alluded to the Generation as one of the "opportunist minority cliques that failed at the last general election to win the support of the people." Aidit declined to comment on the cabinet's composition the morning it was announced. But that evening, having digested the situation, the Politburo endorsed the cabinet as the "only way out" of the predicament confronting the country (and, doubtlessly, the PKI). Aidit apparently recognized that he was at a point of no return in his affair with Sukarno, that the Communists had little choice but to accept the cabinet. Moreover, there was a national council to be formed and in the selection of "functional" groups, the PKI, in view of its front organizations, would inevitably play a noteworthy role.

Sukarno's method of forming the cabinet drew criticism from Hatta, Natsir, Sjahrir, and even the PNI. Natsir termed Sukarno's behavior "unconstitutional," and Hatta publicly asked: "Can a constitutional President who is irresponsible, although holding the rank of formateur and supreme commander, retain the state's highest authority?" Parliamentary speaker Sartono, the prominent prewar PNI leader, criticized the President for violating the interim Constitution but felt his action "justified because of the state of emergency"; Sjahrir felt similarly.

Indonesian democracy had been delivered a serious blow. Shortly thereafter, Sukarno toured Java, citing Soviet Russia's "guiding of the masses" as an example for Indonesia's "new-style democracy." For the PKI, the future appeared filled with promise and peril.

21

New-Style Democracy

The "new-style democracy" was inaugurated in Indonesia, on May 6, 1957. By decree, Sukarno established a National Advisory Council composed of functional groups empowered to offer advice "both at the request of the government and on its own initiative," the advice to be "conveyed" to the cabinet by the President. On June 15, the Djuanda cabinet unanimously approved Sukarno's selection of forty-five members to the Council. They embraced twelve known Communists and fellow travelers, including representatives of SOBSI, BTI, LEKRA, PERBEPSI, GERWANI, and Pemuda Rakjat among those representing such functional groups as labor, peasants, artists, ex-independence fighters, women, and youth. But the Communists were a minority; the Council was dominated by radical nationalists, among them Iwa Kusumasumantri and Mohammed Padang, the irrational leader of the Progressives. Significantly, too, the armed forces were drawn into the new-style democracy. Sukarno named the chiefs of the army, navy, air force, and state police to the council as "sociomilitary" representatives.

Although Djuanda professed to believe that the advice of the Council was not binding on the government and that the cabinet continued to be responsible to parliament ("the repository of the people's sovereignty"), in practice the Council, i.e. Sukarno, exercised veto power over the government, even on the appointment of ambassadors. Thus, through a series of steps that began shortly after his tour of the Communist world, Sukarno put into operation a system of government that would not have been possible if he had been forced to rely on majority opinion.[1] Sukarno's coup presaged the liquidation of the parliamentary system and the phenomenal growth of the Communist mass movement. Sukarno refuted this interpretation; Roeslan Abdul Gani denounced it as "a canard [that] must be denied."[2]

In an obvious act of symbolism, Sukarno coordinated the inauguration of the Council with the arrival of Marshal Kliment Y. Voroshilov, the Soviet chief of state whom Khrushchev denounced as a "Stalinist" at the Twenty-first Party Congress in October, 1961. Voroshilov's good-will mission—an outgrowth of Sukarno's Russian tour—was an immediate success. On May 7, the day after his arrival, the Soviet President reaffirmed Moscow's "support of the just and rightful claim of the people of Indonesia to the return of a part of Indonesia—West Irian." Sukarno beamed. He and his guest toured Java and flew to Bali and Medan aboard the Illyushin jet that Voroshilov had presented to Sukarno as a gift during the latter's Russian visit. The pair shared the same platform, literally and figuratively. Sukarno, embracing Voroshilov, repeatedly declared: "There are many common grounds between us, especially in the struggle against colonialism and imperialism." The crowds cheered, particularly the Communists. Clearly, Sukarno was transferring his party "allegiance" from the PNI to the PKI. Still annoyed with Nationalist defiance the year before in the selection of a cabinet, he was determined to teach the PNI a tactical lesson. At the time the parties were in the field again campaigning for seats in regional and municipal councils.

The impact of the Sukarno-Voroshilov tour on the election results in Java was devastating:

Djakarta (June 22)		East Java (July 29)	
Masjumi	153,709	NU	2,999,785
PKI	137,305	PKI	2,704,523
PNI	124,955	PNI	1,899,782
NU	104,892	Masjumi	977,443
Central Java (July 17)		West Java (August 10)	
PKI	2,706,893	Masjumi	1,841,030
PNI	2,235,714	PKI	1,087,269
NU	1,771,556	PNI	1,055,801
Masjumi	714,722	NU	597,356

In Central Java the Communists registered majorities in fourteen of the province's eighteen municipalities and regencies; in East Java the story was similar. Invariably the PKI registered gains at the expense of the PNI. In Djakarta, the PKI picked up 45,000 votes; the PNI lost 50,000 votes. In Surabaya, the PKI picked up 26,000 votes; the PNI lost 24,000. And so it went. In seaports and inland cities—Semarang, Surabaya, Madiun, Magelang, Malang, and Soerakarta—the Communists registered absolute majorities. Significantly, however, the figures for the Masjumi and NU were largely static, an indication of firm Islamic strength and a harbinger of civil war on Java should the Communists bid for power.

The real victor, of course, was Sukarno. Aidit was so confident about the outcome of the election that during the campaign, for the first time since 1952, the PKI openly assailed the PNI as the party of "corruption." Nor did Aidit underestimate Sukarno's role in the Communist sweep. Although he conceded that "to some extent" the Communist triumph was due to the PKI's efficient organization and the Voroshilov tour, he said that the overriding factor was "the Party's unreserved support of Sukarno's nation-saving device." [3] Aidit also interpreted the PKI victory as an affirmation of Khrushchev's parliamentary thesis that "under certain conditions" the Communists could attain power by parliamentary means. He said the election results pointed the way to a peaceful transition from a semicolonial society to a people's democracy. "In other words," Aidit concluded, "if everything depends on the Communists, we would follow the peaceful way."

Aidit had cause for exuberance. But as with the PNI, and everyone else who had fallen along the political wayside since 1945, the PKI was in Sukarno's embrace. The concept of guided democracy was admittedly vague; suppose Sukarno abandoned elections and parties as "Western-imported devices"? Already there were unmistakable signs of a Tan Malaka revival, evidence that Sukarno was developing a new faction as a counterpoise to the PKI. The veteran Tan Malaka leader Adam Malik openly observed: "In contradiction to the fears expressed by the foreign press, 'guided democracy' will check the expansionism of the Communist Party." [4] Nevertheless, Aidit had reason to be confident. In victory he was magnanimous. In areas where the Communists registered absolute majorities, he offered to share power "in a spirit of cooperation" with "those parties supporting Sukarno's conception." It was an invitation to the PNI to be swallowed; it was also a maneuver by the PKI to avoid sole responsibility for the deepening economic crisis on Java.

But the PNI was shaken. The Nationalists denounced their "pact of cooperation" with the PKI, and on August 5 attacked the Communists as a "double-faced party, because half of its leaders are in Moscow and the other half in Indonesia." The PNI's English-language daily, the *Indonesian Observer*, declared on August 13 that the "alarm bell has been sounded" and that the non-Communist parties should cooperate, since the differences among them "were purely sentimental and hardly fundamental." On August

22, the *Indonesian Observer* described the PKI electoral gains as a "warning" and called for a popular front "against the march of Communism." Others observed that if the Communist trend continued, the PNI would be reduced to the position of a minority party in the 1960 general elections. In East Java, the PNI ascribed the Communist showing to promises of free distribution of land and said Aidit's willingness to sacrifice district headships in areas where the PKI received an absolute majority was motivated by the knowledge that the Party could not carry out its campaign promise of free land. At no time, however, did the PNI criticize Sukarno's role in the Communist successes.

The religious scholars were also shaken. On September 20, the NU participated in an All-Indonesia Conference of Moslem Scholars at Palembang that adopted a resolution calling on the Christian population to join with the Moslems to "form a solid bulwark in the struggle against atheism." The conference proposed a ban on the PKI, a suggestion that prompted Aidit on October 9 to observe that the legal existence of the Communists was a characteristic of Indonesian democracy and that only parties violating that democratic principle should be outlawed.

In the dissident outer islands, Sukarno's tour with Voroshilov, followed by the Communist showing at the polls, generated another violent reaction. In Sumatra and Sulawesi, the authorities arrested local Communist leaders.* To their demands for a restoration of the Sukarno-Hatta partnership and greater regional autonomy, the rebellious civil-military councils now added a call for the removal of Communists from the government. In Djakarta, the crisis atmosphere deepened. On July 5 and 30, grenades exploded outside PKI and SOBSI headquarters, probably at the behest of the elusive Lubis and the Darul Islam. A reconciliation between Sukarno and Hatta was imperative. On September 11, Djuanda succeeded in arranging for a national conference of all parties except the Communists. Aidit, realizing that a Sukarno-Hatta rapprochement was an unlikely prospect, appeared unconcerned. The fact that Sukarno consented to a conference without the PKI was sufficient proof. His assessment was correct; the conference failed to resolve the differences between the cosigners of the proclamation of independence and those between the outer islands and the central government.

* In provincial elections held in South Sumatra on December 1, 1957, the Masjumi polled 555,276 votes; PKI, 228,965; PNI, 187,042; NU, 113,888. In South Kalimantan, elections held on February 20, 1958, showed the following results: NU, 282,691 votes; Masjumi, 188,606; PKI, 22,283; PNI, 18,566.

Sukarno was not perturbed. As the result of his power play he felt unfettered. He saw Irian as a common denominator that would unite the country. "We shall restore our unity," he declared.[5] "There may be differences of opinion among us, but with regard to the struggle to regain West Irian we are one." Sukarno now turned the clock back to the Natsir cabinet.

As early as May 29, Djuanda had forewarned parliament that the government was contemplating "other" forms of struggle for Irian. The "other" form materialized on July 29, when Sukarno installed a "youth corporation," the Youth-Military Cooperation Body (BKSPM), composed of representatives of the army and the youth organizations associated with the PNI, Masjumi, NU, and PKI, including the PKI's Pemuda Rakjat (half its members were said to have been drilled by PERBEPSI). At that time, the Communist block in the National Council was advocating extreme measures against the Dutch in Irian. The PKI favored a military course of action in anticipation of Communist-bloc moral and material support, i.e., "rockets" and "volunteers." SOBSI publicly offered to organize paramilitary formations to fight the Dutch, and Aidit openly called for "direct armed attack on Irian." [6] But although the intention was there, the capability was lacking, and the National Council settled on measures short of war: an assault on the Dutch community and on the Dutch economic position in Indonesia.

In 1949, there had been 200,000 Netherlanders in Indonesia, two-thirds of whom were Eurasian, largely white-collar workers and technicians. The Dutch economic investment in Indonesia was then estimated at $2 billion. In the intervening years, the Dutch community had dwindled to 46,000 (16,000 in Djakarta) and Dutch economic holdings to $1.3 billion. The former colonial power was in the process of gradual self-liquidation. It was against this background in August that the BKSPM prepared for an intensive anti-Dutch campaign on Irian to coincide with the fourth Indonesian attempt to wrest control of Irian through the General Assembly. On September 27, the BKSPM defined as its purpose the rekindling of "the spirit of the August revolution to bring the outside world to a sense of reality." The next day, a "Liberate Irian" drive was unleashed (primarily on Java, the outer islands being largely indifferent). Roving bands of youth painted "Irian or Death!" on Dutch homes and establishments. Shopkeepers and stall-owners were warned not to sell to the Dutch.

As the gangs moved through the streets in the weeks that followed, Indonesia's democratic leadership was appalled. On November 6, Natsir felt constrained to warn that if the anti-Dutch campaign was not controlled, Irian might not be obtained. He criticized the scribbling of indecent words on Dutch buildings, calling it incompatible with the Indonesian character. The next day, *Harian Rakjat* denounced Natsir for attempting to "save colonialism." The leaders of the Masjumi and moderate parties were the recipients of threatening letters and telephone calls. The police were standing by passively as bands of youths congregated on street corners in the vicinity of the homes of Natsir and other Masjumi leaders. Sukarno, meanwhile, incited the crowds. On November 7, he warned that unless Indonesia acquired Irian "we will resort to methods that will startle the world." Twelve days later, Sukarno delivered an inflammatory speech before a mass rally at Djakarta organized by the Action Committee for the Liberation of West Irian, a government body composed largely of irrational radical nationalist elements, including such notorious figures as "General" Mustopo. Hatta, ailing, sent a message to the outdoor meeting and appealed to the population to fight "seriously" for Irian. "Daubing people's houses and intimidating people harm our struggle," he said. In the hope of forestalling a general-strike action that would further impair the economy, Hatta proposed a nationwide five-minute work stoppage as a demonstration of unity.

Then, on November 29, the General Assembly voted forty-one to twenty-nine, with eleven abstentions, in favor of a mild resolution proposed by Indonesia and eighteen members of the Afro-Asian bloc. The resolution requested the Secretary-General to "assist the parties concerned as he deems it appropriate" in resolving the Irian question. The vote fell thirteen short of the two-thirds majority required for passage. In New York, Foreign Minister Subandrio said: "We have no alternative but to resort to action outside the United Nations." The action was not long in coming.

Failure at the U.N. was a signal for an attempt on Sukarno's life. The next day, a group of anti-Communist terrorists, later linked to Colonel Lubis, hurled four grenades at Sukarno as he visited the Tjikini public school; 9 persons were killed and 150 wounded, mostly children. Sukarno was unhurt. *Pravda* accused the United States of complicity,[7] and the Soviet Embassy offered medical assistance to the victims.[8] The terrorists were apprehended and tried; three were executed and one sentenced to twenty years.

The day after the Tjikini incident, the government declared a twenty-four-hour general strike against Dutch firms, a ban on Dutch-language publications, and the cancellation of KLM landing rights in Indonesia. New slogans appeared: "Murder the Dutch." "Fry Dutch children." By now, Sukarno, the Communists, and the intransigent radicals had so aroused literate and illiterate passions by mob oratory and the creation of a fictitious sense of emergency that the Djuanda government lost control of the situation.[9] On December 4, without the knowledge of the cabinet, a labor union of the Royal Packet Shipping Company (KPM), the principal interinsular shipping line, seized control of the firm's main office at Djakarta and hoisted a red flag. The seizure was organized by Joop Mamesha, a leader of the Indonesian People's Workers Union (KBKI), a PNI affiliate headed by Ahem Erningpradja, a prominent labor leader and radical nationalist in parliament who had broken with SOBSI. Although the Communist-controlled Seamen and Dockworkers' Union (SBPP), a SOBSI affiliate, was the dominant KPM union, the KBKI branch kept the Communists uninformed about their plans.[10] Aidit and the SOBSI were undoubtedly as surprised as the government, but moved quickly to advantage.

The following day Djuanda ordered the closure of Dutch consulates and the expulsion of the Dutch. "The sooner all Dutchmen leave, the better," Justice Minister A. G. Maengkom declared. That same day, SOBSI affiliates seized Dutch estates, banks, and trading companies. The following morning, Djakarta was decorated with red flags. The government was shocked—and alarmed by the implications. Djuanda appealed for an end to the seizures. SOBSI ignored the appeal and the following day occupied the offices of three more Dutch banks and other properties. On December 10, the cabinet announced that it would assume control of the Netherlands-seized estates in order to prevent "other people," presumably the Communists, from doing so. Ironically, the pronouncement was delivered by the BTI Minister of Agriculture. Three days later, Nasution ordered a complete halt to the seizures and threatened severe punishment if the order was disobeyed. But again SOBSI defied the government amid indications that the Communists planned the seizure of foreign (non-Dutch) firms. On December 15, the army arrested several SOBSI leaders. A struggle for power appeared in the making between the army and the PKI.

Throughout the anti-Dutch campaign, Moscow and Peking had exhorted the Indonesians to greater effort: As late as January 3, 1958, the Peking *People's Daily* applauded Indonesia for having "done right and done well." For Aidit, the situation was more promising than ever. But when the army ordered an end to the seizures, and the military began arresting Communist front leaders, Aidit found himself at a crossroad. To defy the army would mean a direct clash with the government, perhaps prematurely, and an

abandonment of the prevailing Right strategy; moreover, with the
outer islands in "rebellion," the Communists would be isolated on
Java, a precarious situation especially since the SEATO powers
controlled the seas. Yet the situation for the PKI was extraordinar-
ily favorable. The Communists were in the national council and
were making impressive electoral gains; the economic situation
bordered on chaos; the government could not operate the seized
companies without SOBSI assistance. By exercising restraint, there
was the possibility of power by default. Aidit was forced to choose
between Trotsky's thesis of "immediate action regardless of the
consequences" and Lenin's dictum, "get strong first, everything
else afterward." In the face of the developing revolutionary situation, Aidit held his hand. Thus on December 16, one observer was
able to report that "without doubt [the Communists] are better organized than the government in Java, but whether they would
want power at this time is doubtful, especially since they know
the outlying areas would immediately declare their autonomy." [11]
And two months later, another observer reported that "Communist strategy now is to play the game in low key. While ostensibly
supporting Djakarta, the Communists are blaming the government
for all the present troubles when they campaign at the village level.
They are consolidating their hold on the Javanese population." [12]
Two steps forward, one step backward. Time, so it would seem to
Aidit, favored the Communists.

The action against the Dutch disrupted distribution, shipping,
and communications. As the *Times of Indonesia* commented
Christmas week: "Because the West Irian issue is a matter of absorbing national concern, no one has summoned up enough courage to criticize action taken either by the government or by individuals and organizations lest the critic find himself branded as
a national or pro-Dutch." On December 28, Hatta broke the silence. In an open letter, he charged that the Irian campaign had
"hurt Indonesia more than the Dutch" and asked whether it was
necessary for the Indonesian people to make such sacrifices to
speed the return of Irian. "The Dutch economy here must be
liquidated," he said, "but not in a fashion that will cripple us."
He attacked the government for failing to provide KPM and KLM
with a notice of the termination of their services while arrangements were made for their replacement. Sjafruddin Prawiranegara,
the former head of the underground emergency government of
the republic, 1948-49, and now the governor of the Bank of
Indonesia, denounced the seizures as creating chaos in the monetary field, stagnation in trade, and runaway inflation.

The short-sighted nature of the anti-Dutch campaign was clearly demonstrated in March, 1958, when the government returned thirty-seven vessels to KPM that had been impounded at the height of the anti-Dutch campaign. SOBSI "regretted" the government's decision, but Djuanda had no alternative. KPM was in the process of collecting insurance from Lloyds in excess of the real value of the ships, which were of pre-World War II vintage. To fill the gap, Djakarta turned to other sources for shipping, notably Russia and Japan. As early as December 10, the government asked Japan for 100,000 tons of shipping, and on March 17 the first of ten Soviet ships arrived as part of a $100-million credit extended to Indonesia during Sukarno's Soviet visit and ratified by parliament on February 7, 1958, as the economic crisis deepened. Thus Indonesia senselessly replaced the influence of a small West European kingdom with that of two Asian nations possessing great power ambitions.

From the outset of the "people's action," Sukarno, brooding over the Tjikini incident, remained in seclusion. On December 11, the President reappeared in public and offered this solace: "Although we face shortages of food and clothing, our revolutionary spirit of 1945 will be renewed." On January 5, drawn and tired, Sukarno went abroad for a rest. Sixteen days later, in a letter to Palembang's *Batang Hari Sembilan*, Sjafruddin—who had left Djakarta for Sumatra with Natsir and other prominent leaders "because I am not prepared to become the victim of wild animals in human form"—wrote: "The opportunity freely to express opinions no longer exists [in Indonesia]. In such anarchy naturally the door is closed to democratic elements."

The burgeoning rebel movement in the outer islands was preparing to put an end to corruption, demagogy, and Communist infiltration by establishing a rival government at Bukittingi, the capital of Sumatra in the revolutionary years 1945–48. The Indonesian revolution had come full circle.

22

"Rightist Symptoms"

Wisdom counseled restraint in the outer islands as Indonesia entered 1958. The dissidents possessed preponderant economic power, arms, and high-caliber political leadership. They included three former heads of government: Sjafruddin (1948–49), Natsir (1950–51), and Harahap (1955–56). By contrast, the area controlled by Djakarta, notably Java, was in disarray. The anti-Dutch campaign had disorganized the economy; the army and the PKI faced each other with suspicion; nationalists and religious scholars were alarmed by the dimensions of the Communist mass movement unleashed during the anti-Dutch drive, particularly the Party's control over street gangs. Clearly, the rebels were ahead on points; it was a question of letting the clock run out. But the rebels calculated on a tour de force, Sukarno's collapse as a consequence of economic chaos or a palace revolution.[1] In forcing Sukarno's hand, the insurgents miscalculated. They lost the initiative.

From Padang, West Sumatra, on February 10, the dissidents demanded that within "five times twenty-four hours" the Djuanda cabinet return its mandate, Hatta and the Sultan of Jogjakarta establish a national working cabinet pending elections, and Sukarno "resume his constitutional status." The ultimatum was accompanied by a "Charter of Struggle" that denounced guided democracy as a camouflage for personal rule and prelude to a Communist take-over, described the liquidation of Dutch economic interests without government approval as "irresponsible" and part of a Communist pattern to weaken the economy, and alleged that Djakarta was incapable of controlling "sinister forces" in the capital "running wild, organizing seizures, slandering, intimidating, and using other forms of terror."

On February 11, Djuanda rejected the ultimatum out of hand. Four days later, coinciding with Sukarno's return from abroad, the dissidents proclaimed the Revolutionary Government of the Republic of Indonesia (PRRI) with its seat at Bukittingi. The PRRI pledged to "govern on the basis of the Charter of Struggle and to transfer the leadership of the [PRRI] government to Hatta and Hamengkubuwono at any time they expressed readiness and willingness to assume that leadership." Clearly, the rebel administration was not separatist. Sjafruddin was named Premier and Finance Minister; Harahap, Defense and Justice Minister; Sumitro, Trade and Communications Minister; Colonel Simbolon, Foreign Minister. Natsir, the chairman of the Masjumi, remained aloof; later, in a reorganization of the PRRI, he became Vice Premier.*

In Djakarta, the passive intellectual opposition to Sukarno, led by Hatta and Sjahrir, resolutely opposed the precipitous action lest it turn Sukarno and Java toward the Communists, and in the process polarize Indonesia into Communist and anti-Communist camps, transforming the archipelago into a cradle of East-West conflict. The major non-Communist parties, alarmed at the specter of foreign intervention, denounced the rebellion as "unconstitutional" and warned that it was "strictly an internal affair"; the Masjumi was the only party that considered the Djuanda administration "unconstitutional" as well. In general, the parties favored a peaceful settlement. Their hopes resided in Hatta, who conferred with Sukarno between February 20 and March 4 in an effort to work out a compromise.

The prospect of Hatta in a government appalled the Communists. The PKI dreaded either a "phony war" that would lead to a "hawker's bargain" or a protracted armed conflict that might isolate Java. For the PKI, a swift suppression of the revolt was imperative. As Aidit observed, the "annihilation of the rebels . . . will, if achieved swiftly, greatly push forward the development of the revolutionary situation." He added: "If the annihilation of the rebels can be achieved within a short space of time . . . the reactionaries and imperialists will have lost one of their important bases, and more favorable conditions will be created for the Indonesian people to implement President Sukarno's concept 100 per cent." [2]

Strikingly, the interests of Sukarno and the armed forces coincided with those of the Communists at this time. With Irian

---

* On March 8, 1960, the PRRI was renamed the Federal Republic of Indonesia, or Union of Indonesian States (PRI).

momentarily spent, the army confident of victory, and the President a primary target of the rebellion, Sukarno—and Nasution—also favored an armed showdown. Accordingly, on March 11, Djakarta's forces attacked Pakenbaru, Central Sumatra. The PRRI forces withdrew into the jungles without offering resistance or scorching the American-owned (Caltex) oil fields in the area, the focal point of the initial air-borne assault. On May 6, Bukittingi fell and Sjafruddin disappeared into the same jungle that had concealed him from the Dutch a decade before. On June 9, Djakarta's amphibious forces invaded North Sulawesi and seventeen days later, in the hardest fighting of the campaign, occupied the PERMESTA* capital of Menado, a recruiting ground for the pre-war Dutch colonial army. The operations, commanded by Indonesian officers who had received their advance military training in the United States,† assumed the characteristics of all military campaigns in Indonesia since 1942: rapid advances and light resistance, if any—an aftermath of desultory guerrilla warfare.

Militarily, the insurrection had failed. The rebellion had been generated primarily by intellectuals lacking organized rice-roots support and the prerequisite fanaticism to wage civil war. The rebels were militarily unprepared despite their abundance of weapons and doubtlessly were surprised by Sukarno's decision to fight. The PRRI had failed to ensure Hatta and the Sultan's endorsement before embarking on the adventure. The Darul Islam in Atjeh and elsewhere was not inclined to assist a reformist Moslem leadership in partnership with predominantly Christian North Sulawesi; indeed, the PRRI Foreign Minister had led Djakarta's military campaign against Atjeh since 1953. Within the rebel movement there was also dissension between proponents of a secularist and Islamic-orientated state. On Sumatra, the east and south were immobilized by the presence of large Javanese migrant populations who considered the rebellion "anti-Javanese"; Kalimantan and East Indonesia, with the exception of North Sulawesi and the Halamaheras, were prepared to feint but not fight. The rebels also relied on foreign support, which was haphazardly organized and withdrawn when the PRRI failed to offer "serious" resistance. The impression that the insurgents enjoyed foreign assistance proved a psychological hazard in central-government areas

---

* The Sulawesi rebel council was called the Universal Charter of Struggle (PERMESTA).
† E.g., Colonel Achmad Jani, who commanded the Sumatra invasion. He later became Second Deputy to Nasution and promoted to major general; in January, 1962, he was put in command of Irian operations.

where anti-Djakarta sentiment was high. Western domination was still too recent for comfort.

At the onset, the rebellion strained Indonesian-American relations almost to a breaking point.[3] United States prestige in the period preceding the rebellion was already at a low ebb: There had been Little Rock in September; Sputnik in October; the United States' abstention on Irian in November; and the abrupt recall of Ambassador John M. Allison on January 21. Allison had urged Washington to apply pressure on the Dutch to move towards an Irian settlement while putting pressure on Indonesia to respect Dutch economic interests—the Linggadjati-Renville formulas. Allison considered Sukarno a perpetual revolutionary who exploited Irian for its revolutionary mass appeal. He felt Irian provided Aidit a natural link to Sukarno. Allison wanted to dissolve that link. But if Sukarno was a perpetual revolutionary, would Irian really satisfy him? The State Department declined in principle to place pressure on a NATO ally for Sukarno's benefit. This, however, begged the question. At issue was whether relinquishing Irian was of greater benefit to Sukarno or to the non-Communist world. On March 10, the day before fighting developed, Howard P. Jones, the chief of the U.S. Foreign Operations Mission to Indonesia (1954–55), presented his credentials to Sukarno as Allison's successor, the fourth American envoy within eight years.*

During the next three months, in quest of "peace and stability," the American position seesawed. On February 11, the day after Sjafruddin's ultimatum, Dulles told a news conference that the United States "would like to see in Indonesia a government which is constitutional" and observed that Sukarno's concept "may not quite conform with the provisional constitution." By May 20, however, Dulles expressed the conviction that "the situation in Indonesia can be and should be dealt with as an Indonesian problem . . . by the Indonesians without intrusion from without." The readjustment in American policy reflected a fundamental Dulles decision to contain the Indonesian war, for by then, the conflict embodied the ingredients of an East-West clash.

Sufficient evidence exists, including eyewitness accounts in the Anglo-American press, to confirm that the PRRI received tacit foreign assistance.[4] Regular arms drops over rebel territory precluded erratic arms profiteering. In some broad respects, the role of the United States in the PRRI rebellion was comparable to that of the United States and others in the Cuban affair in 1961. At best, the "intervention" was uncoordinated, reflecting moral uncertainty, confusion, and indecision.

* At this writing, Ambassador Jones still is in Indonesia.

For example, the crucial first seven weeks of the civil war were merely a shadow war on Sumatra. Then, as if by afterthought, the complexion of the campaign altered when two B-26s and two Mustangs strafed shipping, closed the Royal Dutch Shell (BPM) oil refinery at Balikpapan,* and bombed Macassar. On April 30, Djuanda charged that American "soldiers of fortune" piloted the aircraft. On May 2, Sukarno warned Washington "not to play with fire" and accused the United States of pushing Indonesia into the Communist fold. The following day, the Foreign Ministry threatened to air the question of intervention at the United Nations. Doubts about the participation of Americans in the affair, at least unofficially, were removed on May 18, when a B-26 was downed near Ambon and Allan Lawrence Pope, the aircraft's American pilot, was captured.† Many recalled the August revolution, when Americans flew for the republic.

On Java, the issue of intervention provided the Communists with an opportunity. Aidit marshaled his fronts for a massive anti-American campaign. On May 1, the PKI sent a telegram to Ambassador Jones threatening action against American economic interests in Indonesia. Three days later, the Communists organized a rally against "foreign intervention" as a prelude to a mammoth "SEATO Hands Off!" demonstration planned for May 7. Aidit labored to develop a popular front against "imperialist aggression." But despite Aidit's moderation since the preceding December, the Communists had apparently overplayed their hand during the daubing campaigns, intimidation of the opposition, and unauthorized seizures of property. The PNI and NU declined to participate in the rally, incurring PKI wrath. The PNI realized that Aidit was unleashing a "Hate America" wave so as to create a revolutionary situation and that it was not inconceivable that the Communists planned to provoke direct American intervention. The army and Djuanda felt similarly and postponed, then canceled, the demonstration.

Aidit was again confronted with the alternative of open conflict or tactical retreat. Again he withdrew. It would have been ludicrous for the Communists to defy the army as it suppressed an anti-Communist hard core, particularly since many senior army officers sympathized with the rebels' aims but disapproved of their methods. Aidit's problem, like that of the loyal opposition and

---

* This was a joint Anglo-Dutch enterprise and, therefore, had not been seized in 1957. (Sukarno has treated the oil industry gingerly. It is a primary, regular source of foreign exchange for Djakarta.)

† Pope was convicted and sentenced to death on April 29, 1959. On July 2, 1962, he was released, as a gesture of good will toward the U.S., in the midst of the Irian negotiations.

the government, but for different reasons, was to avoid the snare of portraying the civil war in Communist and anti-Communist terms—the strategy of the PRRI. Thus the PKI adopted the slogan: "Not Communist and Anti-Communist, but Democracy and Anti-democracy, National and Anti-national." [5] Aidit was realistic: Already the cabinet held that the suppression of the PRRI was not inspired by anti-anti-Communism but by the dynamics of nationalist unity and survival.[6]

But neither Moscow nor Peking were inclined to lose the momentum generated by the Sukarno-Djuanda charges of intervention. Thus on May 15, following the postponement of the "SEATO Hands Off" demonstration, Peking formally announced its preparedness to furnish Indonesia "such assistance, within its ability, as may be requested by the Indonesian government." The Chinese initiative was followed two days later by a Soviet declaration that non-Communist intervention posed a threat to peace that the Soviet Union cannot ignore. The Russians, however, raised the threat of "neither rockets nor volunteers," as they had done at Suez.

Chronologically, the threat of "volunteers" was first introduced at Seoul on March 31 by Syngman Rhee. South Korea's patriarch criticized the United States' failure to recognize the PRRI and assailed Dulles' "hands-off policy" in Indonesia.[7] Rhee offered the PRRI "volunteers," but neither Djakarta nor Bukittingi took his "exclusive interview" seriously; nor did Rhee follow up the offer with a formal declaration. Peking's maneuver, however, drew an immediate, unambiguous reply. On May 23, with the U.S. 7th Fleet patrolling the Taiwan Strait, Taipeh warned that it would consider the presence of " 'volunteers' in the South China Sea as a threat to the security of Taiwan" and would interdict their movement. Correctly or not, it appeared that the non-nuclear allies of America and Russia leaned toward the "internationalization" of the civil war—an internationalization, events demonstrated, that neither Washington nor Moscow was prepared to accept in Indonesia in 1958.

With the rebels on Sumatra displaying little disposition to fight, and with Djakarta displaying awareness of the threat posed by the PKI on Java, the United States was confronted with the choice of unreservedly supporting the PRRI or, overlooking past indiscretions, buttressing the central government. A decision was urgent: On May 6, the first shipment of MIG-16 jet trainers arrived on Java, a hint of future Soviet arms shipments.* Only the year before,

---

* Within a year, MIG-17's were operating against the rebels. See Macassar dispatch, Antara, May 19, 1959.

the United States had refused an Indonesian request for $600-million worth of arms on credit. Now Sukarno resubmitted the request, implying that Washington's acceptance would demonstrate American nonintervention, at least officially, and that a refusal would compel Indonesia to turn to Moscow.

On May 21, the United States eased an embargo on arms sales to the belligerents and the following day announced the shipment of 37,000 tons of rice to Java. These measures, coupled with Dulles' May 20 statement and coincident with the termination of PRRI air activity, signalized an agonizing reappraisal of American policy in Indonesia. The delivery of arms marked a turning point, Foreign Minister Subandrio conceded, but he believed the political evaluation leading to the transaction to be of more importance for the future relationship between the two countries than the arms themselves. In August, the first American arms shipments were ferried to Djakarta by Globemaster, "solely for the maintenance of internal security," according to a State Department announcement of August 19. Within six months, the United States re-equipped 20 Indonesian battalions (160,000 men). The arms shipments disillusioned the rebels, who had revised their strategy and now planned for a long-term, undramatic war of attrition. On July 28, the PRRI attacked Bukittingi, and on September 22, the rebels temporarily reoccupied Sibolga, a West Sumatran port. But the stirring of "serious" resistance, patterned on the style of the Indonesian infiltration of Dutch-occupied Jogjakarta in February, 1949, came too late. Yet American policy was a stopgap at best. When the United States declined Sukarno's request for heavy weapons in 1960–61 for deployment against Irian, Khrushchev rapaciously consented.

The American re-evaluation reflected the judgment that Nasution offered the best prospect for stability. The Dutch seizures, followed by the civil war, had immeasurably deepened the army's participation in the governing process. Some called it a "creeping coup";[8] for example, 4,000 army officers administered the former Dutch properties. Washington was impressed by both the army's technical and political capabilities—reflected in the military operations—and Nasution's moves to prevent the Communists from advancing their own interests as the army engaged the PRRI. The Action Committee for the Liberation of West Irian, controlled by radical nationalists and Communists, was dissolved and replaced by a West Irian National Liberation Front under Nasution's chairmanship; the army prohibited parades, censored speeches, and barred the red flag on May Day; banned wall-writing as a "political weapon"; established the Indonesian Veterans'

Legion, proscribing all other veteran organizations, including PERBEPSI; and even prohibited an elaborate PKI welcome at the airfield for a new Soviet Ambassador, Boris Volkov.[9] Djuanda also reshuffled the cabinet on June 25, dissolved the Mobilization Ministry, which had financed the myrmidons of the anti-Dutch campaign, and demoted Hanafi to a state minister. The Sultan was invited to join the government but declined. The now politically sophisticated PNI, influenced by Ali, launched a vigorous anti-Communist campaign. It accused Aidit of attempting to draw nationalists into a popular front to serve Moscow's Cold War interests while destroying the PNI in the wake of the bankruptcy of the Masjumi and PSI. The old-line nationalists had parted with the Communists.

Significantly, perhaps, within a month of the revolt, the PKI sensed that the army, the cabinet, and the other parties would try to drown the PKI in the backwash of the campaign against the PRRI. At the sixth plenary session of the Central Committee (March 3–April 4, 1958), Aidit warned against "hawkers' bargains" between Djakarta and Washington, between the army and the PRRI,

> between the die-hard bourgeois elements and the right nationalist elements so as to "contain Communism," to "save Java from the red danger," and for "the safety of the free world." By means of these base agreements, consciously or otherwise, the right-nationalist elements are deviating from the general political line of the nationalists. . . . In brief, the slogan "anti-Communism" at the present stage of history in our country is nothing but a slogan to split national unity, a slogan to weaken the anti-imperialist struggle that is now intensifying, and a slogan to destroy democracy.[10]

Aidit foresaw, too, that Sukarno and the army might "learn the lessons of Egypt": Dissolve parties and parliament, annul elections—"the policy of a bourgeoisie that has lost all reason." Suddenly Western-imported, bourgeois, parliamentary democracy acquired urgency among Marxist-Leninists: "The Indonesian Communists and people stand firmly by their conviction that however bad democracy may be in practice, it is much better than fascism," [11] Aidit said.

The sixth plenary session ended with a reshuffle of the Party hierarchy in which the Left group appeared strengthened. An Executive Committee was formed as the Party's supreme body, and the triumvirate of Aidit, Lukman, and Njoto expanded into a quadrumvirate with the elevation of Sudisman, a member of the Lukman group, from the Politburo. The Secretariat was enlarged to include Sudisman, Jusuf Adjitorop, Peris Pardede, Siswojo, Anwar Sanusi, Anwar Kadir, and Djokosudjono. Adjitorop was also named to the Politburo. Finally, the Central Committee was enlarged with the appointment of the following candidate members to full membership: Utarjo, Tjugito, Anwar Sanusi, Anwar Kadir, and Ruslan Kamaludin. Sanusi's rise was swift.

On August 17, barely six months after the rebellion, the PKI was thoroughly disturbed. The Party contended that the

> American imperialists, together with the domestic reactionaries, have been trying to overcome their defeat [in Sumatra] by means of making approaches to middle-of-the-road groups [PNI] and by reviving anti-Communist propaganda. . . . The task of the Indonesian people today is to resist and defeat these tactics, which are in actual fact no different from imperialist intervention. If we fail to defeat these new kinds of intervention, it will mean that what the PRRI-PERMESTA failed to achieve will be achieved quite peacefully by means of these new tactics.[12]

This was the first suggestion that perhaps some objectives of the PRRI could be realized in the postmilitary phase—indeed, within a year, the PKI felt constrained to openly denounce "peace talk."

The August 17 statement again vigorously defended parliamentary processes and warned that a postponement of the general elections scheduled for 1959 would abet the Masjumi and PSI by "preserving the position that they now unrightfully hold in parliament." Aidit did not participate in drafting the statement; that same day, he returned from his first tour behind the Iron Curtain since Hungary, professed that "there is no such thing as a 'crisis of Communism,'" and joined in urging opposition to a postponement of elections. But the screws were tightened and Aidit must have appreciated the nature of the crisis confronting the Party. On September 22, Djuanda postponed the elections for a year in view of unsettled conditions. *Harian Rakjat* termed the decision "a great disappointment."

In Party circles "the burning question" on Aidit's return was whether the political line would alter. On September 19, the Central Committee conferred on "the rightist symptoms of the national bourgeoisie." Khrushchev, Aidit, and the Right prevailed. Njoto, who abided by "the wing of the Party led by Aidit," and himself only recently returned from China, spoke for the Executive Committee.[13] Njoto acknowledged that "the most decisive question is the relationship between the progressive forces [Communist] and the middle-of-the-road forces [non-Communist], and especially the relationship between the proletarian party [PKI] and the national bourgeois parties [PNI, etc.]." As a demonstration of Party harmony, Njoto cited the conclusion "drawn by Comrade Lukman": first, strike harder blows at the "diehards" (PRRI, Masjumi, PSI) and thereby reduce the "possibility of the middle-of-the-road forces turning toward them"; and, second, "patiently and resolutely and by means of concrete actions, convince the middle-of-the-road forces that our enemy, the enemy of the Indonesian people, is still the imperialists [West] together with their compradores [Masjumi]" and that "therefore national unity must be strengthened." But how? Njoto cited Irian [Sukarno]. Through Irian, he said, the Party would consolidate a "national united front that includes all anti-imperialist classes and groups."

To escape the army by following Sukarno's footsteps was to tread a narrow path. Guided democracy could lead to a burial of the PKI with the party system. But the Communists had no alternative. The PKI certainly could not challenge the army while the PRRI rebellion smoldered; significantly, the PRRI leadership remained at large, its forces largely intact. The lightning victory promised by Nasution and urged by Aidit had not materialized. Moreover, Aidit was under pressure from the Left faction within the Party to counter the army's anti-Communist drive. On October 27, the PKI seized the initiative with a call for a "100 per cent" implementation of the Sukarno concept, including formation of a *gotong royong* cabinet with PKI participation. Aidit probably reasoned that with the Communists in the cabinet, the Party would be immune from the army. Aidit described guided democracy as "antimilitary dictatorship of the individual and antiliberalism." Therefore, he contended, those who rejected Sukarno's plan were "antinational, and proliberal, i.e., promilitary and proindividual dictatorship." And he concluded: "The only way to defeat military or individual dictatorship and liberalism is to implement Sukarno's guided democracy. . . . At the moment there is no other way for Indonesia [for the PKI]. At this moment, this is the most revolutionary policy."

On November 21, at the seventh plenary meeting of the Central Committee, Aidit went further. He proposed "special powers" for Sukarno to carry out his plan. The plenum no sooner concluded than the peripatetic Aidit again departed for Moscow, on this occasion to attend the twenty-first Party Congress, at which Khrushchev glossed over Sino-Soviet differences and moved a step further in replacing the monolithic unity of the Communist camp with the concept of "a single Commonwealth" of Communist states, apparently a device to ensure Soviet direction of the international movement by numbers, since the majority of "socialist" states contiguous to Russia were occupied by the Red Army. The Chinese, at best, could muster the support of North Vietnam and North Korea (where their own Red Army exercised preponderant influence), and perhaps Albania, which dwelled in isolation between "revisionist" Yugoslavia and NATO Greece. During Aidit's travels, Ho Chi-minh arrived in Djakarta, apparently on a dual mission both to cultivate Sukarno and to assess the situation in Indonesia in Aidit's absence. Ho approved of Aidit's road. On March 26, en route from Moscow, Aidit visited Ho at Hanoi and came away "extremely satisfied with the unanimity reached on all the questions discussed." [14] More important than sterile communiqués, Aidit's broad policies remained unchanged in the months ahead.

23

A Cult of Personality

Pending the development of his own political organization in the guise of a national front, Sukarno relied primarily on the support of the rival army and PKI, the most disciplined and powerful organizations on Java, to further his concept of guided democracy. On February 20, 1959, he resumed his forward motion with a summons to the nation to return to the constitution of 1945. A rebirth of the original charter, he believed, would revive the romanticism of 1945 and heal the nation's wounds. The response to his invitation was a foregone conclusion; the day before, the army had enthusiastically endorsed his course.

The 1945 constitution provided for a strong executive. The President appointed and discharged ministers and ruled without parliamentary interference for five years. Sovereignty was vested in a People's Congress, which met at least once every five years to lay down the broad lines of state policy. The Congress was composed of a People's Representative Council, a legislature that met at least once a year, and representatives of both the regions and "corporations," i.e., functional groups.* The constitution also provided for the establishment of a Supreme Advisory Council, which functioned as a Presidential cabinet. In addition to proposing a return to '45, Sukarno suggested a limitation on parties and an amended election law permitting the election of functional groups to parliament. Sukarno declined to partake in demonstra-

---

* The term "corporation" was employed in translation of the Constitution and (Sjahrir's) Political Manifesto as late as in the Emergency Edition, 1949. The PKI prefers the word "group." For PKI translation, see *Review of Indonesia,* August, 1959.

tions supporting his proposals. "The people," he said, "will have to decide for themselves." [1]

The Communists reluctantly endorsed a return to the former constitution and reserved judgment on the other proposals. The PKI's uncertainty was reflected in the Party slogan: "Hold high and defend the basic rights and democratic freedoms of the people! Defend the freedom of the people's organization!" The slogan betrayed Aidit's concern that a return to 1945 would lead to a burial of the Party system. The non-Communist press criticized Communist reservations as PKI infidelity to Sukarno. The PKI characterized the attacks as "Trotskyite-inspired," ostensibly Tan Malakist in origin. Within a week, however, the Party reversed itself and announced enthusiastic support for the Sukarno program. The PKI praised the scheme for opening the way to the President to take executive powers into his own hands. Thus the Communists continued in the competition for Sukarno's favor. Thereafter, the army and the PKI, in Aidit's words, became "the foremost supporters" of a return to 1945.[2] But the Communists apparently felt their posture to be unconvincing. "Some people say that the PKI supports the policy of back to the 1945 constitution because it has no alternative," Aidit observed. "Yes, indeed, and not only for the PKI. There is no alternative for all Indonesian patriots." [3]

On April 22, Sukarno submitted his plan to the constituent assembly sitting at Bandung. The President observed that "in all fields we are deteriorating—and deteriorating continuously," and advised the assembly "not [to] waste time, energy, and thinking" in deliberating over the text of the 1945 charter but to reinstate it "as is." Sukarno, however, introduced modifications. He proposed the creation of a national front—"a mass generator"—to assist the President in the execution of policies that "cannot be entrusted to political parties." But he pledged: "The political parties will not be dissolved." He reassured the army of a prominent role by reserving the right to appoint thirty-five members of the armed forces to the new parliament as a functional sociomilitary group. He appeased the Moslem scholars, who had considered the constituent assembly a vehicle for advancing Islamic political concepts in the drafting of a constitution, by proposing that the assembly recognize the "Djakarta Charter" as a historic document insolubly linked to the old constitution. The Charter, drawn on June 22, 1945, obliged the nation's Moslems to observe Islamic law; since almost all Indonesians, including Sukarno, nominally profess Islam, this could conceivably have deep implications.

Indonesia's "continuing deterioration" notwithstanding, Sukarno two days later departed on a world tour confident that the assembly would abide by his wishes. But almost immediately, a struggle developed between the non-Islamic and Islamic factions. The Masjumi and NU sought to incorporate the Charter's obligation directly into the constitution. Islam was at a point of no retreat. Tension mounted. On May 30, the 468-member chamber rejected Sukarno's plan by 47 votes; on June 1, by 48 votes; on June 2, 49 votes. Under the assembly's rules, a proposal was discarded if it failed to pass by a two-thirds majority after 3 ballots. Wilopo, the chairman of the constituent body, announced that the proposal had been dropped and the current session adjourned. Roeslan Abdul Gani, still Sukarno's principal adviser but being pressed in that role by an emerging Subandrio, cited the assembly's action as "voting democracy" and not "democracy by consultation" (*musjawarah*). He asked: "Is absolute justice two plus one or half plus one?" That same day, June 2, with Sukarno in Hollywood lunching with film personalities,[4] Nasution acted. He ordered a temporary prohibition on political activity to preserve "public order." Rumors of a military coup swept Indonesia. But the rumors were unfounded; unless compelled by circumstance, Nasution was loath to assume responsibility for the "continuing deterioration."

On June 29, Sukarno returned from abroad. In 1957, Sukarno had said that he could not neglect the 6 million votes of the PKI; now he would neglect the 15 million votes of the parties who rejected his proposals. On July 5, by decree, Sukarno dissolved the constituent assembly and reinstated the constitution of 1945. The next day, Djuanda returned his mandate. Four days later, Sukarno appointed a ten-man "inner cabinet" with himself as Prime Minister; Djuanda as Chief Minister and Minister of Finance; Nasution as Minister of Security and Defense; Saleh as Minister of Development; Yamin as Minister of Social and Cultural Affairs. Seven ex-officio ministers were appointed, including the chiefs of the armed forces (Nasution for a second time). Sukarno also named twenty-six "junior" ministers, among them Erningpradja (Labor); Saleh, also for a second time (Basic Industries and Mines); Sadjarwo (Agrarian Affairs); and Prijono (Education). Later, Iwa joined the cabinet.* There were no overt Communists in the cabinet. The government adopted a three-point

---

* On March 21, 1960, Prijono was downgraded to Minister of Basic Education and Culture, and Iwa named Minister of Higher Education and Science. Working in tandem, they have since oriented Indonesia's educational system toward the Soviet bloc, introducing Soviet texts, redirecting the flow of Indonesians studying abroad, etc.

program that accurately reflected the situation in Indonesia after a decade of sovereignty: (1) Satisfy the people's need for food and clothing in the shortest possible time; (2) maintain the security of the people and the state; (3) continue the struggle against economic imperialism and political imperialism (West Irian).

Then, on July 30, Sukarno named a forty-six-member Provisional Supreme Advisory Council (Deperas), empowered under the constitution to "advise on matters submitted to it by the President and [exercising] the right to submit proposals to the government." The Council included Aidit, Njoto, Sutomo Atomo, Siauw Giok Tjhan, and such radical nationalists and Tan Malaka sympathizers as Adam Malik, Iwa Kusumasumantri, Mohammed Padang, and Mrs. Rasuna Said. Sukarno also named a seventy-seven-member National Planning Council (Depernas).* Yamin was appointed chairman; a Communist, Sakirman, third vice chairman. Other members included Wikana, Tjoa Sik Ien, and, Semaun, a figure out of the dim past, who was named a representative of the "intelligentsia-scholars" functional group.† Both the advisory and planning council included representatives from BTI, SOBSI, GERWANI, SAKTI, LEKRA, PERBEPSI, and Pemuda Rakjat as functional groups. The next day Sukarno authorized the parliament to continue, pending elections in 1962—the first indication that elections had again been postponed. On August 1, the ban on political activity was lifted. The nation was confronted by a *fait accompli*. Sukarno emerged as President, Commander in Chief, Prime Minister, and Chairman of the Supreme Advisory Council. On December 16, 1959, he acquired the title Supreme War Administrator; on January 1, 1961, the appellation, "the Greater Leader of the Revolution"; and on January 20, 1961, "Supreme Leader of the National Front." A year later he also became Supreme Commander of the West Irian Liberation Command. The PKI, of course, emerged entrenched in the new structure. They were in a difficult position, however, being re-

* Depernas drafted an Eight-Year Plan, which was officially launched by Sukarno on January 1, 1961. The only comment necessary, perhaps, was Yamin's announcement at Bandung on August 13, 1960, that the Plan is divided into 8 parts, 17 volumes, and 1,945 paragraphs (shades of August 17, 1945!).

† Semaun returned to Indonesia on December 12, 1956, after spending thirty-three years in Russia, where he had acquired a Russian family and Russian citizenship, served as Third Vice Premier of the Soviet Republic of Takjikistan, and, during the revolutionary Indonesian postwar period, worked for Radio Moscow. See Malik, *Sovjet Rusia Seperti Jang Saja Lihat*, Djakarta, 1954, p. 62.

sponsible for the government's actions but lacking the power to make decisions.

By now, of course, a central problem confronting the PKI was to what extent the Communists should support the Sukarno program. Should the Communists establish unity with the middle-of-the-road national bourgeoisie no matter at what cost, or should they direct their main blows at those forces? Nor was this problem confined to the PKI. A continuation of the Right strategy posed similar questions in other parties—as reflected later by the Sino-Soviet discord—and by 1957, a year after Khrushchev's denunciation of Stalin had shaken international Communism, the problem of the strategy Communists should adopt toward the non-Communist world had begun to assume epic proportions. In this conflict, Moscow and Peking, for strategic reasons, assumed opposing positions. Before pursuing the PKI's treatment of the problem, we must digress momentarily to trace the impact of the debate on the Communist bloc.

Moscow, confronted with the nightmare of thermonuclear war, advocated a continuation of the post-1952 Right strategy. Peking, suspicious lest a policy of compromise lead to an accommodation with the nuclear West, at China's expense, advocated a turn to the Left. The Chinese could risk an aggressive line. China was less vulnerable than Russia to nuclear weapons. The Chinese possessed no nuclear weapons, and the Korean War had demonstrated that the West was morally incapable of using nuclear weapons against a non-nuclear power, however aggressive. Japan had been the exception that made the rule; in 1945, the bomb was still an unknown quantity, certainly in political and psychological terms.

At Moscow, on November 14–16, 1957, the debate over strategies in the nuclear-missile age was joined. A compromise was explored. The outcome was a Joint Declaration by Twelve Communist Parties and Workers' Parties of the Communist bloc and a Peace Manifesto, signed by sixty-four Communist parties, including the PKI. The documents sought to smooth over the differences between Moscow and Peking. The conclave defined and obscured the nature of the debate in Marxist-Leninist terminology. But it was patently clear that the debate was inconclusive. The Declaration, endorsed by the Manifesto, approved the Chinese position that "the main danger at present [to Communists] is revisionism or, in other words, Right-wing opportunism, which, as a manifestation of bourgeois ideology, paralyzes the revolutionary energy of the working class."

But in the same breath, the session concluded that dogmatism "can also be the main danger at different phases of development in one Party or another [and that] it is for each Communist Party to decide what danger threatens it more at a given time."

On balance, Khrushchev and the Right won the day. Aidit subsequently confirmed this interpretation in a statement on December 8, 1957. Aidit held that "both of these documents will definitely be warmly welcomed . . . by all people who have no interest in there being a war," i.e., the nuclear powers.

The meeting no sooner dispersed than the debate began anew within the Communist world. In November, 1960, a new effort was made to iron out differences at the Meeting of Eighty-one Communist and Workers' Parties in Moscow. In contrast to 1957, Peking appeared to gain an edge, however slight, over Moscow. A Marxist-Leninist distinction emerged between "national bour-geois" states born of "bourgeois democratic revolutions," such as the United Arab Republic, Mexico, and India, and "independent national democracies" such as Cuba.*

The session concluded that in the "bourgeois" states "fascism is expanding in new forms, that dictatorial methods of government combine with fictitious parliamentary practices that have been stripped of democratic content and reduced to pure form," where-as in the "independent national democracies" conditions were being created "for passing on to the tasks of Socialist revolution."

As defined by the Communists, an "independent national de-mocracy" is

> a state consistently defending its political and economic independ-ence, fighting against imperialism and its military blocs, and against military bases on its territory, a state fighting against new forms of colonialism and the penetration of imperialist capital, a state re-jecting dictatorial and despotic methods of government [toward Communists], a state in which the people [read Communists] are guaranteed broad democratic rights and freedom (freedom of speech, press, association, and assembly, and freedom to create political parties and social organizations), the opportunity to achieve agrarian reforms and the realization of other aspirations in the field of demo-cratic and social reorganization and the opportunity of participating in shaping state policy.[5]

---

* Interestingly, perhaps, the term "national democracy" was first used by Sukarno (see p. 288). A September 25, 1959, decision by the Deperas recog-nizing Sukarno's August 17, 1959, speech as Indonesia's Political Manifesto describes the Indonesian Revolution as "national and democratic . . . a com-mon revolution of all classes and groups who oppose imperialism-colonialism [read West]."

Clearly, or so it would appear, the definition is not wholly applicable to contemporary Indonesia. Yet the Communist Left and Right professed to believe otherwise. As early as May 23, 1960, six months before the Moscow meeting, the Lao Dong (Communist) Party of North Vietnam declared in a fortieth anniversary message to the PKI that "although still facing many difficulties and hardships [the PKI will] assuredly achieve the *national democratic revolution*, wipe out completely colonialism from Indonesia and contribute to the defense of Asian and world peace." [6] Hence, although Indonesia may not yet be there, she is on the way. Nor is this view held exclusively by Ho Chi-minh. The Russians assume a similar position. Thus, writing in *Kommunist*, the Soviet Party journal in May, 1961, B. N. Ponomarev bunches together Cuba, Guinea, Ghana, Mali, and Indonesia as countries developing "the economic independence" necessary for transition to an "independent national democracy." Ponomarev has apparently been impressed by the emerging corporate structure of Sukarno's guided democracy, the sequestration of Dutch and Chinese properties, state controls over imports and exports, the development of the state sector of the economy, and the establishment by the state of food and clothing shops.

It should be noted that the developing conflict between Moscow and Peking over strategy and tactics, the question of how far Communists should travel in collaborating with "bourgeois nationalism," is not a new dilemma for the Marxist-Leninist world. At the second Comintern congress in 1920, the Communists faced a similar problem and straddled the fence—with disastrous consequences—as Moscow and Peking are doing at present. On that occasion, Lenin proposed a new term, "national revolutionaries," as distinct from the "bourgeois democratic revolutionaries." The term has since fallen into disuse. Lenin defined it as follows:

> We Communists should, and will, support bourgeois liberation movements in the colonial countries only when these movements are really revolutionary, when the representatives of these movements do not hinder us in training and organizing the peasants and the broad masses of the exploited in a revolutionary spirit. [7]

It is in this historic context that the power struggle between Moscow and Peking has developed; so has the conflict between the PKI's Right and Left wings. It is significant, perhaps, that in the developing dispute between Moscow and Peking, the Indonesian Communists would appear to fall between the two ideological positions. Indeed, Indonesia under Sukarno would become one of the few areas in the underdeveloped Afro-Asian world where Moscow and Peking would share the same policies—the endorsement of Sukarno's guided democracy and the encouragement of his plan to forcibly "liberate" West Irian. In a broad sense, with Moscow and Peking agreeing that Indonesia is on the path leading toward an "independent national democracy," Indonesia and the PKI may have become a testing ground for Sino-Soviet rivalry in Southeast Asia.

But of immediate practical concern to the PKI by mid-1959, however, was whether to characterize the armed forces as middle of the road or diehard. Between August 5 and 7, 1959, an eighth plenary meeting of the Central Committee, preparatory to a Sixth Party Congress scheduled for August 22, analyzed the question. Aidit hedged. He described burgeoning army influence under guided democracy as a "negative factor," but suggested that "antipopular and antidemocratic" factions within the army would be ultimately "purged" (Aidit's word). He observed that the army was young (barely fifteen years old), revolutionary in composition, and lacking in tradition—somewhat misleading since its roots were in the Japanese occupation, not the August revolution. He proposed an infiltration, a modified Amir-PERBEPSI concept for a people's defense. He deemed it "imperative that more people should be mobilized to participate, under the leadership of government troops, in defending national security and in thoroughly eliminating remnant rebel cliques." Aidit recognized that the civil war had forced Nasution to expand the army, lower requirements, draft questionable elements, and rely increasingly on former ill-disciplined irregulars. The worst characteristics of the army had therefore been strengthened at the expense of organization, discipline, and authority. As a consequence, in some rural areas, local "war lords" abused their powers, the efforts of Nasution and his staff to correct the situation, notwithstanding. Aidit skillfully probed this weakness, intensifying the Party's campaign to "arouse, mobilize, and organize the peasantry." Indeed, in April, 1959, the PKI held its *first* National Peasant's Conference, rather belatedly for a party of "workers and peasants" then in its thirty-ninth year. The conference unfolded a "reform" land program reflecting the positions adopted at the Fifth Congress and, significantly, focused for the first time on the Party's line in "arousing, organizing, and leading the millions of fishermen in the struggle for better living conditions, democracy and full national independence," i.e., "national democracy." [8] Farmers and fishermen: This promises to be the Communist response to the challenge of the army, particularly after the passing of Sukarno. If this is a reasonable analysis of

Communist strategy in the 1960's, the implications are enormous. Developing the PKI position in rural peasant areas requires little elaboration. In the case of the fishermen, however, ít appears that the Party is determined to secure a hospitable coastline, an indispensable escape hatch in an insular nation, a reliable line of communications and supplies; in a broad sense, an "active sanctuary," particularly in the event of a voluntary or involuntary showdown with the army with Sukarno's passing or if the Party should be dissolved and/or absorbed by a Sukarno National Front during his rule.

In this light, therefore, Moscow's growing interest in Indonesian maritime affairs is noteworthy: the provision of Russian and East European freighters in 1958 after the expulsion of the KPM; the first good-will visit by Soviet warships to Java in 1959; Soviet rocket tests in the central Pacific and credits for the construction of an Oceanographic Institute at Ambon in 1960; the visit of the Supreme Commander of the Soviet Navy, and the transfer of ten gunboats to the Indonesian Navy (ALRI) in 1961; the stepped-up delivery of naval weapons, including W-class submarines, 1962. In some measure, coupled with the gradual evolution of Cuba as a first major island outpost of the Communist world, Soviet-bloc naval activity in the Indonesian archipelago may be designed to impress on insular Indonesia that the Soviet Union is emerging from the confinement of the Eurasian heartland as a maritime power.[9]

In any event, PKI infiltration of the system of guided democracy apparently encouraged Aidit to believe that the relative strength of the PKI had risen compared to that of the army. Nasution, however, was anxious to disabuse Aidit of this interpretation. On August 13, the army ordered the PKI's Sixth Congress canceled. Two days later Aidit publicly challenged Nasution: "We are going ahead." In this test of wills, Sukarno performed the role of mediator, restoring the balance of power. He promoted a compromise. The Congress was postponed, not canceled. When the Congress convened (September 7–14), army controls were so stringent that Reuters described the convocation as "a private meeting"; over Radio Moscow, Afrin termed it a "brilliant event." The Congress' main theme was: "Strengthen, Expand, and Renew the Party." With army stenographers present, the congress deliberated on ideological shortcomings and adopted a revised constitution that stressed discipline and organization. A fifty-point minimum program was adopted whose first point stated: "Further intensify the struggle for the liberation of West Irian by means of organizing our forces at home, building up all national potentials, modernizing the equipment of the Army, the Navy and the Air Force and by obtaining international solidarity, to face all possibilities." [10]

Aidit probably reasoned that a Soviet-armed adventure against the Dutch in Irian constituted the PKI's trump against the "antipopular and antidemocratic" elements in the army. But there was always that lingering uncertainty in dealing with the flexible, elusive Sukarno. The President addressed the Congress—perhaps the only chief of state in the non-Communist world to attend a Communist Party congress—and delivered what could be interpreted as a polite warning: "As the Javanese saying goes, you are all relatives of the same family, and if you die, it is I, as a member of the family, who will mourn the loss."

Every stage of the deteriorating political situation had been accompanied by the deepening economic crisis: ruinous inflation, dwindling estate production, declining imports, widespread shortages in consumers' and industrial goods, and mounting expenditures for military operations.[11] The scope of economic disaster was dramatized by the fact that in 1959, Indonesia imported 35,000 tons of fish(!) and purchased 604,200 tons of rice abroad to become the world's largest rice importer. (In 1960, Indonesia imported 961,990 tons.) In desperation, the government in August froze bank deposits of over 25,000 rupiahs and devalued bills of over 100 rupiahs to one-tenth of their value. Overnight, the drastic measures reduced the 32.3 billion rupiahs in circulation by 1 billion. But the central bank was obliged to grant credits to companies left without working capital, and by December the amount of money in circulation had spurted to 39.4 billion rupiahs.* Loss of confidence in the rupiah spread; inflation accelerated. Perhaps the clearest picture of the inflationary impact of strident nationalism on the economy since the advent of the first Ali cabinet is mirrored in these statistics:[12]

$$(1953 = 100)$$

	Rice	Sugar	Meat, fish, eggs	Coconut oil	Textiles	Cigarettes
1953	102	99	107	90	99	103
1954	104	103	115	94	163	100
1955	152	104	151	112	127	117
1956	161	108	148	94	117	123
1957	342	142	179	225	184	161
1958	348	164	237	356	379	208
1959	292	184	345	496	1001	278

* On August 27, 1959, Radio Moscow applauded the fiscal "reform" as barring Western control of the economy.

In this depressing situation, Sukarno resorted increasingly to the fabrication of slogans as palliatives. On August 17, 1959, he introduced a Political Manifesto (MANIPOL), a turgid potpourri of undefined "nationalist" and "socialist" terms, whose five pillars were USDEK (the initial letters of the Indonesian words for the 1945 constitution, Indonesian socialism, guided democracy, guided economy, and the Indonesian identity). MANIPOL's objective was "Socialism à la Indonesia." On November 10, Hero's Day, the Supreme Advisory Council adopted MANIPOL as the main line of the state's policy "in the struggle of the Indonesian people to consummate their revolution which bears a *national* and *democratic* character." (Italics added.) Sukarno invented other words, i.e., RESOPIM, formed from the Indonesian words for revolution, socialism, and leadership, and NASAKOM, a combination of the words nationalism, religion, and communism. Under RESOPIM, NASAKOM would implement MANIPOL and bring USDEK to fruition. Indonesia had developed a new political language. Sukarno also sought to revive a New Life Movement, which he had inaugurated in 1957 and which had failed to arouse the people.* The parallels between postwar Indonesia and prewar China were striking.

In Indonesia, slogans were not enough. The failure of the monetary reforms and the ensuing economic dislocation begged for popular diversion. The expulsion of the Dutch had removed the most likely candidate; next best were the Chinese. Since the Chinese provided the PKI with a primary source of revenue and the Chinese mainland was Communist, an anti-Chinese campaign could also be construed as anti-Communist. It is not unlikely that the government's decision to launch an anti-Chinese movement was also influenced by external developments. The Indonesian campaign coincided with rising tension between Peking and her neighbors and restiveness within China itself: the smothering of Tibet (Mao's Hungary); Chinese incursions along the Indian border; exigent demands on the Himalayan states; ideological discord with Russia; Mao's weeding of his garden where only the year before a hundred flowers had bloomed and a hundred thoughts contended; a great leap forward transformed into a great leap backward.

In November, the "inner cabinet," from which the PKI had been excluded, approved Presidential Regulation No. 10, prohibit-

---

* In February, 1945, the Japanese had undertaken a similar program. So had Chiang Kai-shek in China in February, 1934, and lately the Ngo Dinh Diem government in South Vietnam. Such movements inevitably betray a regime's insecurity.

ing aliens in rural areas from operating retail trade effective January 1, 1960. Local war administrators were empowered to "liquidate" alien enterprises and order them from the area in the interests of "security," if warranted—as it apparently was, particularly in West Java and the Riau archipelago, the Java-Singapore-Sumatra triangle. To avoid misunderstanding, Djuanda explained that the prohibition on aliens—who were almost exclusively Chinese—involved basic economic policy within the framework of the guided economy. Clearly, Sukarno endorsed the campaign.

As China and Indonesia engaged in a vitriolic propaganda war, it became plain that for a regime founded on universalist Marxist dogma, Peking's reaction to the Indonesian program betrayed Chinese nationalist rather than supranationalist class interests. China accused Indonesia of "colonialism," "imperialist racism," etc. Indonesia retorted by turning the Chinese argument on the Indian frontier dispute against the Chinese and in the process succeeded in beating the Western dog: There are no issues between China and Indonesia except those inherited from a colonial past.[13] During the acrimonious exchange, Moscow remained outwardly uncommitted. Indonesian intellectuals, including those in the PRRI leadership, endorsed the anti-Chinese measures but condemned the methods employed—intimidation, insufficient notice to the Chinese, and the lack of preparation for filling the ensuing void in the rural economy. In some areas, Chinese were forcibly evacuated, and instances of police and army brutality are known to have occurred. In West Kalimantan, Chinese Communist and Nationalist organizations joined forces to oppose the regulation. By mid-1960, 40,000 Chinese had been repatriated and tens of thousands more put on waiting lists.

The Communists were apparently caught unawares, although—in tacit recognition that it inevitably would become embroiled in the Chinese question—the PKI, particularly since the 1953–54 "purge," had pressed the line that Indonesian citizens of Chinese racial origin play an important role in the national struggle against imperialism and that Indonesians of Chinese ancestry must therefore be protected by the government in the competition against foreign capital. The PKI's first reaction to the anti-Chinese drive was that Sukarno's order was not being implemented "in the spirit of MANIPOL."[14] The PKI, however, demonstrated solidarity with China and in the process collided with nationalist sentiment at every level of Indonesian society. Aidit attempted to divert the campaign by charging that the principal sources of economic difficulty were "the big foreign enterprises of the imperialists that monopolized Indonesia's economy, such as Stanvac,

Caltex, BPM"—that is, the oil companies that in fact constituted Sukarno's primary source of foreign exchange. "Do not fight a cat just because you are afraid to fight a tiger," Aidit chided.[15]

Other than authorizing the creation of cooperatives to fill the vacuum left by the displaced Chinese retailers, who also served as rural bankers, pawnbrokers, distributors, and wholesalers, the government lacked a plan of action. The expulsion of Chinese was as impetuous as the expulsion of the Dutch and, initially at least, as harmful to the Indonesian people. The popular political interpretation was that the PKI's defense of the Chinese had seriously impaired Communist popularity in the villages. Aidit, however, felt otherwise:

> The PKI has consistently preached that the economy must be in Indonesian hands. The peasants know this. But we must prepare for the day. The removal of Chinese from the villages served only to dislocate the village economy. I am a villager. I have two eggs. To whom do I sell? The Chinese. And if there are no Chinese? I sell to nobody. Many villagers realize this now. The Chinese question helps us.[16]

Nor was this only a Communist viewpoint. A PRRI analysis of the situation observed that power groups would move for advantage in filling the vacuum and that "the danger comes specifically from powerful rural organizations under the political direction of the Communists," such as the BTI.[17]

A by-product of the economic drive, however, was a new initiative at resolving "double nationality": the principle that "once a Chinese always a Chinese"—*jus sanguinis,* an unwritten law in China since antiquity and a written law since 1909. In revolutionary postwar Indonesia there was a disposition to be done with the archaic concept. Thus on April 10, 1946, the Sjahrir cabinet adopted a "passive" citizenship act bestowing Indonesian citizenship on all Chinese who had resided in Indonesia for five years and had not renounced Indonesian citizenship. Sjahrir favored the assimilation of the Chinese with a view to removing a source of social and political tension at home and abroad. In 1949, under The Hague accord, a similar "passive" system was applied to the Chinese. Under the passive system between 1949 and 1951, about 400,000 Chinese opted for Chinese citizenship and twice that number for Indonesian citizenship (the remaining 1.5 million were Chinese-born and therefore automatically regarded as aliens). But the "passive" systems of the Sjahrir and Hatta eras were opposed by the ultranationalists who preferred an "active" system under which the Chinese would be compelled publicly to renounce Chinese citizenship before acquiring Indonesian citizenship. Few Chinese, it was surmised, would renounce their ancestral homeland. Thus future economic measures against the Chinese could be directed at "foreigners" and not "second-class" Indonesian citizens and could therefore be technically defended before the bar of world opinion as not racially discriminatory.

On April 22, 1955, in the glow of "the spirit of Bandung," Indonesia and China concluded a dual-citizenship agreement based on the "active" system, discussed earlier. The Chinese apparently also favored retaining a large body of Chinese citizens in Indonesia and, in the process, an established political position in the largely underpopulated archipelago. Nonetheless, the Sunario-Chou pact was inconclusive; Article 14 permitted either party to annul the treaty after twenty years and presumably reopen the potentially explosive question. In Indonesia, particularly among the Chinese who felt that under the "passive" system they could retain the illusion. of "double citizenship" at least among themselves, there was a strong reaction against the treaty, and ratification was delayed. But in the climate of 1959, Indonesia insisted on ratification. China complied on January 20, 1960, apparently in the hope of mitigating the harshness of the anti-Chinese campaign. Tension subsided. China appeared anxious to end the quarrel, motivated by need for PKI support in its rift with Moscow and for Indonesian good-will in the drive to isolate India. On January 10, 1961, in Tokyo's *Economist*, Deputy Premier Ch'en Yi expressed regret that "normal relations with Indonesia were marred" and explained that "we are only anxious to protect the lawful rights of Chinese merchants." He added: "We tell them to disband any Communist Party among them. If they want to hold membership in a Communist Party, they should do so by going home. . . . We are encouraging them to become citizens of their residence countries." Thereafter he visited Djakarta; the two nations signed a friendship treaty in April; Sukarno visited Peking in June; and China extended Indonesia a $30 million credit in September. In 1980, of course, relations may be "marred" anew.

The immobilization of the Communist mass organizations as demonstrated by a failure to employ the strike weapon as the economic crisis worsened, coupled with the anti-Chinese campaign, the growth of army influence, and the rising prominence of Tan Malaka's former aides in the development of guided democracy, imperiled the PKI's erstwhile position of strength.

Aidit departed for Hungary and an unpublicized meeting in December, 1959, with Khrushchev.[18] In Budapest, Aidit apparently persuaded Khrushchev to move up his announced visit to Southeast Asia in 1960. Aidit may have reasoned that a Khrushchev visit would ease the pressure on both China and the PKI and demonstrate "international proletarian solidarity." On January 5, Indonesia officially disclosed that Khrushchev would arrive within six weeks. Four days earlier, the PKI had opened an offensive against the government. A New Year's message criticized the anti-Chinese campaign, the extension of martial (i.e., army) law and the inner cabinet's monetary policies. In Aidit's absence, Lukman directed the Party. In rapid succession, GERWANI, SOBSI, Pemuda Rakjat, and other Communist fronts demonstrated in January at Djakarta, Cheribon, Bandung, and Semarang to protest against the spiraling cost of living. At Surabaya, rumors of another devaluation generated panic. In central Java, leaflets were distributed calling for a 50-per-cent reduction in prices. Significantly, the PKI campaign was confined to Java.

Nasution sensed the nature of the campaign, and on January 23 accused "subversive elements" of generating a panic psychology. Four days later, Sukarno urged severe punishment, including the death penalty, for economic saboteurs. On February 10, the day Aidit returned from behind the Iron Curtain, the Central Committee renewed the attack. Whether Lukman's campaign was designed to demonstrate the Party's revolutionary mood and capabilities for the benefit of Khrushchev (and Aidit), or whether the Communists simply sought to exploit the good will radiated by the impending Khrushchev visit to criticize the government and thereby ease tension within the Party, is conjectural. Whatever the case, on February 16, two days before Khrushchev's arrival, the PKI treated the Soviet leader's impending arrival as rescue. The Politburo described the visit as signifying "the thawing of the Cold War imported by the imperialists into our country to hinder the struggle of the people of Indonesia to forge national unity and to strengthen the anticolonialist and peace-loving international front." The reference to the Cold War should be read in the army-PKI context, not in terms of the East-West conflict.

Khrushchev's arrival had been preceded by a massive propaganda effort—the tour of a Soviet soccer team, a Soviet circus, and, interestingly, the release of a film depicting Khrushchev's "triumphant" tour of the United States. His eleven-day sojourn in Indonesia was a blend of successes and failures. He shunned references to the Chinese question and, to Sukarno's growing consternation, avoided endorsing Indonesia's Irian claim until February 25. In effect, Khrushchev tacitly warned Sukarno that Soviet support on Irian was under constant review and should not be taken for granted. Without Soviet-bloc diplomatic, propaganda, and military assistance—even merely the threat it posed to Holland's allies—Sukarno must have realized that the acquisition of Irian would be immeasurably more formidable a task.

In a speech on February 22 before the student body of Gadja Mada University at Jogjakarta, where Khrushchev scored impressively with a "wave-of-the-future" speech, the Soviet leader had words—or so one could fairly interpret—for both the Right and Left within the PKI. Khrushchev endorsed Aidit's Rightist strategy by citing the Indonesian maxim, "A peaceful buffalo is much stronger than a predatory tiger." But he also reminded Aidit of Lenin's admonition that the strength of a Communist movement is not judged by numbers but by militancy. "The Communist Party is not a grocery store where the more customers you attract, the more soap, rotten herring, or other spoiled goods you sell, the more you gain," he said.

Khrushchev's most difficult moment came before parliament on February 26. The deputies had been in rebellious mood since the dissolution of the constituent assembly and had objected to Sukarno's rule by fiat. In particular, they opposed a decree that prohibited government officials of the six highest ranks from holding membership in a political party and that empowered Sukarno to appoint provincial and regency heads without regard to elections. The former seriously impaired the PNI, the latter both the PKI and the non-Javanese areas. Distressed by Sukarno's growing dictatorial powers, the big four parties had called on the President in November to submit his decrees to parliament as proposed legislation. Sukarno refused. In a letter to the house on December 1, he said that if the President was empowered to reinstate the 1945 constitution by decree, he was empowered to issue decrees related to its implementation. It was against this background that parliament seized on the Khrushchev visit to stage a silent demonstration against Sukarno's authoritarian drift. The deputies sat motionless during Khrushchev's speech; when he referred to Irian, only the PKI, to its embarrassment, broke into applause. Indonesia was serving notice on Khrushchev—and the PKI—that Sukarno's obsession with Irian also had political limitations. Sukarno was infuriated by this act of defiance by the last vestige of the democratic system under which the revolution against the Dutch had been fought and won.

Parliament's behavior notwithstanding, the Khrushchev visit concluded on a satisfactory note. In a joint communiqué, Sukarno subscribed largely to Khrushchev's positions on international issues while Khrushchev endorsed Indonesia's "right and claim" to Irian, and extended Indonesia a $250-million credit at 2.5 per cent interest to be repaid over a twelve-year period at the completion of individual projects. The credit raised Sino-Soviet-bloc assistance to Indonesia since 1955 to $509 million, including credit for such nonproductive, inflationary, but visible ventures as the construction of a 100,000-seat sports stadium for the 1962 Asian games, complete with public tennis courts, swimming pools, and athletic fields. By comparison, since 1950, the first year of Indonesian sovereignty, the United States had given the islands $428.6 million in grants and loans, largely dispersed on intangibles designed to bolster the failing economy, including loans totaling $47.5 million on January 28, the eve of Khrushchev's arrival, which Sukarno cited as evidence of Indonesian "solvency."

Khrushchev's visit, however, failed to thaw the "imported Cold War." On February 28, the day before his departure, SOBSI's Njono handed Khrushchev's interpreter a sealed envelope and was promptly arrested and detained for two days on the ground that his action was unauthorized. The letter's contents have never been divulged. Moreover, Khrushchev no sooner departed than Sukarno moved against the parliament. The big four, including the PKI, were now united in opposition to the government's draft budget. It was a performance in the highest tradition of *gotong royong, musjawarah,* and *mufakat,* but Sukarno was unimpressed. On March 5, he dissolved parliament for failing to live up to "the spirit of . . . guided democracy and the Political Manifesto." Two days later, parliament adjourned to the singing of the national anthem and shouts of "Long live democracy!" "Long live the Republic of Indonesia!" The democratic eclipse in Indonesia had entered the umbra phase.

Two days later there was a new attempt on Sukarno's life. A pilot trained in the U.A.R., Lt. Daniel Maukar, one of six selected to provide Khrushchev with an air escort during his tour, attacked the palace in a MIG-17, wounding eighteen persons, including four in the palace compound. Sukarno escaped unscathed. Maukar crashed, was captured, linked to the PRRI, and sentenced to death. The incident appeared to act as a catalytic agent on Sukarno. He hastened with even greater determination to complete the scaffolding for his guided democracy. By the end of March he implemented a series of decrees promulgated on December 30–31 and announced on January 12–13. One provided for the appointment of a people's congress. Another repealed the 1945 Sjahrir-Hatta ordinance legalizing political parties and empowered the President to "ban or dissolve political parties," inspect the parties' administration, finances, and properties, and barred a party from receiving "aid from or to give aid to any foreign quarter, in any form or manner." A third edict authorized the President to establish a National Front (Front Nasional) "to mobilize and unite the revolutionary forces in society" and to finance the Front partially "from government subsidies." The decrees gave the PKI pause for serious concern, but the Communists were powerless to reverse the process without challenging Sukarno. Moreover, there was always the prospect that the disciplined PKI would eventually acquire control over Sukarno's political machine.

Thus, on March 27, Sukarno established a 261-member *gotong royong* parliament under the 1945 constitution, consisting of 130 representatives from 9 political parties and 131 representatives from 21 functional groups. The PNI was awarded 44 seats (compared to 57 in the former parliament); NU, 36 (45); PKI, 30 (39); Protestants, 6 (8); Catholics, 4 (6); PSII 5, (8); Perti, 2 (4); Murba, 2 (2), and Partindo, 1. Partindo was a crypto-Communist splinter that advocated maintaining the PNI-PKI alliance, had broken from the PNI on August 5, 1958, and adopted the name of the radical wing of the prewar PNI, naming K. Werdojo and Asmara Hardi as its leaders. Among the functional groups were representatives of the armed forces, police and village guards, SOBSI, SARBUPRI, GERWANI, ex-PERBEPSI, BTI, Permuda Rakjat—and the Generation of '45. The Communists emerged with 65 members in parliament. The next day Sukarno installed a National Front preparatory committee, composed of the chairman of the major parties, including Aidit, and such figures as Saleh, Yamin, Erningpradja, Hanafi, and Pandu Wiguna. The week before, Sukarno bestowed on the Generation of '45 the task of "completing the revolution" and attaining "Indonesian socialism." Between March 16 and 19, 1,500 representatives of the burgeoning movement attended a Greater All-Indonesia Conference at which they claimed to be the only political grouping "true" to the 1945 proclamation since its promulgation—i.e., free from the taint of Linggadjati, Renville, The Hague agreement, Madiun, the Darul Islam, PRRI, etc.—and rededicated themselves to that undefined and unending "struggle against imperialism, colonialism, fascism, and feudalism." In 1961, the National Front grew. It was installed on January 20; absorbed the West Irian Liberation Front three days later; was relieved from participation in future elections on March 11; and established regional branches on March 23. Clearly, as guided democracy developed, Sukarno was increasingly relying on four powerful and antagonistic blocs: the army, NU, the PKI, and that curious collection of irrational ultranationalists, the "national Communists." Sukarno was constructing an intricate system of checks and balances whose combination he alone possessed.

In the competition against the army and the Generation of '45, the PKI—at least for the record—welcomed the new parliament as "a major victory for the democratic forces over the forces of reaction who had waged a ferocious campaign against parliament." [19]

Indeed, the "forces of reaction" had offered resistance to Sukarno but hardly of "ferocious" nature. On March 24, fifteen members of the inactivated parliament representing the Masjumi, Sjahrir Socialists, Protestants, Catholics, IPKI, the PSII, Perti, and NU (the latter three indirectly through the chairman of the Moslem League) formed the Democratic League. The League opened a campaign against Sukarno's violation of "democratic principles" and during April and May, with Sukarno abroad on another world tour, established branches on Java and the outer islands. The army looked the other way. Nasution was displeased by Sukarno's exclusion of IPKI from the parliament (Sukarno later corrected the oversight) and by Sukarno's inclusion of the PKI in the trappings of guided democracy. On May 23, the fifty-second anniversary of the founding of Budi Utomo, a League manifesto declared that the occasion marked not only "national reawakening" but the "struggle for democracy." The League was short-lived. The sharks swam after the little fishes. The Generation of '45 criticized the League for "sowing confusion [while] we are confronted with an armed challenge by the Dutch in West Irian," * and the PKI assailed the League as "reactionary, desperate, and brazen . . . the black forces of reaction."

On June 24, Sukarno returned from abroad, ignored the League, and installed his new parliament. Sukarno, however, succumbed to the restiveness of the Islamic factions and named twenty-two additional members of parliament, largely orthodox religious leaders. It was a hollow performance. Then, on August 15, Sukarno installed a People's Congress composed of 94 regional representatives, 232 functional representatives, and the 283 members of parliament. Since the Congress was a repository of the people's sovereignty and—democracy by consultation notwithstanding—elects the President by "majority vote," [20] the Congress could theoretically elect Sukarno's successor. Sukarno named Saleh Acting Chairman and Ali Sastroamidjojo (PNI), K. H. Idham Chalid (NU), Aidit (PKI), and Colonel Wiljuo (army)

---

* This was a reference to the "Karel Doorman," a Dutch aircraft carrier dispatched to Netherlands New Guinea on May 16, 1960.

as Deputy Chairmen, in that order. Their appointment recalled Sukarno's 1945 testament, i.e., NASAKOM plus Tan Malaka. Saleh (who might be considered Tan Malaka); Ali (Wongsonegoro—nationalism); Chalid (Iwa—ostensibly Islam); and Aidit (Sjahrir—Marxism). The only new element was the army. The comparisons have obvious defects, but in Indonesia the spirit and not the letter is paramount.

Rule by decree came easy to Sukarno. In the development of his system, he conspicuously ignored the Masjumi and Sjahrir Socialists and it therefore is not surprising that, on August 17, 1960, he dissolved both parties. In the months that followed, Sukarno banned the Democratic League and "imported" organizations ranging from the Rotary to Rosicrucians. He also dissolved the Boy Scout movement, headed by the Sultan of Jogjakarta and re-formed it as the Pioneers (Pramuka) with himself as "chief pioneer." On the sixteenth anniversary of Indonesian independence; surveying his structure, Sukarno concluded that "the conditions for the journey are complete." He described his system as the "New Ordering," affixing the suffix to avoid an apparent comparison with Japan's "New Order." Yet, he confided, the New Ordering was only a "stepping stone" in a two-stage transition toward his vague "socialism à la Indonesia." Irresistibly, in 1961–62 Sukarno advanced toward the creation of labor, youth, peasant, and women "corporations" ostensibly under the guidance of the consolidating National Front. In each instance, the PKI contributed a well-knit organization. The crucial question in Indonesia was whether the Communists would devour the corporations or whether the corporations would swallow the Communists and demonstrate the validity of a basic Sukarno thesis, shared by a majority of Indonesian intellectuals, namely, that the PKI rank and file is composed predominantly of radical nationalists and not genuine Communists—a thesis, incidentally, shared by many intellectuals and observers in assessing the development of the Communist Party of China before it came to power.

24

A Double Game

Barely two months after Khrushchev's departure, the Communists resumed their political offensive with great intensity. Whether the vigor of the Communist action originated with Khrushchev or merely had his approval, or whether perhaps it was undertaken without either his knowledge or endorsement—hardly likely given the character of the Indonesian Communist Party—is conjectural. Whatever the case, Aidit apparently concluded that the moment was appropriate for a reshuffle of the government and the broadening of the PKI's role in the shaping of policy by its inclusion in the "inner cabinet."

Aidit may have been motivated by restiveness within the Party or by the specter of the emerging National Front. Khrushchev's visit had provided the Party with a psychological lift, imparted a new spirit of power, purpose, and "international proletarian solidarity." Aidit's failure to keep pace with the mood slowed the movement's centripetal motion, a dangerous development for an authoritarian organization whether of the Right or Left. A renewal of the political offensive would also serve to demonstrate the Party's vitality and put Sukarno on notice that the PKI was not a scout movement that could be dissolved by pen stroke. Moreover, there was always a possibility that a militant action would excite Sukarno's revolutionary emotionalism and push him further Left, thereby lessening the influence of the moderate army leadership under Nasution.

Appropriately, the PKI opened its offensive on May Day, focusing attention on the unchecked rise in the cost of living, the growth of "fascist" army influence, and the curtailment of the civil liberties exercised under the old bourgeois democracy. A SOBSI manifesto proposed "mass actions" to alleviate the economic situation and, stirring ultranationalist embers, called for the "liquidation" of the "economic interests of big foreign imperialists." From behind this screen, the labor federation assailed the army's "harmful" policies, citing as an example Nasution's order canceling Lebaran (Islamic New Year) bonuses, and charged that in practice army-operated state enterprises "still resemble ordinary private commercial businesses." SOBSI's manifesto also accused the government of suppressing "democratic liberties in general and the freedom of the press in particular," the latter a reference to increasing military harassment of the Communist press. SOBSI held that without civil liberties, "the masses cannot be mobilized to assist the realization of the Government programs." [1] Lifting a leaf from Deuteronomy, SOBSI solemnly declared: "Workers do not live by rice alone; they also need democracy."

The tempo of the Communist campaign accelerated in June. Njono and other PKI-SOBSI officials embarked on a tour of Java, instructing local branches to line up the countryside behind the May Day slogan: "Under the Banner of Unity Continue the Mass Actions for Food and Clothing for Democracy." The Communists called for a 25-per-cent increase in wages and a 50-per-cent reduction in prices. In July, the campaign attained climactic proportions. On July 8, on the eve of the first anniversary of the Sukarno-Djuanda cabinet, the Politburo struck a hard blow—its most stern criticism of an administration since the Sukiman era. In a lengthy evaluation of the cabinet's performance, the Communists concluded that the government had dismally failed to carry out its three-point program and that a cabinet reshuffle was imperative. The Politburo developed the theme that Sukarno was not at fault but had been misguided, misused, and misled by "certain" ministers. The Communists also appealed to Sukarno to terminate the state of martial law under which "compradore elements" and "bureaucratic capitalists" had suppressed civil liberties. The latter term, novel to the Marxist-Leninist lexicon, specifically referred to the army officers and government officials operating the former Dutch properties that had been nationalized in gradual stages since July, 1959. The Politburo charged that working conditions in the former Dutch enterprises were worse under Indonesian supervision than under "imperialist" management.

Now the Politburo openly said what had been persistently whispered in Djakarta for months: Nasution was seeking an accommodation with the rebels. According to rumor, Nasution had secretly appealed to the PRRI commanders to return to the fold to fight the common foe: the Communists. It was said that Nasution had couched his appeal in a call for unity as a prerequisite for the recovery of Irian. Against this background, the Politburo cited "stagnation in the field of security" and said: "The basic errors that brought about the stagnation in security were that officials responsible for security did not spend the greater part of their energy and thought on liquidating counterrevolutionary rebel cliques, but on preventing the development of revolutionary and democratic movements led by the PKI."

This was at the core of Aidit's offensive, reflecting deepening anxieties in the Communist camp. No effort was made to soften the charge other than to observe that Leftist criticism is constructive and Rightist criticism destructive, albeit as seen through the distortion of the Marxist-Leninist looking glass.

At this stage there is overlapping between the forward momentum of the Communist drive and the reaction of the army. But to appreciate the real nature of Aidit's objectives it is necessary to trace the PKI's developing line one stage further.

In an article that may have been prepared in July and that appeared in the August issue of the Central Committee's *Review of Indonesia*, Aidit delivered a crude assault against "agents" of the Masjumi and Sjahrir Socialists "who poisoned the Indonesian political atmosphere." He wrote that the creative energies released by guided democracy, which the Communists wholeheartedly and enthusiastically endorsed, could only encompass the people "if all this filth is removed and cast away, both by bold action from above [Sukarno] as well as under pressure from below [PKI]." In effect, Aidit proposed an alliance between Sukarno and the Communist mass organizations. Aidit backed his proposal with the observation that the previous August Sukarno had accepted the thesis that a revolution from above was not a revolution because the people did not participate (Madiun? PRRI?), whereas a revolution from below was rebellion. Aidit said:

> We know that President Sukarno does not want a rebellion, even a revolutionary rebellion, and that he draws the revolutionary consequences from this attitude, namely *that revolution must also proceed from above.* [Aidit's emphasis] If this is not the case, revolutionary rebellion becomes a necessity, in the same way as our armed rebellion in connection with the Proclamation of Independence on August 17, 1945, was [a necessity]. This is the opinion of every revolutionary.

Aidit obviously was telling Sukarno that the PKI could not restrain its followers unless Sukarno assumed a more revolutionary posture, purged "antipopular and antidemocratic" elements from the army and government, and gave the Communists license for development as in the 1945–48 and 1952–57 periods. For Sukarno's benefit, Aidit analyzed what he purported to be the position of five groups toward MANIPOL (Sukarno): (1) The Communists and progressives who conscientiously and consistently try to put the Manifesto into practice; (2) the masses, who have no proper understanding of ideology but follow others in approving the Manifesto; (3) those (presumably the PNI) who waver because they fear state control over the economy will whittle the private sector; (4) those (presumably Nasution) who profess to agree but sabotage the Manifesto; and (5) the Masjumi, PSI, PRRI, Darul Islam, and their ilk who reject the Manifesto.

The post-May Communist offensive was accompanied on Java by what one correspondent described as a "cold war." [2] There were reports of minor armed incidents between Communists and non-Communists in Central-East Java, the PKI stronghold; reports that the Communists had transformed the Jogjakarta-Soerakarta-Semarang triangle into a retreat in the event of a showdown with the army; that Sudisman had been authorized to form a clandestine organization. These measures were presumably provided for under Article 70 of the Party's constitution, which stated: "If the Party is unable because of circumstances to function in the normal way, the forms of organization and the methods of work shall be determined by the Central Committee." The unanswered question, however, was whether the Central Committee judged the situation on Java in 1960 as "normal" or "abnormal."

Whatever the case, with Communist strategy and tactics undergoing a revision, the army appeared anxious to provoke a showdown. Eight days after the July 8 evaluation appeared, *Harian Rakjat* was temporarily banned, the Politburo statement suppressed on pain of fine or imprisonment, and Aidit, Lukman, Njoto, Sudisman, and Sakirman detained and/or interrogated between July 16 and 30. The Party leadership was asked 679 questions; their replies covered 190 typed pages. The crackdown on the Party press and leadership in the capital served as a springboard for demonstrations sponsored by the army between July 28 and August 6 at Palembang, South Sumatra, and Bandjermasin, South Kalimantan. The demonstrators demanded a ban on the PKI. On August 2, Aidit emerged from eight consecutive days of interrogation ("Very fatiguing," he said.) and summoned the Party to "close ranks" and remain "vigilant." The situation was rapidly disintegrating. As in the previous August, Sukarno restored a balance of power by rallying to the defense of the Communists, and he chose to do so at the Ninth PNI Congress, on July 25. The PNI had been in decline since the end of the second Ali cabinet. The Nationalists had lost a considerable following to the PKI during the 1958 provincial elections, been weakened by the withdrawal of the Partindo faction, and shaken by Sukarno's nonparty decree. Alluding to the waning influence of the PNI, Sukarno criticized its leadership for their "Communist phobia" and lectured: "I do not fear the Communists. I have no Leftist phobia. . . . I and the PKI have many differences, but we also share similar views with regard to anticolonialism, anti-imperialism, the fate of the workers and peasants, the West Irian struggle." *

Three days later, at the formal presentation of a Lenin Peace Prize, Sukarno resumed the attack with a blanket denunciation of "Leftist phobia." The Prize had been awarded to Sukarno as "one of the most outstanding leaders of independent Asia who actually pursues an independent foreign policy aimed at strengthening universal world peace." The announcement of the award had been made on May 4, three days after the SOBSI manifesto signaled the Communist offensive.

Sukarno's defense of the PKI had restored the uneasy balance of power between the army and the PKI. But his dissolution of the Masjumi and PSI three weeks later upset the balance again, or at least so the army interpreted it. Nasution reacted more sharply than ever. On August 26, the army countered by imposing a ban on the activities of the PKI and its fronts, including SOBSI, BTI, GERWANI, LEKRA, and Pemuda Rakjat in South Kalimantan; in South Sumatra on August 29; and in South Sulawesi on August 30. In West Java, on August 27, the army uncovered a Communist "double organization" in the Tasikmalaja area and began arresting PKI and BTI leaders. The Communists had apparently established a parallel administration at the village level installing "village councils" with tax powers, somewhat on the style of Kartosuwirjo's Darul Islam. Significantly, the army had acted in non-Javanese areas, largely in the outer islands, although the main Communist thrust had centered on Djakarta and Central-East Java. On September 4, the Politburo replied with an appeal to "all members and sympathizers of the PKI to redouble their vigilance [and] above all else . . . foil all provocations."

Relations between the army and the PKI, simmering since 1958, appeared to be bubbling over. But as long as Sukarno was uncommitted, neither camp could assume the initiative with confidence. Nasution's hesitancy on Java was a hint, perhaps, that

* He repeated this theme at a special PKI Congress in April, 1962, at which the Communists endorsed MANIPOL.

he did not exercise unlimited control over the army; it was said, for example, that Saleh, when he was Veterans' Minister, had developed a base in the army by the judicious use of patronage and that the army on Java was divided in its loyalty to Nasution. In any event, sometime between September 5 and 13, Aidit had a private confrontation with Sukarno. Aidit played his trumps. He impressed on Sukarno that the PKI was the largest, most efficient, best-disciplined and -organized, most popular and powerful political organization on Java, and that Sukarno could ill afford to lose such a source of strength. "What Indonesia requires is unity," Aidit later recounted.[3] "Sukarno needs the PKI to support national unity. I made this clear to him during our September talks." Aidit warned Sukarno that a conflict between the army and PKI on Java would serve only to benefit Sukarno's bitterest domestic foes, the PRRI leadership still at large in the outer islands. Aidit said:

There are twenty-one provinces in Indonesia and the army has temporarily suppressed our activities in three. Their policy is unrealistic. Indonesia is moving ever leftward. Look at the roll call. What happened to Sjahrir, Hatta, Natsir, Sjafruddin, etc.? There is much foolish talk about the character of our armed forces. But it should not be forgotten that our army is new; that it is not an Indian or U.A.R. army that was there before; that Sukarno exercises great influence on the ranks and has rejected military dictatorship. Remember we did not possess an army fifteen years ago.

And he emphasized:

The army cannot succeed in destroying either Sukarno or the PKI. If we are destroyed, what follows will be worse. The army knows this. So does Sukarno. We are loyal to the republic, loyal to the President, the Political Manifesto, and the Pantjasila. We are uncorrupted. During 1958, not one member of the PKI joined the anti-Sukarno rebellion. We remained steadfastly loyal to the President by deeds, not only words, and Sukarno knows it.[4]

Aidit also returned to a familiar theme: the main enemy of Indonesia were the Dutch, not the PKI. An army-PKI clash on Java would drain Indonesia's national vitality and enhance the Dutch position in Irian. Clearly, then, in a showdown between the army and the PKI, Sukarno's position would be impaired, national unity shattered, and Sukarno's archenemies at home and abroad strengthened. Aidit said later: "Following my talks with the President, after the Affair of the Three Souths, I think the army understands us and we understand the army." [5]

As evidence of Communist good faith, Aidit urged Sukarno to accelerate the campaign for the recovery of Irian and apparently promised unlimited Soviet assistance for the "liberation" of the Dutch colony. As a comparable act of good faith, Aidit argued, Nasution had no alternative but to accept this outstretched hand and turn eastward against Irian.

Aidit may have reasoned that an invasion of Irian would divert the army's attention from the Communists to the Dutch while a revolutionary situation was developing on Java. A war with the Dutch would serve as a pretext for the total mobilization of the country and thereby conceivably lead to the arming of the Pemuda Rakjat, whose membership now totaled 1 million and whose organization, significantly perhaps, was declared an official arm of the PKI and incorporated into the Party constitution at the Sixth Congress. A war would also generate a new wave of ultranationalist sentiment that would infect all layers of society, including the armed forces. Of course, if an armed invasion of Irian misfired, Nasution and his staff would suffer national disgrace and Sukarno would have no choice other than dismiss them, removing the PKI's most formidable adversaries at this stage of the Party's growth and development. A war would also inject the Cold War directly into Indonesia and deepen Sukarno's dependence on Soviet-bloc propaganda, diplomatic, economic, and military support. An Irian war would draw the United States from its neutralist posture, and, with or without Dutch and Australian pressure, compel Washington to oppose Indonesia's forcible seizure of Irian and thereby tacitly support a "colonial" position. Aidit may have also reasoned that the inflationary impact of a war would accelerate the deterioration of the economy and conceivably lead to Djakarta's economic collapse, a situation the PKI alone would be in a position to exploit.

If the Communists foresaw advantages in an Irian war, so did the army. An attack on Irian would redress a national grievance by force, a method in itself appealing to the military. A war in Irian would provide Nasution with the opportunity of removing disaffected units from Java. The liquidation of the Irian issue would dissolve the "natural link" between Aidit and Sukarno and make Sukarno increasingly dependent on the army for support. The armed forces, of course, would benefit from an arms-modernization program sponsored by the Soviet Union. And whether a conflict materialized or not, the preparations for war would also provide a pretext for the return of the PRRI forces to the lap of the republic. This, of course, was the obvious loophole in the

Communists' otherwise well-constructed plan to ease army pressure on the Party and create the conditions for an inevitable Communist bid for power.

Sukarno, of course, was obsessed with Irian and eager to avail himself of the opportunity of turning against the Dutch. An Irian war would dispel antagonisms between the army and the PKI—at least momentarily—and in any event would ensure Sukarno's continuing leadership. Moreover, as with the Communists, but for different considerations, Sukarno may have reasoned that rattling a Soviet saber would draw the United States into the dispute—a primary Sukarno objective for a decade—and induce Washington to put pressure on the Dutch to relinquish the territory. Once the United States became embroiled in the dispute, Washington would have to act in the Indonesian interest to prevent Moscow and the PKI from exploiting American support of the Dutch. Certainly the prospect of a war in the Southwest Pacific that could transform the area into an arena of East-West conflict would be unattractive to the United States, the leading Pacific power, and its Pacific allies, the Philippines, Australia, and New Zealand. Naturally, assuming Indonesia's acquisition of Irian, whether by peaceful or forcible means, Sukarno's prestige would soar. Whether, however, because of renewed army-PKI tension or because of a worsening economy, Sukarno would later seek another diversion to avoid realities—for example, a campaign against Portuguese Timor—was another matter.

Indonesia had been actively moving toward an armed struggle in Irian since 1954.[6] But it was not until July 21, 1960, at a session of the Supreme Advisory Council attended by Sukarno, Nasution, and Aidit, that the "principle of confrontation of all our national forces with Dutch imperialism-colonialism" was formally adopted as state policy. This was followed on August 17 by a break in diplomatic relations with the Netherlands and Sukarno's summons to the country to move forward "to the liberation of West Irian, to the eradication of imperialism from Indonesian soil, to full independence, to Indonesian socialism." Significantly, perhaps, these moves coincided with the precipitous rise in army-PKI tension.

In October, following the Sukarno-Aidit dialogue, Nasution and Aidit accompanied the President on his journey to the summit at the United Nations, where Sukarno renewed his friendship with Khrushchev and Khrushchev greeted Aidit as a comrade-in-arms. On a side visit to the Pentagon, Nasution revived an earlier request for heavy war material. The United States refused the request, but to retain Nasution's good will agreed to provide additional small arms for Indonesia's ground forces, which had grown to an estimated 400,000 men, the largest armed force in Southeast Asia. Nasution's conscience cleared, he turned to the Kremlin, and, on January 2, 1961, arrived in Moscow at the head of an arms mission. At the airport, Nasution was welcomed by Marshal Rodion Y. Malinovsky, the Soviet Defense Minister, who promptly affirmed Soviet determination to assist Indonesia in "repulsing any threat" arising from the Dutch, a fairly safe commitment since the Dutch garrison in Irian consisted of fewer than 5,000 effectives and a Dutch community of about 18,000 persons, largely Eurasian administrators who had left Java in 1949–50 and 1957–58. Malinovsky's statement, however, was prominently displayed in Djakarta's controlled press and was cited as further proof in ultranationalist circles, if any was needed, that the Dutch, in collusion with NATO and SEATO, plotted aggressive war against Indonesia.

Nasution's four-day mission to Moscow was singularly triumphant. Mikoyan described Sukarno as an "ardent fighter for peace" and termed the liquidation of colonialism "a sacred Lenin command." Khrushchev declared that "the time will come soon" to exclude Irian from the Dutch Kingdom. The terms of the arms pact were not made public, but considering the brevity of Nasution's trip it appears that the accord had already been negotiated and that Nasution had flown to Moscow for the pomp and circumstance. On January 6, an Indonesian diplomat at Bonn claimed that Moscow had provided Indonesia with an arms credit of $400 million. A more realistic but still substantial figure may have been about $250 million, raising the total Sino-Soviet military and economic investment in Indonesia's future to about $800 million, the largest Communist assistance program in non-Communist Asia. Interestingly, the Indonesian team at Moscow included such figures as Adam Malik, now the Ambassador to the Soviet Union, and Air Marshal Suriadarma, who had long harbored alternating Tan Malakist and PKI sympathies.* On his return to Djakarta, Nasution described the pact as evidence of Moscow's "unconditional support" of Indonesia "in the struggle against colonialism." As dramatic proof that Russia and Indonesia faced a common foe, Moscow dispatched a note to The Hague on January 7, the day after Nasution departed for Djakarta, and warned that with the arrival of American nuclear warheads in Holland on December 1, the Netherlands had become "the first

---

* Sukarno has pursued a policy of sending envoys to the Sino-Soviet bloc who have Tan Malaka links. Sukarni, the former Murba chairman, is now Ambassador to Peking.

government in Europe to agree to the actual turning of its country
into an American nuclear base" and that the Dutch should be
aware that they had assumed a "terrible risk."

In Indonesia, Sukarno turned up the thermostat. In March and
September, the Dutch announced the capture of armed Indonesian infiltrators along the marshy West Irian coastline. On
April 13, meeting at Bandung, the fourth session of the Afro-
Asian People's Solidarity Organization, a Communist-dominated,
nongovernmental front, accused NATO and SEATO of providing
the Dutch with military aid in the "preservation of their colonial
domination of West Irian." On the night of June 7, while President Kennedy reported to the American people on his "sober"
talks with Khrushchev at Vienna, Khrushchev and Sukarno, who
had returned to Moscow in the course of another world tour,
danced and sang to the strains of "Indonesia is free, cha, cha,
cha." Three days later, at a Soviet-Indonesian friendship rally,
Sukarno observed that Russia, unlike the West, welcomed "Indonesia's determination to fight for Irian." Khrushchev inter-
rupted: "We are not only happy about it but we are ready to
demonstrate it, too."

On July 3, the first shipment of heavy Soviet war material
emerged at the Indonesian end of the pipeline with the arrival
of TU-16 long-range jet bombers flown from Russia by Indonesian
crews. Five days later, the Indonesian navy announced plans to
establish a guided-missile school, and in the months that followed
the arrival of Soviet arms for Java—accompanied by Soviet technicians and military instructors—accelerated markedly as Indonesia assembled an impressive offensive striking force composed
of MIG-19's and MIG-21's. On August 17, 1961, Sukarno announced that the dispute had entered a "decisive stage."

In Holland there was a growing disposition to yield Irian—but
not to Djakarta. On October 9, declaring itself irrevocably determined to terminate its history as a colonial power, the Dutch
circulated a proposal for the "internationalization" of Irian under
the United Nations on the "sole condition that the right of self-
determination of the Papuans be guaranteed." The Dutch withdrew the resolution, however, at the insistence of the United
States, which felt that "there is no purpose to be gained by an
attempt to ignore, as does the Netherlands draft resolution, the
claim of Indonesia to sovereignty over the territory." [7] A compromise resolution, submitted by the Brazzaville group of thirteen
African states in close association with France, proposed that if
Indo-Dutch talks on Irian failed by March 1, a United Nations
commission should explore an interim international administration

of the disputed territory without prejudicing the right of 700,000 Papuans to "self-determination." Indonesia bridled at the suggestion of self-determination, however oblique. Indonesia held that the principle was inapplicable in Irian because the disputed territory was rightfully a part of the republic. Djakarta denounced the Brazzaville resolution as a "Dutch camouflage." Although avoiding direct participation, Indonesia induced India to introduce a neutralist nine-power resolution that called for Indo-Dutch talks under the aegis of the U.N., thereby avoiding the issue of self-determination. From Semarang, on November 10, Sukarno warned that "we shall fight for West Irian with or without the United Nations" and told a cheering crowd that "later all of you here will be heroes." On November 28, the rival resolutions were put to a vote at the Sixteenth General Assembly. Both failed to muster the two-thirds majority required for passage. The Brazzaville resolution, however, received a simple majority, 53 votes in favor, 41 against, and 9 abstentions; the Indonesian version was blocked 41-40-21. In 1957, when the Assembly had 81 members, Indonesia's position had attracted 42 votes; 4 years later, with the Assembly's roll expanded to 103 members, Indonesia had received 41 votes. Encouraged by this apparent weakening of the Indonesian case, the Dutch proceeded with their plan for Irian's "self-determination" and on December 1 changed the name of the territory from Netherlands New Guinea to West Papua, unfurled a Papuan flag, and provided an "All-Papuan National Committee" with a national anthem. Professing equal encouragement, Radio Indonesia declared that the outcome of the U.N. debate had strengthened Indonesia's claim to Irian, and on November 30, Sukarno announced that the "decisive moment" was at hand for the "liberation" of the territory, and that "I shall give my command in the near future." Sukarno now asserted that the world had become a battleground between "emerging new forces" and "established old forces" and that the conflict raged not only in Irian but also in Berlin, Laos, Taiwan, South Vietnam, Algeria, Angola, and Katanga. "At the moment the emerging new forces triumph," he declared, "all conflicts will disappear." Against this turbulent background, and with a view to forestalling an outbreak of hostilities, President Kennedy on December 9 assumed the initiative and in a letter to President Sukarno appealed for a peaceful settlement of the dispute. Sukarno was elated: The United States had been drawn into the dispute. Sukarno replied that if there was a war it was the responsibility of the Dutch, and Subandrio, emerging on December 13 from a ninety-minute talk with Ambassador Jones, asserted: "This has become a problem between Indonesia and the United States." At Jogjakarta six days later, on the thirteenth anniversary of the Dutch seizure of the former republican capital—and twenty-four hours after India invaded Goa, Damão, and Díu—Sukarno ordered a "total mobilization" and commanded: "Hoist the red-and-white in West Irian." Whether Sukarno seriously planned an Irian assault or not, Nehru's action had made the acquisition of Irian a matter of face for Sukarno, not only at home but also abroad. On December 23, Aidit enthusiastically responded by pledging the PKI's 2 million members for active service; Pemuda Rakjat announced that its members were ready to enter training camps, receive arms, and join in the struggle to wrest Irian from the Dutch.

If the Dutch were troubled by Indonesian belligerence, and adjoining Malaya, the Philippines, and Australia unsettled by the prospect of a hot war over Irian that could conceivably excite an East-West conflict, developments within Indonesia during 1961 could hardly be reassuring to Moscow and the PKI. Rebel surrenders appeared to keep pace with the accelerated tempo of Sukarno's Irian campaign. Colonel Kawilarang and his forces on Sulawesi surrendered to government troops on April 15; Hussein, Simbolon, and Lubis surrendered on Sumatra on June 23, July 27, and August 22, respectively; Sumual on Sulawesi, October 29. The capitulations bore the characteristics of a class reunion and were accompanied by rebel dress parades, welcoming speeches by loyalist commanders, news conferences, and banquets. Invariably, the returning rebels professed that their decision to lay down arms was "not unrelated to Irian." In several instances, the rebels were permitted to retain their arms and formations. In May, Nasution made a personal tour of the former rebel areas and on May 15, in North Sulawesi, after welcoming Kawilarang to the fold, called on the people to remain "alert against certain elements." On May 24, on Sumatra, Nasution held that although the people of the outer islands in 1958 had lost confidence in Djakarta, the government had restored that confidence and was determined to face "anyone" threatening the republic. Lest there be a misunderstanding, on July 7–11, IPKI held its Third Congress and warned that NASAKOM was being undermined by "a certain group." While the group was never defined, the reference was widely interpreted as applying to the PKI. Significantly, the surrenders were confined at first only to the PRRI's military leadership. The primary political leadership remained hesitant. Nasution and Djuanda, however, prevailed on Sukarno to issue a "last appeal" to the rebels on August 17. Sukarno promised general amnesty to all insurgents who surrendered before October 5, 1961, and signed the following oath of allegiance: "I swear allegiance to the Constitution, to the Political Manifesto, which has become the policy of the state, to the country and the nation, to the revolution and the Great Leader of the Revolution."

To the bewilderment and consternation of Sukarno and his closest advisers, the Communists and the ultranationalist cliques around him, the political leaders of the PRRI surrendered virtually en masse—Sjafruddin and Harahap on August 28; Natsir, September 27. By October 5, the PRRI rebellion was at an end. In a sense, the *status quo ante bellum* had been restored. In one stroke, Nasution had repaired the armed balance of power between Java and the outer islands. The PRRI capitulation occurred while Sukarno was abroad attending the Belgrade conference of non-aligned powers. After the meeting he flew to Washington to present the conference's views to President Kennedy, his third visit to Washington within a year.* Aidit, who accompanied Sukarno, expressed misgiving over the surrender. "Sjafruddin acted on instructions from the CIA," he said,[8] a view which Sukarno's closest advisers professed to share. Doubtlessly, the PRRI capitulation confirmed the Communists' worst fears of the year before that the "bureaucratic capitalists" and "compradore elements" had struck a hawker's bargain.

Thus, correctly or not, the impression is that the principal power factors in contemporary Indonesia were engaged in a "double game": the army preparing for war in Irian while restoring the internal military balance of power; the Communists providing Sukarno with unreserved support while preparing for an inevitable third armed struggle for power; and Sukarno cultivating the support of both the army and the PKI while pursuing the development of a National Front to perpetuate his personal rule. As if to further roil the situation, there has been a hint—and only a hint—that Aidit has reacted to the rebel surrenders by seeking an accommodation with the emerging Tan Malaka forces. On August 22, 1961, for example, in a curious ceremony, a delegation composed of the extremist elements that participated in the 1945 Sukarno-Hatta kidnapping, returned to the President the original copy of the proclamation of independence that had moved surreptitiously from hand to hand in the intervening years. Of interest is that the delegation included two of Tan Malaka's former

* On October 6, 1960, he had visited President Eisenhower; on April 24, 1961, President Kennedy; and on September 12, 1961, Kennedy once more. On each of these visits, Sukarno was accompanied by Aidit and other PKI leaders. In 1960, he introduced Aidit to President Eisenhower. For each of these visits, Sukarno rented a foreign commercial jet at a cost of $200,000.

aides, Sjamsu Harajaudaja and Sudijono Djojoprajitno—and Aidit.

Given the fluid situation obtaining in Indonesia at the outset of 1962, it would be rash to attempt to forecast the outcome of this interplay of forces. But, incontestably, the Indonesian republic is approaching the most critical turning point in its troubled history. Yet that juncture is unlikely to be arrived at until the question of Sukarno's succession arises as an immediate issue.*

The deepening of the internal crisis in Indonesia in 1961–62 also coincided with portents that the PKI may be entering a new phase in its relationship with Moscow amid signs that the Party's restive Left wing may be preparing to challenge Aidit's leadership. In part, these developments were by-products of the ideological Cold War between Moscow and Peking.

In 1957, in the aftermath of Hungary, as differences of opinion arose between Moscow and Peking, as implied in the Joint Declaration and Peace Manifesto drafted that year, Aidit assumed the role of mediator—with a pro-Moscow bias. He was suited to the task. In Indonesia there was no dispute between Moscow and Peking. The twin citadels of Communism warmly endorsed Sukarno's guided democracy and encouraged intimate relations with Djakarta. Thus, as the fissure between Moscow and Peking widened, Aidit moved to dispel suggestions of tensions within the Communist camp. On February 8, 1959, speaking over Radio Moscow as the leader of the PKI delegation to the Twenty-first Congress of the CPSU, Aidit asserted: "Imperialist theoretical and ideological speculations, those of the Yugoslav revisionists included, on the difference of opinion between the Communists of the Soviet Union and China are pure fabrications."

And at the Twenty-second Congress in October, 1961, when differences between Moscow and Peking burst into the open, Aidit—in a message drafted on the eve of the Congress—cited both the Soviet Union and China as "inspiring examples for the people of Indonesia" and praised the peoples and leadership of the Communist bloc "headed by the Soviet Union."

The PKI's inclination to gloss over, if not discount, differences between Moscow and Peking was understandable for a party thirsting for, but not yet in, power. It would seem axiomatic that divisions within the Communist world tend to sow seeds of controversy and strengthen divisive tendencies within individual Communist parties, or "national branches," as they were now being

---

* A sixth attempt on Sukarno's life was made on May 19, 1962, during Idul Adha (Sacrifice Day) prayers in Djakarta. The attempt was ascribed to the Darul Islam. Kartosuwirjo was apprehended in June and executed in September.

called by Moscow. This was particularly true of parties like the PKI that were bedeviled by assorted heresies.

The most obvious theoretical problem for the PKI was the revival of the Murba under the banner of Sukarno's guided democracy; indeed, Sukarno's "Socialism à la Indonesia" posed another bedevilment. Yet another was the increasingly warm relationship between Sukarno and Tito, who had demonstrated that a Marxist-Leninist could seize power, establish a Communist dictatorship without surrendering national independence, profess neutralism, and, in the bargain, extract substantive economic and military assistance from the West—more than $2.6 billion from the United States alone, "the main country of capitalism."

At the outset, the struggle between Moscow and Belgrade served as an ideological exercise for the PKI. But in 1956, when Sukarno visited Yugoslavia for the first time, Titoism became a painful reality for Indonesia's Communists. How painful was brought home to the PKI on December 23, 1958, when Tito arrived in Djakarta for a nine-day state visit. The PKI's position was delicate. Criticism of Tito implied criticism of Sukarno's foreign policy. Worse, as it later developed, with the participation of Communists in Sukarno's guided democracy, the PKI's attacks on Titoism only served to draw the fire of the PNI–Murba-oriented press. *Merdeka* and its English-language companion daily, the *Indonesian Observer*, repeatedly challenged the right of Communists in official government positions to criticize a friendly power.

Even so, PKI criticism of Yugoslavia was restrained and moderate after Stalin's passing—in line with Khrushchev's effort at a *détente* with Belgrade. The PKI did not criticize the Yugoslav Communist League for stating, as did the PKI—and Khrushchev—that there is more than one road to Communism and that each country must take into account national peculiarities. Rather, the PKI attacked the League for placing "too much stress on national peculiarities" and for failing to recognize Marxist-Leninist "laws of revolution and socialist construction." [9] As a consequence, the PKI chided the Yugoslavs for straying toward national-bourgeois ideology. This in turn gave rise to a new Communist definition of "neutralism" in the Cold War, e.g., "the [policy] that is being pursued by Indonesia is aimed at freeing itself from the camp of imperialism, and the other being pursued [by] Yugoslavia is aimed at breaking all links with the camp of socialism." [10] In addition to the question of heresy raised by the Murba's national Communism, Sukarno's Socialism à la Indonesia, and Indonesia's informal alliance with Tito, Aidit was also confronted with Party factionalism. His central problem was rising dissatisfaction within the Party with the Right strategy, a restlessness that fed on the ideological discord between Moscow and Peking.

Aidit's difficulty with his Left wing, dating back to 1953, had assumed such proportions by 1959 that he was compelled openly to concede the Party's deep division. On January 11, 1959, in an address at the Party's "People's University," * he flayed the Left. As in 1953, he sought to blunt their countercharge of "Right-wing opportunism" leveled against him by emphasizing the Maoist content of his strategy. By doing so, he tacitly acknowledged a developing alliance between Peking and the Party's Left. On this occasion, he described the Indonesian revolution as "national and democratic in character" and reaffirmed his basic Rightist strategy of uniting the "progressive forces with the middle-of-the-road forces." His goal, he reiterated, was the creation of a national front composed of workers, peasants, the petty bourgeoisie, and the national bourgeoisie—Mao's four-class bloc, the popular-front strategy the Communists employed in China after 1936. Aidit then turned on those "well-intentioned people who want the Indonesian revolution to proceed rapidly," proclaiming the need for a "socialist revolution now." He said: "Such demagogy is very dangerous and can have very bad consequences for the revolutionary movement. The consequence is, among other things, the emergence of fear among the national bourgeoisie [Sukarno?] with the result that they become hostile to the [Communist] revolution, or become more hostile than they were previously." [11]

He thereupon assailed the party's Left as "criminal demagogues" whose enthusiasm impaired the development of a four-class bloc. "With these 'Left' slogans," he said, paraphrasing the Stalin of 1925, "these demagogues are striking against the genuine Left-wingers."

Then in 1960, in the course of an interview with this author, Aidit discussed the prospects of the PKI in terms that might be easily applied to his problem of leadership within the Party. "Time is with us," he said. "In our view, there is no question about this. We are in no hurry. Indeed, the country runs faster than we do." Was it possible that the Party was running faster than he did? Certainly, the overnight development of a mass party, by intermingling ultranationalist slogans with vistas of a Communist nirvana, may have given rise to expectations among the

---

* The University opened in Djakarta on September 25, 1958, for the training of Party cadres and functionaries. Prijono attended the opening as Minister of Education, thereby denoting official government approval.

rank and file that Aidit found increasingly difficult to control. Nor would this be the first time in the history of the PKI that an uncontrollable spin to the Left had developed.

Indeed, on the eve of the Twenty-second Congress, there was evidence that the spin was gathering momentum. In August, Alimin circulated a harsh, disjointed attack on Aidit's "Right-wing opportunism" within the Party. Alimin apparently sensed a shift in line and balance of power within the Party and, as in 1956, after Khrushchev's first denunciation of Stalin, moved to exploit the opening in another effort to re-establish his leadership. Aidit dismissed Alimin's effort as "crude and amusing." [12] On the Party's Left there was a similar disposition to treat Alimin, now in his mid-sixties, with equal distaste and contempt. But however coarse the Alimin maneuver, it was symptomatic of discontent within the Party with Aidit's leadership.

Amidst these circumstances, Aidit flew to Moscow to attend the Twenty-second Congress. At that momentous session, Khrushchev accelerated his progress of de-Stalinization with the removal of Stalin's mummy from Lenin's crypt, a chilling performance for a society in possession of 50-megaton bombs and Vostoks capable of immediate delivery to any point on the earth. Khrushchev also exacerbated his dispute with China in a by-play with Albania. Khrushchev denounced the Tirana regime of Enver Hoxha, the First Secretary of the Central Committee of the Albanian Workers' Party, which had come to power largely through the assistance of Tito's partisans. Hoxha, who later employed the Stalin-Tito quarrel as a cover for the liquidation of internal rivals on charges of "Titoism," had become increasingly alarmed by Khrushchev's prolongation of the Right strategy. Hoxha feared it would lead to an accommodation between the Kremlin and Tito and, in turn, to his own downfall.

Aidit played his hand cautiously at the Congress, reflecting awareness of Party discord at home. He tacitly refrained from endorsing Khrushchev's policies on de-Stalinization and Albania and reaffirmed his fidelity to Moscow in cryptic fashion. A strange dialogue ensued at the Congress between Khrushchev and the chairman of the largest Communist Party in the non-Communist world. "As a mighty tree with deep roots does not fear any storm, so the new socialist world does not fear any adversity or shock," Khrushchev told the delegates. And Aidit replied: "Relations between Indonesia and the Soviet Union are now blossoming rapidly, like flowers in the spring. The spring of friendship between Indonesia and the Soviet Union will be eternal because no matter what the weather is, spring is always spring." [13]

Aidit's need to exercise caution at Moscow was confirmed by developments within the PKI on his return to Djakarta. The Central Committee of the PKI convened at Party headquarters December 30–31, 1961, to hear Aidit's report on the Congress. The meeting adopted a resolution that conspicuously refrained from criticizing Albania. Instead, the resolution appealed to both Moscow and Peking to abide by the Joint Declaration and Peace Manifesto of 1957, which was weighted in Moscow's favor, and the 1960 Statement of Eighty-One Parties, which was weighted in Peking's favor. Thus, the Indonesian Communists implied criticism of both parties.

The PKI went a step further and openly criticized the behavior of both the Russians and Chinese. Taking Khrushchev to task for publicly airing the question of Albania, the Party declared: "There should be no precedent for a Communist Party and a Labor Party to criticize each other in a Congress. Such an approach cannot simplify—even less solve—problems, and it is not in agreement with the 1960 Communist Declaration, which demands mutual contact and consultation on urgent issues." [14]

The reference to "consultation" reflected Aidit's pique at Khrushchev's failure to take him and other Party leaders into his confidence, as explicitly provided for in the 1960 pact, before unleashing the assault on Albania. But at the same time, Aidit also criticized Peking's attack on Khrushchev's de-Stalinization program. The PKI held that de-Stalinization was an "internal affair" of the Soviet Party and therefore not subject to intra-Party comment. Thus the PKI again displayed an aptitude for tightrope-walking reminiscent of the PKI's performance during the incubation period of the Stalin-Trotsky conflict. Nonetheless, on balance, considering the iron discipline demanded by Moscow of all Communists since the Second Comintern Congress in 1920, the PKI gave the almost imperceptible impression of leaning in the general direction of Peking—or at least leaning almost as imperceptibly away from Moscow. The PKI may have felt it necessary to placate growing rank-and-file dissatisfaction with the Party's policy of "appeasement" of Sukarno and the army, or, in part, to assuage the Chinese minority, which continued to provide the Party with a principal source of revenue and administrative know-how. More likely, the PKI probably felt that in terms of stages of development and of revolutionary ardor, the Party stood closer to Peking than Moscow.

As for Aidit himself, he may have gone along with the criticism of Moscow on Albania as a momentary tactical aberration. The Albanian question was meaningless in the Indonesian context.

Both Moscow and Peking were in accord that Indonesia under Sukarno was an "independent national democracy" in which the conditions for a Communist assumption of power were ripening. Should the PKI come to power, the Party doubtlessly would revert wholly to Moscow's embrace for the strategic reasons Aidit tactfully suggested in 1953.

The December meeting, concluding on New Year's Eve, provided the PKI with a pretext for peace-making in the Communist world. The Party dispatched season's greetings to fraternal parties and sounded a call for bloc unity. Of particular interest was the cable sent to Hoxha. Signed by Aidit, the message expressed the hope that "1962 may be a year of world Communist unity." But Hoxha's reply was less sanguine about the prospects for world Communist unity. In a cable released at Tirana on January 8, 1962, Hoxha returned the hope that 1962 would be "a year of new and even greater victories in the struggle . . . against contemporary revisionism and every other manifestation of opportunism." This was far removed from the joint Hoxha-Aidit statement of January 26, 1960, following Aidit's visit to Albania after his clandestine meeting with Khrushchev in Hungary the preceding month. On that occasion, the Albanian and Indonesian leaders reaffirmed "the leadership of the CPSU [as] the decisive force and the vanguard of socialism, the source of experience and knowledge for all Communist and Workers' Parties in the application of Marxism-Leninism."*

In Djakarta, although unsubstantiated at this writing, the impression in early 1962 was that these developments may eventually herald the gradual passing of the PKI's leadership into the hands of the militant Left. Sudisman, a disciple of Lukman, and now chairman of the Party Secretariat, was said to be in the ascendancy. However speculative this may be, there was little doubt that Sudisman's stature within the Party had risen appreciably after attending the Moscow conclave of Communist parties in 1957, and visiting Pyongyang and Peking on his return home. It is not inconceivable that his subsequent appointment to head

* Curiously, on February 16, 1962, Radio Tirana broadcast receipt of an undated cable from Aidit ("end of 1961") in which the Third Plenum of the Central Committee of the PKI replied to an Albanian anniversary message sent on the occasion of the thirty-fifth anniversary of the 1926 PKI rebellion, which said the Indonesian Communists "feel strengthened by the support of your people and Party, by the people and the Communist and Workers' Parties of the world and the powerful Socialist [Communist] camp, led by the glorious vanguard, the Soviet Union." Did this reflect an Albanian retreat in its quarrel with Moscow, or a PKI decision to leap from the fence and rejoin Khrushchev? At this time we can only speculate.

the Party's underground apparatus and develop a Communist re-doubt in Central Java may have provided him with the oppor-tunity to build his own power base within the Party. The hard fact is that the PKI's failure to endorse Moscow's Albanian policy marked the first time since 1925 that the Party has been known to be deliberately out of step with the Kremlin. At that time, it will be recalled, the Party ignored Stalin's warning against dog-matism and sectarianism and consequent "isolation from the masses." The result was the abortive 1926 revolt. But the 1960's are not the 1920's, and the critical question today is to what degree the Party may be "isolated from the masses." Nobody can say with confidence, least of all Aidit and Njoto, Lukman and Sudisman.

At this writing, Sukarno's power play on Irian has succeeded handsomely. On January 5, 1962, a first wave of armed Indonesian guerrillas parachuted into the jungle cover of West Irian.* In succeeding months other waves followed. The small Dutch gar-rison encountered little resistance in mopping them up. But the developing assault was only in its initial phase. It was accom-panied by a flow of heavy Soviet war material to Indonesia, in-cluding jet bombers, submarines, motor torpedo boats, and am-phibious craft. The publicized shipments were accompanied by a crescendo of shrill war propaganda from Djakarta, Moscow, and Peking. Intimidated by the expanding Communist role in Sukarno's developing war of liberation, the U.S. impressed on The Hague the necessity, if not desirability, of ceding the disputed territory to Indonesia to avoid wide-scale hostilities in the Southwest Pacific; in part, perhaps, the American attitude was also guided by a grow-ing realization that the Dutch position in Irian was politically unjustifiable and, short of a major conflict, militarily untenable. Washington named Ellsworth Bunker, a former Ambassador to India, to negotiate the Dutch retreat; technically, Bunker acted as the agent of U Thant, the Acting Secretary General of the U.N., thereby committing the prestige of the world organization to a settlement.

As in 1949, the intervention of the U.S. in negotiations between the Dutch and Indonesians proved decisive. On August 15, a settlement was signed at the U.N.; Subandrio affixed his signature to the accord on behalf of Indonesia, and Van Roijen, now the Ambassador to the U.S., on behalf of the Netherlands. The

---

* That same day, in a naval encounter off Irian, the Dutch sank an Indo-nesian torpedo boat and damaged another; Suriadarma was relieved of his command for having failed to provide air cover.

agreement provided for a Dutch transfer of the administration of West Irian to a United Nations Temporary Executive Authority (UNTEA) by October 1. The U.N. authority was empowered to transfer "all or part of the administration to Indonesia" after May 1, 1963.* For its part, Djakarta pledged to permit the inhabitants of West Irian to exercise the right of free choice, *ex post facto*, by 1969, in deciding "(a) whether they wish to remain with Indonesia; or (b) whether they wish to sever their ties with Indonesia." [15]

Irian had proved an avoidable tragedy for all concerned, with the probable exception of the overwhelming majority of Papuans, who, barely emerging from the Pleistocene epoch, were oblivious to the dispute. Dutch colonialism in Asia had reached a predictable dead end; Holland doubtlessly would be the better off for it: so would the whole of the Western world. The Australians, despite their explicit interest in West Irian since 1949, did nothing at the critical moment except deplore Indonesia's use of force as a means of conquest or as a lever in the negotiations. The Malayans and the Filipinos were publicly relieved by the removal of a source of regional tension but privately disquieted by Indonesia's military build-up under Soviet auspices and by rash expansionist talk in Djakarta.

In truth, the agreement was a measure of the bankruptcy of Western policy. In 1945, the West had failed to support the inalienable Indonesian right to independence. Similarly, the West had failed to support the Sjahrir-Hatta program of democratization in the emerging republic, although the British moved in that direction at Linggadjati, and the U.S. and Australia during the Renville and Hague conferences. In the years after 1949, until the demise of Harahap in 1956, the West lost many opportunities for transferring Irian to responsible, constructive, progressive Indonesian leadership. When the West finally acted, it did so negatively, in response to burgeoning PKI and Moscow influence in Indonesia, coincident with the Communist thrust in Laos and South Vietnam. Irian was then handed over to a discredited Indonesian regime facing economic chaos. Worse, the transfer occurred under the aegis of the U.N. in what many observers felt was a reward for aggression contrary to the lofty principles embodied in the U.N. Charter. From the Indonesian viewpoint, above all, Irian had proved a ghastly tragedy. Sukarno brilliantly demonstrated that the Hattas, Sjahrirs, Natsirs, and Sjafruddins—and the democratic forces surrounding them—were wrong in opposing his methods of acquiring the territory. Sukarno secured Irian, as

* West Irian's complete transfer to Indonesia by that date is a foregone conclusion.

he pledged he would—albeit at the cost of wrecking the economy, snuffing out representative government, trampling on civil liberties, mortgaging Indonesia's future to Soviet arms shipments, and providing the Communist Party with a rare opportunity to develop a base of mass power in the islands.

Yet, such are the fortunes of destiny, that the Irian settlement, however belated, has nonetheless driven Moscow, Peking, and the PKI onto a precarious ledge. The Communists have been quick to perceive this state of affairs. On July 20, for example, amid rumors of an impending negotiated settlement, Mikoyan flew to Djakarta in an apparent effort to impress on Sukarno the desirability of acquiring Irian forcibly. Four days later, Mikoyan abruptly terminated his scheduled one-week sojourn in Indonesia. The following day, Radio Moscow, in a broadcast to Indonesia, warned that "U.S. mediation on West Irian [is] a trick . . . a wicked and treacherous game" and that "as is known, the plan of U.S. diplomat Bunker carries a number of pitfalls with which the colonialists try to . . . delay the transfer of West Irian to its rightful owner." Earlier, when the prospects of a peaceful settlement had first brightened, Aidit echoed the basic Peking line in Asia in 1961–62, i.e., "the Kennedy Administration is more aggressive than its predecessor, the Eisenhower Administration."

A myriad of questions arise in the wake of the settlement. By his own admission, Sukarno is a romantic enraptured by revolution for revolution's sake.[16] In which direction will he now turn? Logically, the Irian settlement should remove a source of external preoccupation and redirect his attention to the deteriorating internal situation. But will it? There are serious doubts. And what of the armed forces? Past experience shows the difficulty of trying to "rationalize" the Indonesian armed forces. With the Dutch windmill in Irian dismantled, what purpose is there in Indonesia's maintaining a huge and costly military establishment? Moreover, dissatisfaction in the army is widespread. In April, 1962, for example, when soup kitchens were publicly set up in Djakarta, the pay and rations of troops were cut in a move to alleviate the acute rice shortage. And what about the Communists? The Irian settlement severed the umbilical cord between Communism and nationalism in Indonesia. The accord has removed the principal issue that the PKI has skillfully exploited for a decade to excite base nationalist emotions. Aidit, in his first post-Irian comment, weakly groped toward a new political line. Writing in *Harian Rakjat* on August 17, 1962, he held that Indonesia was now confronted by three tasks: "firstly, to consolidate the victory already achieved . . . by strengthening the National Front and further clearing out the remains of Communist-phobia; secondly, to overcome the difficulties in the economy . . . ; and thirdly, to oppose neocolonialism bravely—that is, to oppose the imperialist intrigues to enslave the Indonesian people indirectly through investment, subversion, and infiltration into politics, the military, and culture." Aidit's explanation for the Irian agreement is correspondingly weak. "The United States and Holland," he said, "are willing to resolve the West Irian question peacefully because they hope to achieve their aims through the practice of neocolonialism."

Similarly, Moscow has also displayed irritation over the *peaceful* settlement. On that same August 17, Radio Moscow conceded that the Irian agreement "is, of course, a great victory for the peace-loving republic of Indonesia," but alleged that "plans were afoot in the West to use UNTEA against Indonesia." Knocking down its hastily erected straw man, Moscow proclaimed with Khrushchevian vigor: "If such plans exist, we can tell their authors: 'Your efforts are in vain, gentlemen!'"

Doubtlessly the combined interests of Moscow, Peking, and the PKI would best be served at this stage by encouraging a new "colonial" adventure—Timor, perhaps, or ideally, East Irian. Although the latter development is clearly against the Indonesian interest, since it would embroil Djakarta with Australia and is therefore remote and improbable, East Irian is historically—in the geographic, ethnic, and cultural sense—linked to West Irian. A straw indicative of the future PKI wind may have been cast in the following commentary over Radio Moscow on Feb. 23, 1962, as Indonesia accelerated its military campaign for West Irian:

> People in East New Guinea and the nearby islands who are witnessing the approaching moment of the unavoidable downfall of Dutch colonialism are intensifying their struggle against the Australian colonists for complete independence and freedom of their country. The West Irian people's struggle for reunification with the Indonesian republic and the struggle of those in East New Guinea for freedom are both anticolonial movements. The Dutch colonists and their friends in Australia, in their colonial plundering, look with great fear at the approaching storm.

Clearly, with a resolution of the West Irian dispute, the principal protagonists in the contemporary Indonesian drama—Sukarno, the armed forces, and the PKI (and therefore Moscow)—are feeling their way cautiously.

A built-in danger in the Irian settlement is that Sukarno may now tack westward in search of substantial Western aid to salvage his ruined economy. As an inducement, perhaps, he may even turn on the PKI and, in the process, repudiate his arms debt to

Moscow. It would be folly for the West to reward such opportunism. A program of Western assistance would not only dishearten the democratic opponents of Sukarno's regime, many of whom are now in jail, others under surveillance, but would also drive the PKI into an underground opposition from where they could fan the smoldering fires of popular discontent. In such a situation, the West would find itself backing the wrong horse. Western errors of omission and commission have been manifest in Indonesia for more than a decade; they would be compounded by shoring up the incumbent regime and, therefore, the *status quo.* The West should continue to disengage. Indonesia's internal problems can only be solved by Indonesians, and only from within, not without.

Epilogue

For forty years, the fortunes of the Indonesian Communist Party have alternatively ebbed and flowed. Indonesia's Communists have never obscured their objective: power; the establishment of an Indonesian "people's democracy"; the creation of a Communist society, i.e., a revolution "in one form or another" that brings about a dictatorship of the Communist Party; the abolition of private ownership in a country that the Communists concede to be a "country of small bourgeoisie, meaning a country in which small, privately owned enterprises—especially in the field of agriculture—are rampant"; the establishment of public ownership of all the basic means of production; the reorganization of agriculture into collectives, if not communes; the planned development of the national economy; the suppression of civil liberties; the suppression of representative government. Such a society, the PKI reassures the frustrated and the easily led, is a society where there is no exploitation of man by man, a Communist society.

The Indonesian Communists are convinced that they ride the crest of the future, their path lighted by a shower of Soviet Sputniks. A red star hovers on the Javanese, if not Indonesian, horizon. Aidit has cause for confidence: Within a decade the PKI's membership has soared from 7,910 to 2 million, thus making the PKI the largest Communist Party in the non-Communist world. The PKI has 272 branches; every island of consequence has an Island Committee and an elaborate honeycomb of cells, each cell propagating the Communist line and the Communist myth of inevitability to family, friend, and foe alike. The PKI has also developed a forest of fronts whose total membership is more than

10 million, including 4 million peasants in the BTI. Every conceivable "functional" group in Sukarno's guided democracy has its PKI counterpart either above or below ground. If an exception makes the general rule, the exception is the PKI's failure since Madiun to develop a legal paramilitary front. The Party sought to arm the Pemuda Rakjat in the name of Irian's "liberation"—but the army has been wary of such a wafer-thin stratagem. If the Party could gain direct control of the armed forces, or failing in that, neutralize the army's effectiveness by encouraging "war lordism" or by subverting ill-paid troops, the Party would be on the threshold of power.

In the pursuit of that power, the Communists on Java have been heartened by developments on another island on the other side of the world. The PKI has been lifted to ecstatic heights by the "victorious revolution in Cuba" which "provides important lessons and experiences for the Indonesian people" and "sets a good example for Indonesia." These lessons were spelled out as early as 1959 at the Sixth Party Congress:

> In the present international situation, it is not impossible for a small island-nation, even though geographically isolated and close to the center of world imperialism, to win a revolution, to overthrow a reactionary tyrannical military power [Nasution?] that bows down in servitude to U.S. imperialism and that is helped by the imperialists, and to establish a *national, democratic,* and *independent* government.[1]

And a year later, Aidit added:

> The prospects for a peaceful transition to socialism, as laid down by Khrushchev at the Twentieth Soviet Party Congress, are the brightest and the opportunities most bountiful in two countries; namely, Cuba and Indonesia.[2]

Nor is this sanguine interpretation held only by the PKI leadership. For the moment at least, as noted earlier, both Moscow and Peking profess to believe that Indonesia is treading the path leading to an "independent national democracy" and thereby creating the conditions for Communist revolution.

But are the PKI and Moscow overly optimistic? Is the Indonesian Communist movement as strong as they suggest, or is it a paper tiger, as illusory a force as in 1926 and 1948? Is the PKI in a position to ascend to power in the near future "by one form or another"? Have the Communists been deceived by Sukarno or have they misread his Political Manifesto? It seems unlikely. The PKI must realize that although a thousand Communist flatterers sit within his orbit, other than by folly or miscalculation

—neither of which can be completely ruled out—Sukarno has no intention of putting the PKI into power. Nor is it likely that the PKI misread his Political Manifesto, which may characterize the Indonesian revolution as "national and democratic" but bars "the founding of a proletarian dictatorship."

Has Aidit, like Alimin and Musso before him, or Khrushchev, like Zhdanov before him, misjudged the strength of Indonesian Communism? Perhaps the PKI's hopes ride on the deepening economic crisis. In 1961, the worsening economic crisis kept pace with Sukarno's alarums and excursions over Irian. The cost of living in Djakarta alone spurted 500 per cent in the last six months of 1961. On Christmas Day, rice all but disappeared from the free market as Sukarno issued his "last command" for the conquest of Irian. The government—shades of China in the 1940's—warned that persons "disrupting the nation's economy" would be executed. In 1962, inflation galloped. Yet an economic collapse in Indonesia is not likely for some time yet; in the rural areas, where the masses of the people live, a barter economy prevails, and although conditions worsen, the rural areas are largely insulated from the money economy and chaos in the towns and seaports. Moreover, having survived in recent years largely on sequestered Dutch and Chinese properties, Djakarta can be expected to continue to survive on Soviet and Western handouts—and on oil. Neither Moscow nor Washington can wholeheartedly withdraw from the assistance race for fear that the other will move to fill the vacuum; on October 26, 1961, for example, the United States injected another 55,000 tons of rice into Djakarta. And whereas the oil companies have conspicuously refrained from building new refineries in Indonesia—they have built them in neighboring Malaya, the Philippines, and Australia, although Indonesia is the largest oil producer between the Middle East and California—Indonesian crude oil continues to provide Djakarta with its minimum foreign-exchange requirements. Thus, although economic collapse is not improbable, Djakarta may manage to survive for a considerable period. China survived for a generation or more, and in Indonesia winter is unknown, as are the kind of floods and famines that have beset China.

Whatever the case, despite its impressive assets, the Indonesian Communists also are burdened by a number of liabilities. The PKI, for example, is wholly dependent on Sukarno and/or the mass support of a distinct ethnic group, the Javanese. And despite their overwhelming numbers, the Javanese are confined largely to Central and East Java and to small enclaves, notably Djakarta and the south and east coasts of Sumatra. However, as long as two-thirds of the archipelago's people dwell on Java while the other islands produce two-thirds of the country's wealth, and as long as Indonesia seeks to impose a highly centralized regime from Djakarta (i.e., Java), it is obvious that Indonesia will continue in the throes of political, economic, and social upheaval.[6] This unrest—which doubtlessly will be resolved one day by transmigration and the development of a federal republic—would persist if there were no Communist challenge. But the Communist challenge only serves to intensify it. Thus the tensions between Djakarta and the outer islands serve as a built-in mechanism against Communist expansionism. Nor is the situation on Java as favorable for the Communists as it would appear from afar. The Sundanese border on Djakarta on three sides, and in East Java, the stronghold of the orthodox NU, Islam poses a formidable barrier to a PKI takeover. Indeed, the most powerful of all Javanese, the Sultan of Jogjakarta, the only Javanese leader of national stature who commands the respect and loyalty of both Javanese and non-Javanese, is in the democratic camp and outside the pale of the authoritarianism of either the Right or Left.

Aside from its ethnic characteristics, the composition of the Communist mass movement also casts shadows over the PKI's prospects. The Party machine is operated largely by the small bourgeoisie whose interests, or so one would assume, run counter to Marxist-Leninist ideology. In an analysis of the PKI structure, Darsono, for example, has observed that many of the PKI's branch leaders are "still dominated by superstition [by] traditional mysticism"[3]—Sjahrir's assessment in the 1930's. Darsono also makes the point that the Communists have attracted a mass movement not because the masses have endorsed the Communist program, but because the Communists have promised an Amalthean horn of plenty, including land to the tiller on overcrowded, land-hungry Java, and the peasantry is unaware that the Communists know that they cannot fill this cornucopia. The PKI has also nurtured a myth of incorruptibility and cultivated the impression that the other parties have impoverished the people by corruption, and that if the people wish to improve living conditions, they have no choice but to elect the PKI. Thus the PKI appears to offer an alternative to the corruption and demoralization that has marked the system of guided democracy that they have enthusiastically supported. Here, then, is a success story of having one's cake and eating it, too. The parallel between Indonesia and pre-Communist China is disturbing.

Thus the PKI's prospects sway first this way, like a sea forced by the tide to combat the wind, and then the other, like the selfsame sea forced to retreat by the fury of the wind. In such a situation little can be said with even a professed air of expertise. It appears probable, however, that with the passing of Sukarno, either naturally or by assassination, his system of guided democracy, a creature of his own ego, will crumble. Autocratic rule is unpopular among Indonesia's educated classes; beneath the surface it runs against the democratic grain inherent in the national movement. Moreover, at this writing, the system has failed to produce a successor with the charismatic appeal and authority to follow in Sukarno's track. For Indonesia, the passing of Sukarno will mean the passing of an era.

In the confusion that arises after Sukarno's demise, the army is likely to flow into the void. It is not improbable either that the army will turn to the only popular figures capable of providing an aura of hope for the future and a semblance of republican unity between Java and the outer islands—either the Sultan or Hatta and, in either case, with Sjahrir quietly in the background. Such a development could foreshadow a return to power of the democratic forces that shaped and won the Indonesian struggle for independence. Aidit is aware of this possibility and doubtlessly has made his calculations. At the Sixth Party Congress, Aidit expressed the Communists' fear that

> even though the reactionary leaders and adventurers of the PRRI-PERMESTA have met with failure, the reactionaries and political adventurers are still sufficiently numerous in our country, and there is still Mr. Hatta, who can become a means for trying to get the Indonesian people to drown by means of forming a reactionary cabinet . . . or by the establishment of a military dictatorship or a one-man dictatorship.[4]

The danger may arise, however, that if the army fills the Sukarno vacuum, the military will move against the PKI. The army may drive the PKI underground and into the opposition, if Sukarno's National Front has not already done the job for them. A development of this nature would thrust the party leadership into the hands of the Left or Peking faction and provide the Communists with the opportunity to proclaim themselves in the vanguard of Indonesia's democratic forces in the struggle for civil liberties and representative government and to lead a guerilla war. To ban the PKI at this late stage would therefore be imprudent and ill advised. The time to have outlawed the PKI was 1948–52. The Communists, by their support of Sukarno's corrupt, demoralized, and inept nationalist regime, have been discredited in educated and intellectual circles. Driving the PKI underground would provide the Party with the conditions for recovery. Indonesia's most prudent method of dealing with the Communists, perhaps, would be an exposure of their demagogy and the hollowness of their "nationalistic" pretensions. The PKI should not be outlawed but systematically curbed. The Indonesian people should be told about Stalin's Russia, as recounted by Khrushchev; about living conditions in China and North Vietnam; of repression in Hungary and North Korea; of a wall in Berlin and terror in Tibet. The Indonesian people should be told of the relatively rapid economic and social advances registered in nearby Malaya and the Philippines, while Indonesia stagnates. The Indonesian people should be told that the West possessed a nuclear monopoly between 1945 and 1949 and employed it for peace, not war; that the Bolsheviks seized a Russia that already had an industrial and technical base; that Tito's Communism has "succeeded" only with billions in United States aid. The list of self-evident truths about Communism is interminably long. The PKI should be cauterized by sunlight.

Whatever follows Sukarno, it is indisputable that Indonesia, endowed with people, land, climate, and resources, has squandered its assets. As a land, it lies in reputation sick. Yet it would the sicker be if the country's democratic leaders and the emerging student generation lost their sense of dedication and destiny in attaining the lofty ideals of the nationalist movement. What Indonesia requires most if the Communist challenge is to be turned back is not a return to the spirit of '45—the burning desire for independence from foreign rule which has always been there—but a return to the spirit of Jogja, where democracy flowered in Indonesia's shining hour. Sjahrir set the tone in *Our Struggle*: "Democracy, not nationalism, should be the primary objective of our revolution." Indonesia must now prepare for a new phase and a new struggle if what was lost after the revolution is to be rewon. Should her democratic leaders fail to accept the challenge, the path to power for the Communists will be cleared. In Hatta's words, "To uphold democracy, then, is a moral duty, for the disappearance of democracy means the disappearance of an independent Indonesia." [5]

Indonesia may have drifted far from her revolutionary ideals. But she has not abandoned them.*

* How far she has drifted is illustrated by the arrest of Sjahrir and others on January 16, 1962, as the internal Indonesian crisis deepened. On August 17, 1962, in a conversation at New Rochelle, N.Y., Subandrio said: "They have no place in our society."

Notes

Introduction: THE SETTING

(pp. ix–xviii)
1. U.S. Congress, *Khrushchev on the Shifting Balance of World Forces: A Study* (86th Cong., 1st sess.; Sen. Doc. 57 [Washington, D.C., 1959]), pp. 1–4.
2. U.S. Congress, *Staff Consultation with General Charles A. Willoughby, Former Chief of Intelligence, Far Eastern Command* (85th Cong., 1st sess.; H.R., [Washington, D.C., 1957]), p. 3.
3. D. N. Aidit, *Indonesian Society and the Indonesian Revolution* (Djakarta, 1958), p. 8.
4. Department of Economic Affairs, Central Bureau of Statistics, *Statistical Pocketbook of Indonesia, 1941* (Batavia, 1941), p. 1. Djakarta claims the same area (including Irian) as the former N.E.I.
5. Robert F. Emery, "Agricultural Production Trends and Problems in Indonesia," *Far East Survey*, August, 1960.

Chapter 1—THE ROAD FROM SEMARANG

(pp. 3–12)
1. D. N. Aidit, *The Birth and Growth of the Communist Party of Indonesia* (Djakarta, 1958), p. 4. The official Party history up to 1954.
2. Bernard H. M. Vlekke, *Nusantara, A History of the East Indian Archipelago* (Cambridge, Mass., 1945), p. 9.
3. H. J. Van Mook, *The Stakes of Democracy in Southeast Asia* (New York, 1950), p. 115.
4. J. T. Petrus Blumberger, *De Communistische Beweging in Indië* (Haarlem, 1935). The author acknowledges indebtedness to Blumberger, on whose work he has freely drawn for these early chapters. Blumberger died in April, 1961.
5. Tan Malaka, *International Press Correspondence* (hereinafter referred to as *Inprecor*) (Vienna), August 16, 1923, p. 607.
6. Aidit, *op. cit.*, p. 9.
7. Jane Degras, (ed.), *The Communist International, 1919–1943* (London, 1956), I.

Chapter 2—An Infantile Disorder

(pp. 13–26)

1. Stalin address of May 18, 1925, University of the Peoples of the East.
2. Ruth T. McVey, *The Development of the Indonesian Communist Party and Its Relations with the Soviet Union and the Chinese People's Republic* (Cambridge, Mass., July 16, 1954.)
3. Harry J. Benda and Ruth T. McVey, "The Communist Uprisings of 1926–27," in *Indonesia: Key Documents* ("Translation Series," Modern Indonesia Project) (Ithaca, N.Y.; 1960), p. 136.
4. *Ibid.*, p. 42.
5. Alimin interview, Soerakarta, November 4, 1947.
6. *Inprecor*, November, 1926, p. 1,429.
7. *The Communist International Between the Fifth and Sixth World Congresses, 1924–28* (London, July, 1928).
8. Soetan Sjahrir, *Out of Exile* (New York, 1949).
9. Clifford Geertz, *The Religion of Java* (Chicago, Ill., 1960). A penetrating study of the *abangan* (pre-Hindu), *prijai* (Hindu), and *santri* (Islamic) cultures of Java. Guy J. Pauker, in his article "The Role of Political Organizations in Indonesia," *Far East Survey*, September, 1958, speculates, on the basis of Geertz' research, that the growth of Communism in Java is limited to non-*santri* elements.
10. B. Schrieke, "The Causes and Effects of Communism on the West Coast of Sumatra, in *Indonesian Sociological Studies, Selected Writings* (The Hague and Bandung, 1955), Part I, pp. 132–33.
11. Benda and McVey, *op. cit.*, p. 65.
12. James W. Gould, "Communism in Indonesia" (Unpublished paper, December 17, 1952).
13. D. N. Aidit, *The Birth and Growth of the Communist Party of Indonesia*, pp. 11–12.
14. *Pendorong* (Medan), November 12, 1954.
15. Sardjono interview, Jogjakarta, October, 1947.
16. *Review of Indonesia* (Djakarta), December, 1958.
17. F. Tielman, *International Spectator* (The Hague), May 30 and July 11, 1951.
18. *Review of Indonesia*, November, 1958, p. 12.
19. *Regeerings Voorlichtings-Dienst*, Documentary B–1 (Batavia), January 24, 1946.
20. Van Mook, *op. cit.*, p. 116.
21. J. H. Brimmell, *Communism in South East Asia* (London and New York, 1959), p. 86.
22. *Review of Indonesia*, I, No. 2 (1951), 88.
23. Party Council PNI, "Manifesto of Marhaenism" (Djakarta, 1954).
24. Sjahrir, *op. cit.*, p. 210.

Chapter 3—The "Illegal-PKI"

(pp. 27–32)

1. Iskandar Tedjasukmana, *The Political Character of the Indonesian Trade Union Movement* (Ithaca, N.Y., 1959), p. 15.
2. Aidit, *The Birth and Growth*, p. 17. There is no other evidence of this program at present, however.
3. Malcolm D. Kennedy, *A History of Communism in East Asia* (New York, 1957), p. 210.
4. Sjahrir, *Out of Exile*, p. 211.

5. McVey, *The Development of the Indonesian Communist Party*, p. 18.
6. Aidit interview, New York, October 3, 1960. "Nusantara," a Javanese word used in the fifteenth century to mean "the outer world" as seen from Java and Bali, was employed by nationalists in the Twenties to mean "Indonesia." See Vlekke, *Nusantara* (rev. ed.; Chicago, Ill., 1960), p. 400. Aidit may have acquired the name for propaganda purposes. Aidit is commonly reported to be of part Chinese or Arab origin, which he vehemently denies. He declines to give his exact birthplace.

Chapter 4—ASIA FOR THE ASIANS

(pp. 33–43)
1. Trotsky, *The First Five Years of the Communist International* (New York, 1945) I, 132.
2. Sardjono interview.
3. Aidit interview.
4. M. A. Aziz, *Japan's Colonialism and Indonesia* (The Hague, 1955), p. 228.
5. International Military Tribunal of the Far East (hereafter cited as IMTFE), Doc. 2756. The author covered part of the "Tojo Trial," including this phase.
6. IMTFE, Doc. 6912, p. 23.
7. Sjahrir, *Out of Exile*, p. 246.
8. IMTFE, Doc. 5762.
9. Decrees 2, 3, and 23, issued March 8, 20, and July 15, 1942, respectively, by the 16th Imperial Japanese Army.
10. IMTFE, Doc. 5733.
11. Sjahrir, *op. cit.*, p. 247.
12. Aidit interview.
13. IMTFE, Doc. 2756.
14. Aziz, *op. cit.*, p. 60. Maeda was also the Japanese naval attaché in Amsterdam when the Germans invaded. See Anderson, *Aspects of Indonesian Politics Under the Japanese Occupation, 1944–45* (Ithaca, N.Y., 1961).
15. Tan Malaka, *Dari Pendjara ke Pendjara* (n.d.).
16. Aidit interview.
17. *Ibid.*
18. Aidit, *op. cit.*, p. 35.

Chapter 5—THE AUGUST REVOLUTION

(pp. 44–58)
1. Sjahrir, policy statement made in Djakarta, November 14, 1945, in *Keesing's Contemporary Archives* (London, 1946), p. 7,812.
2. Johan Fabricius, *Java Revisited* (London, 1947), p. 155.
3. Aidit interview. Armed bands ran amok (a Malay word, incidentally) during the *bersiap* ("be prepared," "be ready") period, often attacking defenseless Eurasians, Dutch, and Chinese. The republic deplored the excesses. Many of the intransigent radicals who gathered around Sukarno after 1957 actively participated in the terror.
4. Halim in *Het Inzicht* (Purworedjo), August 13, 1946. *Het Inzicht* was a Sjahrir underground paper.
5. Draft program, Fifth Congress, Part III, Sec. 4.
6. Aidit interview.
7. Sjahrir, in *Keesing's Contemporary Archives*, p. 7,813.
8. For the possibility that the Communists are using similar tactics in

Africa today, see Walter Z. Laqueur "Communism and Nationalism in Tropical Africa," *Foreign Affairs,* July 1961.

9. Ruth T. McVey, "The Soviet View of the Indonesian Revolution" ("Interim Reports Series," Modern Indonesia Project) (Ithaca, N. Y., 1957), p. 3.
10. Aidit interview.
11. Sardjono interview.
12. Alimin interview.
13. Charles Bidien, *Far East Survey,* December 5, 1945. See also p. 65 of this study.
14. Darusman interview, September 21, 1947, Jogjakarta.
15. McVey, *op. cit.,* p. 16.

Chapter 6—THE FIRST COLONIAL WAR

(pp. 59–62)
1. Virginia Thompson and Richard Adloff, *The Left Wing in Southeast Asia* (New York, 1950), p. 178. In reality, the Communists possessed the dominant voice, since the PKI had infiltrated the leadership of the Socialist and Labor parties.
2. Aidit, *Aidit Accuses Madiun Affair* (n.d.).

Chapter 7—THE ROAD TO MADIUN

(pp. 63–79)
1. See McVey, *The Calcutta Conference and the Southeast Asian Uprisings* (Ithaca, N. Y., 1958); Frank N. Trager, *Marxism in Southeast Asia* (Stanford, Calif., 1959), pp. 263–73.
2. Aidit, *Aidit Accuses Madiun Affair*—Aidit's defense on February 25, 1955, against charges of libeling Hatta. On March 31, Aidit was sentenced by a district court to ninety days in jail.
3. *Ibid.,* p. 16.
4. Amir interview, Jogjakarta, February 20, 1948.
5. McVey, *op. cit.,* p. 12.
6. Hatta interview, May 31, 1948.

Chapter 8—MADIUN

(pp. 80–101)
1. Aidit, *Aidit Accuses Madiun Affair,* p. 16–17.
2. John Coast, *Recruit to Revolution* (London, 1952), p. 158.
3. *Revolusioner* (Jogjakarta), August 19, 1948; Aidit, *op. cit.,* p. 26; S. P. Derita, *Lima Minggu Sebelun Madiun Affair* (Medan, 1948). The Derita volume is available in the U. S. Library of Congress.
4. *Antara News Bulletin,* August 18, 1948.
5. *Aneta News Bulletin,* September 1, 1948.
6. *Ibid.,* September 10, 1948.
7. Van Mook, *op. cit.,* p. 259.
8. A. P. dispatch, September 19, 1948.
9. Aidit, *The Birth and Growth,* p. 32.
10. Van Mook, *op. cit.,* p. 259.
11. George McTurnan Kahin, *Nationalism and Revolution in Indonesia* (Ithaca, N. Y., 1952) pp. 270–71. The author is deeply indebted to him, having drawn in particular on chapters 4–11 of this classic.
12. Radio Gelora Pemuda (Madiun) broadcast, September 8, 1948.
13. SOBSI Manifesto, September 8, 1948.

14. UP dispatch, Jogkarta, September 16, 1948.
15. Suripno, "Why We Lost," *Mutiara* (Djakarta) June, 1949. Authentic memoirs.
16. Aidit, *The Birth and Growth*, pp. 33–36.

Chapter 9—CHAOS IN THE FIELD

(pp. 102–19)
1. UP dispatch, Jogkarta, December 12, 1948.
2. UP dispatch (Hatta interview; Jogjakarta), December 5, 1948.
3. Raymond ("Turk") Westerling, *Challenge to Terror* (London, 1952), p. 140.
4. *Sin Po* (Djakarta), September 10, 1949.
5. Netherlands Army Information Service: Darul Islam dossier, released November 1, 1949; NP. 55/DIR/Secret/M (detailed account on Kartosuwirjo and the rise of the DI).
6. Aidit, *The Birth and Growth*, p. 26.
7. *Kedaulatan Rakjat* and *Nasional* (Jogjakarta); both July 13, 1949. *Press Review*, Delegation Republic of Indonesia (Djakarta), July 29, 1949.
8. Even the Dutch conceded such clashes. See LVD communiqué, January 6, 1949, 18:30 hours Java time, on PKI-Masjumi clashes in East Java.
9. Aidit, *op. cit.*, p. 34.

Chapter 10—THE LEFT MODIFIED

(pp. 120–32)
1. UP dispatch, Jogjakarta, September 4, 1949.
2. John H. Kautsky, *Moscow and the Communist Party of India* (New York, 1956), pp. 8–13.

Chapter 11—THE CHINESE QUESTION

(pp. 133–36)
1. A guess; most guesses vary from 1.8 to 3.5 million. See Victor Purcell, *The Chinese in Southeast Asia* (London, 1951), Chapter vii; Donald E. Willmott, *The National Status of the Chinese in Indonesia*, 1900–58 "Interim Report Series," (Ithaca, N. Y., 1961); A. J. Muaja, *The Chinese Problem in Indonesia* (Djakarta, circa 1956).
2. Memorandum (mimeographed), *Chung Hua Tsung Hui*, Batavia, September 15, 1947.

Chapter 12—CROSSROAD

(pp. 137–52)
1. Arnold Mononutu, Information Minister; UP dispatch, February 4, 1950.
2. UP dispatch, December 30, 1949.
3. PSI circles felt Hatta was too close to Cochran. See Lawrence S. Finklestein, "Indonesia's Record in the United Nations," *International Conciliation*, November, 1951.
4. L. Metzemaekers, "The Western New Guinea Problem," *Pacific Affairs*, June 1951, p. 139.
5. Mochtar Lubis, "The Indonesian Communist Movement Today," *Far Eastern Survey*, November, 1954.
6. Aidit interview.
7. *Short biography of D. N. Aidit*, Fifth Party Congress, Djakarta, March, 1954.

8. Angkatan Communist Muda, the Generation of Communist Youth, a Left-deviationist grouping led by Ibnu Parna that opposed Linggadjati and splintered from the PKI, later advocated a "Greater Indonesia" embracing Timor, Malaya, East New Guinea, etc. In 1952, ACOMA split over a reconciliation with the PKI, which Parna opposed as "Right-deviationist." In 1956, Parna visited China and North Korea.

Chapter 13—The August Razzia

(pp. 153–65)
1. Draft program, Fifth Party Congress (prepared by the Plenum of Central Committee of the PKI, October, 1953), Part III, Section 1.
2. *Harian Rakjat* (Djakarta), April 23, 1953.
3. Aidit, *The Birth and Growth*, p. 38.
4. UP dispatch, December 30, 1949.
5. See "Indonesian Tumult Tests U.S.," *Christian Science Monitor*, December 22, 1954; also, "Indonesia Reaffirms Neutralist Policy," *ibid.*, August 18, 1954.

Chapter 14—Stalin Veers Right

(pp. 166–70)
1. Nineteenth Congress of the CPSU (b), October 5–14, 1952, Moscow, as reported in *Collected Documents*, Ministry of Information, Djakarta, December 17, 1952.
2. *Ibid.*

Chapter 15—The Turn in the Road

(pp. 171–85)
1. Aidit, *Indonesian Society and the Indonesian Revolution*, p. 57.
2. Draft program, Fifth Party Congress, October, 1953.
3. Aidit, *The Birth and Growth*, p. 39.
4. *The New York Times*, July 25, 1952.
5. Statement of the Central Committee of the PKI, December 29, 1952.
6. See the *Christian Science Monitor* for the period November–December, 1952; see also *The New York Times*, November 22, 1952, Section 4.
7. *Antara News Bulletin*, May 15, 1952.
8. *Ibid.*
9. Aidit, *The Birth and Growth*.

Chapter 16—Bourgeois Alliance

(pp. 186–98)
1. James M. Gavin, *War and Peace in the Space Age: A New Approach* (New York, 1958), p. 157.
2. *Antara News Bulletin*, July 13, 1953.
3. Ibid., December 17, 1954.
4. PIA, December 17, 1954; Pedomon, December 16, 1954. Aneta, the former Netherlands Indies News Agency, passed into Indonesian control in May, 1950, and became Persbiro Indonesia Aneta; and, later, PIA.
5. Radio Moscow, 21:30 hours, July 24, 1953.
6. PIA, July 31, 1953.
7. Statement of the Central Committee of the PKI, August 26, 1953.
8. *Antara News Bulletin*, February 25, 1954.
9. In joint interview with Edward Tan, AP, July 5, 1953.
10. Publicly confirmed by Antara, October 7, 1953.

11. Ferdinand Tobing (SKI), Minister of Information, in speech of November 2, 1954.
12. Statement by Masjumi Executive Council, November 13, 1954.
13. See *The Christian Science Monitor* dispatches for the period June 26, 1954–October 25, 1954.
14. Robert C. Bone, Jr., *The Dynamics of the Western New Guinea (Irian Barat) Problem* ("Interim Report Series,") (Ithaca, N. Y., 1958).

Chapter 17—AIDITISM
(pp. 199–206)
1. Second Plenary Session of the Central Committee of the PKI, November 8–10, 1954. See *Review of Indonesia*, Supplement, November 20, 1954.
2. Draft Program, Fifth Party Congress, Part II.
3. *Ibid.*
4. *Tentang Tan Ling Djie-ism*, Central Committee of the PKI (Djakarta, 1954).
5. Conrad Brandt, Benjamin Schwartz, and John K. Fairbank, *A Documentary History of Chinese Communism* (Cambridge, Mass., 1953), pp. 260–75.
6. Draft Program, Fifth Party Congress.
7. Aidit, *Indonesian Society*, p. 8.

Chapter 18—TOWARD A MASS MOVEMENT
(pp. 207–14)
1. *Harian Rakjat*, December 7, 1954, published the letter accompanying his application.
2. Draft Program, Fifth Party Congress, Part I, Section 1.
3. *Ibid.*, Part II, Section 3.
4. For a rosy view, see Ralph Parker, *Indonesian Impressions* (New Delhi, 1955).

Chapter 19—COMPRADORE RULE
(pp. 215–22)
1. Aidit, "The General Elections and the Tasks of the Indonesian Communist Party," *For a Lasting Peace, for a People's Democracy* (Bucharest), September 9, 1955.
2. Aidit, in a speech at Singaradja, April 27, 1955.
3. *Singapore Standard*, October 11, 1955.
4. Sal Tas, "Which Way Indonesia?," *New Leader*, October 24, 1955.
5. Herbert Feith, *The Indonesian Elections of 1955*, ("Interim Report Series,") (Ithaca, N. Y.), p. 24.
6. *Antara News Bulletin*, November 20, 1955.
7. Mohammed Hatta, "Indonesia Between the Power Blocs," *Foreign Affairs*, April, 1958.

Chapter 20—SPIRITUAL CRISIS
(pp. 223–36)
1. PIA, July 27, 1956.
2. For details, see Ali's report to Parliament, December 12, 1956.
3. John Foster Dulles' news conference, Djakarta, March 13, 1956.
4. Hatta, "Indonesia's Misguided Democracy," *New Leader*, November 10, 1960. The phrase "guided democracy" may have been invented by

Chaerul Saleh while he was studying abroad. See *Antara News Bulletin*, January 30, 1957.
5. *Christian Science Monitor*, July 25, 1956.
6. Bernard Vlekke (ed.), *Indonesia in 1956* (The Hague, 1957).
7. Hasan Muhammad Tiro, *Demokrasi Untuk Indonesia*, Atjeh. For English translation, see JPRS:6318 (Washington, D.C., U.S. Joint Publications Research Service).
8. PIA, January 21, 1957.
9. Louis Fischer, *The Story of Indonesia* (New York, 1959), p. 225.
10. PIA, March 2, 1957.
11. James Wilde, AP dispatch, Djakarta, March 2, 1957.

Chapter 21—NEW-STYLE DEMOCRACY

(pp. 237–45)
1. Denis Warner, "Indonesia: Growing Opposition to Sukarno's Gotong Royong," *The Reporter*, June 13, 1957.
2. Roeslan Abdul Gani, "Indonesia's National Council: The First Year," *Far East Survey*, July, 1958.
3. PIA, June 29, 1957.
4. *Antara News Bulletin*, April 17, 1958.
5. PIA, September 29, 1957.
6. Diah, *Indonesian Observer* (Djakarta), November 5, 1957.
7. *Pravda*, December 7, 1959.
8. *Antara News Bulletin*, January 8, 1960.
9. *Christian Science Monitor*, December 28, 1957.
10. Sitompoel, *Indonesian Spectator* (Djakarta), January 15, 1958.
11. Warner, *Christian Science Monitor*, December 16, 1957.
12. Sol Sanders, "Civil War Comes Nearer in the Indies," *Business Week*, February 22, 1958.

Chapter 22—"RIGHTIST SYMPTOMS"

(pp. 246–56)
1. *PRRI Bulletin*, July–August, 1959, No. 5. An English-language clandestine publication, issued irregularly.
2. *Documents of the Sixth Plenum of the Central Committee of the Communist Party of Indonesia* (Djakarta, 1958), p. 1.
3. *Indonesian Spectator*, April 1, 1958.
4. E. g., Keyes Beech, *Chicago Daily News*, April 8, 1959; *The Economist* (London), May 3, 1958.
5. *Documents of the Sixth Plenum* . . . , p. 42.
6. PIA, April 2, 1958.
7. Interview, Jim G. Lucas, *New York World-Telegram & Sun*, April 1, 1958.
8. Haldore Hanson, "A Gamble on 'Guided Democracy,'" *The Reporter*, July 23, 1959.
9. Ronald Stead, *Christian Science Monitor*, December 8, 1958.
10. *Documents of the Sixth Plenum* . . . , p. 47.
11. *Ibid.*, p. 49.
12. *Review of Indonesia*, September, 1958, p. 4.
13. *Ibid.*, October, 1958, p. 33. Njoto apparently shifted to the Left after his Peking sojourn.
14. *Ibid.*, April–May, 1959.

Chapter 23—A Cult of Personality

(pp. 257–76)
1. *Indonesian Observer*, April 13, 1959.
2. PIA, May 3, 1959.
3. Aidit, "Consolidate the Forces of the People," *Review of Indonesia*, June–July, 1959.
4. *The New York Times*, June 3, 1959. Dispatch datelined Los Angeles.
5. *Pravda*, December 6, 1960.
6. *Nhan Dan* (Hanoi), May 23, 1960.
7. V. I. Lenin, *Works* (4th Russian ed.; Moscow, XXXI, 1941–51), 217.
8. See also *Material for the Sixth National Congress of the Communist Party of Indonesia* (Djakarta, 1958), p. 19.
9. Paul Wohl, *Christian Science Monitor*, November 12, 1960, and April 20, 1961.
10. *Material for the Sixth National Congress of the Communist Party of Indonesia*, p. 100.
11. *Economic Developments in the Far East and Oceania* (Washington, D.C.: U.S. Department of Commerce), Part I, No. 60–67.
12. International Monetary Fund, Washington, D.C.
13. Statement by Foreign Minister Subandrio, January 29, 1960. Subandrio was identified with Sjahrir and the intellectual Left in 1945. He broke with the Socialists when the Amir and Sjahrir wings split in 1948, and has been a prominent Sukarnophile since 1952. He served as Ambassador to London, and Moscow, and has been Foreign Minister since 1960. He also serves as chief coordinator of military-civil intelligence.
14. *Indonesian Observer*, November 23, 1960.
15. *Review of Indonesia*, March, 1960.
16. Aidit interview.
17. Sumitro, *Searchlight on Indonesia*, December 23, 1960. One of several penetrating monographs on Indonesia's economy, mimeographed and secretely circulated by the PRRI.
18. *Suluh Indonesia*, December 12, 1959; *Indonesian Observer*, December 14, 1959.
19. *Review of Indonesia*, July, 1960.
20. Chapter 2, Article 2, Section 2 of Constitution of the Republic of Indonesia.

Chapter 24—A Double Game

(pp. 277–300)
1. *Review of Indonesia*, May, 1960.
2. Bernard Kalb, *The New York Times*, May 27, 1961; also see Tillman Durdin, October 14, 1951.
3. Aidit interview.
4. *Ibid.*
5. *Ibid.*
6. *Christian Science Monitor*, November 27, 1954. As early as January 8, 1951, the PKI advocated armed action; see *Antara News Bulletin*, same date.
7. General Assembly debate (November 22, 1961), A/PV, 1061, p. 73.
8. Aidit interview held in New York, September 15, 1961.
9. Njono in *Review of Indonesia*, October, 1958, pp. 31–32.

10. *Harian Rakjat,* December 30, 1958.
11. Aidit interviews, 1960.
12. *Ibid.,* 1961.
13. Radio Moscow, October 21, 1961.
14. *Christian Science Monitor,* January 25, 1962.
15. U.N. Document A/L 393.
16. August 17, 1960, speech.

EPILOGUE

1. *Review of Indonesia Supplement,* September–October, 1959.
2. Aidit interview, 1960.
3. Darsono, "The Indonesian Communist Party," *Eastern World,* December, 1957.
4. *Materials for the Sixth National Congress of the Communist Party of Indonesia,* p. 35.
5. Hatta, "Indonesia's Misguided Democracy," *loc. cit.*
6. See *The Economist,* May 3, 1958.

Bibliography

AIDIT, D. N. *Aidit Accuses Madiun Affair*. n.d. Preface datelined Djakarta, March, 1955. Aidit's defense against charges of libeling Hatta took place on February 25, 1955.

——— "Djalan ke Demokrasi Rakjat Bagi Indonesia" ("The Road to a People's Democracy"), *Bintang Merah* (October–November, 1953). Paper delivered at the October 6, 1955, plenary session of the Central Committee of the PKI.

——— *Indonesian Society and the Indonesian Revolution*. Djakarta: Jajasan Pembaruan, 1958.

——— "Lessons from the History of the C.P.I. Djakarta," *Review of Indonesia*, Supplement (June, 1960).

——— *Pilihan Tulisan D. N. Aidit* (*The Selected Writings of D. N. Aidit*). 2 vols. Djakarta: Jajasan Pembaruan, n.d. An English translation is available in Library of Congress, Washington, D.C.

——— *Tentang Tan Ling Djie-isme* (Concerning Tan Ling Djie). Djakarta: Departemen Agitprop, CC Partai Kommunis Indonesia, 1954.

ANDERSON, BENEDICT R. O'G. *Some Aspects of Indonesian Politics Under the Japanese Occupation, 1944–45*. ("Interim Report Series," Modern Indonesia Project, Southeast Asia Program.) Ithaca, N. Y.: Cornell University, 1961.

Antara News Bulletin. Djakarta. Published daily by the Antara News Agency, founded in 1938. It has been, alternately, under Murba and PKI influence.

BARNETT, A. DOAK. *Echoes of Mao Tse-tung in Djakarta*. American Universities Field Staff. ADB–6–55, May 21, 1955.

BENDA, HARRY J. "The Communist Rebellions of 1926–27 in Indonesia," *Pacific Historical Review*, May, 1955.

——— and McVEY, RUTH T. "The Communist Uprisings of 1926–

318   Bibliography

27," in *Indonesia: Key Documents*. ("Interim Report Series.")
Ithaca, N. Y.: Cornell University, 1960.

Bintang Merah (Red Star). Djakarta: Jajasan Pembaruan. Published
monthly by the Sekretariat Agit-Prop of the PKI.

BLUMBERGER, J. T. PETRUS. De Communistiche Beweging in Neder-
landch-Indie (The Communist Movement in the Netherlands
Indies) (2nd ed.) Haarlem: Tjeenk Willink en Zoon, 1938. A
classic on the formative period of the PKI. Unfortunately, it has
not yet been translated into English.

*Buku Putih tentang Peristiwa Madiun (White Paper Concerning the
Madiun Event)*. Djakarta: Sekretariat Agitasi-Propaganda CC
PKI, n.d. (circa 1955). Withdrawn as libelous shortly after
publication.

BRANDT, CONRAD, SCHWARTZ, BENJAMIN, and FAIRBANK, JOHN K.
A Documentary History of Chinese Communism. Cambridge,
Mass.: Harvard University Press, 1952.

BRIMMELL, J. H. *Communism in South East Asia: A Political Analysis*,
London and New York: Oxford University Press, 1959.

COLLINS, J. FOSTER. "The U.N. and Indonesia," *International Conciliation*, March, 1950.

COMPTON, BOYD R. *Indonesian Communism*. American Universities
Field Staff. BRC–25–55, February 1, 1955.

CROZIER, BRIAN. *The Rebels*. London: Chatto & Windus, 1960.

DARSONO. "The Indonesian Communist Party," *Eastern World*,
December, 1957.

DEGRAS, JANE (ed.). *The Communist International, 1919–1943*, Vol.
I: *1919–1922*. London and New York: Oxford University Press,
1956.

DERITA, S. P. *Lima Minggu Sebelum Madiun Affair (Five Weeks
Before the Madiun Affair)*. Medan: Toko Buku Sarkawi, n.d.
Preface dated October, 1949.

*Documents of the Sixth Plenum of the Central Committee of the
Communist Party of Indonesia*. Djakarta: Jajasan Pembaruan,
1958.

DJOJOHADIKUSUMO, SUMITRO. *Searchlight on Indonesia*. n.p., 1959.
A secret PRRI monograph.

EBON, MARTIN. *World Communism Today*. New York: McGraw-Hill
Book Company, 1948.

EUDIN, XENIA JOUKOFF. *Soviet Russia and the East, 1920–1927: A
Documentary Survey*. With Robert C. North ("Hoover Library
Series," No. 25.) Berkeley, Calif.: Stanford University Press,
1957.

FAGG, DONALD. *Modjokuto Study*. Cambridge, Mass.: Center for
International Studies, Massachusetts Institute of Technology,
1956. A penetrating look into PKI tactics at the village level.

FEITH, HERBERT. *The Indonesian Elections of 1955*. ("Interim Report
Series.") Ithaca, N. Y.: Cornell University, 1957. Contains
excellent statistics.

FINKELSTEIN, LAWRENCE S. "Indonesia's Record in the United Nations," *International Conciliation*, November, 1951. Discusses PKI policy in 1950–51.

GEERTZ, CLIFFORD. *The Religion of Java*. Chicago: The Free Press of Glencoe, Ill., 1960. A fine study of Islamic, Hindu, and animist influences in Java.

General News Agency Bulletin. New York.

GOLDBERG, HARRY. "Indonesia's New Rule," *The New Leader*, July 20, 1959.

GOULD, JAMES W. "Communism in Indonesia." Unpublished paper, December 17, 1952.

H. A. "A Brief Sketch of Indonesian-Chinese Relations," n.p., n.d. (circa 1946). Typescript in English; circulated by the Indonesian Ministry of Information.

Harian Rakjat (People's Daily). Djakarta, Official PKI daily.

HATTA, MOHAMMED. *Indonesia's Misguided Democracy*. Reprinted in *The New Leader*, October 10, 1960.

HINDLEY, DONALD. "The Indonesian Communists and the CPSU Twenty-Second Congress, *Asian Survey*, March, 1962.

History of the Chinese in Indonesia, n.p., n.d. Circulated by the Indonesian Ministry of Information.

HUNT, R. N. CAREW. *The Theory and Practice of Communism*. New York: The Macmillan Company, 1951.

Ilmu Marxist (Marxist Science). Djakarta: Jajasan Pembaruan. An official PKI quarterly.

International Press Correspondence (Inprecor). Vienna, Third Communist International. Invaluable source for PKI tactics in the late twenties—particularly November 25 and December 30, 1926; January 13, April 14, August 12, and December 8, 1927; January 5, and October 4, 1928.

JOSEY, ALEX. *Socialism in Asia*. Singapore, 1958.

KAHIN, GEORGE MCTURNAN. *Nationalism and Revolution in Indonesia*. Ithaca, N. Y.: Cornell University Press, 1952. A modern classic.

———. "Resistance in Indonesia," *Far Eastern Survey*, February 23, 1949.

———. "The Communist Revolt in Java: The Crisis and Its Aftermath," *ibid.*, November 17, 1948.

KATTENBURG, PAUL M. *Communism in Indonesia*. ("Foreign Policy Reports Series.") December 15, 1948.

KAUTSKY, JOHN H. *Moscow and the Communist Party of India*. New York: John Wiley & Sons, 1956.

KENNEDY, MALCOLM D. A *History of Communism in East Asia*. New York: Frederick A. Praeger, 1957.

Kapartaian di Indonesia (Parties of Indonesia). Djakarta: Kementerian Penerangan, n.d. (circa 1951). An excellent handbook on parties in the Acting Council of People's Representatives (parliament).

LUBIS, MOCHTAR. "The Indonesian Communist Movement," *Far Eastern Survey* (November, 1954). The author, who was the publisher of the defunct *Indonesian Raya,* has been either in prison or under house arrest in recent years.

MALIK, ADAM. *Soviet Russia seperti jang saja liaht (What I Saw in Soviet Russia).* Djakarta: N. V. Pustaka and Penerbit Endang, 1954. Adam Malik is a Tan Malaka aide who visited Russia in 1952 and is now the Indonesian Ambassador to Moscow.

MALAKA, TAN. *Dari Pendjara ke Pendjara (From Jail to Jail),* 3 vols. The third volume has been suppressed. For a summary, see Willard A. Hanna, WAH–1–59, American Universities Field Staff, New York, April 6, 1959.

————. *Massa Actie (Mass Action).* Jogjakarta: n.p., 1947.

————. *Parlemen Atau Sovjet? (Parliament or Soviet?).* Semarang: PKI–CC, 1921.

Manifesto of Marhaenism. Djakarta: Party Council Partai Nasional Indonesia, n.d. (circa 1953).

Manipol and Uzdek in Questions and Answers. n.d. (circa 1961). Prepared and distributed by the Permanent Indonesian Delegation to the United Nations.

Materials of the Sixth National Congress of the Communist Party of Indonesia. Djakarta: Agitation and Propaganda Department of the CC of the C.P.I. (PKI), n.d. Preface dated December 8, 1958.

MCVEY, RUTH T. *The Calcutta Conference and the Southeast Asian Uprising.* ("Interim Report Series.") Ithaca, N. Y.: Cornell University, 1957. Miss McVey is a leading American scholar on the PKI; her work alternates disconcertingly between brilliance and naïveté.

————. *"The Development of the Indonesian Communist Party and Its Relations with the Soviet Union and the Chinese People's Republic.* Cambridge, Mass.: Massachusetts Institute of Technology, 1954.

————. *The Soviet View of the Indonesian Revolution* ("Interim Report Series.") Ithaca, N. Y.: Cornell University, 1958.

Memorandum Outlining Acts of Violence and Inhumanity Perpetrated by Indonesian Bands on Innocent Chinese Before and After the Dutch Police Action Was Enforced on July 21, 1947. Batavia: Chung Hua Tsung Hui (Federation of Chinese Associations).

Mimbar Kommunism (Communist Platform). Djakarta: Jajasan Pembaruan. Official PKI bimonthly.

MINTZ, JEAN S. "Marxism in Indonesia," in Frank N. Trager, *et al., Marxism in Southeast Asia.* Berkeley, Calif.: Stanford University Press, 1959.

MOES, J. E. "Trade Unionism in Indonesia," *Far Eastern Survey,* February, 1959.

MOSSMAN, JAMES. *Rebels in Paradise.* London: Jonathan Cape, 1961.

MUAJA, A. J. *The Chinese Problem in Indonesia.* Djakarta: New Nusantara Publishing, n.d. (circa 1956).

MUSSO. *Djalan Barua untuk Republik Indonesia (A New Road).*

Djakarta: Jajasan Pembaruan, 1953. Reprint of Musso's 1948 *Road*.

"National Economic Seminar," *Review of Indonesia*, No. 4–5 (April–May, 1959).

New China News Agency. *Anti-Chinese Atrocities in Indonesia*. Peking: July 3, 1960. Contains articles from the Chinese press, 1959–60.

Njoto. "Some Matters Concerning Yugoslavia and Indonesia Considered from the Philosophical Point of View," *Review of Indonesia*, October, 1958.

Overstreet, Gene D., and Windmiller, Marshall. *Communism in India*. Berkeley and Los Angeles: University of California Press, 1959.

Parker, Ralph. *Indonesian Impressions*. New Delhi: People's Publishing House, 1955. An analysis of Indonesia by a Communist sympathizer who attended the Bandung Conference.

PIA Bulletin. Djakarta.

PKI dan Perwakilan (PKI and Parliament). Djakarta: Jajasan Pembaruan. An official PKI quarterly.

PRRI publications. *The Voice of New Indonesia; Informations; Voice of New Indonesia; Monthly Review*. Printed clandestinely by the PRRI between October, 1958, and March, 1960.

Pauker, Guy J. "Current Communist Tactics in Indonesia," *Asian Survey*, May, 1961.

Purcell, Victor. *The Chinese in Southeast Asia*. London: Oxford University Press, 1951.

Raliby, Osman. *Documents Historica: Sedjarah Dokumenter dari Pertumbuhan dan Perdjuangan Negara Republik Indonesia. (Historical Documents: Documentary History of the Growth and Struggle of the Republic of Indonesia)*. Djakarta, 1953.

Report of the Committee New Guinea 1950, Parts I–IV. Scheveningen, Holland: The Secretariat of the Netherlands-Indonesian Union, 1950.

Review of Indonesia. Djakarta: Jajasan Pembaruan. An official English-language PKI magazine that first appeared, in mimeographed form, in August, 1954. (The first Soviet Embassy in Djakarta opened the following month.) It is likely that the magazine was in part designed to surmount the Russian-Indonesian language barrier. The magazine appeared irregularly in 1960 and was suspended by the authorities (read Army) in 1961. See February, 1959, issue for a detailed report on PKI publishing activities in Indonesia.

Sacks, Milton. "Communism and Regional Integration," in Phillips Talbot, ed., *South Asia in the World Today*. Chicago: University of Chicago Press, 1950.

———. "The Strategy of Communism in Southeast Asia," *Pacific Affairs*, September, 1950.

Schrieke, B. "The Causes and Effects of Communism on the West

Coast of Sumatra", in *Indonesian Sociological Studies, Selected Writings*. The Hague and Bandung: W. van Hoeve, 1955. (Originally published in 1928.)

SJAHRIR, SOETAN. *Nationalism and Internationalism* (2nd ed.). Rangoon. U Hla Agung. September, 1953. A brilliant analysis.

————. *Out of Exile*. Translated by Charles Wolf, Jr. New York: John Day Co., 1949. Letters written in exile.

————. *Perdjuangang Kita* (*Our Struggle*). n.p., n.d. (Mimeographed, circa November, 1945.) The political manifesto of the Indonesian revolution.

SWEARINGEN, RODGER. *Red Flags in Japan*. Cambridge, Mass.: Harvard University Press, 1952.

TEDJASUKMANA, ISKANDAR. *The Political Character of the Indonesian Trade Union Movement*. ("Interim Report Series.") Ithaca, N. Y.: Cornell University, 1959. Iskandar Tedjasukmana is a former Minister of Labor.

The Voice of Free Indonesia—Historical Survey of the Indonesian National Movement. Djakarta: Indonesian Office of Youth Affairs, Foreign Relations Branch, May 4, 1946.

THOMPSON, VIRGINIA, and ADLOFF, RICHARD. *The Left Wing in Southeast Asia*. New York: William Sloane Associates, 1950.

TIELMAN, F. "De Partai Kommunis Indonesia de Stem van Moskou" ("The Indonesian Communist Party, the Voice of Moscow"), *International Spectator* (Amsterdam), May 30 and July 11, 1951.

TIRO, HASAN MUHAMMAD. *Demokrasi Untuk Indonesia* (*Democracy for Indonesia*). n.p., n.d. (preface datelined Penerbit Seulawah, Atjeh, September, 1958.) Available in English translation in Library of Congress, Washington, D. C. Tiro is a former official of the Indonesian Embassy in Washington, D.C. He resigned in 1953, after the Atjeh revolt, and on February 8, 1960, was named the PRRI representative to the U.N.

TINKER, IRENE, and WALKER, MILLIDGE. "Indonesia's Panacea: 1959 Model," *Far Eastern Survey*, December, 1959.

U. S. CONGRESS. *The Strategy and Tactics of World Communism*. (80th Cong., 2nd sess.; H. R. Dec. 619.) Washington, D. C.: Government Printing Office, 1948.

————. *The Communist Conspiracy, Strategy and Tactics of World Communism*. (84th Cong., 2d sess; H.R. Dec. 2,243.) Washington, D. C.: Government Printing Office, 1956. An excellent documentation.

VAN DER KROEF, JUSTUS M. "Agrarian Reform and the Indonesian Communist Party," *Far Eastern Survey*, January, 1960.

————. "Communism in Indonesia," *Problems of Communism*, November–December, 1958.

————. "Communist Policy and Tactics in Indonesia," *The Australian Journal of Politics and History*, November, 1959.

————. "Indonesian Communist Policy and the Sixth Party Congress," *Pacific Affairs*, September, 1960.

VAN MOOK, H. J. *The Stakes of Democracy in Southeast Asia.* New York: W. W. Norton and Company, 1950.

WILLMOTT, DONALD E. *The Status of the Chinese in Indonesia.* ("Interim Report Series.") Ithaca, N. Y.: Cornell University, 1956. (A revised edition was published in 1961 under the title *The National Status of the Chinese in Indonesia, 1900–1958.*)

Index

Abbas, Siradjudin, 190
Abduljahat, 190n
Abdulmadjid, 33, 56–57, 84, 90, 94, 109
Abikusno, 105, 190
Acheson, Dean, 111
ACOMA, 151, 311n
Action Committee for the Liberation of West Irian, 242, 252
Adjitorop, J., 183, 208
Affair of the Three Souths, 281–82
Afrin, Georgi, 69, 72, 207
Afro-Asian People's Solidarity Organization, 286
Aidit, Dipa Nusantara, 69–70, 169, 175, 275, 277, 293, 314; East New Guinea, ix; youth, 30–31, 35; and Sukarno, 38, 41–43, 279–81, 282–84, 296–97; jailed, 48; and Jussuf, 55; on 1926 and 1945, 21, 53; on Madiun, 99, 101; on Musso, 85; and Alimin, 148, 151–52, 228, 293; travels, 150–51, 181, 183–85, 199–206 passim, 219–20, 223, 256, 270–71; Fifth Congress, 207–10; on Three Trends, 212; "five-class bloc," 220; on de-Stalinization, 228; and Tan Ling Djie, 230
Aidit, Mrs. Tanti, 209n
Albania, 20, 204, 256, 293–96
Algeria, 107, 287
All-Indonesian Association of Former Strugglers, see PERBEPSI

All-Indonesian Central Organization of Labor, see SOBSI
All-Indonesian Conference of Moslem Scholars, 240
All-Indonesian Women's Movement, 209n
All-Papuan National Committee, 287
Allison, John M., 249
Angkatan Indonesia Baru, see Menteng 31 group
Angola, 107, 249
Anticolonial Day, 209
Anwar, A. Z., 208
Armed forces: guerrilla tactics, 74–75; and Tan Malaka, 115; PKI strategy, 130; American arms, 161; Iwa intrigues, 213–14; rise of "fascism," 277, 283; Soviet arms, 284–85, 298; see also Madiun rebellion; October 17 Affair; August 13 Affair; Affair of the Three Souths
Asian and Pacific Peace Conference, 176
Association of Eastern Youths, 31
Atjeh Rebellion, 191–92, 205, 248
Atomo, Sutomo, 259
August 13 Affair, 226
Australia, viii, ix, 14, 34, 63, 127, 143–44, 146–47, 164, 284, 297, 299, 303; Country Party of, 143; Labour Party of, 143; Liberal Party of, 143

Baars, A., 7
Bachtaruddin, 208

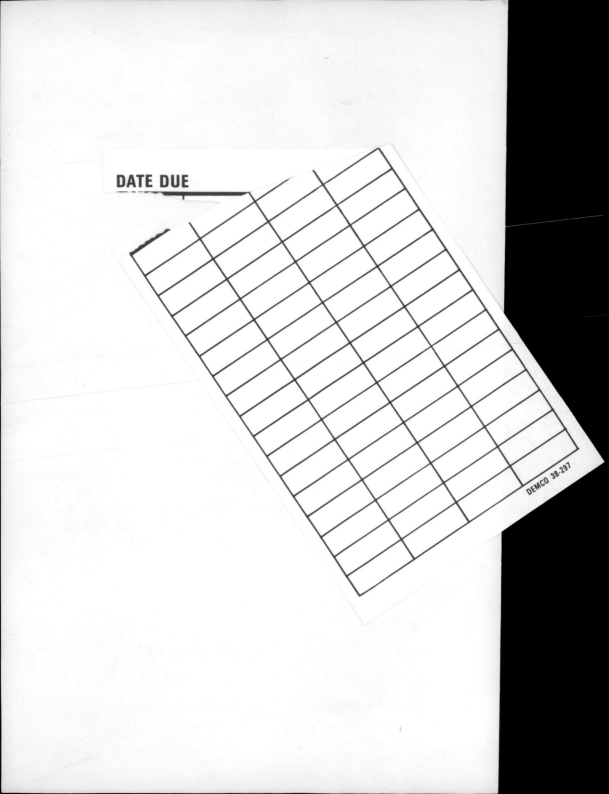

DATE DUE

DEMCO 38-297